# CONTENTS

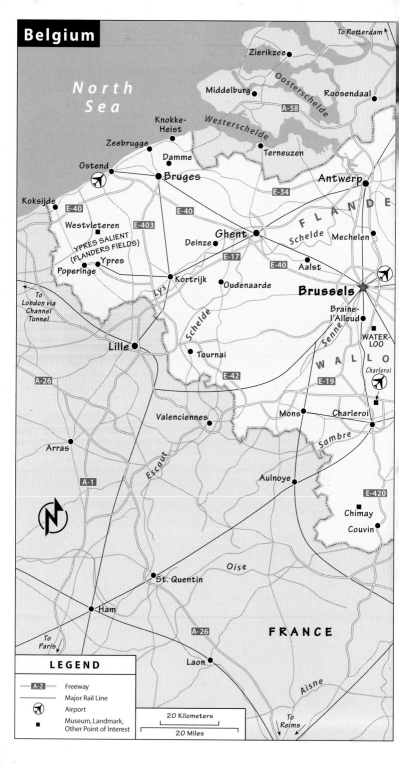

# Belgium

**North Sea**

To Rotterdam

Zierikzee

Middelburg

Oosterschelde

Roosendaal

A-58

Westerschelde

Knokke-Heist

Zeebrugge

Terneuzen

Damme

Ostend

Bruges

Antwerp

E-34

FLANDE

Koksijde

E-40

Schelde

Mechelen

Westvleteren

E-403

E-40

Ghent

YPRES SALIENT (FLANDERS FIELDS)

Deinze

E-17

E-40

Aalst

Ypres

Poperinge

Lys

Kortrijk

Oudenaarde

Brussels

Braine-l'Alleud

WATER-LOO

Senne

To London via Channel Tunnel

Schelde

Tournai

WALLO

Charleroi

Lille

E-42

E-19

Charleroi

A-26

Valenciennes

Mons

Charleroi

Sambre

Arras

Aulnoye

E-420

A-1

Chimay

Couvin

Oise

St. Quentin

Ham

FRANCE

A-26

To Paris

Laon

Aisne

To Reims

## LEGEND

A-2 — Freeway

— Major Rail Line

✈ Airport

■ Museum, Landmark, Other Point of Interest

20 Kilometers

20 Miles

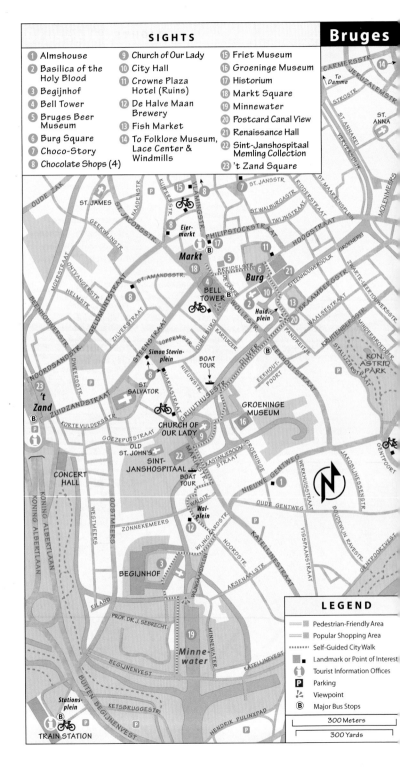

# SIGHTS

**Bruges**

1. Almshouse
2. Basilica of the Holy Blood
3. Begijnhof
4. Bell Tower
5. Bruges Beer Museum
6. Burg Square
7. Choco-Story
8. Chocolate Shops (4)
9. Church of Our Lady
10. City Hall
11. Crowne Plaza Hotel (Ruins)
12. De Halve Maan Brewery
13. Fish Market
14. To Folklore Museum, Lace Center & Windmills
15. Friet Museum
16. Groeninge Museum
17. Historium
18. Markt Square
19. Minnewater
20. Postcard Canal View
21. Renaissance Hall
22. Sint-Janshospitaal Memling Collection
23. 't Zand Square

## LEGEND

- Pedestrian-Friendly Area
- Popular Shopping Area
- Self-Guided City Walk
- ■ Landmark or Point of Interest
- Tourist Information Offices
- **P** Parking
- Viewpoint
- **B** Major Bus Stops

300 Meters

300 Yards

# Rick Steves

# BELGIUM:
## BRUGES, BRUSSELS, ANTWERP & GHENT

# Welcome to Rick Steves' Europe

Travel is intensified living—maximum thrills per minute and one of the last great sources of legal adventure. Travel is freedom. It's recess, and we need it.

I discovered a passion for European travel as a teen and have been sharing it ever since—through my tours, public television and radio shows, and travel guidebooks. Over the years, I've taught thousands of travelers how to best enjoy Europe's blockbuster sights—and experience "Back Door" discoveries that most tourists miss.

Written with my talented co-author, Gene Openshaw, this book offers you a balanced mix of Belgium's lively cities and cozy towns, from medieval Bruges to slick, fashion-forward Antwerp. It's selective: Rather than listing dozens of Flemish art museums, we recommend only the best ones. And it's in-depth: Our self-guided museum tours and city walks provide insight into the country's vibrant history and today's living, breathing culture.

We advocate traveling simply and smartly. Take advantage of our money- and time-saving tips on sightseeing, transportation, and more. Try local, characteristic alternatives to expensive hotels and restaurants. In many ways, spending more money only builds a thicker wall between you and what you traveled so far to see.

We visit Belgium to experience it—to become temporary locals. Thoughtful travel engages us with the world, as we learn to appreciate other cultures and new ways to measure quality of life.

Judging by the positive feedback we receive from our readers, this book will help you enjoy a fun, affordable, and rewarding vacation—whether it's your first trip or your tenth.

Have a *prachtig* trip! Happy travels!

Rick Steves

# INTRODUCTION

Digging into a dish of mussels while seated on a sunny square beneath the outline of a lacy medieval spire...you're in Belgium.

This book presents the best of Belgium—its great cities, fine food, rich history, and sensuous art, as well as the modern scene that makes Belgium the face of Europe today. You'll see the predictable biggies and experience a healthy dose of Back Door intimacy.

Bruges is the Belgium of the past—a wonderfully preserved medieval gem that once was one of the largest cities in the world. Once mighty, now mighty cute, it comes with fancy beers in fancy glasses, lilting carillons, and filigreed Gothic souvenirs of a long-gone greatness.

The thriving towns of Ghent and Antwerp—also former medieval powerhouses—demonstrate how the country has rebounded to again be a global trendsetter. Design-forward Antwerp offers interesting contrasts, from its high-fashion couture scene to its racy red light district. In the university town of Ghent, you'll find a richly detailed Renaissance altarpiece amid a vibrant urban landscape.

And finally, there's Brussels: the unofficial capital of the European Union, with a low-rise Parisian ambience that exudes joie de vivre. With the finest town square in the country (if not the Continent), a chocolate shop on every corner, a French taste for class and cuisine, and a smattering of intriguing museums, it's equally ideal for a quick stopover as it is for a multiday visit. Wherever you go, find time to leave the quaint-but-touristy central square to wander the back streets. You'll find a Belgium that's lived-in, a bit funky, and authentic.

Belgium is ready for you. Like sampling a flavorful praline in

INTRODUCTION

a chocolate shop, that first enticing taste just leaves you wanting more. Go ahead, it's OK...buy a whole box of Belgium.

# Planning Your Trip

This section will help you get started planning your trip—with advice on trip costs, when to go, and what you should know before you take off.

## TRIP COSTS

Five components make up your trip costs: airfare to Europe, transportation in Europe, room and board, sightseeing and entertainment, and shopping and miscellany.

**Airfare to Europe:** A basic round-trip flight from the US to Brussels can cost, on average, about $1,000-2,000 total, depending on where you fly from and when (cheaper in winter). Consider saving time in Europe by flying into one city and out of another; for instance, into Brussels and out of Amsterdam. If you're sticking to Belgium, you're never more than about two hours from Brussels' international airport. Overall, Kayak.com is the best place to start searching for flights on a combination of mainstream and budget carriers.

**Transportation in Europe:** For getting around, you're best off enjoying tiny Belgium's excellent and affordable train system. Trains travel several times hourly between its major cities. It costs about $10 for a ticket from Ghent to Brussels. If you plan to rent a car, allow at least $250 per week, not including tolls, gas, and supplemental insurance. If you need the car for three weeks or more, leasing can save you money on insurance and taxes. If your travels extend beyond Belgium, a short flight can be cheaper than the train (check www.skyscanner.com for intra-European flights).

**Room and Board:** You can thrive in Belgium on $125 a day per person for room and board. This allows $20 for lunch, $30 for dinner, and $70 for lodging (based on two people splitting the cost of a $140 double room that includes breakfast). That leaves you $5 for *frieten*, beer, or chocolate. To live and sleep more elegantly, I'd propose a budget of $145 per day per person ($20 for lunch, $40 for dinner, $5 for snacks, and $80 each for a $160 hotel double with breakfast). Students and tightwads can enjoy Belgium for as little as $60 a day ($30 for a bed, $30 for meals and snacks).

**Sightseeing and Entertainment:** In big cities, figure about $10-15 per major sight (Royal Museums, Rubens House, climbing Bruges' bell tower); $5-10 for minor ones (beer tour or chocolate museum); $10-20 for guided walks, boat tours, and bike rentals; and $30-60 for splurge experiences such as concerts, special art exhibits, and big-bus tours. An overall average of $25 a day works

# Belgium at a Glance

▲▲▲**Bruges** Perfectly pickled Gothic city with charming cobbles, cozy squares, dreamy canals, divine chocolate, and unbeatable beer.

▲▲**Brussels** Urbane capital of Belgium, the European Union, and NATO, with one of Europe's grandest squares, colorful urban zones, and a beloved statue of a little boy peeing.

▲▲**Antwerp** Gentrified port city with excellent museums, Belgium's best fashion, and an engaging mix of urban grittiness and youthful trendiness.

▲**Ghent** Pleasant, lively university city with historic quarter and breathtaking Van Eyck altarpiece in its massive cathedral.

**Flanders Fields** Infamous WWI battlefields near Ypres with artillery craters, memorials, and cemeteries amid pastoral pastures and fine museums.

for most people. Don't skimp here. After all, this category is the driving force behind your trip—you came to sightsee, enjoy, and experience Belgium.

**Shopping and Miscellany:** Figure $1-2 per postcard, tea, or ice-cream cone. Shopping can vary in cost from nearly nothing to a small fortune. Good budget travelers find that this category has little to do with assembling a trip full of lifelong and wonderful memories.

## SIGHTSEEING PRIORITIES

So much to see, so little time. How to choose? With affordable flights from the US, minimal culture shock, almost no language barrier, and a well-organized tourist trade, Belgium is a good place to start a European trip. Depending on the length of your trip, and taking geographic proximity into account, here are my recommended priorities for a great week in Belgium:

| | |
|---|---|
| 2 days: | Bruges |
| 4 days, add: | Brussels and Ghent |
| 6 days, add: | Antwerp |
| 7 days, add: | Flanders Fields (near Bruges) plus time to just slow down |

## WHEN TO GO

For tourist hotspots like Bruges, peak season is summer, especially June and early July. Business towns like Brussels, Antwerp,

INTRODUCTION

and Ghent tend to be more crowded in spring and fall. With long days, lively festivals, and sunny weather, summer is a great time to visit despite the crowds in places like Bruges. It's rarely too hot for comfort. Plus, Brussels' fancy business-class hotels are deeply discounted in the summer.

Late spring and fall are also pleasant, with generally mild weather and lighter tourist crowds (except during holiday weekends—see "Holidays and Festivals" in the appendix).

Travel from late October through mid-March is cold and wet, as coastal winds whip through the low, flat country. It's fine for city visits, but smaller towns and countryside sights feel dreary. Some sights and TIs keep shorter hours, and many outdoor activities vanish altogether.

## Before You Go

You'll have a smoother trip if you tackle a few things ahead of time. For more information on these topics, see the Practicalities chapter (and www.ricksteves.com, which has helpful travel tips and talks).

**Make sure your passport is valid.** If it's due to expire within six months of your ticketed date of return, you need to renew it. Allow up to six weeks to renew or get a passport (www.travel.state.gov).

**Arrange your transportation.** Book your international flights. Figure out your main form of transportation within Belgium: It's worth thinking about buying train tickets online in advance, getting a rail pass, or renting a car. (You can wing it once you're there, but it may cost more.)

**Book rooms well in advance,** especially if your trip falls during peak season or any major holidays or festivals.

**Consider travel insurance.** Compare the cost of the insurance to the cost of your potential loss. Check whether your existing insurance (health, homeowners, or renters) covers you and your possessions overseas.

**Call your bank.** Alert your bank that you'll be using your debit and credit cards in Europe. Ask about transaction fees, and get the PIN number for your credit card. You don't need to bring euros for your trip; you can withdraw euros from cash machines in Europe.

**Use your smartphone smartly.** Sign up for an international service plan to reduce your costs, or rely on Wi-Fi in Europe instead. Download any apps you'll want on the road, such as maps, translation, transit schedules, and Rick Steves Audio Europe (see sidebar).

**Rip up this book!** Turn chapters into mini guidebooks: Break the book's spine and use a utility knife to slice apart chapters, keep-

---

### 🎧 **Rick Steves Audio Europe** 🎧

My Rick Steves Audio Europe app makes it easy to download audio content to enhance your trip. Enjoy my audio tours of many of Europe's top destinations and a library of insightful travel interviews from my public radio show with experts from Belgium and around the globe. The app and all of its content are entirely free. (And new content is added about twice a year.) You can download the app via Apple's App Store, Google Play, or Amazon's Appstore. For more info, see www.ricksteves.com/audioeurope.

---

ing gummy edges intact. Reinforce the chapter spines with clear wide tape; use a heavy-duty stapler; or make or buy a cheap cover (see Travel Store at www.ricksteves.com), swapping out chapters as you travel.

**Pack light.** You'll walk with your luggage more than you think. Bring a single carry-on bag and a daypack. Use the packing checklist in the appendix as a guide.

## Travel Smart

If you have a positive attitude, equip yourself with good information (this book), and expect to travel smart, you will.

**Read—and reread—this book.** To have an "A" trip, be an "A" student. Note opening hours of sights, closed days (for example, many museums in Bruges are closed on Mondays), crowd-beating tips, and whether reservations are required or advisable. Check the latest at www.ricksteves.com/update.

**Be your own tour guide.** As you travel, get up-to-date info on sights, reserve tickets and tours, reconfirm hotels and travel arrangements, and check transit connections. Visit local tourist information offices (TIs). Upon arrival in a new town, lay the groundwork for a smooth departure; confirm the train, bus, or road you'll take when you leave.

**Outsmart thieves.** Pickpockets abound in crowded places where tourists congregate. Treat commotions as smokescreens for theft. Keep your cash, credit cards, and passport secure in a money belt tucked under your clothes; carry only a day's spending money in your front pocket. Don't set valuable items down on counters or café tabletops, where they can be quickly stolen or easily forgotten.

**Minimize potential loss.** Keep expensive gear to a minimum. Bring photocopies or take photos of important documents (passport and cards) to aid in replacement if they're lost or stolen. Back up photos and files frequently.

**Guard your time and energy.** Taking a taxi can be a good value if it saves you a long wait for a cheap bus or an exhausting walk across town. To avoid long lines, follow my crowd-beating tips, such as making advance reservations, or sightseeing early or late.

**Be flexible.** Even if you have a well-planned itinerary, expect changes, strikes, closures, sore feet, bad weather, and so on. Your Plan B could turn out to be even better.

**Attempt the language.** Many Belgians—especially in the tourist trade and in cities—speak English, but if you learn some Dutch or French, even just a few phrases, you'll get more smiles and make more friends. Practice the survival phrases near the end of this book, and even better, bring a phrase book.

**Connect with the culture.** Interacting with locals carbonates your experience. Enjoy the friendliness of the Belgian people. Ask questions; most locals are happy to point you in their idea of the right direction. Set up your own quest for the best local beer, lace doily, or handmade praline. When an opportunity pops up, make it a habit to say "yes."

Belgium...here you come!

# BELGIUM

Belgium falls through the cracks. Wedged between Germany, France, and the Netherlands, and famous for waffles, Smurfs, and a statue of a little boy peeing, it's no wonder it can get lost in the mix.

But Belgium rewards with richer sights than you might expect—and fewer tourist crowds. You'll encounter some of Europe's finest cuisine, including the best beer, creamiest chocolates, and tastiest French fries. Belgium's town squares bristle with soaring spires and warm-brick gables. Its museums house lush paintings celebrating the glories of everyday life. From funky urban neighborhoods to tranquil convents, from old-fashioned lace to high-powered European politics—little Belgium delights.

With nearly 950 people per square mile, Belgium is the second most densely populated country in Europe (after the Netherlands). When viewed from space, Belgium shines at night as a single patch of light—a phenomenon NASA astronauts call the "Belgian Window."

Despite its small size, Belgium is diverse. It's divided—linguistically, culturally, and politically—between French-speaking Wallonia in the south and Dutch-speaking Flanders in the north, with bilingual Brussels in between. ("Flemish," the Dutch spoken in Belgium, is even more guttural than textbook Dutch—insert your own "phlegmish" pun here.) And, because of its international business and political connections, more than 25 percent of its residents are foreigners who speak English as their common language.

Belgium is at the crossroads of Western Europe, where Romance languages meet the German world, and where the Protestant north meets the Catholic south. It was born as a merchant entity in medieval times (c. 1300-1500), when energetic traders made it one of Europe's richest, most cosmopolitan, and sophisticated lands. On the other hand—located as it is in the cross fire

BELGIUM

# Belgium

North Sea

NETHERLANDS

GERMANY

Zeebrugge
Ostend • Damme
Bruges
YPRES
SALIENT
(FLANDERS FIELDS) Ghent
F L A N D E R S
Ypres
Antwerp
Brussels
Hasselt • Maastricht
Waterloo • Leuven • Aachen
B E L G I U M
Liège
Lille • Spa
Charleroi • Namur Meuse
W A L L O N I A
Bastogne
FRANCE
A R D E N N E S
LUXEM-
BOURG Trier
Luxembourg
City

50 Kilometers
50 Miles

between larger powers—it's also been Europe's battlefield. From Charlemagne to Napoleon, from the Habsburgs to Germany in two world wars, this country has paid a heavy price.

But tiny Belgium has survived by producing savvy business-people and excellent linguists, and by welcoming new trends. I recently asked a local, "What is a Belgian?" He said, "We are a melting pot. We're a mix culturally: one-third English for our sense of humor, one-third French for our love of culture and good living, and one-third German for our work ethic."

Belgians have a directness that some find refreshing (and others find brusque). They revel in their wry, sardonic sense of humor—it can be hard sometimes to tell whether they're putting you on. The art of the comic strip is deeply respected—the Smurfs and Tintin were created by Belgians. If you ask twentysomething Belgians what career they're pursuing, and they say "comic books," nobody snickers. Belgians are said to be born with a "brick in their stomach"—meaning they feel a deep-seated need to own a house, decorate it just so (hence the abundance of furniture shops), and invite their friends for dinner. Belgians are social, meeting up at sidewalk cafés or cozy pubs after work. On a beautiful spring day, it might seem like nobody here has a job—they're all outside drinking beer.

Belgium flies the flag of Europe more vigorously than any

# Belgium Almanac

**Official Name:** Royaume de Belgique/Koninkrijk België, or simply Belgique in French and België in Dutch.

**Population:** About 11.5 million Belgians are packed into their little country—58 percent are Flemish, 31 percent are Walloon, and 11 percent are "mixed or other." About three-quarters are Catholic, and the rest are Protestant or other.

**Latitude and Longitude:** 50°N and 4°E. The latitude is similar to Calgary, Canada.

**Area:** With only 12,000 square miles, it's slightly smaller than the state of Maryland, and one of the smallest countries in Europe.

**Geography:** Belgium's flat coastal plains in the northwest and central rolling hills make it easy to invade (just ask Napoleon or Hitler). There are some rugged hills and ridges in the southeast Ardennes Forest. The climate is temperate.

**Biggest Cities:** Antwerp has a half-million inhabitants, Ghent has 250,000, and little Bruges has almost 120,000. Brussels has 170,000 people in the city proper, but 2 million in the capital region.

**Economy:** With few natural resources, Belgium imports most of its raw materials and exports a large volume of manufactured goods, making its economy unusually dependent on world markets. It can be a sweet business—Belgium is one of the world's top exporters of chocolate. It's prosperous, with a Gross Domestic Product of nearly $526 billion and a GDP per capita of about $46,000. As the "crossroads" of Europe, Brussels is the headquarters of NATO and the de facto capital of the European Union.

**Government:** Belgium is a parliamentary democracy, and its official head of state is King Philippe. Voting is compulsory. An average of 90 percent of registered voters participate in general elections (compared with 55 percent in the US).

**Flag:** Belgium's flag is composed of three vertical bands of black, yellow, and red.

**The Average Belgian:** The average Belgian is 41 years old and will live to be 81. He or she is also likely to be divorced—Belgium has the highest divorce rate in Europe, with 70 for every 100 marriages. Beer is the national beverage: On average, Belgians drink 20 gallons a year, just behind the Dutch and just ahead of the Brits.

other place on the Continent. There's a feeling of being at the center of global events. But even with a thousand years of history behind it, the country seems determined to write a new chapter in its long and illustrious tale.

# BRUGES

# ORIENTATION TO BRUGES

*Brugge • Bruges*

With pointy gilded architecture, stay-a-while cafés, vivid time-tunnel art, and dreamy canals dotted with swans, Bruges is a heavyweight sightseeing destination. It's also a joy: Where else can you ride a bike along a canal, munch mussels and wash them down with the world's best beer, savor heavenly chocolate, and see Flemish Primitives and a Michelangelo, all within 300 yards of a bell tower that jingles every 15 minutes? And do it all without worrying about a language barrier?

The town is Brugge (BROO-ghah) in Dutch, and Bruges (broozh) in French and English. Its name comes from the Viking word for "wharf." Right from the start, Bruges was a trading center.

In the 11th century, the city grew wealthy on the cloth trade. As the middleman in the sea trade between northern and southern Europe, Bruges was an economic powerhouse and became one of the biggest cities in the world (as large as London, for a time). By the 14th century, it was the most important cloth market in northern Europe.

In the 15th century, while England and France were slugging it out in the Hundred Years' War, Bruges was the favored residence of the powerful Dukes of Burgundy—and at peace. Commerce and the arts boomed. The artists Jan van Eyck and Hans Memling had studios here.

But by the 16th century, the harbor had silted up and the economy had collapsed. The Burgundian court left, Belgium became a minor Habsburg possession, and Bruges' Golden Age abruptly ended.

For generations, Bruges was a backwater. In the 19th century, a new port, Zeebrugge, brought renewed vitality to the area. And in the 20th century, tourists discovered the town. These days,

Bruges seems to be a particularly hot destination among British people—for whom it's an easy weekend getaway.

Today, Bruges prospers because of tourism, but even with the crowds, it's the kind of place where you don't mind being a tourist. Just an hour west of Brussels by train, this uniquely well-preserved Gothic city is a handy gateway to Europe.

## PLANNING YOUR TIME

Bruges needs at least two nights and a full, well-organized day. With one day—other than a Monday, when the Groeninge and Sint-Janshospitaal museums are closed—a speedy visitor could try this ambitious Bruges blitz (which is outlined in my Bruges City Walk):

| | |
|---|---|
| 9:30 | Climb the bell tower on the Markt (Market Square). |
| 10:00 | Tour the sights on Burg Square. |
| 11:30 | Tour the Groeninge Museum. |
| 13:00 | Eat lunch and buy chocolates. |
| 14:00 | Take a short canal cruise. |
| 14:30 | Visit the Church of Our Lady and see Michelangelo's *Madonna and Child*. |
| 15:00 | Tour the Memling collection inside Sint-Janshospitaal (St. John's Hospital). |
| 16:00 | Catch the De Halve Maan Brewery tour (can reserve in advance). |
| 17:00 | Relax in the Begijnhof courtyard. |
| 18:00 | Ride a bike around the quiet back streets of town or take a horse-and-buggy tour. |
| 20:00 | Enjoy the low light of magic hour on the Markt, then lose the tourists and find dinner elsewhere. Finish the evening with a unique Belgian beer in a local pub. |

If this schedule seems too ambitious, skip the bell tower and the brewery—or stay another day.

# Overview

The tourist's Bruges is less than one square mile, contained within a canal (the former moat). Nearly everything of interest and importance is within a convenient cobbled swath between the train station and the Markt (Market Square; a 20-minute walk). Most tourists are concentrated in the triangle formed by the Markt, Burg Square, and the Church of Our Lady; outside of that tight zone, the townscape is sleepy and relatively uncrowded. Many of my charming recommended accommodations lie just beyond this zone.

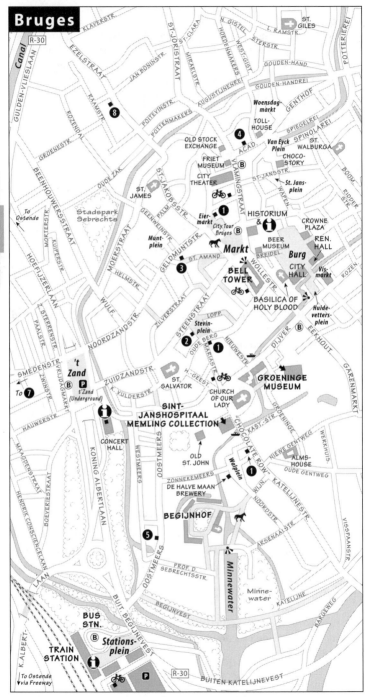

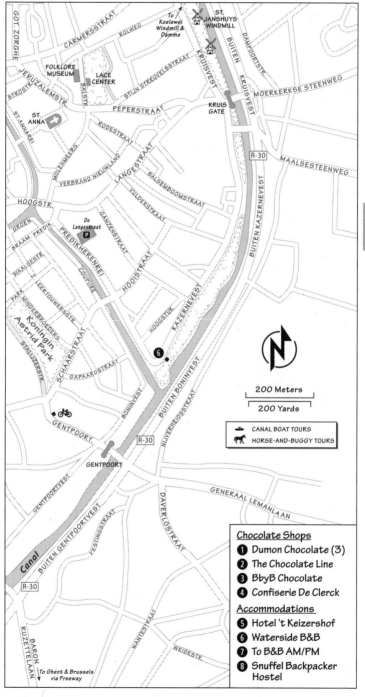

Chocolate Shops
1 Dumon Chocolate (3)
2 The Chocolate Line
3 BbyB Chocolate
4 Confiserie De Clerck

Accommodations
5 Hotel 't Keizershof
6 Waterside B&B
7 To B&B AM/PM
8 Snuffel Backpacker Hostel

## TOURIST INFORMATION

The main TI, called **In&Uit** ("In and Out"), is inconveniently located in the big, red concert hall on the square called 't Zand (Mon-Sat 10:00-17:00, Sun until 14:00, 't Zand 34, tel. 050-444-646, www.brugge.be). Better-located branches are at the **train station** and on the **Markt,** sharing a building with the Historium museum (both open daily 10:00-17:00). Look for the *Bruges City Guide* (€5, map, walking tour routes, sights/services), the free English-language *What's On Guide* (train schedules, events), and the free "Use-It" map (tips for backpackers and the young-at-heart, also downloadable at www.use-it.travel).

## ARRIVAL IN BRUGES

**By Train:** Bruges' train station is situated in a clean, parklike setting, where travelers step out the door and are greeted by a taxi stand and a roundabout with center-bound buses circulating through every couple of minutes. Coming in by train, you'll see the bell tower that marks the main square (Markt, the center of town). The station has a TI branch, ATMs, and lockers.

The best way to get to the town center is by **bus** (for details, see "Getting Around Bruges," later). A **taxi** from the train station to most hotels is about €10-15.

It's a 20-minute **walk** from the station to the center. To reach the Markt, cross the busy street and canal in front of the station, head up Oostmeers, and turn right on Zwidzandstraat. You can rent a **bike** at the station for the duration of your stay, but other bike-rental shops are closer to the center (see "Helpful Hints," later).

**By Car:** Driving in town is very complicated because of the one-way system. The best plan for drivers: Park at the train station, visit the TI there, and rent a bike or catch a bus into town.

Park in front of the train station in the handy two-story garage (€3.50 for 24 hours). The parking fee includes a round-trip same-day bus ticket into town for up to four people in your car (show parking ticket to staff at Lijnwinkel ticket office just outside the station).

There are pricier underground parking garages at the square called 't Zand and around town (€9/day, all well-marked). Paid street parking is limited to four hours.

## HELPFUL HINTS

**Sightseeing Tips:** The "Museumpas" **combo-ticket** is a good deal (available at the 't Zand TI and city museums; see the next chapter for details). If you're in Bruges on a **Monday,** when several museums are closed, consider the following activities or attractions: bell-tower climb on the Markt, Begijnhof, De Halve Maan Brewery tour, Basilica of the Holy Blood, City Hall's Gothic Room, Bruges Beer Museum, Historium, chocolate shops and museum, and Church of Our Lady. You can also join a boat, bus, or walking tour, or rent a bike and pedal into the countryside.

**Market Days:** Bruges hosts markets on Wednesday morning (on the Markt) and Saturday morning ('t Zand). On good-weather Saturdays, Sundays, and public holidays, a flea market hops along Dijver in front of the Groeninge Museum. The fish market *(vismarkt)* sells souvenirs daily and seafood Wednesday through Saturday mornings until 13:00.

**Bookstore:** A good travel bookstore (which carries my guidebooks) is at #12 on the Markt.

**Laundry:** Bruges has several self-service launderettes. Ask your hotelier for the nearest, but one of the most central is **The Laundrette** (daily 10:00-22:00, Mon from 12:00, next to Hotel Marcel at Niklaas Desparsstraat 5, tel. 050-335-502, www.thelaundrette.be).

**Bike Rental:** Rates are generally the same around town (about €4-5/hour, €13-15/day, more for specialty bikes).

**Bruges Bike Rental** is central and cheap, with friendly service and long hours (show this book to get student rate—€10/day, no deposit required—just ID, daily 10:00-20:00, free child seats, behind the far-out iron facade at Niklaas Desparsstraat 17, tel. 050-616-108, www.brugesbikerental. be). **Fietsen Popelier Bike Rental** is also good (electric bikes available, 24-hour day is OK if your hotel has a safe place to store bike, no deposit required, daily 10:00-19:00, sometimes open later in summer, free Damme map, Mariastraat 26, tel. 050-343-262, www.fietsenpopelier.be). **Koffieboontje Bike Rental** is just under the bell tower on the Markt (tandem bikes available, daily 9:00-22:00, free child seats, Hallestraat 4, tel. 050-338-027).

**De Ketting** is less central, but cheaper than most (Mon-Fri 10:00-18:00, Sat-Sun from 12:30, Gentpoortstraat 23, tel. 050-344-196, www.deketting.be). **Fietspunt Brugge** is a big outfit at the train station (7-speed bikes available, Mon-Fri 7:00-19:00, Sat-Sun 9:00-20:00, just outside the station and to the right as you exit in the huge bicycle parking garage, tel. 050-396-826).

**Best Town View:** The bell tower overlooking the Markt rewards those who climb it with the ultimate Bruges view.

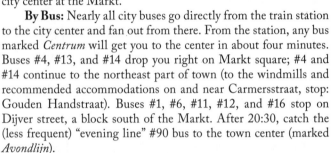

## GETTING AROUND BRUGES

Because the city is easily walkable, most visitors won't need a bus or taxi except for traveling between the train station and the city center at the Markt.

**By Bus:** Nearly all city buses go directly from the train station to the city center and fan out from there. From the station, any bus marked *Centrum* will get you to the center in about four minutes. Buses #4, #13, and #14 drop you right on Markt square; #4 and #14 continue to the northeast part of town (to the windmills and recommended accommodations on and near Carmersstraat, stop: Gouden Handstraat). Buses #1, #6, #11, #12, and #16 stop on Dijver street, a block south of the Markt. After 20:30, catch the (less frequent) "evening line" #90 bus to the town center (marked *Avondlijn*).

If traveling from the city center back to the train station, catch any bus labeled *Station*. The handiest stop is Stadsschouwburg, two blocks north of the Markt on Vlamingstraat, right across from the City Theater—buses stopping here all go to the station (every five minutes).

A bus **ticket** is €3 and good for an hour. At the train station, you can buy tickets at the Lijnwinkel shop that's curbside, just outside the station (cash or credit card; buy as many tickets as you need in advance); or simply hop on (with exact change) and pay the driver. If you're going to Antwerp and/or Ghent and plan to use public transportation there as well, consider the **10-ride ticket** for €16. You can use it in all three cities (and anywhere else in Flanders), and you can share the ticket with others. Though various day passes are available (such as a 24-hour pass for €6), there's really no need to buy one for your visit. Bus info: www.delijn.be.

**By Taxi:** You'll find taxi stands at the station and on the Markt (€10-15/first 2 kilometers; to get a cab in the center, call 050-333-881).

# Tours in Bruges

## Boat Tours

The most relaxing and scenic (though not informative) way to see this city of canals is by boat, with the captain narrating. All companies offer essentially the same thing: a 30-minute route (roughly 4/ hour, daily 10:00-17:00), a price of €8 (cash only), and narration in three or four languages. Qualitative differences are because of individual guides, not companies. Let them know you speak English to ensure you'll understand the spiel. Two companies give the group-rate discount to individuals with this book: **Boten Stael** (just over the canal from Sint-Janshospitaal at Katelijnestraat 4, tel. 050-332-771) and **Gruuthuse** (Nieuwstraat 11, opposite Groeninge Museum, tel. 050-333-393).

## Bike Tour

**QuasiMundo Bike Tours** leads daily five-mile bike tours around the city (€28, RS%, 2.5 hours, departs March-Oct at 10:00, in Nov only with good weather, no tours Dec-Feb). For more details and contact info, see their listing under "Near Bruges," next page.

## City Minibus Tour

**City Tour Bruges** gives a rolling overview of the town in an 18-seat, two-skylight minibus with dial-a-language headsets and video support (€20, 50 minutes, pay driver). The tour leaves every 30 minutes from the Markt (10:00-19:00, until 18:00 in fall, fewer in winter, tel. 050-355-024, www.citytour.be). The narration is slow-moving, but the tour is a lazy way to cruise past virtually every sight in Bruges.

## Walking Tour

The **TI** arranges two-hour walks through the core of town (€12.50, 4/week July-Aug, Sat only in off-season, depart from TI on 't Zand Square at 14:30, see schedule at www.visitbruges.be). Though earnest, the tours are heavy on history and given in two languages, so they may be less than peppy. Still, to propel you beyond the pretty gables and canal swans of Bruges, they're good medicine. In the off-season, the TI occasionally organizes "winter walks"—ask.

### Local Guides
**Sylvie Brems** gives three-hour walks (€120) and full-day tours (€240), and organizes guided tours of Ypres and WWI battle-fields (mobile 0478-822-978, sylvie.brems@gmail.com). You can also hire a guide through the **TI** (typically €75 for a two-hour tour, reserve at least one week in advance).

### Horse-and-Buggy Tour
The buggies around town can take you on a clip-clop tour (€50, 35 minutes; price is per carriage, not per person; seats five; buggies gather in the Markt).

## NEAR BRUGES
Popular tour destinations from Bruges are Flanders Fields (famous WWI sites about 40 miles to the southwest; see that chapter for more information) and the picturesque town of Damme (four easy-to-bike miles to the northeast).

### Quasimodo Countryside Tours
This company offers those with extra time two entertaining, all-day bus tours through the rarely visited Flemish countryside. A Flanders Fields tour concentrates on WWI battlefields, trenches, memorials, and poppy-splattered fields (Tue-Sun at 9:15, no tours Mon or in Jan, 8 hours, visit to In Flanders Fields Museum not included). Another tour focuses on Flanders' medieval past and rich culture, with tastes of chocolate, waffles, and beer (departs Mon, Wed, and Fri at 9:15, 8 hours, no tours Dec-mid-Feb). Be ready for lots of walking.

Tours cost €69.50, or €59.50 if you're under 26 (cash preferred, includes sandwich lunch, make required reservation online, at TI, or by calling 050-370-470, www.quasimodo.be).

### Bike Tours
For do-it-yourself bike tours, see my bike ride to the historic town of Damme (page 38). My self-guided walk from the Markt to the moat is also good fun on a bike (page 27). For bike rental shops in Bruges, see "Helpful Hints," earlier.

**QuasiMundo Bike Tours** offers a daily "Border by Bike" tour through the nearby countryside to Damme (€28, €16 if you already have a bike, RS%, reservations required, March-Oct, departs at 13:00, 15 miles, 4 hours, tel. 050-330-775, www.quasimundo.com). Meet at QuasiMundo's office at Predikherenstraat 28 (be there 10

minutes before departure). Jos, who leads most departures, is a high-energy and entertaining guide.

Charming Mieke of **Pink Bear Bike Tours** takes small groups on an easy and delightful 3.5-hour guided pedal along a canal to Damme and back, finishing with a brief tour of Bruges. English tours go daily through peak season and nearly daily the rest of the year (€27, €18 if you already have a bike, RS%, meet at 10:25 under bell tower on the Markt, tel. 050-616-686, www. pinkbear.be).

# SIGHTS & EXPERIENCES IN BRUGES

While Bruges has several worthwhile museums and churches, the ultimate sight here is the town itself. After seeing the essential sights, I enjoy slowing down and savoring the city, whether it's getting lost on the back streets, away from the lace shops and waffle stands, taking a bike ride along a quiet canal, learning about beer from passionate locals, or sampling chocolate at one of Bruges' fine chocolatiers. This chapter covers both the top sights and best experiences Bruges has to offer.

**Sightseeing Pass:** The 't Zand TI and city museums sell a "Museumpas" combo-ticket for €28 (valid for 3 days at 16 locations). Because the Groeninge and Sint-Janshospitaal museums cost €12 each, you'll likely save money with this pass if you plan to see at least one other covered sight.

## Sights in Bruges

These sights are listed by neighborhood, covering the area around the Markt (Market Square) and Burg Square; the cluster of sights south of the Markt; and the less touristy area northeast of the core.

### ON OR NEAR THE MARKT

All of these sights (except the Historium) are described in greater detail in the 📖 Bruges City Walk chapter—including details on visiting the interiors of the Basilica of the Holy Blood, the City Hall's Gothic Room, and Renaissance Hall.

#### ▲Markt (Market Square)

The crossroads of Bruges is one of the most enjoyable town squares in Belgium—and in this country, that's really saying something. In Bruges' heyday as a trading center, a canal came right up to this

# Bruges at a Glance

▲▲**Bell Tower** Overlooking the Markt—the modern heart of the city—with 366 steps to a fine view and carillon close-up. **Hours:** Daily 9:30-18:00, last entry at 17:00. See page 24.

▲▲**Burg Square** Sight-filled historic square with impressive architecture. See page 25.

▲▲**Groeninge Museum** Top-notch collection of mainly Flemish art. **Hours:** Tue-Sun 9:30-17:00, closed Mon. See page 26.

▲▲**Church of Our Lady** Tombs and church art, including Michelangelo's *Madonna and Child.* **Hours:** Mon-Sat 9:30-17:00, Sun from 13:30. See page 26.

▲▲**Sint-Janshospitaal Memling Collection** Art by the greatest of the Flemish Primitives, displayed in a medieval hospital. **Hours:** Tue-Sun 9:30-17:00, closed Mon. See page 26.

▲▲**Begijnhof** Peaceful medieval courtyard and Beguine's House museum. **Hours:** Courtyard—daily 6:30-18:30; museum—Mon-Sat 10:00-17:00, closed Sun, shorter hours off-season. See page 27.

▲▲**De Halve Maan Brewery Tour** Fun beer tour. **Hours:** Tours on the hour Sun-Fri 11:00-16:00, Sat until 17:00. See page 33.

▲**Historium** Multimedia exhibit re-creating the sights, sounds, and smells of 1430s Bruges. **Hours:** Daily 10:00-18:00. See page 24.

▲**Basilica of the Holy Blood** Romanesque/Gothic church housing a relic of the blood of Christ. **Hours:** Daily 9:30-12:00 & 14:00-17:30. See page 25.

▲**City Hall** Beautifully restored Gothic Room from 1400, plus the Renaissance Hall. **Hours:** Daily 9:30-17:00 (Renaissance Hall closes 12:30-13:30). See page 25.

▲**Folklore Museum** Well-presented exhibits of life in Bruges' industrious Golden Age. **Hours:** Tue-Sun 9:30-17:00, closed Mon. See page 31.

▲**Bruges Beer Museum** History of Belgian beer and brewing, with tastings. **Hours:** Daily 10:00-17:00. See page 34.

▲**Choco-Story: The Chocolate Museum** The delicious story of Belgium's favorite treat. **Hours:** Daily 10:00-17:00. See page 37.

square. And today it's still the heart of the modern city. The square is ringed by the frilly former post office, enticing restaurant terraces, great old gabled buildings, and the iconic bell tower. Under the bell tower are two great Belgian-style French-fry stands. The streets spoking off this square are lined with tempting eateries and shops.

### ▲▲Bell Tower (Belfort)

Most of this bell tower has presided over the Markt since 1300, serenading passersby with cheery carillon music. The octagonal lantern was added in 1486, making it 290 feet high—that's 366 steps. The view is worth the climb...and probably even the pricey admission. Some mornings and summer evenings, you can sit in the courtyard or out on the square to enjoy a carillon concert (for details, see page 93).

**Cost and Hours:** €12; daily 9:30-18:00, last entry at 17:00 is strictly enforced—best to show up before; pay WC in courtyard, tel. 050/448-767.

### ▲Historium

I despise the Disneyfication of Europe, but this glitzy sight right on the Markt is actually entertaining—and it takes a genuine interest in history. It's pricey and cheesy—sort of "Pirates of the Belgianean" (or maybe "Hysterium")—but it immerses you in the story of Bruges in a way a textbook cannot.

**Cost and Hours:** €14, includes audioguide, virtual-reality option is more, daily 10:00-18:00, last entry one hour before closing, may be too creepy for kids, Markt 1, tel. 050-270-311, www. historium.be.

**Visiting the Museum:** The 35-minute audioguide tour leads you from room to room as it tells the story of medieval Bruges in the time of the painter Jan van Eyck. Using giant video screens, animatronic mannequins, fake fog, and even smell-o-vision, the rooms re-create life in Bruges during its heyday in the 1430s, bringing to life the gritty harbor, the sensuous (R-rated) bath houses, and Van Eyck's studio. The story is engaging and—most important—rooted in real history, providing beauti-

fully rendered glimpses of a medieval age when Bruges was a bustling and important metropolis.

You emerge into a small museum that's as good an introduction to the city's history as you'll find in Bruges. Don't miss the panoramic terrace overlooking the Markt. One floor down, the

Duvelorium, a self-described "grand beer café" (see details on page 90), lets you enjoy a pricey beer on the terrace with that same great view.

## ▲▲Burg Square

This opulent, prickly-spired square is Bruges' civic center, the historic birthplace of Bruges, and the site of the ninth-century castle of the first count of Flanders. It's home to the Basilica of the Holy Blood and City Hall (both described next). Today, it's an atmospheric place to take in an outdoor concert while surrounded by six centuries of architecture.

### ▲Basilica of the Holy Blood (Heilig-Bloedbasiliek)

Originally the Chapel of Saint Basil, this church is famous for its relic of the blood of Christ, which, according to tradition, was

brought to Bruges in 1150 after the Second Crusade. The lower chapel is dark and solid—a fine example of Romanesque style. The upper chapel (separate entrance, climb the stairs) is decorated Gothic. An interesting treasury museum is next to the upper chapel.

**Cost and Hours:** Church-free, treasury-€2.50, daily 9:30-12:00 & 14:00-17:30; Burg Square, tel. 050-336-792, www.holyblood.com.

### ▲City Hall (Stadhuis)

This complex houses several interesting sights, including a room full of old town maps and paintings, and the highlight—the grand, beautifully restored **Gothic Room** from 1400, starring a painted and carved wooden ceiling adorned with hanging arches. Your ticket also covers the less impressive **Renaissance Hall** (Brugse Vrije) next door, basically just one ornate room with a Renaissance chimney (separate entrance—in corner of square at Burg 11a).

**Cost and Hours:** €6, daily 9:30-17:00 (Renaissance Hall closes 12:30-13:30); tel. 050-448-743, www.brugge.be.

## SOUTH OF THE MARKT

The following sights are covered in more detail in either a separate self-guided tour or walk chapter. Also in this area is the De Halve Maan Brewery, with an excellent beer tour (described later, under "Experiences in Bruges").

## ▲▲Groeninge Museum

This museum houses a world-class collection of mostly Flemish art, from Memling to Magritte. While there's plenty of worthwhile modern art, the highlights are the vivid and pristine Flemish Primitives. (In Flanders, "Primitive" simply means "before the Renaissance.") Flemish art is shaped by its love of detail, the egos of its merchant patrons, and the power of the Church. Lose yourself in the halls of Groeninge: Gaze across 15th-century canals, into the eyes of reassuring Marys, and through town squares littered with leotards, lace, and lopped-off heads.

**Cost and Hours:** €12, more for special exhibits, ticket also covers nearby Arentshuis Museum (described on page 68); Tue-Sun 9:30-17:00, closed Mon; Dijver 12, tel. 050-448-743, www.brugge.be.

📖 See the Groeninge Museum Tour chapter.

## ▲▲Church of Our Lady (Onze-Lieve-Vrouwekerk)

This imposing church brims with reminders of the wealth of medieval Bruges. Its prized possession is a delicate *Madonna and Child* sculpture, said to be the only Michelangelo statue to leave Italy in his lifetime (a Belgian cloth merchant with connections in Italy shipped the statue home in 1506). Note that the church is undergoing a major, years-long renovation, during which parts of the interior will be closed to visitors. It's supposed to be finished by 2020—but it might take a miracle.

**Cost and Hours:** Entry to the rear of the church is free. To get into the main section costs €4; Mon-Sat 9:30-17:00, Sun from 13:30; Mariastraat, tel. 050-448-711, www.brugge.be.

For more on the church, see the 📖 Bruges City Walk chapter.

## ▲▲Sint-Janshospitaal Memling Collection (St. John's Hospital)

This former monastery is one of the oldest hospital buildings in Europe. Besides preserving medieval wards where monks and nuns cared for the sick, its museum has a fine collection of artworks from the monastery chapel. Hans Memling, the greatest of the Flemish Primitives, created his *St. John Altarpiece* triptych for the hospital; you'll also see his miniature, gilded-oak shrine to St. Ursula. Your ticket includes entry to the skippable old pharmacy (Apotheek) in a nearby building.

**Cost and Hours:** €12, Tue-Sun 9:30-17:00, closed Mon, across the street from the Church of Our Lady, Mariastraat 38, tel. 050-448-743, www.brugge.be.

📖 See the Sint-Janshospitaal Memling Collection Tour chapter.

### ▲▲Begijnhof

The courtyard called the Begijnhof was once enclosed by buildings inhabited by members of a lay sisterhood, the Beguines. Though the original buildings are no longer there, the atmosphere may still make you want to don a habit and fold your hands as you walk under its wispy trees and whisper past its modest little homes. For a good slice of Begijnhof life, walk through the simple Beguine's House museum.

**Cost and Hours:** Courtyard-free, daily 6:30-18:30; museum-€2, Mon-Sat 10:00-17:00, closed Sun, shorter hours off-season; museum is left of entry gate.

**Nearby:** Just south of the Begijn-hof is the waterway called **Minnewater,** an idyllic world of flower boxes, canals, and swans.

For more on the Begijnhof and Minnewater, see the 📖 Bruges City Walk chapter.

## NORTHEAST OF THE MARKT

The less touristy streets north and east of the Markt are worth a wander—they don't suffer from the intense crowd congestion of the main Markt-Burg-Church of Our Lady thoroughfare.

### ▲Markt to the Moat Stroll

This tranquil walk takes you along postcard canals and through sleepy residential areas to the moat, where you can climb up inside a working windmill. The walk takes about 20 minutes (longer if you enter the sights). It's also great on a bike and can be extended with a longer ride to Damme (described later).

**➋ Self-Guided Walk:** From the Markt, head up Vlaming-straat (with the bell tower at your back, exit straight ahead up the top-right corner of the square).

**Vlamingstraat:** Two short blocks up this street, on the left, you'll spot the stately, Neo-Renaissance-style **City Theater** (Stadsschouwburg). Notice how atypically broad this street is for claustrophobic Bruges. That's because several old buildings were torn down to build this theater in 1869. This was a time of Flemish cultural revival—when Dutch-speaking people began to take pride in what differentiated them from the dominant French-speaking Belgians—and Dutch-language theater was an important symbol

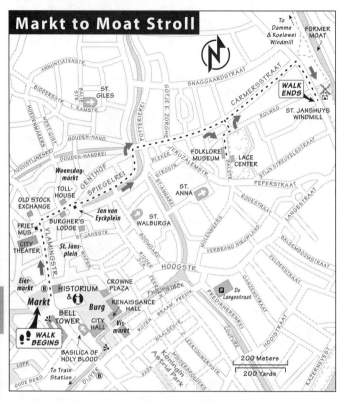

**Markt to Moat Stroll**

of Flemish pride. Notice the large plaza in front of the main entrance, dating from a time when classy horse carriages would drop off well-heeled theatergoers. French speakers wish actors a hearty "break a leg!" with the expression, *"Je te dis merde!"* ("I say crap to you!"). Back then, more *merde* meant more horse carriages...and a bigger audience.

• *A few steps past the theater, on the left, notice the* **Friet Museum**, *dedicated to the esteemed fry (described later in the chapter). A bit farther up and also on the left, look for the angled building set slightly back from the street, with yellow bricks and narrow windows. This marks a small square known as...*

**Oude Beursplein** (Old Stock Exchange): While Amsterdam likes to lay claim to inventing the stock market, Bruges' actually predates it. (See the old sign reading *Huis Ter Beurze*—House of the Stock Market.) In the mid-13th century, the Van der Beurse family built an inn here and offered discounted beers to passing merchants on their way between the tollhouse (which we'll see soon) and the Markt. Gradually these hangouts began to host more formalized trading of goods and services. Much of this business took place out in this square; traders would scurry under awnings in case of bad weather. To kick off these meetings amid this chaos, they'd ring a bell, which is still used today to start and end stock trading sessions. And to this day, in most European languages, some variation of the word "Beurse" (*Börse, borsa,* etc.) means "stock market." (Conveniently, the family name also means "purse.")

Just after the old stock market, turn right up Academiestraat. The big building near the end of the street on your right is the **Burghers' Lodge** (Poortersloge)—a meeting place of the local businessmen, similar to today's Rotary clubs. Pause at the building's ornate doorway, just before the square. Just above, notice the Latin message in golden letters with a few seemingly random capitalized letters; if you add them up, they represent the year of the building's reconstruction after a devastating fire (VIXXCIVVIVMD-VIVI—1655).

• *You'll pop out into a square called...*

**Jan Van Eyckplein:** A large **statue** honors the painter in the middle of this charming waterfront square. In this bilingual city,

he's identified twice: the Dutch *Jan van Eyck* on the side facing you, and the French *Jean van Eyck* on the side facing the canal.

On the left side of the square, you can't miss the building with the big, fire-engine red doors. Sure enough, this was once the firehouse. But before that, it was the **tollhouse** *(tolhuis).* Although this canal once went all the way to the Markt (and water still runs under this square), entering vessels had to pause here to pay duties. Today it's the library and archive for the province of West Flanders.

The extremely skinny facade just left of the tollhouse (with the four carved figures over the red door) is the **Dockworkers' House** (Pijndershuisje). Above the door, notice the detailed carvings showing hardworking stevedores hunched beneath heavy loads. It's no wonder the Dutch word for this thankless occupation was *pijnder*—"one who feels pain."

As the entry point for trade into the city, this neighborhood was an eclectic zone of sailors from around the world. Many international dockworkers lived in little enclaves near here. Looking at a map, you'll see street names that echo this past: Spanjaardstraat ("Spaniard Street"), Biskajer-plein ("Basque Square"), and Engelsestraat ("English Street").

Facing the canal, find the brick house on the left corner. On the upper story, a **statue of Mary** stands in a niche, next to an old lamp. In the 18th century, when Bruges was in decline and in need of beautification, local authorities made landowners a deal: If they added a statue of Mary to their house, the city would install a gas light to illuminate it (the homeowner benefited from more light and security). Many burghers took them up on the offer, and more than 350 statues of Mary continue to decorate the city (many still with a lamp nearby). Once you start looking for them, you'll see them everywhere.

• *From here, enjoy a stroll through a...*

**Residential Canal Zone:** From the square, head straight along the canal (left side), simply enjoying the serene scenery. When you hit the wide cross-canal, jog left, cross the bridge, and continue straight up Carmersstraat. At the fifth street on the right—tiny Korte Speelmansstraat—you're a short block from the **Folklore Museum** and the **Lace Center** (both described later). After detouring there, backtrack to Carmersstraat and carry on straight until you pop out at the dike that separates Bruges from the old moat that surrounds it.

• *Sitting on top of the dike is the...*

**St. Janshuys Windmill:** In its heyday, bustling Bruges had 28 windmills, mostly used to grind grains. Built in 1770, this one was

funded by several local bakers. Notice how its narrow base allows it to swivel to catch the prevailing wind. Windmill keepers had to be as skilled at riggings as sailors—ready to cover the blades with canvas when the conditions were right. If you're curious about how this remarkable old technology operated, you can climb up the steep ladder-like stairs to enter the windmill (€4, Tue-Sun 9:30-12:30 & 13:30-17:00, closed Mon and Sept-April, tel. 050-448-743). In the top section, you'll see the mighty gears and appreciate how wind power not only spun the giant millstones, but also harnessed pulleys to hoist up heavy sacks of grain from the ground below. The grain steadily trickled into the ever-spinning millstones, which ground it and poured it down the spout, in the lower area of the windmill. There it was bagged and hoisted down to send off to the awaiting baker.

• *If you're on foot, you can keep strolling and explore the moat and other* *nearby windmills, including the tourable **Koelewei Windmill** (covered by St. Janshuys ticket, different style and an interesting complement but open only July-Aug). When you're ready to head back, retrace your steps—and consider detouring to the Folklore Museum and Lace Center, if you haven't yet visited these.*

*If you're on a bike, you can turn left and head up along the moat— past three more windmills—before you angle off to the right and head for Damme (see directions later, under "Bike Ride to Damme").*

### ▲Folklore Museum (Volkskundemuseum)

While "folklore" usually indicates farming lifestyles and colorful costumes, urbane Bruges dedicates its Folklore Museum to the occupations that kept the city humming through its industrious Golden Age. It's a well-presented little slice of Bruggian life, with modern exhibits filling a row of eight charming, interconnected 17th-century almshouses.

**Cost and Hours:** €6, €10 combo-ticket with Lace Center; Tue-Sun 9:30-17:00, closed Mon; Balstraat 43, tel. 050-448-764, www.brugge.be. To find it, ask for the Jerusalem Church.

**Visiting the Museum:** As you enter, borrow the English descriptions, which bring each room to life. You'll see a schoolhouse; workshops for a cobbler, clogmaker, and barrelmaker; a grocery; and exhibits featuring devotional objects and pipes.

In the garden courtyard, you can play a traditional folk game, then head back up to the main building to see the rest of the collection: the late-19th-century inn/pub (In de Zarte Kat—look for the resident black cat), a typical living room, fragrant candy shop, pharmacy, hatmaker, tailor, costume collection, and more.

### Lace Center (Kant Centrum)

Across the street from the Folklore Museum, this lace museum and school lets you learn about lacemaking and then see lace being made.

**Cost and Hours:** €6, €10 combo-ticket with Folklore Museum; Mon-Sat 9:30-17:00, closed Sun, demonstrations usually 14:00-17:00, come when the demonstrations are scheduled; tel. 050-330-072, Balstraat 16, www.kantcentrum.eu.

**Visiting the Lace Center:** Your tour starts with a brief movie about the history of lace (and why it was regarded as women's work). Next are exhibits explaining the different ways to make lace. A computer lets you try different techniques for making lace yourself—it ain't easy.

# Lace

Beginning in the 1500s and especially throughout the 1600s, lace collars, sleeves, headdresses, and veils became fashionable with members of royalty, the aristocracy, and the Catholic Church. All this fine lace was made by hand—and was expensive. For a time, lacemaking was a significant part of several European economies. Even so, it was primarily a cottage industry, with women working from their homes, using patterns and threads supplied to them by lace dealers. The lacemakers made little money for their effort, but the industry helped many peasant families support themselves (the lace dealers, however, became wealthy from the trade).

Men stopped wearing lace with the French Revolution of 1789, when suddenly lace for men seemed undemocratic and unmanly. Around 1800, machines replaced human hands, and except for ornamental pieces, the demand for lace died out.

These days, handmade lace is usually also homemade—produced by dedicated, sharp-eyed hobbyists who love their work. Lacemakers create their own patterns or trace tried-and-true designs. It requires total concentration to follow the intricate patterns. Producing a piece of lace by hand is time-consuming—which is why a handmade tablecloth can easily sell for €250 and up.

There are two basic kinds of lace: bobbin lace (a specialty in Bruges) and needle lace. To make bobbin lace, the lacemaker juggles many different strands tied to bobbins, "weaving" a design by overlapping the threads. Needle lace is more like sewing. The lacemaker uses a threaded needle to make loops and knots on top of a pattern in a fancy design. To see lace being made, drop by a demonstration at the Lace Center.

The payoff is upstairs in the demonstration room, where ladies chat merrily while making lace, usually using the bobbin technique perfected in Bruges. Observe as ladies toss bobbins madly while their eyes go bad. They follow mazelike patterns with a forest of pins to help guide their work.

Lace handiwork is on sale in the gift shop, along with materials for making lace on your own.

**Nearby:** Just down the street from the Lace Center is a lace shop with a good reputation, **'t Apostelientje** (generally 10:00-12:00 & 13:30-17:00 but closed Tue morning, Sun afternoon, and all day Mon, Balstraat 11, tel. 050-337-860).

# Experiences in Bruges

Bruges has some top-notch museums, but many of its charms are experiential: beer drinking, chocolate tasting, and bike riding.

## BEER

Much as wine flows through all aspects of French or Italian cuisine, Belgians prize beer above all else. Bruges offers a wide variety of places to sample brews, one of the most accessible and enjoyable brewery tours in Belgium, and an interesting museum on beer. For more on Belgian beers, see the "Eating" section of the Practicalities chapter. For recommendations on shops where you can buy bottles, see page 92.

### Pubs and Beer Halls

Hoisting a glass of beer is a quintessential ▲▲▲ Bruges experience. Here, pubs are not just pubs, they're destinations, and places in the old center—which you'd think would be overrun by tourists—are the proud domain of locals, who are happy to educate you on the (sometimes) hundreds of choices. I've listed some of my favorite spots to sample Bruges beer starting on page 87.

### ▲▲De Halve Maan Brewery Tour

Belgians are Europe's beer connoisseurs, and this handy tour is a great way to pay your respects. The only working, family brewery in Bruges, De Halve Maan pro-duces two beers: Brugse Zot ("Fool from Bruges") and Straffe Hendrik ("Strong Henry"). They also give entertaining and informative 45-minute tours. Avoid crowds by visiting early or late.

During your tour, you'll learn that "the components of the beer are vitally necessary and contribute to a well-balanced life pattern. Nerves, muscles, visual sentience, and healthy skin are stimulated by these in a positive manner. For longevity and lifelong equilibrium, drink Brugse Zot in moderation!" You'll also hear about their new beer pipeline that runs two miles underground to their bottling plant (it was partially crowdfunded).

Their bistro, where you'll drink your included beer, serves quick, hearty lunch plates daily and dinner Thu-Sat. You can eat indoors with the smell of hops, or outdoors with the smell of hops. This is a good place to wait for your tour or to linger afterward.

**Cost and Hours:** €10 tour includes a beer; tours run on the hour Sun-Fri 11:00-16:00, Sat until 17:00; smart to book online as tours can fill up—and you get a minor discount; lots of steep steps but a great rooftop panorama; Walplein 26, tel. 050-444-222, www.halvemaan.be.

### ▲Bruges Beer Museum

With a red-carpet entrance just off the Markt, this homage to beer's frothy history overlooks the square from the top of the former post office.

**Cost and Hours:** €9, €15 ticket includes three tastings, daily 10:00-17:00, Breidelstraat 3, tel. 050-699-229, www.mybeerexperience.com.

**Visiting the Museum:** Head up three flights of steep stairs to the museum's entrance, where you'll get an iPad and headphones to tour the exhibit and learn about the history of beermaking. The most interesting section is on the top floor, where you can run your hands through raw hops, yeast, and barley while getting a step-by-step guide to modern brewing.

When you've had your historical fill, saunter down to the bar and trade the iPad for three tokens good for your choice of tasting-size beers from a rotating list of 16 local drafts. The bar offers Markt views and is also open to the public (ticket not required).

## CHOCOLATE

Bruggians are connoisseurs of fine chocolate. You'll be tempted by chocolate-filled display windows all over town. While Godiva is the best big-factory/high-price/high-quality brand, there are plenty of smaller family-run places in Bruges that offer exquisite handmade chocolates. All of the following chocolatiers are proud of their creative varieties and welcome you to assemble a 100-gram assortment of five or six chocolates.

A rule of thumb when buying chocolate: Bruges' informal "chocolate mafia" keeps the price for midrange pralines quite standard, at about €28 per kilogram (or €2.80 for 100 grams). Swankier and "gastronomical" places (like The Chocolate Line or BbyB) charge significantly more, but only aficionados may be able to tell the difference. On the other hand, if a place is priced well *below* this range, be suspicious: Quality may suffer.

By the way, if you're looking for value, don't forget to check the supermarket shelves. Since the country is the largest producer of raw chocolate, Belgium's stores always have a wall of quality chocolate. Try Côte d'Or Noir de Noir for a simple bar of pure dark chocolate that won't flatten in your luggage.

### ▲Chocolate Shops

Katelijnestraat, which runs south from the Church of Our Lady, is "Chocolate Row," with a half-dozen shops within a few steps.

Locals rarely buy chocolate along here (as the prices are marked up for tourists), but this is a convenient place to shop. For locations, see the map on page 14.

**Dumon:** Perhaps Bruges' smoothest, creamiest chocolates are at Dumon, just off the Markt (a selection of 5 or 6 chocolates  are a deal at €2.80/100 grams). Nathalie Dumon runs the store with Madame Dumon still dropping by to help make their top-notch chocolate daily and sell it fresh. The Dumons will happily describe their chocolates to you—and they do it with an evangelical fervor. Try a small mix-and-match box to sample a few out-of-this-world flavors, and come back for more of your favorites. The family runs the original location just north of the Markt at Eiermarkt 6 (Wed-Mon 10:00-18:00, closed Tue, old chocolate molds on display in basement, tel. 050-346-282). A bigger, glitzier Dumon branch is at Simon Stevinplein 11. While technically their flagship store, it lacks the charm of the original—but they produce similar chocolates, offer additional types of pralines, and have a full coffee-and-hot-chocolate bar (daily 10:00-18:30, tel. 050-333-360). A third, less-interesting branch is farther south, at Walstraat 6.

**The Chocolate Line:** Locals and tourists alike flock here to taste the *gastronomique* varieties (pricey at about €7/100 grams) concocted by Dominique Persoone—the mad scientist of chocolate. His unique creations mix chocolate with various, mostly savory, flavors. Even those that sound gross can be surprisingly good: Havana cigar (marinated in rum, cognac, and Cuban tobacco leaves), Deadly Delicious (a chocolate skull filled with raspberry and hazelnut paste), wine vinegar, fried onions, lime/vodka/passion fruit, wasabi, and tomatoes/olives/basil. The kitchen—busy whipping up 80 varieties—is on display in the back. Enjoy the window display, refreshed monthly (Tue-Sat 9:30-18:30, Sun-Mon from 10:30, between Church of Our Lady and the Markt at Simon Stevinplein 19, tel. 050-341-090).

**BbyB:** This chichi, top-end chocolate gallery (whose name stands for "Babelutte by Bartholomeus," for the Michelin-starred restaurateur who owns it) lines up its pralines in a minimalist display case like priceless jewels, each type identified by number. If you don't mind—or actually enjoy—the pretense, the chocolates are top-notch (about €5 for a 5-flavor sleeve, €10 for a sleek 10-flavor sampler box; Tue-Sat 10:00-18:00, closed Sun-Mon; Sint-Amandsstraat 39, tel. 050-705-760, www.bbyb.be).

# A Brief History of Chocolate

While Belgium's chocolatiers rake in the euros today, their customers are just the latest in a long line of chocoholics.

Ancient Central American indigenous groups—from the Aztecs to the Mayans to the Olmecs—indulged in cocoa products for centuries; the earliest evidence of cocoa consumption dates to around 2000 BC. Cocoa was so prized that some societies used it as currency.

In 1519, the Aztec emperor Montezuma served Spanish conquistador Hernán Cortés a cup of hot cocoa (xocoatl) made from cocoa beans, which were native to the New World. It ignited a food fad in Europe—by 1700, elegant "chocolate houses" in Europe's capitals served hot chocolate (with milk and sugar added) to wealthy aristocrats. By the 1850s, the process of making chocolate candies was developed, and Belgium, with a long tradition of quality handmade luxuries, was at the forefront.

Cocoa comes from a big orange fruit that grows primarily in the tropical climates of Central and South America. The fruit's gooey pulp and beans are scooped out and left to ferment, then sun-dried for two weeks. The beans are roasted, creating "nibs"—the essence of cocoa.

Chocolate straight from the bean is very bitter, so nibs are processed into cocoa paste or cocoa butter, and the byproduct is ground again to make cocoa powder. Cocoa butter and cocoa paste are mixed together and sweetened with sugar to make chocolates. (Dark chocolate has a higher concentration of cocoa paste, while milk chocolate has more cocoa butter as well as milk powder.)

Europeans created the first chocolate bar in 1847. In 1876, a Swiss man named Henry Nestlé added concentrated milk, creating milk chocolate. And in 1912, Swiss confectioner Jean Neuhaus invented the Belgian praline in Brussels. Later innovators perfected the process, among them the Greek-American chocolatier Leonidas Kestekides, who started his internationally renowned company in Belgium.

Belgians divide their confections into two categories: **Truffles** have soft, crumbly chocolate shells filled with buttercream, while **pralines** are made of a hard chocolate shell with a wide range of fillings—totally different from the sugar-and-nuts French praline.

Belgians take chocolate seriously, and rightly so: It's an essential—and delicious—part of the economy.

**Confiserie De Clerck:** Third-generation chocolatier Jan sells his handmade chocolates for about €1.50/100 grams, making this one of the best deals in town. Some locals claim his chocolate's just as good as at pricier places, while others insist that any chocolate this cheap must be subpar—taste it and decide for yourself. The time-warp candy shop itself is so delightfully old-school, you'll want to visit one way or the other (Mon and Wed-Sat 10:00-18:00, closed Sun and Tue, Academiestraat 19, tel. 050-345-338).

## ▲Choco-Story: The Chocolate Museum

This kid-friendly museum with lots of artifacts fills you in on the production of truffles, bonbons, hollow figures, and solid bars of chocolate.

**Cost and Hours:** €8, includes chocolate bar; various combo-tickets include the Lamp Museum, Friet Museum, and Diamond Museum; daily 10:00-17:00, last entry 45 minutes before closing; where Wijnzakstraat meets Sint Jansstraat at Sint Jansplein, three-minute walk from the Markt; tel. 050-612-237, www.choco-story-brugge.be.

**Visiting the Museum:** Head up the stairs by the gigantic chocolate egg to follow the chronological exhibit, tracing 4,000 years of chocolate history. You'll discover why, in the ancient Mexican world of the Maya and Aztec, chocolate was considered the drink of the gods, and cocoa beans were used as a means of payment.

Higher up, you'll learn how chocolates are made and how Belgian pioneers perfected the process. And on the top floor, you'll view a delicious little video and learn more about the big-name Belgian chocolatiers (including some less-than-subtle product placement for Belcolade, which owns this museum). The finale is downstairs in the "demonstration room," where—after a 10-minute cooking demo—you get a taste.

**Related Sights:** The owners of the Chocolate Museum operate two similarly hokey but endearing museums that are open the same hours. Neither one is worth its €7 individual admission, but both are cheap add-ons with one of the Chocolate Museum's combo-tickets.

The museum owner's wife got tired of her husband's ancient lamp collection...so he opened the **Lamp Museum** (Lumina Domestica) next door. While obscure, it's an impressive and well-described collection showing lamps through the ages.

The same folks also run the **Friet Museum,** a few blocks away (at Vlamingstraat 33, www.frietmuseum.be). While this fun-loving and kid-friendly place tries hard to elevate the story of the potato, this is—for most—one museum too many. Still, it's the only place in the world that enthusiastically tells the story of French fries, which, of course, aren't even French—they're Belgian.

## BIKING

The Dutch word for bike is *fiets* (pronounced "feets"). And though Bruges' sights are close enough for easy walking, the town is a treat for bikers. A bike quickly gets you into dreamy back lanes without a hint of tourism. Take a peaceful evening ride through the town's nooks and crannies and around the outer canal. Consider keeping a bike for the duration of your stay—it's the way the locals get around. You can try one of the following rides, or ask at the rental shop for maps and ideas (see "Bike Rental" on page 17 for more info).

### ▲Markt to the Moat Ride

My self-guided walk from the Markt to the Moat (see listing earlier) is equally as fun on a bike. As this area is less touristy, it's less congested and easy to navigate on a bike. When you reach the end of the described route, you can circle the moat in either direction on the fine bike paths or continue riding, following the route described next.

### ▲Bike Ride to Damme

For the best short bike trip out of Bruges, pedal four miles each way to the nearby town of Damme. You'll enjoy a whiff of the countryside and see a working windmill while riding along a canal to a charming (if well-discovered) small market town. While Damme is cute, it's sleepy, with little to see—take this ride mostly as an excuse to pedal through the countryside, between canals and farm fields. Allow about two hours for the leisurely round-trip bike ride and a brief stop in Damme. The Belgium/Netherlands border is a 40-minute pedal (along the same canal) beyond Damme.

• *Head east from Bruges' Markt through Burg Square and out to the canal. (Or, for a more entertaining route, follow the directions under my "Markt to the Moat Stroll," earlier.) At the canal, circle to the left, riding along the former town wall and passing four windmills (including the St. Janshuys Windmill, described earlier). After the last windmill, at Dampoort, turn right across the second of two*

SIGHTS & EXPERIENCES IN BRUGES

*bridges (at the locks), then continue straight along the north/left bank of the Damme Canal (via Noorweegse Kaai/Damse Vaart-West).*

**The Damme Canal** (Damse Vaart): From Dampoort you'll pedal straight and level along the canal directly to Damme. There's no opportunity to cross the canal until you reach the town. The farmland to your left is a polder—a salt marsh that flooded each spring, until it was reclaimed by industrious local farmers. The

Damme Canal, also called the Napoleon Canal, was built in 1811 by Napoleon (actually by his Spanish prisoners) in a failed attempt to reinvigorate the city as a port. Today locals fish this canal for eels and wait for the next winter freeze. Old-timers have fond memories of skating to Holland on this canal—but nowadays such a hard freeze is a rare event (ask locals about the winter of 2008-2009).

**Schelle Windmill** (Schellemolen): Just before arriving in Damme, you'll come upon a working windmill that dates from 1867. This one is ingeniously designed so just the wood cap turns to face the wind—rather than the entire building. If it's open, climb up through the creaking, spinning, wind-powered gears to the top floor (free, Sat-Sun 9:30-12:30 & 13:00-18:00, closed Mon-Fri and Oct-March).

In its day (13th-15th century), Bruges was one of the top five European ports...and little Damme was important as well. But its once-bustling harbors silted up, and the sea retreated. Pause atop the bridge just beyond the windmill, with the windmill on your right and the spire of Bruges' Church of Our Lady poking up in the distance. It's easy to imagine how, at Napoleon's instructions, the canal was designed to mimic a grand Parisian boulevard—leading to the towering church back in Bruges.

• *From here, the canal continues straight to Holland. (If tempted...you're a third of the way to the border.) Instead, cross the bridge and follow Kerkstraat, which cuts through the center of town, to Damme's main square and City Hall.*

**Damme:** Contemporary Damme is now a tourist center—a tiny version of Bruges. It has a smaller but similar City Hall, a

St. John's Hospital, and a big brick Church of Our Lady. Five hundred years ago, Damme must have been rolling in herring money—its City Hall is made of French limestone rather than the more typical Belgian brick (like other buildings around here). Originally the ground floor was a market and fish warehouse, with government offices upstairs.

• *Continue on Kerkstraat as it leads two blocks farther to the Church of Our Lady. Along the way, you could side-trip to the left, down Pottenbakkersstraat, which takes you to a quaint little square called Haringmarkt (the Herring Market that made Damme rich in the 15th century). The trees you see from here mark the lines of the town's long-gone 17th-century ramparts. Returning to Kerkstraat, continue on to the big church.*

**The Church of Our Lady:** This church, which rose and fell with the fortunes of Damme, dates from the 13th century. Inside are two Virgin Marys: To the right of the altar is a 1630 wooden statue of Mary, and to the left is Our Lady of the Fishermen (c. 1650, in a glass case). Over the nave stands Belgium's oldest wooden statue, St. Andrew, with his X-shaped cross.

Outside, behind the 13th-century church tower, is a three-faced, modern fiberglass sculpture by the Belgian artist Charles Delporte. Called *View of Light*, it evokes three lights: morning (grace), midday (kindness), and evening (gentleness). If you like his work, there's more at a nearby gallery.

• *To return to Bruges, continue past the church on Kerkstraat. Just before crossing the next bridge, follow a scenic dirt lane to the right that leads you back to the Damme Canal (and Damse Vaart-Zuid). Take this road back to Bruges. If you want a change of pace from the canal, about half-way back turn off to the left (at the white bridge and brick house), then immediately turn right on Polderstraat and follow the smaller canal back to the outskirts of Bruges.*

# BRUGES CITY WALK

Bruges is made for walking. In just a couple of hours, you can get the lay of the land, pop in to a few sights, and mentally bookmark others to come back to later. On this walk, we'll get a sampling of what makes Bruges, Bruges. It's a city with a thousand years of history, and its citizens preserve their buildings and carry on their traditions with pride.

We'll start on the vast square with a towering bell tower that shows off the Golden Age of the 1400s, when Bruges was one of the richest cities on earth. We'll see art by Memling and Michelangelo, oak pilings from Bruges' foundations, the pious home of cloistered women, and maybe even a few drops of Christ's blood. Along the way you can sample local beer, watch swans glide beneath willow trees, and enjoy postcard views of a tranquil city reflected in a quiet canal.

## Orientation

**Length of This Walk:** Allow two hours for the walk, plus more time for touring sight interiors.

**Sightseeing Tip:** If you're planning to visit all the sights listed on this walk, consider buying the "Museumpas" combo-ticket (see page 17; the pass is sold at City Hall and the Renaissance Hall, near the start of the walk).

**Bell Tower:** €12, daily 9:30-18:00, last entry at 17:00 is strictly enforced.

**Basilica of the Holy Blood:** Church-free, treasury-€2.50, daily 9:30-12:00 & 14:00-17:30.

**City Hall and Renaissance Hall:** €6 ticket includes City Hall's Gothic Room and Renaissance Hall; daily 9:30-17:00 (Renaissance Hall closes 12:30-13:30).

**Church of Our Lady:** Free to glance down the nave, €4 to see art-filled apse and choir; Mon-Sat 9:30-17:00, Sun from 13:30.

**Sint-Janshospitaal Memling Collection:** €12, Tue-Sun 9:30-17:00, closed Mon.

**De Halve Maan Brewery Tour:** €10, tours run on the hour Sun-Fri 11:00-16:00, Sat until 17:00 (smart to book ahead).

**Begijnhof:** Courtyard-free, daily 6:30-18:30; museum-€2, Mon-Sat 10:00-17:00, closed Sun, shorter hours off-season.

# The Walk Begins

### ❶ Markt (Market Square)

Ringed by the frilly-spired post office, lots of restaurant terraces, great old gabled buildings, and the massive bell tower, this is the modern heart of the city.

The square is adorned with **flags:** There's the lion flag of Bruges (red, white, and blue) and the lion flag of Flanders (yellow and black)—Bruges is the capital of the region of Flanders. There's also the flag of Belgium (black, yellow, and red) and the flag of the European Union (blue with yellow stars). Visitors from all over Europe and the world roam the square. More than ever, in peak season, there are large cruise groups following the numbered ping-pong paddles of their guides.

Imagine this square back in the 1300s, during Bruges' glory days as a trading city. Back then (before the geography changed), Bruges was a major seaport, with a harbor that connected it to the open sea. Here on the Markt, a canal came right up to the square. Boats once moored next to where the Historium and TI stand today.

Cranes (powered by humans in hamster wheels) loaded and unloaded the boats. Right next to the dock, there was a vast warehouse where businessmen from all nations stored and traded goods. Most of the old buildings are gone, but on the opposite side of the square, locate the rectangular-shaped house with the modern gold ball on top—this is **Bruges' oldest house** (15th century). In former times, farmers shipped their cotton, wool, flax, and hemp to the port at Bruges. The industrious locals would spin, weave, and dye it into a finished product, then load it onto boats to ship throughout the known world.

By 1400, Bruggians were trading more refined goods, such as trendy clothes, tapestries, chairs, jewelry, and cotton-rag paper—a

# Bruges City Walk

**CANAL BOAT TOURS**
**HORSE-AND-BUGGY TOURS**

WALK BEGINS

1. Markt
2. Bell Tower
3. Burg Square
4. Basilica of the Holy Blood
5. City Hall
6. Renaissance Hall
7. Ruins in Crowne Plaza Hotel
8. Blinde-Ezelstraat
9. Fish Market
10. Huidevettersplein
11. Postcard Canal View
12. Picturesque Bridge
13. Church of Our Lady
14. Sint-Janshospitaal Memling Collection
15. De Halve Maan Brewery
16. Begijnhof
17. Minnewater

WALK ENDS

200 Meters
200 Yards

**BRUGES CITY WALK**

relatively new innovation (replacing parchment) made in Flanders. One of the Continent's first bookmakers worked here in Bruges.

The **statue** depicts two friends, Jan Breidel and Pieter de Coninc, who helped put this city on the world map. It's the year 1302, and clutching sword and shield, they look toward France, preparing to lead the citizens of Bruges against their French oppressors. The rebels identified potential French spies by demanding they repeat two words—*schild en vriend* (shield and friend)—only

Flemish locals (or foreigners with phlegm) could pronounce them. The French knights, thinking that fighting these Flemish peasants would be a cakewalk, wore their dress uniforms into battle. But the Flemish cleverly used hooks to pull the knights from their horses, scoring the medieval world's first victory of foot soldiers over cavalry, and of common people over nobility. The peasants had a field day afterward scavenging all the golden spurs from the fallen soldiers. And with that, Flanders won its freedom in what came to be called the Battle of the Golden Spurs.

Want a coffee? Consider the **Café-Brasserie Craenenburg** on the Markt (at #16). The building has been here since the 15th century, and it's been a café since 1905. Most of the square's "typical" old buildings were actually rebuilt in the 19th century. As Bruges recovered from centuries of decline, the city fathers wanted to return it to its former medieval glory. They built in an exaggerated medieval style called Neo-Gothic, full of spiky spires, fanciful towers, lacy stonework, and leering gargoyles. (This pre-Martin Luther style was also a political statement for this Catholic town.) The result is a medieval-era town that actually looks medieval—or "more Gothic than Gothic," as Bruges is often described.

• *Turn your attention to the...*

## ❷ Bell Tower (Belfort)

This bell tower has stood over the Markt since 1300. The octagonal lantern was added in 1486, making it 290 feet high. The tower displays many different architectural elements: medieval crenellations, pointed Gothic arches, round Roman arches, flamboyant spires, and even a few small flying buttresses (two-thirds of the way up).

At the base of the tower is another compelling feature—**Belgian fries.** Try some from either of the takeout stands. While the fries come with an array of exotic sauces, traditionally Belgians dip in mayonnaise—while kids and Americans enjoy ketchup.

Enter the courtyard. The public sits on benches here to enjoy free **carillon concerts** (normally Wed, Sat, and Sun at 11:00, plus mid-June-mid-Sept Mon and Wed at 21:00—see the posted schedule). A pay WC is in the courtyard.

The tower has 47 bells that chime periodically. Every 15 minutes, the carillon plays a little ditty. This is done mechanically, through the action of a giant barrel and movable tabs (like a barrel

organ or player-piano roll). At other times, there's a human caril-
lonneur who plays concerts, using a keyboard and foot pedal (like
an organist). In fact, playing the carillon is so strenuous that the
musician needs to use fists and feet, rather than fingers.

You can **climb the tower** (though the price is steeper than
its 366 steps). Just before you reach the top, peek into the carillon
room to see the mechanisms.
Be there on the quarter hour,
when things ring (the bell
experience is best at the top
of the hour). Atop the tower,
survey Bruges. On the horizon, you can see the towns
along the North Sea coast.

• *Back out on the square, get
oriented. Steenstraat, the
people-packed main shopping
street, stretches from in front of the belfry to the big 't Zand Square,
and eventually all the way to the train station. Geldmuntstraat, a block
northwest of the square, has fun shops and eateries you might check out
later.*

*Now, facing the bell tower, turn left (east) onto Breidelstraat, and
thread yourself through the lace and waffles to...*

## ❸ Burg Square

For over a thousand years, this opulent square has been Bruges'
historical birthplace, political center, and religious heart. Today

it's still the place where the citizens of Bruges carry on timeless
traditions in local festivals and
parades.

Pan the square counter-
clockwise to see six centuries
of architecture. You'll go from
Romanesque (the interior of
the fancy, gray-and-gold Basilica of the Holy Blood, in the
corner), to the pointed Gothic arches and prickly steeples of the
white sandstone City Hall, to the well-proportioned windows of
the Renaissance Hall (next door, under the gilded statues). Continue spinning, past the park, until you reach the elaborate 17th-
century Baroque Provost's House (at the head of Breidelstraat).
Now backtrack to the modern Crowne Plaza Hotel, which sits atop
thousand-year-old ruins (we'll visit shortly).

Dominating the square is **City Hall,** a symbol of Bruges'
proud independence. The facade's 49 statues feature several key fig-

## Bruges History

**Beginnings:** The city is founded in the 800s as a safe haven from Viking raiders.

**1100s Piety:** The relic of the Holy Blood makes Bruges a major pilgrimage destination.

**1200s Growth:** With its harbor on an inlet, Bruges begins trading with oceangoing ships as far as England (for raw wool) and the Mediterranean.

**1300s Independence:** Flanders wins its independence from France.

**1400s Golden Age:** This is Bruges' glory time, when trade, textile manufacture, pioneering painters, and a population of 150,000 make it one of Europe's greatest cities.

**1500s Changes:** Bruges and Flanders become part of the vast Habsburg empire—both augmenting the city and diminishing its independence.

**1600s Decline:** The harbor silts up, and trade routes shift, beginning two centuries of decline.

**1800s Inertia:** Bruges is a poor, rundown village adrift in an Industrial Age world. But its very backwardness inspires an idea...

**1900s Revival:** The citizens revamp the medieval (and medieval-looking) city, attracting visitors from around the world.

ures in Bruges' history. Baldwin I (bottom row, fourth statue from left) built a fort here in the 9th century, founding Bruges. Thierry of Alsace (in the upper-right tower) grabs his sword, hoping to secure the holy relic that would put Bruges on the pilgrimage map.

• *Let's go see the relic. Approach the gray building decorated with gold statues in the corner of Burg Square.*

## ❹ Basilica of the Holy Blood

The gleaming knights and ladies on the church's facade remind us that this church was built (c. 1150) by a brave Crusader to house the drops of Christ's blood he'd brought back from Jerusalem. The relic is still here today, and it still connects the people of Bruges to their roots.

**Visiting the Basilica:** Start by entering the ground-level lower chapel through the door labeled *St.-Basiliuskapel.*

**Lower Chapel:** The stark and dim decor reeks of the medieval piety that drove crusading Christian Europeans to try to free the Holy Land from Muslim rule. With heavy columns and round arches, the style is pure

## The Legend of the Holy Blood

Several drops of Christ's blood, washed from his lifeless body by Joseph of Arimathea, were preserved in a rock-crystal vial in Jerusalem. In 1150, the patriarch of Jerusalem gave the blood to a Flemish soldier, Thierry of Alsace, as thanks for rescuing his city from the Muslims during the Second Crusade. Thierry returned home and donated it to the city. The old, dried blood suddenly turned to liquid, a miracle repeated every Friday for the next two centuries, and verified by thousands of pilgrims from around Europe who flocked here to adore it. The blood dried up for good in 1325.

Every year on Ascension Day, Bruges' bankers, house-wives, and waffle vendors put on old-time costumes for the parading of the vial through the city. The slow-mo parade involves 1,700 locals and 50 floats: Crusader knights re-enact the bringing of the relic, Joseph of Arimathea washes Christ's body, and ladies in medieval costume with hair tied up in horn-like hairnets come out to wave flags. It takes 1.5 hours to watch the entire processional trudge past from beginning to end. Most of the remaining Bruges citizens just take the day off.

Romanesque. Step into the annex to see somber statues of Christ being tortured and entombed, plus a 12th-century relief panel over a doorway—it shows St. Basil (a fourth-century scholar-monk) being baptized by a double-jointed priest, and a man-size dove of the Holy Spirit. Now let's visit the place where the holy relic is kept.

• *To reach the upper chapel, go back outside and up the staircase.*

**Upper Chapel:** This chapel is as bright and cheery as the lower one was dim. After being gutted by secular-humanist French revo-lutionaries in 1799, the upper chapel's original Romanesque decor was re-done by 19th-century Romantics in a Neo-Gothic style. The nave is colorful, with a curved wooden ceiling, painted walls, a round pulpit carved from a single massive oak, and stained-glass windows of the dukes who ruled Flan-ders, along with their duchesses.

The **big painting** stretching be-hind the main altar tells the story of how the Holy Blood got here. Find Thierry of Alsace, count of Flanders (kneeling at lower left), the Crusader knight who brought the relic here. Having helped defend Bethlehem *(Bethlema)* and Jerusalem *(Hierosolyma)* from Muslim incursions, he kneels before the grateful Christian patri-arch of Jerusalem, who rewards him with the relic. Thierry returns home (right) and kneels before Bruges' bishop to give him the vial of blood. This church was built to display the relic for the hordes of believers who flocked to see it and feel its miraculous powers.

The **relic** itself—some red stuff preserved inside a clear, six-inch tube of rock crystal—is kept in the adjoining room (through the three arches). It's in the tall, silver tabernacle on the altar. (Each Friday—and many other days as well—the tabernacle's doors will be open, so you can actually see the vial of blood.) On holy days, the relic is shifted across the room and displayed on the throne under the canopy.

• *For more on the relic, step into the adjoining treasury (requires a ticket).*

**Treasury:** Here you can see the impressive gold and silver, gem-studded, hexagonal **reliquary** (c. 1600, left wall) that the vial

of blood is paraded around in on feast days. The vial is placed in the "casket" at the bottom of the three-foot-tall structure. Flanking the shrine are paintings of the Brotherhood of the Holy Blood. For centuries, this 31-member fraternity has tended the shrine and organized the pageantry. The Brotherhood is still in action today, and it's their job to carry the reliquary on their shoulders, parading it through the city streets on special occasions.

Elsewhere in the room are the Brotherhoods' **ceremonial objects:** necklaces, chalices, and so on. A centuries-old hunting horn is used to sound the alarm every year on the anniversary of the murder of a Flemish nobleman 100 yards from here, back in 1127 (which coincidentally allowed Thierry to take power). You may also see a fine tapestry, a remnant of Bruges' glory days of textile manufacture.

Finally, find the **small lead box** holding a broken glass tube. This is a replica of the precious rock-crystal vial that holds the blood of Christ. The lead box once protected the vial of blood from Protestant extremists (1578) and French revolutionaries (1799) bent on destroying what, to them, was a glaring symbol of Catholic mumbo jumbo.

• *Go back out into the square.*

## ❺ City Hall (Stadhuis)

Built in about 1400, when Bruges was a thriving bastion of capitalism with a population of 35,000, this building served as a model for town halls elsewhere, including Brussels. The white sandstone facade is studded with half-ton statues of knights, nobles, and saints with prickly Gothic steeples over their heads. A colorful double band of coats of arms includes those of Bruges (Brugghe) and Dunkirk (Dunquerke). Back then, Bruges' jurisdiction included many towns in present-day France. The building is still the City Hall; on Fridays and Saturdays, it's not unusual to see couples arriving here to get married.

**Visiting City Hall:** The ground-level lobby leads you to a **picture gallery** (free, closed Mon) with scenes and portraits from Belgium's history, from the Spanish king to the arrival of Napoleon, shown meeting the mayor here at the City Hall in 1803.

• *You can pay to climb the stairs for a look at the...*

**Gothic Room:** Some of modern democracy's roots lie in this ornate room, where, for centuries, the city council has met to discuss the town's affairs. In 1464, one of Europe's first parliaments, the Estates General of the Low Countries, convened here. The fireplace at the far end is inscribed with a 1305 proclamation: "All the artisans, laborers...and citizens of Bruges are free—all of them."

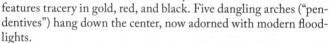

The elaborately carved and painted wooden ceiling (a Neo-Gothic reconstruction from the 19th century) features tracery in gold, red, and black. Five dangling arches ("pendentives") hang down the center, now adorned with modern floodlights.

The late-19th-century Romantic **wall murals** depict episodes in the city's history. Start with the largest painting along the left wall, and work clockwise.

In the **big painting on the left wall,** everyone cheers, flags wave, trumpets blare, and dogs bark, as Bruges' knights, dressed

in gold with black Flemish lions, return triumphant after driving out French oppressors and winning Flanders' independence. The Battle of the Golden Spurs (1302) is remembered every July 11.

Next, the **painting on the fireplace wall** shows cardinals in red flocking to this elaborate ceremony. In what may have been Bruges' high-water mark, Philip the Good of Burgundy (seated, in black) assembled his court here in Bruges and solemnly founded the knightly Order of the Golden Fleece (1429).

Next, the Crusader knight, Thierry of Alsace, returns from the Holy Land and kneels at the entrance of St. Basil's Chapel to present the relic of Christ's Holy Blood (c. 1150).

On the **right wall,** a nun carries a basket of bread in this scene from Sint-Janshospitaal (St. John's Hospital).

A town leader stands at the podium and hands a sealed document to a German businessman, renewing the Hanseatic League's business license. Membership in this club of trading cities was a key to Bruges' prosperity.

As peasants cheer, a messenger of the local duke proclaims the town's right to self-government (1190).

The mayor visits a Bruges painting studio to shake the hand of Jan van Eyck, the great Flemish Primitive painter (1433). Jan's wife, Margareta, is there, too. In the 1400s, Bruges rivaled Florence and Venice as Europe's cultural capital. See the town in the distance, out Van Eyck's window.

Bruges' book printer sells his wares—the first English-language books printed on the Continent (in 1474).

City fathers grab a ceremonial trowel from a pillow to lay the fancy cornerstone of the City Hall (1376). Bruges' familiar towers (before the lantern was added to the bell tower) stand in the background.

The city's best-known medieval poet gazes out the window for inspiration.

On the **back wall,** it's a typical market day at the Halls (the courtyard behind the bell tower). Arabs mingle with Germans in fur-lined coats and beards in a market where they sell everything from armor to lemons.

And finally, a bishop blesses a new canal (1404) as ships sail right by the city. This was Bruges in its heyday, before the silting of the harbor. At the far right, the two bearded men with moustaches are the brothers who painted these murals.

**Adjoining Room:** Old paintings and maps show how little the city has changed through the centuries. Find one well-known **map** (in pale white, aqua, and gold, on the left wall). It shows in exquisite detail the city as it looked in 1562. Find the bell tower, the Church of Our Lady, and Burg Square, which back then was bounded on the north by a cathedral. Notice the canal (on the west) leading from the North Sea right to the Markt. A moat encircled the city with its gates, unfinished wall, and 28 windmills (four of which sur-

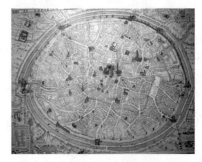

vive today). The mills pumped water to the town's fountains, made paper, ground grain, and functioned as the motor of the Middle Ages. Most locals own a copy of this map that shows how their neighborhood looked 400 years ago.

• *Leaving City Hall, turn right and go to the corner of the square to enter...*

## ❻ Renaissance Hall (Brugse Vrije)

This elaborately adorned mansion has served Bruges as a governing palace, a courthouse, and (today) as the city archives. The white facade with gold and red trim dates from the 1720s. Notice the crowned heads, each with their unique personality.

**Visiting the Hall:** Go inside to find the elaborately decorated Renaissance Hall. If you're into heraldry, it's fascinating. If not, you'll wonder where the rest of the museum is.

This ornate room was where the town's burghers met. They'd sit on the green benches around the perimeter, under a lavish wood-beamed ceiling and surrounded by tapestry-covered walls. The big green table at one end is where they played medieval snooker. (Actually, it was the dais for the presiding bigwigs.)

The highlight of the room is the grand **fireplace mantelpiece** carved from oak by Bruges' Renaissance Man, Lancelot Blond-

eel, in 1531. In the center of it stands the most powerful man in Europe—Holy Roman Emperor Charles V. His crown, sword, and orb symbolize his power—as does his bulging codpiece. (The hall may also display another, more human bust of Charles.)

Charles had recently freed Bruges (yet again) from French rule, making the city part of his pan-European Habsburg empire, so the city fathers honored him here. They also included their hometown duke (to the left), who was related to Charles. The duke's crown, orb, and codpiece mirror those of Charles, indicating the family jewels were well-guarded. By making the connection to the Holy Roman Emperor clear, this carved family tree helped substantiate the power of Bruges' nobility. You'll also see the double-eagle emblem (above Charles and elsewhere in the room), the Habsburg family symbol. The other coats of arms belong to the many European nobles under Charles' powerful reign. Check out the expressive little cherubs.

Notice the **painting** that stands nearby. It depicts this very same hall you're standing in: There's the fireplace, the same paneled walls, and the raised green table where justices sat in judgment. The painting shows the room in action in 1659, as the lace-collared judges hear the pleas of a repentant man before deciding his punishment. One of the judges is about to pull that long chain to ring a bell and seal his fate.

• *Leaving the building, walk straight ahead and hook around the cream-colored building to your right.*

## ❼ Ruins in the Crowne Plaza Hotel

One of the old town's newest buildings (1992) sits atop the ruins of the town's oldest structures—the original fort that established Bruges. In the late 9th century, when Viking ships regularly docked here to rape and pillage, Baldwin I (also known as Iron Arm) built a fort *(castrum)* to protect his Flemish people. In 950, the fort was converted into St. Donatian's Church, which became one of the city's largest. That church was destroyed in the 1800s during Napoleon's invasion (leaving nothing but a park bordering Burg Square). In the 20th century, the Crowne Plaza rose over the ruins, but only on the condition that visitors be allowed to see them.

**Visiting the Ruins:** Ask at the hotel's reception desk to see the archaeological site (ruins of the fort and the church). If there's no conference in progress, they'll let you walk down the stairs and have a peek.

In the basement, the modern conference rooms are lined with old stone walls and display cases of objects found in the ruins of earlier structures. Trace the history.

See thousand-year-old oak pilings, carved to a point, once driven into this former peat bog to support the original fort and shore up its moat. Next, see paintings that show the church that replaced it. The curved stone walls you walk among are from the foundations of the ambulatory around the church altar.

A document (*Vente de Materiaux,* posted back where you entered) announces the "sale of material" when Napoleon destroyed the church in the early 1800s and auctioned off the bricks. A local builder bought them, and now the pieces of the old cathedral are embedded in other buildings throughout Bruges.

Display cases around the room show what modern archaeologists found around here—the refuse of a thousand years of habitation: pottery, animal skulls, rosary beads, dice, coins, keys, thimbles, pipes, spoons, and Delftware. There's also a 14th-century sarcophagus painted with the Crucifixion on the west end and a Virgin and Child on the east.

• *Back on Burg Square, find the passageway by Renaissance Hall. This alley is called...*

### ❽ Blinde-Ezelstraat

At the alley's entrance—on the corner of City Hall—is a **statue of the Virgin Mary** known to locals as Our Lady of the Inkpot.

In past times, locals nodded to the statue as they passed, and she is still the protector of the town council.

Head down the alley. Midway down on the left side (thigh level), see an original **iron hinge** from the city's south gate, back when the city was ringed by a moat and closed nightly at 22:00. On the right wall, at eye level, a square black patch shows you just how grimy the city had become before a 1960s cleaning. Despite the cleaning and a few fanciful reconstructions, the city today looks much as it did in centuries past.

The name "Blinde-Ezelstraat" means "Blind Donkey Street." Perhaps in medieval times, the donkeys, carrying fish from the North Sea on their backs, were stopped here so that their owners could put blinders on them. Otherwise, the donkeys wouldn't cross the water between the old city and the fish market.

From the end of the alleyway, look back and up for a nice photo-op of the Goldfinger family standing atop the alley's sky bridge.

• *Step onto the bridge over one of Bruges' many canals. This particular canal was the 13th-century city moat around the old town. What would you name a city built atop water? How about "Brugge"—old Flemish for "bridge"? Crossing the bridge, on your left are the arcades of the...*

### ❾ Fish Market (Vismarkt)

The North Sea is just 12 miles away, and the fresh catch is sold

here. Locals love the shrimp—cooked on the boat before arriving at the market. Today this once-thriving market has mostly crafts and souvenirs... and the big catch is the tourists (fish market open Wed-Sat 6:00-13:00, closed Sun-Tue; souvenir market open daily).

• *Take an immediate right (west), entering a courtyard called...*

## ❿ Huidevettersplein

This tiny, picturesque, restaurant-filled square was originally the headquarters of the town's skinners and tanners. The lions atop the

square's lone column hold the tanners' logo. On the facade of the Hotel Duc de Bourgogne, four old relief panels above the windows show scenes from the leather trade—once a leading Bruges industry. First, tan the hide in a bath of acid; then, with tongs, pull it out to dry; then beat it to make it soft; and, finally, scrape and clean it to make it ready for sale.

• *Continue a few steps to Rozenhoedkaai street, where you can look back to your right and get a great...*

## ⓫ Postcard Canal View

The bell tower reflected in a quiet canal lined with old houses—this view is the essence of Bruges. Seeing buildings rising straight

from the water makes you understand why this was called the Venice of the North. Can you see the bell tower's tilt? It leans about four feet. The tilt has been carefully monitored since 1740, but no change has been detected.

As you face the view, to your left (west) down the Dijver canal (past a flea market on weekends) looms the huge spire of the Church of Our Lady, the tallest brick spire in the Low Countries. Between you and the church is Europa College, a prestigious post-graduate institution that has produced many well-known "Eurocrats"—diplomats, lawyers, and economists who run the European Union.

• *Walk ahead, toward the steeple of Our Lady. About 100 yards ahead, on the left, is the copper-colored sign that points the way to the* **Groeninge Museum**. *This sumptuous collection of paintings highlights Bruges' own Flemish Primitives, with all their glorious detail (📖 see the Groeninge Museum Tour chapter).*

*Continue another half-block past the Groeninge Museum. At Dijver 16, turn left into a quiet courtyard. You'll pass by the entrance to* *the **Arentshuis Museum** (covered at the end of the Groeninge Museum Tour chapter). Continue through the courtyard to the far right corner, where you'll find a...*

## ⑫ Picturesque Bridge

Standing atop this tiny stone bridge over a little canal, take in the scene and savor its beauty. Start with the back end of the church,

admiring Our Lady's big buttresses and round apse. Panning clockwise, find a teeny-tiny window at the corner of a building—a toll-keeper's lookout. Below that, at canal level, you could snap a photo of your travel partner at the iron bars. Continue panning until you find the old relief panel of a boat (directly behind you). Next comes the old wooden house along the canal. Finally, in the garden, there's a bust of Juan Luis Vives (1492-1540), the Spanish-born resident of Bruges whose writings on the connection between the body and the soul made him the "father of psychology."

• *Cross the bridge, veer left along the hedge-lined path, and find the church entry on the right.*

## ⑬ Church of Our Lady (Onze-Lieve-Vrouwekerk)

This towering brick church stands as a memorial to the power and wealth of Bruges in its heyday. Step inside. While you can stand

in the back and marvel at its interior, to get a close-up look at its historic tombs and art—including a Michelangelo—you'll need to pay for a ticket. As the church is undergoing a major renovation, some parts may be closed to visitors, and your tour may follow a different route than I describe.

**Visiting the Church:** Enter and stand in the back to admire the Church of Our Lady—whitewashed walls below,

gray stone midway up, and a red-brick ceiling above. Its 14th- and 15th-century stained glass was destroyed by iconoclasts, so the church is lit more brightly today than originally. Like most churches in Belgium, this one is Catholic. The medieval-style screen (topped with the organ) once divided the clergy from the commoners who gathered here in the nave. Worshippers are still attended by 12 Gothic-era statues of apostles, each with his symbol and a grandiose Baroque wooden pulpit, with a roof that seems to float in midair. It was from this fancy perch that the priest would interpret the word of God.

**_Madonna and Child_ by Michelangelo:** Pay and pass through the turnstile, entering first a chapel featuring a small marble Mi-

chelangelo statue. The delicate sculpture is somewhat overwhelmed by its ornate Baroque niche. It's said to be the only Michelangelo statue to leave Italy in the artist's lifetime, bought in Tuscany by a wealthy Bruges businessman, who's buried in the same chapel (to the right).

As Michelangelo chipped away at the masterpiece of his youth, _David,_ he took breaks by carving this one in 1504. Mary, slightly smaller than life-size, sits while young Jesus stands in front of her. Their expressions are mirror images—serene, but a bit melancholy, with downcast eyes, as though pondering the young child's dangerous future. Though they're lost in thought, their hands instinctively link, tenderly. The white Carrara marble is highly polished, something Michelangelo only did when he was certain he'd gotten it right.

**Tombs at the High Altar:** Two statues lying tits-up atop coffins mark the tombs of the last local rulers of Bruges: Mary of Burgundy and her father, Charles the Bold. The dog and lion at their feet are symbols of fidelity and courage. Underneath the tombs are the actual excavated gravesites with mirrors to help you enjoy the well-lit, centuries-old tomb paintings.

These tombs represent the point in time when the city began its slow, four-century decline. Charles the Bold died prematurely, in war, in 1477. And in 1482, 25-year-old Mary tumbled from her horse and died. She left behind a toddler son and a husband who was heir to the Holy Roman Empire. The twin deaths meant Bruges now belonged to Austria, and would soon be swallowed up by the empire and ruled from Vienna by Habsburgs—who didn't understand or care about its problems. Meanwhile, Bruges' North Sea port silted up, and trade routes shifted to Antwerp and Amsterdam. The city was eventually mothballed—until this sleeping beauty of Flemish towns was rediscovered by modern-day tourists.

BRUGES CITY WALK

The first tourists were Americans and Canadians who came in the wake of World War I to visit the graves of loved ones in nearby cemeteries.

**Rest of the Church:** To the left of the painted altarpiece is a wooden balcony on the wall. It's part of the Gruuthuse mansion next door, and once provided that noble family with prime seats for Mass.

To the right of the altarpiece is a side chapel with fascinating 14th-century tombs found during excavations. Some are painted with images of Mary as Queen of Heaven (on a throne, carrying a crown and scepter) and Mother of God (with the Baby Jesus on her lap). Since Mary is in charge of advocating with Jesus for your salvation, she's a good person to have painted on the wall of your tomb. The tombs also show lots of angels—generally patron saints of the dead person—swinging incense burners.

• *Near the church on Mariastraat is the entrance to perhaps the city's most visit-worthy museum. Note that there are two entrances to this complex—a passageway, and a door 20 yards farther south. You want the door, which leads to the museum.*

## ⑭ Sint-Janshospitaal (St. John's Hospital)

The former wards and church of Sint-Janshospitaal are home to a museum with two delightful elements. First there's a look at the one-time hospital's main hall, filled with displays on medieval medicine. But the real highlight here is a collection of masterpieces by Hans Memling, the German painter who made his artistic mark in Bruges. (□ See the Sint-Janshospitaal Memling Collection Tour chapter.)

• *Leaving the museum, turn right and go about 30 paces to enjoy a fine canal view. Before you is one of many canal tour boat companies. (As they share city waterways, they all have the same price and standards.) The canal here was part of the city moat. Standing here in the 15th century, you would have just left town through the Maria Gate. Continue on down Katelijnestraat. After about 50 yards, turn right and go down a tiny lane, Stoofstraat. This was "Stove Street"—where the neighborhood's public bathhouse stood—which in times past served (like ancient Roman baths) as a place to bathe, work out, and socialize. Stoofstraat leads into the pleasant square called Walplein, where you'll find the...*

## ⑮ De Halve Maan Brewery

If you like beer, take a tour here. On busy days, tours can fill up, so you may want to reserve a spot online in advance (see page 33).

• *Leaving the brewery, head right, then turn right on Wijngaartstraat. You'll reach a **horse-head fountain,** where the horse-and-buggy horses stop to drink. From the fountain, turn right and pause in the center* *of a picturesque pedestrian bridge. Before you, above the gate, a sign reads* Sauve Garde—*you are entering the protection of the sisters and leaving the jurisdiction of the city. The relief above shows St. Elizabeth taking care of the handicapped. Walk through the gate and, as the lacy charm of Bruges crescendos, enter the...*

## ⑯ Begijnhof

Begijnhofs (buh-*H*INE-hof) were built to house women of the lay order, called Beguines. Though obedient to a mother superior, they

did not have to take the vows of a nun. They spent their days deep in prayer, spinning wool, making lace, teaching, and caring for the sick. The Beguines' ranks swelled during the Golden Age, when so many women were widowed or unwed due to the hazards of war and overseas trade. The order of Beguines offered such women a dignified place to live and work. When the order died out, many begijnhofs were taken over by towns for subsidized housing. Today, single religious women live in the small homes. Benedictine nuns live in a building on the far side.

There are several sights here. You can tour the simple **museum** to get a sense of Beguine life. It's a typical Beguine's residence—kitchen, dining room, bedroom—with period furniture (spinning wheel, foot warmer). Don't miss the bedroom out back across the tiny cloister. The "Liturgical Center" is little more than a gift shop.

In the **church,** enjoy the peaceful interior, with its carved pulpit and tombstones on the floor. The altar has corkscrew columns and a painting of the Beguines' patron, St. Elizabeth. On the right wall is an 800-year-old golden statue of Mary. The rope that dangles from the ceiling is yanked by a nun to announce a sung vespers service. The Benedictine nuns gather at 11:55, proceed through the garden, and sing and chant a cappella in the choir of the church. The public is welcome for this service.

• *Exiting the church, turn left, and leave the Begijnhof courtyard. Take your first left, through the gate, to a view of the lake known as...*

## ⑰ Minnewater

Just south of the Begijnhof is Minnewater ("Water of Love"), a

BRUGES CITY WALK

peaceful, lake-filled park with canals, weeping willows, and swans. This was once far from quaint—it was a busy harbor where small boats shuttled cargo from the big, oceangoing ships into town. From this point, the cargo was transferred again to flat-bottomed boats that went through the town's canals to their respective warehouses and to the Markt.

When locals see these swans, they recall the 15th-century mayor—famous for his long neck—who collaborated with the Austrians. The townsfolk beheaded  him as a traitor. The Austrians warned them that similarly long-necked swans would inhabit the place to forever remind them of this murder. And they do. With this sweet little murder story, we end our tour of perhaps the cutest town in Europe.

• *You're a five-minute walk from the train station or a 15-minute walk from the Markt. If you walk back to the town center, consider a detour along Nieuwe Gentweg to visit one of about 20* **almshouses** *in the city. At #8, go through the door marked Godshuis de Meulenaere 1613 into the peaceful courtyard (free). This was a medieval form of housing for the poor. The rich would pay for someone's tiny room here in return for lots of prayers.*

**BRUGES CITY WALK**

# GROENINGE MUSEUM TOUR

*Groeningemuseum*

In the 1400s, Bruges was northern Europe's richest, most cosmopolitan, and most cultured city. New ideas, fads, and painting techniques were imported and exported with each shipload. Beautiful paintings were soon an affordable luxury, like fancy clothes or furniture. Internationally known artists set up studios in Bruges, producing portraits and altarpieces for wealthy merchants from all over Europe.

Understandably, the Groeninge Museum has one of the world's best collections of the art produced in the city and surrounding area. Early Flemish art is less appreciated and understood today than the Italian Renaissance art of the same era. This chapter highlights several masterpieces to give you an introduction to this subtle, technically advanced, and beautiful style. Hey, if you can master the museum's name (*H*ROON-ih-guh), you can certainly handle the art.

As you wander, notice that many artists, having lived and worked in Bruges, included scenes of the picturesque city in their pieces, proving that it looks today much as it did way back when. Enjoy the many painted scenes of old Bruges as a slice-of-life peek into the city and its people back in its glory days.

# Orientation

**Cost:** €12, more for special exhibits, ticket includes entry to nearby Arentshuis Museum (described at the end of this chapter).

**Hours:** Tue-Sun 9:30-17:00, closed Mon.

**Information:** Tel. 050-448-743, www.brugge.be.

**Getting There:** The museum is at Dijver 12, near the Church of Our Lady.

**Length of This Tour:** Allow one hour.

**Starring:** The meticulous details and limpid atmosphere of Flemish Primitive art; Jan van Eyck's *Canon Joris* and *Portrait of Margareta van Eyck;* and Rogier van der Weyden's *Duke Philip the Good.*

# The Tour Begins

The collection fills 10 rooms on one easy floor, arranged chronologically from the 15th to the 20th century. As the collection is far bigger than the actual gallery, some paintings featured here may be rotated out or in a different location.

## GOLDEN AGE MASTERS

• *Starting in Room 1, look for...*

### Gerard David, *Judgment of Cambyses,* 1498

That's gotta hurt.

A man is stretched across a table and skinned alive in a very businesslike manner. The crowd hardly notices, and a dog just

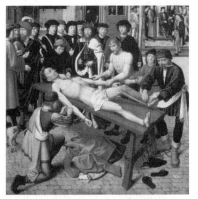

scratches himself. According to legend, the man was a judge arrested for corruption (left panel) and flayed (right panel), then his skin was draped (right panel background) over the new judge's throne.

Gerard David (c. 1455-1523), Memling's successor as the city's leading artist, painted this for the City Hall. City councilors could ponder what might happen to them if they abused their offices.

By David's time, Bruges was in serious decline, with a failing economy and struggles against the powerful Austrian Habsburg family. The Primitive style also was fading. Italian art was popular, so David tried to spice up his retro-Primitive work with pseudo-

*GROENINGE MUSEUM*

Renaissance knickknacks—*putti* (baby angels, over the judgment throne), Roman-style medallions, and garlands. But he couldn't quite master the Italian specialty of 3-D perspective. We view the flayed man at an angle from slightly above, but the table he lies on is shown more from the side.

### Attributed to Hieronymus Bosch, *Last Judgment,* late 15th century

It's the end of the world, and Christ descends in a bubble to pass judgment on puny humans. Little naked people dance and cavort

in a theme park of medieval symbolism, desperately trying to squeeze in their last bit of fun. Meanwhile, some wicked souls are being punished, victims either of their own stupidity or of genetically engineered demons. The good are sent to the left panel to frolic in the innocence of paradise, while the rest are damned to hell (right panel) to be tortured under a burning sky. Bosch paints the scenes with a high horizon line, making it seem that the chaos extends forever.

The bizarre work of Bosch (c. 1450-1516)—who, by the way, was not from Bruges—is open to many interpretations, but some see it as a warning for the turbulent times. He painted during the dawn of a new age. Secular ideas and materialism were encroaching, and the pious, serene medieval world was shattering into chaos. Be aware that this masterpiece is often out on loan and may not be shown in Room 1; ask the attendant if you can't find it.

• *Head to Rooms 2-4 for the following paintings—the core of the collection.*

### Jan van Eyck, *Virgin and Child with Canon Joris van der Paele,* 1436

Jan van Eyck (c. 1390-1441) was the world's first and greatest oil painter, and this is his masterpiece—three debatable but defensible assertions.

Mary, in a magnificent red gown, sits playing with her little baby, Jesus. Jesus glances up as St. George, the dragon-slaying knight, enters the room, tips his cap, and says, "I'd like to introduce my namesake, George (Joris)." Mary glances down at the kneeling Joris, a church official dressed in white.

# Flemish Primitives

Despite the "Primitive" label, the Low Countries of the 1400s (along with Venice and Florence) produced the most refined art in Europe. Here are some common features of Flemish Primitive art.

**Primitive 3-D Perspective:** Expect unnaturally cramped-looking rooms; oddly slanted tables; and flat, cardboard-cutout people with stiff postures. Yes, these works are more primitive (hence the label) than those using later Italian Renaissance perspective.

**Realism:** Everyday bankers and clothmakers in their Sunday best are painted with clinical, warts-and-all precision. Even saints and heavenly visions are brought down to earth.

**Details:** Like meticulous Bruges craftsmen, painters used fine-point brushes to capture almost microscopic details—flower petals, wrinkled foreheads, intricately patterned clothes, the sparkle in a ruby. The closer you get to a painting, the better it looks.

**Oil Painted on Wood:** They were the pioneers of newfangled oil-based paint (while Italy still used egg-yolk tempera), working on wood before canvas became popular.

**Portraits and Altarpieces:** Wealthy merchants and clergymen paid to have themselves painted either alone or mingling with saints.

**Symbolism:** In earlier times, everyone understood that a dog symbolized fidelity, a lily meant chastity, and a rose was love.

**Materialism:** Rich Flanders celebrated the beauty of luxury goods—the latest Italian dresses, jewels, carpets, oak tables—and the ordinary beauty that radiates from flesh-and-blood people.

Joris takes off his glasses and looks up from his prayer book to see a bishop in blue, St. Donatian, patron of the church he hopes to be buried in.

Canon Joris, who hired Van Eyck, is not a pretty sight. He's old and wrinkled, with a double chin, weird earlobes, and bloodshot eyes. But the portrait isn't unflattering; it just shows unvarnished reality with crystal clarity.

Van Eyck brings Mary and the saints down from heaven and into a typical (rich) Bruges home. He strips off their haloes, banishes all angels, and pulls the plug on heavenly radiance. If this is a religious painting, then where's God?

God's in the details. From the bishop's damask robe and Mary's wispy hair to the folds in Jesus' baby fat and the oriental carpet to "Adonai" (Lord) written on St. George's breastplate, the painting is as complex and beautiful as God's creation. The color scheme—red Mary, white canon, and blue-and-gold saints—are Bruges' city colors, from its coat of arms.

Mary, crowned with a jeweled "halo" and surrounded by beautiful things, makes an appearance in 1400s Bruges, where she can be adored in all her human beauty by Canon Joris...and by us, reflected in the mirror-like shield on St. George's back.

### Jan van Eyck, *Portrait of Margareta van Eyck,* 1439

At 35, shortly after moving to Bruges, Jan van Eyck married 20-year-old Margareta. They had two kids, and after Jan died,

Margareta took charge of his studio of assistants and kept it running until her death. This portrait (age 33), when paired with a matching self-portrait of Jan, was one of Europe's first husband-and-wife companion sets.

She sits half-turned, looking out of the frame. (Jan might have seen this "where-have-you-been?" expression in the window late one night.) She's dressed in a red, fur-lined coat, and we catch a glimpse of her wedding ring. Her hair is invisible—very fashionable at the time—pulled back tightly, bunched into horn-like hairnets, and draped with a headdress. Stray hairs along the perimeter were plucked to achieve the high forehead look.

This simple portrait is revolutionary—one of history's first individual portraits that wasn't of a saint, a king, a duke, or a pope, and wasn't part of a religious work. It signals the advent of humanism, celebrating the glory of ordinary people. Van Eyck proudly signed the work on the original frame, with his motto saying he painted it *"als ik kan" (ALC IXH KAN)*..."as good as I can."

### Rogier van der Weyden, *St. Luke Drawing the Virgin's Portrait,* c. 1435

Rogier van der Weyden (c. 1399-1464), the other giant among the Flemish Primitives, adds the human touch to Van Eyck's rather detached precision.

As Mary prepares to nurse her child, Baby Jesus can't contain his glee, wiggling his fingers and toes, anticipating

lunch. Mary, dressed in everyday clothes, doesn't try to hide her love as she tilts her head down with a proud smile. Meanwhile, St. Luke (the patron saint of painters, who was said to have experienced this vision) looks on intently with a sketch pad in his hand, trying to catch the scene. These small gestures, movements, and facial expressions add an element of human emotion that later artists would amplify.

The painting is neatly divided by a spacious view out the window, showing a river stretching off to a spacious horizon. Van der Weyden experimented with 3-D effects like this one (though ultimately it's just window-dressing).

### Rogier van der Weyden, *Duke Philip the Good,* c. 1450

Tall, lean, and elegant, this charismatic duke transformed Bruges from a commercial powerhouse to a cultural one. In 1425, Philip

moved his court to Bruges, making it the de facto capital of a Burgundian empire stretching from Amsterdam to Switzerland.

Philip wears a big hat to hide his hair, a fashion trend he himself began. He's also wearing the gold-chain necklace of the Order of the Golden Fleece, a distinguished knightly honor he gave himself. He inaugurated the Golden Fleece in a lavish ceremony at the Bruges City Hall, complete with parades, jousting, and festive pies that contained live people hiding inside to surprise his guests.

As a lover of painting, hunting, fine clothes, and many mistresses, Philip was a role model for Italian princes, such as Lorenzo the Magnificent—the *uomo universale,* the Renaissance Man.

### Hugo van der Goes, *Death of the Virgin,* c. 1470

This piece may not be on display when you visit. The long death-watch is over—their beloved Mary has passed, and the disciples are dazed with grief, as though hit with a spiritual two-by-four. Each face is a study in sadness, all coping differently—lighting a candle, fidgeting, praying, or just staring off into space. Blues and reds dominate, and there's little eye-catch-

## Oil Paint

Take vegetable oil pressed from linseeds (flax), blend in dry powdered pigments, whip to a paste the consistency of room-temperature butter, then brush onto a panel of whitewashed oak—you're painting in oils. First popularized in the early 1400s, oil eventually overshadowed egg-yolk-based tempera. Though tempera was great for making fine lines shaded with simple blocks of color, oil could blend colors together seamlessly.

Watch a master create a single dog's hair: He paints a dark stroke of brown, then lets it dry. Then comes a second layer painted over it, of translucent orange. The brown shows through, blending with the orange to match the color of a collie. Finally, he applies a third, transparent layer (a "glaze"), giving the collie her healthy sheen.

Many great artists were not necessarily great painters (e.g., Michelangelo). Van Eyck, Rembrandt, Hals, Velázquez, and Rubens were master painters, meticulously building objects with successive layers of paint...but they're not everyone's favorite artists.

ing ornamentation, which lets the lined faces and expressive hand gestures do the talking.

Hugo van der Goes (c. 1430-c. 1482) painted this, his last major work, the same year he attempted suicide. He had built a successful career in Ghent, then abruptly dropped out to join a monastery. His paintings became increasingly emotionally charged, his personality more troubled.

Above the bed floats a heavenly vision, as Jesus and the angels prepare to receive Mary's soul. Their smooth skin and serene expressions contrast with the gritty, wrinkled death pallor of those on earth. Caught up in their own grief, the disciples can't see the silver lining.

### Hans Memling, *The Moreel Triptych,* 1484

Memling (c. 1430-1494), though born in Germany, became Bruges' most famous painter. This triptych (three-paneled altarpiece) fuses the detail of Van Eyck with the balanced compositions of (his probable teacher) Rogier van der Weyden, while introducing his own innovations.

This is perhaps the art world's first group portrait, and everything about it celebrates the family of Willem Moreel, the wealthy two-term mayor of

Bruges. In the center is St. Christopher—patron saint of seafarers—who brought wealth to the merchant Moreel family. He's shown (according to the traditional legend) as a gentle giant graciously carrying Baby Jesus across a river. Christopher is flanked by St. Maurus (the black-robed monk with staff and book) and St. Giles (a hermit whose only companion was a red deer). These two saints represent the family names of Moreel (from Maurus) and his wife.

The true stars of the triptych are not the saints but the earthbound mortals who paid for it. Moreel (left panel) kneels in devotion along with his five sons (and St. William, who was Willem's patron saint). Barbara (right) kneels with their 13 daughters (and her patron saint, Barbara). Memling's skills as a portraitist capture 20 different personalities in this large family. He sets all the figures in a single landscape—note that the horizon line stretches across all three panels. Saints and mortals mingle in this unique backdrop that's both down-to-earth (the castle, plants, and St. Barbara's stunning dress) and ethereal (the weird rock formations and unnaturally pristine light). The glowing Christ child sits at the peak of this balanced composition. Memling creates a motionless, peaceful world that invites meditation. It was perfect for where the triptych originally stood—in the Moreel burial chapel.

### Jan Provoost, *Death and the Miser,* c. 1515

A Bruges businessman in his office strikes a deal with Death. The grinning skeleton lays coins on the table and, in return,

the man—looking unhealthy and with fear in his eyes—reaches across the divide in the panels to give Death a promissory note, then marks the transaction in his ledger book. He's trading away a few years of his life for a little more money. The worried man on the right (the artist's self-portrait) says, "Don't do it."

Jan Provoost (also known as Provost; c. 1465-1529) worked for businessmen like this. He knew their offices, full of moneybags, paperwork, and books. Bruges' materialistic capitalism was at odds with Christian poverty, and society was divided over whether to praise or condemn it. Ironically, this painting's flip side is a religious work bought and paid for by...rich merchants.

## REST OF THE MUSEUM

Breeze through the final rooms to get a quick once-over of Flemish art after Bruges' Golden Age. (The displays in these rooms change often.) As Bruges declined into a cultural backwater, its artists simply copied the trends going on elsewhere: Italian-style Madonnas, British-style aristocrat portraits, French Realist landscapes, Impressionism, and thick-paint Expressionism.

• *After fast-forwarding through the centuries, you may encounter a couple of Belgium's 20th-century masters.*

### Paul Delvaux, *Serenity,* 1970

Perhaps there's some vague connection between Van Eyck's medieval symbols and the Surrealist images of Paul Delvaux (1897-1994). Delvaux gained fame for his pale nudes, dreamily sleepwalking through moonlit, videogame landscapes.

### René Magritte, *The Assault,* c. 1932

Magritte (1898-1967) had his own private reserve of symbolic images. The cloudy sky, the female torso, windows, and a horse-

bell (the ball with the slit) appear in other works as well. They're arranged here side by side as if they should mean something, but they—as well as the title—only serve to short-circuit your thoughts when you try to make sense of them. Magritte paints real objects with photographic clarity, then jumbles them together in new and provocative ways.

• *When you're done touring the museum, consider a visit to the nearby Arentshuis Museum (same ticket and hours as the Groeninge Museum).*

## ARENTSHUIS MUSEUM

This small museum (in the upstairs section) features the art of Frank Brangwyn (1867-1956), who was born in Bruges and built an international career in several fields. Brangwyn's style is accessible and varied. You may see his brooding self-portrait. His specialty was dark engravings of grimy Industrial Age workers and homeless people. You may catch glimpses of Bruges (like the Begijnhof). He also did a series of the *Stations of the Cross*, some large colorful Art Nouveau canvases, and even designed some furniture. He made Bruges proud.

# SINT-JANSHOSPITAAL MEMLING COLLECTION TOUR

Located in one of Europe's oldest surviving hospital buildings, this museum has two parts. First, you see a few rooms of the former hospital, which operated from about 1150 until 1850. You get a glimpse into medieval medicine, with displays of surgical instruments, archival documents, and visual aids. Then you work your way to the collection's climax: several of Hans Memling's glowing masterpieces.

Memling's art was the culmination of Bruges' Flemish Primitive style (see sidebar on page 63). His serene, soft focus, motionless scenes capture a medieval piety that was quickly fading. The popularity of the style made Memling (c. 1430-1494) one of Bruges' wealthiest citizens, and his work was gobbled up by visiting Italian merchants, who took it home with them, cross-pollinating European art.

## Orientation

**Cost:** €12, includes entry to the skippable old pharmacy (Apotheek) in a nearby building and loaner folding chairs (if you'd like to sit and study the paintings).

**Hours:** Tue-Sun 9:30-17:00, closed Mon.

**Getting There:** The museum is at Mariastraat 38, across the street from the Church of Our Lady. There are two entrances to the complex—a passageway and a door, 20 yards farther south. The door takes you to the museum.

**Information:** Tel. 050-448-713, www.brugge.be.

**Length of This Tour:** Allow one hour.

**Starring:** The expansive hospital hall (with displays on medieval medicine) and Memling's *St. John Altarpiece.*

# The Tour Begins

*• After showing your ticket, enter a vast hall. The displays on medieval medicine are all here, with the Memlings at the far right end. In former days, this hall was the...*

## HOSPITAL

Take in the great hall with its sturdy wood-beamed ceiling, stone pillars, and brick walls. Some 500 years ago, this place would have been bustling with doctors and nurses (that is, monks and nuns) attending to the sick. As Bruges was a large city and a major destination for pilgrims (who came to see the Holy Blood relic), the building had to accommodate a lot of patients.

This hall was lined with beds filled with the sick and dying. At the far end was the high altar, which once displayed Memling's *St. John Altarpiece* (which we'll see). Bedridden patients could gaze

on this peaceful, color-ful vision and gain a mo-ment's comfort from their agonies.

Browse the displays. Old paintings show the hospital in former times, and portraits depict its Isaac Newton-looking doctors. One painting by Jan Beerblock—*Zicht op de Oude Ziekenzalen* (1778)—gives an intimate peek at "the old sick hall" in action: Notice that the soup's on, dogs are welcome, a nun administers last rites, and a sedan chair ambulance taxi awaits a pa-tient. (An actual sedan chair ambulance still stands nearby.) Snacks and drinks are served in bed. The floor needs mopping. A VIP clergyman drops in to see that all's OK.

Find the displays of medical implements. There are scalpels, medical books, flasks for testing urine, screws, syringes, and de-

vices more appropriate to a hardware store. It makes you glad for modern medicine. It's clear that medicine of the day was well-intentioned but very crude. In many ways, this was less a hospital than a hospice, helping the dying make the transition from this world to the next.

Religious art (displayed through-out the museum) was therapeutic, addressing the patients' mental and spiritual health. The numerous Crucifixions reminded the sufferers that Christ could feel their pain, having lived it himself. Paintings of saints gave the suffering hope for a miracle. Visions of heaven offered the terminally ill a light at the end of the tunnel.

That's where Memling came in. The hospital hired him to paint works that could bring serenity to the sick.

• *As you continue through the displays (past ominous slabs marking graves of prominent nuns and friars who worked here), you'll find works by Hans Memling. Start by locating a painted box displayed in a free-standing glass case.*

## MEMLING COLLECTION
### St. Ursula Shrine, c. 1489

On October 21, 1489, the mortal remains of St. Ursula were brought here to the church and placed in this gilded oak shrine, built specially for the occasion and decorated with paintings by Memling. Ursula, yet another Christian martyred by the an-cient Romans, became a sensa-tion in the Middle Ages when builders in Germany's Cologne unearthed a huge pile of bones believed to belong to her and her 11,000 slaughtered cohorts.

The church-shaped shrine, carved of wood and covered with gold, has "stained-glass windows" of Memling paintings describing Ursula's well-known legend.

• *"Read" the shrine's story counterclockwise, beginning with the...*

**Left Panel:** Ursula—in white and blue—arrives by boat at the city of Cologne and enters through the city gate. She's on a pil-grimage to Rome, accompanied by 11,000 (female) virgins. That night (look in the two windows of the house in the background, right), an angel appears and tells her this trip will mean her death, but she is undaunted.

**Center Panel:** Continuing up the Rhine (which Memling knew well, having grown up on it), they arrive in Basel and pre-pare to cross the Alps (background, right). Memling condenses the 11,000 virgins to a more manageable 11, making each one pure enough for a thousand.

**Right Panel:** They arrive at the gates of Rome where Ursula falls to her knees before the pope. Kneeling behind Ursula is her fiancé. Ursula has agreed to marry him only if he becomes a Chris-tian and refrains from the marriage bed long enough for her to

MEMLING COLLECTION

---

## Some Memling Trademarks

As you browse the Memling paintings, notice these telltale signs of his work.
- Serene symmetry, with little motion or emotion
- Serious faces that are realistic but timeless, without blemishes
- Eye-catching details such as precious carpets, mirrors, and brocaded clothes
- Glowing colors, even lighting, no shadows
- Cityscape backgrounds

make this three-year pilgrimage as a virgin (making him, I guess, virgin number 11,001).

**Opposite Side—Left Panel:** They board ships to head back home, now joined by the pope. Memling's crowd scenes are hardly realistic—more like a collage of individual poses and faces—but they capture the pomp and ceremony Memling would have seen in Bruges parades.

**Middle Panel:** Back in Cologne, a surprise awaits them—the city has been taken over by vicious Huns. They grab Ursula's hubby, stab him, and he dies in Ursula's arms.

**Right Panel:** The Hun king (in red with turban and beard) woos Ursula, placing his hand over his heart, but she says, "No way." So a Hun soldier draws his arrow and prepares to shoot her dead. Even here, at the climax of the story, there are no histrionics. Even the dog just sits down, crosses his paws, and watches. The whole shrine cycle is as posed, motionless, and colorful as the *tableaux vivants* that may have inaugurated the shrine here in this church in 1489.

In the background, behind Ursula, a Bruges couple looks on sympathetically. This may be Memling himself (in red coat with fur lining) and his wife, Anna, who bore their three children.

• *Now continue to the right and find a black-and-white tiled room where Memling's paintings are displayed. A large triptych (three-paneled altarpiece) dominates the space.*

### St. John Altarpiece, a.k.a. The Mystical Marriage of St. Catherine, 1474

Sick and dying patients lay in their beds in the hospital and looked at this colorful, three-part work, which sat atop the hospital/

church's high altar. The piece was dedicated to the hospital's patron saints, John the Baptist and John the Evangelist (see the inscription along the bottom of the frame), but Memling broadened the focus to take in a vision of heaven and the end of the world.

**Central Panel:** Mary, with Baby Jesus on her lap, sits in a canopied chair, crowned by hovering blue angels. It's an imaginary gathering of conversing saints *(Sacra Conversazione)*, though nobody in this meditative group is saying a word or even exchanging meaningful eye contact.

Mary is flanked symmetrically by the other saints: John the Baptist (to the left) and John the Evangelist (in red); an organist angel (left) matched by a book-holding acolyte; St. Catherine (left) balanced by book-reading St. Barbara. Behind them, classical columns are also perfectly balanced left and right.

At the center of it all, Baby Jesus tips the balance by leaning over to place a ring on Catherine's finger, sealing the "mystical marriage" between them.

St. Catherine of Alexandria, born rich, smart, and pagan to Roman parents, joined the outlawed Christian faith. She spoke out against pagan Rome, attracting the attention of the emperor, Maxentius, who sent 50 philosophers to talk some sense into her—but she countered every argument, even converting the emperor's own wife. Maxentius killed his wife, then asked Catherine to marry him. She refused, determined to remain true to the man she'd already "married" in a mystical vision—Christ.

Frustrated, Maxentius ordered Catherine to be stretched across a large, spiked wheel (the rather quaint-looking object at her feet), but the wheel broke, so they just cut her head off, which is why she has a sword, along with her "Catherine Wheel."

Looking through the columns, we see scenes of Bruges. Just to the right of the chair's canopy, the wooden contraption is a crane used to hoist barrels from barges on Kraanplein.

**Left Panel:** Even this gruesome scene, showing the beheaded John the Baptist with blood still spurting from his severed neck, becomes serene under Memling's gentle brush. Everyone is solemn, graceful, and emotionless—including both parts of the decapitated John. Salomé (in green) receives the head on her silver platter with a humble servant's downcast eyes, as if accepting her role in God's wonderful, if sometimes painful, plan.

**Right Panel:** John sits on a high, rocky bluff on the island of Patmos and, in a vision of the Apocalypse, sees the end of the world as we know it...and he feels fine.

Overhead, in a rainbow bubble, God appears on his throne, resting his hand on a sealed book. A lamb steps up to open the

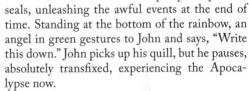

seals, unleashing the awful events at the end of time. Standing at the bottom of the rainbow, an angel in green gestures to John and says, "Write this down." John picks up his quill, but he pauses, absolutely transfixed, experiencing the Apocalypse now.

He sees wars, fires, and plagues on the horizon, the Virgin in the sky rebuking a red dragon, and many other wonders. In the center ride the dreaded Four Horsemen, wreaking havoc on the cosmos (galloping over either islands or clouds). Horseman number four is a skeleton, followed by a human-eating monster head. Helpless mortals on the right seek shelter in the rocks, but find none.

Memling has been criticized for building a career by copying the formulas of his predecessors, but this panel is a complete original. Its theme had never been so fully expressed, and the bright, contrasting colors and vivid imagery are almost modern. In the *St. John Altarpiece*, Memling shows us the full range of his style, from medieval grace to Renaissance symmetry, from the real to the surreal.

• *In the small adjoining room, find more Memlings.*

**MEMLING COLLECTION**

### Diptych of Martin van Nieuwenhove, 1489

Three-dimensional effects—borrowed from the Italian Renaissance style—enliven this two-panel devotional painting. Both Mary and Child and the 23-year-old Martin, though in different panels, inhabit the same space within the painting.

Stand right in front of Mary, facing her directly. If you line up the paintings' horizons (seen in the distance, out the room's windows), you'll see that both panels depict the same room—with two windows at the back and two along the right wall.

Want proof? In the convex mirror on the back wall (just to the left of Mary), the scene is reflected back at us, showing Mary and Martin from behind, silhouetted in the two "windows" of the picture frames. Apparently, Mary makes house calls, appearing right in the living room of the young donor Martin, the wealthy, unique-looking heir to his father's business.

• *Before leaving this area, find, to your right, a...*

### Portrait of a Young Woman, 1480

Memling's bread-and-butter was portraits created for families of wealthy businessmen (especially visiting Italians and Portuguese). This portrait takes us right back to that time.

The young woman looks out of the frame as if she were looking out a window. Her hands rest on the "sill," with the fingertips sticking over. The frame is original, but the banner and Van Eyck-like lettering are not.

Her clothes look somewhat simple, but they were high-class in their day. A dark damask dress is brightened by a red sash and a detachable white collar. She's pulled her hair into a tight bun at the back, pinned there with a fez-like cap and draped with a transparent veil. She's shaved her hairline and plucked her brows to get that clean, high-forehead look. Her ensemble is animated by a well-placed necklace of small stones.

Memling accentuates her fashionably pale complexion and

MEMLING COLLECTION

gives her a pensive, sober expression, portraying her like a medieval saint. Still, she keeps her personality, with distinct features like her broad nose, neck tendons, and realistic hands. She peers out from her subtly painted veil, which sweeps down over the side of her face. What's she thinking? (My guess: "It's time for a waffle.")

• *Special exhibitions are sometimes displayed in a room up the stairs from the main hall. But it's hard to compete with a waffle.*

# BRUGES SLEEPING, EATING & MORE

Bruges is the most inviting town in Belgium for an overnight. This chapter describes the town's top accommodations, eateries, shopping, and nightlife options, as well as train connections to other cities.

## Sleeping in Bruges

Bruges is a great place to sleep, with Gothic spires out your window, little traffic noise, and the cheerily out-of-tune carillon heralding each new day at 8:00 sharp. (Thankfully, the bell tower is silent from 22:00 to 8:00.) Most Bruges accommodations are located between the train station and the old center, with the most distant (and best) being a few blocks to the north and east of the Markt (Market Square).

B&Bs offer the best value, but hoteliers have lobbied City Hall to make it harder to have more than three "official" rooms. Creative B&B owners have found ways to get around the restrictions. For some travelers, short-term, Airbnb-type rentals can be a good alternative.

Bruges is most crowded Friday and Saturday evenings from Easter through October—July and August weekends are the worst. Many hotels charge a bit more on Friday and Saturday, and won't let you stay just one night if it's a Saturday.

I rank accommodations from **$** budget to **$$$$** splurge. To get the best deal, contact my family-run hotels directly by phone or email. When you book direct, the owner avoids a roughly 20 percent commission and may be able to offer you a discount. Book your accommodations well in advance if you'll be traveling during peak season or if your trip coincides with a major holiday or festival (see the appendix). For more information on rates and deals, making reservations, finding a short-term rental, and more, see the "Sleeping" section in the Practicalities chapter.

## HOTELS

**$$$$ Hotel Heritage** offers 22 rooms, with chandeliers that seem hung especially for you, in a solid and completely modernized old building with luxurious public spaces. Warm, inviting, and tastefully decorated, it's one of those places that does everything just right—if you can afford it (breakfast extra, iPad and Nespresso machine in every room, air-con, elevator, sauna, fitness room, free two-hour guided city tour, pay parking, Niklaas Desparsstraat 11, a block north of the Markt, tel. 050-444-444, www.hotel-heritage. com, info@hotel-heritage.com). It's run by cheery and hardworking Johan and Isabelle Creytens.

**$$$ Hotel Adornes** is small and classy—a great value situated in the most charming part of town. This 17th-century canalside house has 20 rooms with full modern bathrooms, free loaner bikes, and a cellar lounge with games and videos (family rooms, elevator, limited free parking—reserve in advance, some street noise, near Carmersstraat at St. Annarei 26, tel. 050-341-336, www.adornes. be, info@adornes.be). Nathalie runs the family business with the help of Kim and Rik.

**$$$ Hotel Patritius,** family-run and centrally located, is a grand, circa-1830 Neoclassical mansion with hardwood oak floors in its 22 stately, high-ceilinged rooms. It features a plush lounge, a chandeliered breakfast room, and a courtyard garden. If you get a room at the lower end of the price range, this can be a great value, or skip breakfast for a lower rate (use code "676PPq" when you book directly for a discount, family rooms, air-con, elevator, coin-op laundry, pay parking, Riddersstraat 11, tel. 050-338-454, www. hotelpatritius.be, info@hotelpatritius.be, cordial Garrett and Elvi Spaey).

**$$ Hotel Botaniek,** quietly located a block from Astrid Park, is a pint-sized hotel with a comfy lounge, renting nine slightly worn rooms—some of them quite big (RS%, family rooms, elevator, Waalsestraat 23, tel. 050-341-424, www.botaniek.be, info@ botaniek.be, Veronika and Brend).

**$$ Canalview Hotel ter Reien** is big and basic, with 26 rooms overlooking a canal in the town center—the water is right outside your window. Ask for a renovated room, which has a larger

# Bruges Accommodations

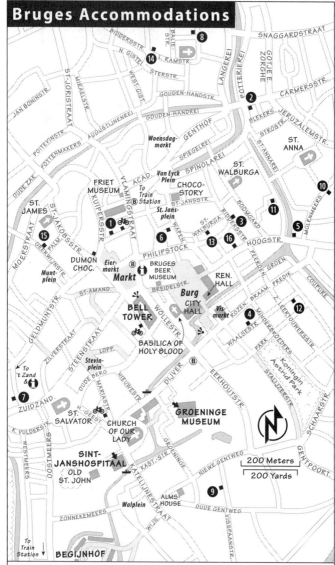

200 Meters
200 Yards

1. Hotel Heritage & Hotel Marcel
2. Hotel Adornes
3. Hotel Patritius
4. Hotel Botaniek
5. Canalview Hotel ter Reien
6. Hotel Cordoeanier
7. Hotel Bla Bla & Passage Hostel
8. Hotel de Pauw
9. The Townhouse
10. La Maison de Nathalie
11. Gastenhuis Sint-Andriescruyse
12. Koen & Annemie Dieltiens B&B
13. B&B Setola
14. Debruyne B&B
15. 't Geerwijn B&B
16. Charlie Rockets Hostel

bathroom, for no extra cost (family rooms, elevator, Langestraat 1, tel. 050-349-100, www.hotelterreien.be, info@hotelterreien.be, Diederik).

**$$ Hotel Cordoeanier,** a charming family-run hotel, rents 22 simple, compact, hardwood-floor rooms on a quiet street two blocks off the Markt. It's one of the best deals in town (RS%, family rooms, breakfast buffet served in their pleasant Café Rose Red, no elevator, patio, Cordoeanierstraat 16, tel. 050-339-051, www.cordoeanier.be, info@cordoeanier.be, Kris).

**$$ Hotel Marcel** has 24 big, boutique rooms with oversized photos of sights around Bruges plastering their ceilings and walls. Breakfast features fresh juice and baked goods served in the hip ground-level café. The location is ideal—on a quiet street a block off the Markt (apartments, some rooms have air-con, elevator, Niklaas Desparsstraat 7, tel. 050-335-502, www.hotelmarcel.be, info@hotelmarcel.be, Sophie).

**$ Hotel Bla Bla,** despite its name, is anything but average. This modern hotel is in a charming old-school building with 12 airy rooms and an updated backyard annex. Uppermost-level rooms reward guests with vaulted ceilings and big bathrooms. It's homey and well-run on a central yet quiet street, and two private courtyards can be enjoyed when the weather is nice (family rooms, includes breakfast when you book directly with hotel and mention Rick Steves, Dweersstraat 24, tel. 050-339-014, www.hotelblabla.com, info@hotelblabla.com, David).

**$ Hotel de Pauw** is tall, skinny, flower-bedecked, and family-run, with eight straightforward rooms on a quiet street next to a church (no elevator, pay parking, Sint Gilliskerkhof 8, tel. 050-337-118, www.hoteldepauw.be, info@hoteldepauw.be, Philippe and Hilde).

**$ Hotel 't Keizershof** is a dollhouse of a hotel that lives by its motto, "Spend a night...not a fortune." (Its other motto: "When you're asleep, we look just like those big fancy hotels.") It's simple and tidy, with seven small, cheery, old-time rooms split between two floors, with a shower and toilet on each level (family rooms, free and easy parking, Oostmeers 126, tel. 050-330-454, www.hotelkeizershof.be, info@hotelkeizershof.be). The hotel is situated in a pleasant area near the train station and Minnewater, a 15-minute walk from the Markt (for location, see the map on page 14).

## BED-AND-BREAKFASTS

These B&Bs, run by people who enjoy their work, offer a better value than hotels. Most families rent out their entire top floor—several rooms and a small sitting area. And most are mod and stylish—they're just in medieval shells. Each is central, on a quiet street, and has lots of stairs. Many places charge a little extra for a one-night stay. It's possible to find parking on the street in the evening (pay 9:00-19:00, two-hour maximum for metered parking during the day, free overnight).

**$$$ The Townhouse** is a classy place about 10 minutes' walk south of the Markt, run by friendly Jason and Sandra. Their four rooms, some with views, are spacious and modern. Breakfast is cooked to order and served in the garden in good weather (parking, Werkhuisstraat 18, tel. 050-615-852, www.thetownhouse.be, bookings@thetownhouse.be).

**$$$ La Maison de Nathalie** hides impeccable contemporary design behind its historic brick facade. Blond wood graces the three rooms, and one has both a bathtub and shower. The public spaces are just as stylish, and the backyard terrace is lovely for breakfast (Molenmeers 34, tel. 0474-113-777, www.lamaisondenathalie.be, info@lamaisondenathalie.be, classy Nathalie).

**$$ Gastenhuis Sint-Andriescruyse** offers warmly decorated rooms with high ceilings in a spacious, cheerfully red canalside house a short walk from the Old Town action. Owners Luc and Christiane treat guests like long-lost family, and proudly share their photo albums with pictures of previous guests (family rooms, some rooms with shared toilet but private bath, cash only, free soft drinks, limited parking, Verversdijk A15, tel. 050-789-168, mobile 0477-973-933, www.gastenhuisst-andriescruyse.be, luc.cloet@telenet.be).

**$$ Koen and Annemie Dieltiens** and daughter Amaryllis enjoy getting to know their guests while sharing a wealth of information on Bruges. You'll eat a hearty breakfast around a big table in their comfortable house (cash only, pay parking, Waalsestraat 40, three blocks southeast of Burg Square, tel. 050-334-294, www.bedandbreakfastbruges.be, koen.dieltiens@skynet.be).

**$ B&B Setola,** run by Lut and Bruno Setola, offers three expansive rooms and a spacious breakfast/living room on the top floor of their house. Wooden ceiling beams give the modern rooms a touch of Old World flair (honor bar, guest kitchen, five-minute walk from the Markt, Sint Walburgastraat 12, tel. 050-334-977, www.bedandbreakfast-bruges.com, setola@bedandbreakfast-bruges.com).

**$ Debruyne B&B,** run by Marie-Rose and her architect husband, Ronny, offers three rooms with artsy, modern decor (check out the elephant-size yellow doors—Ronny's design). The glass walls in the breakfast room open to a cloister-like garden. The architecture is cool, but the hosts are genuinely warm (cash only, minifridge and electric kettle, seven-minute walk north of the Markt, two blocks from the little church at Lange Raamstraat 18, tel. 050-347-606, www.bedandbreakfastbruges.com, mietjedebruyne@yahoo.co.uk).

**$ 't Geerwijn B&B,** run by Chris de Loof, offers homey rooms in the old center. Check out the fun, lofty A-frame room upstairs (cash only, pleasant breakfast room and royal lounge, Geerwijnstraat 14, tel. 050-340-544, www.geerwijn.be, info@geerwijn.be).

**$ Waterside B&B** has two fresh, Zen-like rooms, one floor above a peaceful canal south of the town center (continental breakfast, 15-minute walk from Burg Square at Kazernevest 88, for location see map on page 14, tel. 050-616-686, mobile 0476-744-525, www.waterside.be, mieke@waterside.be, run by Mieke of recommended Pink Bear Bike Tours).

**$ B&B AM/PM** sports three ultramodern rooms in a residential neighborhood just west of the old town (cash only, five-minute walk from 't Zand at Singel 10—see map on page 14, mobile 0486-327-886, www.bruges-bedandbreakfast.com, ampmbruges@gmail.com, artsy young couple Tiny and Kevin). From the train station, head left down busy Buiten Begijnevest to the roundabout. Stay to the left, take the pedestrian underpass, then follow the busy road (now on your left). Just before the next bridge, turn right onto the footpath called Buiten Boevrievest, then turn left onto Singel; the B&B is at #10.

## HOSTELS

Bruges has several good ¢ hostels offering beds in dorm rooms. The American-style **Charlie Rockets** hostel (and bar), a backpacker dive, is the liveliest and most central. The ground floor feels like a 19th-century sports bar, with a foosball-and-movie-posters party ambience. Upstairs is an industrial-strength pile of hostel dorms (private rooms available, breakfast extra, Hoogstraat 19, tel. 050-330-660, www.charlierockets.com, info@charlierockets.com).

Other small and loose places are the minimal, funky, and central **Passage** (private rooms available, Dweerstraat 26, tel. 050-340-232, www.passagebruges.com, info@passagebruges.com) and **Snuffel Backpacker Hostel,** which is less central and pretty grungy, but friendly and laid-back (Ezelstraat 47, tel. 050-333-133, www.snuffel.be, info@snuffel.be).

# Eating in Bruges

Bruges doesn't really have any specialties all its own, but restaurants here excel at all the predictable Belgian dishes: mussels cooked a variety of ways (one order can feed two), fish dishes, grilled meats, and French fries. The town's famous indigenous beers include the prizewinning Brugse Zot ("Bruges Fool"), a golden ale, and Straffe Hendrik, a potent, bitter triple ale.

You'll find plenty of affordable, touristy restaurants on floodlit squares and along dreamy canals. I wouldn't blame you for eating at one of these places, but I prefer the candle-cool bistros that flicker

**BRUGES SLEEPING, EATING & MORE**

# Bruges Restaurants

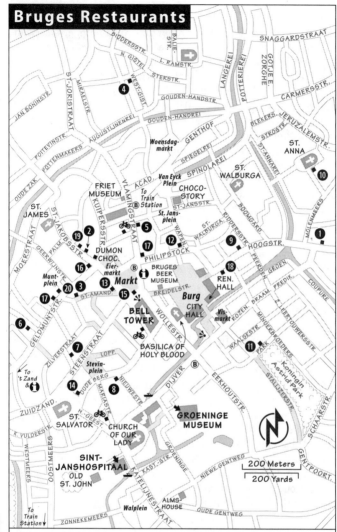

1. Rock Fort
2. Bistro in den Wittenkop
3. Bistro den Amand & Medard Brasserie
4. Tom's Diner
5. Bistro Den Huzaar
6. The Flemish Pot
7. De Hobbit
8. Restaurant de Koetse
9. Carlito's
10. Bistro Sint-Anna
11. L'Estaminet
12. De Plaats
13. Café-Brasserie Craenenburg
14. Chez Vincent
15. Frituur Stands
16. 't Brugsch Friethuys
17. Grocery (2)
18. Chez Albert
19. Lizze's Wafels
20. Gelateria Da Vinci

on back streets or atmospheric beer halls where the pub grub takes a backseat to those famous Belgian brews.

I rank eateries from **$** budget to **$$$$** splurge. For even more advice on eating in Belgium, including details on ordering, dining, and tipping in restaurants, the types of eateries you'll encounter, and Belgian cuisine and beverages, see the "Eating" section of the Practicalities chapter.

## RESTAURANTS

**$$$$ Rock Fort** is a chic spot with a modern, fresh coziness and a high-powered respect for good food. Two young chefs, Peter Laloo and Hermes Vanliefde, give their French cuisine a creative, gourmet twist. At the bar they serve a separate tapas menu (€55 five-tapas special). This place is a winner (Mon-Fri 12:00-14:30 & 18:30-22:00, closed Sat-Sun, reservations recommended, Langestraat 15, tel. 050-334-113, www.rock-fort.be).

**$$$ Bistro in den Wittenkop,** very Flemish, is a stylishly small, laid-back, old-time place specializing in local favorites, where Lindsey serves while Patrick cooks. It's a classy spot to enjoy hand-cut fries, which go particularly well with Straffe Hendrik beer (Mon-Tue and Thu-Sat 12:00-14:00 & 18:00-21:00, closed Wed and Sun, reserve ahead, terrace in summer, Sint Jakobsstraat 14, tel. 050-332-059, www.indenwittenkop.be).

**$$$ Bistro den Amand,** with a plain interior and a few outdoor tables, exudes unpretentious quality the moment you step in. Chef An is enthusiastic about her fair-trade ingredients, which she puts to good use in creative dishes, some with a hint of Asian influence. Portions are splittable and good vegetarian options are always available. It's on a bustling pedestrian lane a half-block off the Markt (Mon-Tue and Thu-Sat 12:00-14:00 & 18:00-21:00, closed Wed and Sun; reservations smart for dinner, Sint-Amandstraat 4, tel. 050-340-122, www.denamand.be, An Vissers and Arnout Beyaert).

**$$$ Tom's Diner** is a trendy, cozy little candlelit bistro in a quiet, cobbled residential area a 10-minute walk from the center. Young chef Tom gives traditional dishes a delightfully modern twist, such as his signature Flemish meat loaf with rhubarb sauce. If you want to flee the tourists and experience a popular neighborhood joint, this is it—the locals love it. Reserve before you make the trip (Tue-Sat 12:00-14:00 & 18:00-23:00, closed Sun-Mon, north of the Markt near Sint-Gilliskerk at West-Gistelhof 23, tel. 050-333-382, www.tomsdiner.be).

**$$$ Bistro Den Huzaar** is somewhat touristy but affordable, serving big portions of Belgian classics. The long dining room stretches back on well-worn wooden floors and a few tables are out on the sidewalk. It's dignified but relaxed (daily 11:30-21:30, five-minute walk north of the Markt at Vlamingstraat 36, tel. 050-333-797).

**$$$ The Flemish Pot** is a busy eatery where enthusiastic chefs Mario and Rik cook up a traditional menu of vintage Flemish specialties—such as rabbit stew—served in little iron pots and skillets. Seating is tight and cluttered, the tourist-oriented menu can be pricey, and service can be spotty. But you'll enjoy huge portions, refills from the hovering "fries angel," a cozy atmosphere, and a good selection of local beers (Wed-Fri 17:30-21:30, Sat-Sun from 12:00, closed Mon-Tue, reservations smart, just off Geldmuntstraat at Helmstraat 3, tel. 050-340-086, www.devlaamschepot.be).

**$$$ De Hobbit,** featuring an entertaining menu, is always busy with happy eaters. For a swinging deal, try the all-you-can-eat spareribs with bread and salad. It's nothing fancy, just good, basic food served in a fun, crowded, traditional grill house (daily 18:00-23:00, family-friendly, Kemelstraat 8, reservations smart, tel. 050-335-520, www.hobbitgrill.be).

**$$$$ Restaurant de Koetse** is handy for central, good-quality, local-style food. It feels a bit formal (stuffy even) and dressy, but don't let that stop you. The cuisine is Belgian and French, with an emphasis on grilled meat, seafood, and mussels (Sat-Wed 12:00-14:30 & 18:00-22:00, closed Thu-Fri, Oude Burg 31, tel. 050-337-680, www.dekoetse-brugge.be, Piet).

**$$ Carlito's** is a good choice for basic Italian fare. Their informal space, with whitewashed walls and tealight candles, is two blocks from Burg Square (daily 12:00-14:30 & 18:00-22:30, patio seating in back, Hoogstraat 21, tel. 050-490-075).

**$$$ Bistro Sint-Anna,** on the eastern edge of town, is a homey little neighborhood place where you can lunch on pasta, tapas, steak, or other yummy dishes in a fresh, modern space on two floors (Tue-Sat 8:30-17:30, Sun until 12:30, closed Mon, St. Annaplein 29, tel. 050-347-800).

**$$ L'Estaminet** is a youthful, jazz-filled eatery, similar to one of Amsterdam's brown cafés. Local students flock here for the Tolkien-chic ambience, hearty spaghetti, and big dinner salads. This is Belgium—it serves more beer than wine. For outdoor dining under an all-weather canopy, enjoy the relaxed patio facing peaceful Astrid Park (Tue-Sun 12:00-24:00, Thu from 17:00, closed Mon, Park 5, tel. 050-330-916).

**$$ De Plaats** offers Bruges' best vegetarian and gluten-free dishes. It's not fancy, but it's welcoming, reasonably priced, and just a bit quirky—like its owner, friendly Frow, who cooks and serves.

Those are even her paintings on the walls (Tue-Fri 12:00-14:00 & 18:00-21:00, Sat dinner only, closed Sun-Mon; Wapenmakersstraat 5, tel. 050-660-366).

**Restaurants on the Markt:** Most tourists seem to be eating on the Markt with the bell tower high overhead and horse carriages clip-clopping by. The square is ringed by tourist traps with aggressive waiters expert at getting you to consume more than you intend. Still, if you order smartly, you can have a memorable meal or drink here on one of the finest squares in Europe at a reasonable price. Consider **$$ Café-Brasserie Craenenburg,** with a straightforward menu, where you can get pasta and beer for €20 and spend all the time you want ogling the magic of Bruges (daily 7:30-23:00, Markt 16, tel. 050-333-402). Or come here just to savor a before- or after-meal drink with the view.

**Cheaper Restaurants Just Off the Markt:** For a similar but less expensive array of interchangeable, tourist-focused eateries, head a few steps off the Markt up **Sint-Amandstraat** (through the gap between Café Craenenburg and the clock tower). You'll pop out into a pleasant little square with lots of choices. The best of these is **Bistro den Amand** (recommended earlier), but if that's full or closed, this is a fine place to browse for something else. **$ Medard Brasserie,** also on this square, serves the cheapest hot meal in town—hearty meat spaghetti for only €6.50 (sit inside or out, Mon-Sat 12:00-20:00, Wed lunch only, closed Sun, Sint Amandstraat 18, tel. 050-348-684).

## PUBS AND BEER HALLS

My best budget-eating tip for Bruges: Stop into one of the city's bars for a simple meal and a couple of world-class beers with great Bruges ambience. Among these listings, Cambrinus puts more emphasis on its food; Café Terrastje, Herberg Vlissinghe, and Pub 't Gezelleke have a small selection of still-substantial meals; and 't Brugs Beertje and De Garre have lighter food and snacks.

**Kemelstraat:** On this street, just west of the Markt, you'll find three nice **$$** options: **De Hobbit** (described earlier, under "Restaurants"), **The Habit** (hearty Belgian food, beer, and Belgians), and the convivial **'t Brugs Beertje,** where you're welcome to sit at the bar and talk with the staff (more than 300 beers—including seasonal brews, very short menu of light meals, cash only, Thu-Tue 16:00-24:00, closed Wed, Kemelstraat 5, tel. 050-339-616).

**Just off the Markt:** Another good place to gain an appreciation for Belgian beer culture is **$$ De Garre** (deh-*H*AHR-reh). Rather than a noisy pub scene, it has a dressy, sit-down-and-focus-on-your-friend-and-the-fine-beer vibe. It's mature and cozy, with light meals (cold cuts, pâtés, and toasted sandwiches) and a huge selection of beers. Heavy beers are the forte: Beer pilgrims flock

# Bruges Beer Halls & Nightlife

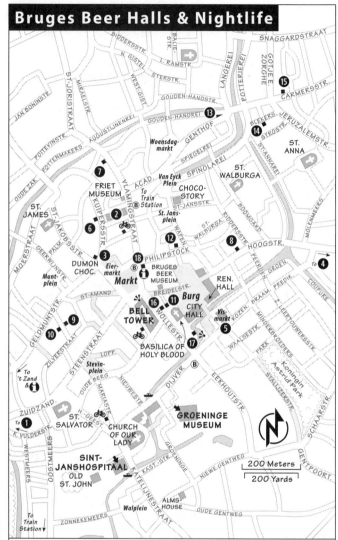

① To Concertgebouw
② Municipal Theater
③ Eiermarkt
④ To Langestraat
⑤ Wijnbar Est
⑥ 't Zwart Huis &
   't Under Ground
⑦ Comptoir des Arts
⑧ Charlie Rockets
⑨ De Hobbit

⑩ The Habit &
   't Brugs Beertje
⑪ De Garre
⑫ Cambrinus
⑬ Café Terrastje
⑭ Herberg Vlissinghe
⑮ Pub 't Gezelleke
⑯ The Bottle Shop
⑰ 2Be Bar
⑱ Duvelorium Grand Beer Café

here, as it's the only place on earth that sells the Tripel van de Garre beer on tap. As it's 12 percent alcohol, there's a three-Tripel limit...and many tourists find that the narrow alley out front provides much-needed support as they start their stumble back home (daily 12:00-24:00, additional seating up tiny staircase, off Breidelstraat between Burg and the Markt, on tiny Garre alley, tel. 050-341-029).

**Rollicking Beer Brasserie:** The touristy but enjoyable **$$$ Cambrinus** is a bright, tight, and boisterous *bierbrasserie*, serving 400 types of beer and good pub grub—the thick beer menu looks like a Bible. It's one of the only places in Bruges to try Westvleteren 12—often voted the world's best beer—but it's pricey. Come here for a lively evening out; it's more high-spirited and accessible than some of Bruges' traditional, creaky old beer halls (daily 11:00-23:00, reservations smart, Philipstockstraat 19, tel. 050-332-328, www.cambrinus.eu).

**In the Gezellig Quarter, Northeast of the Markt:** These **$$** pubs are tucked in the wonderfully *gezellig* (cozy) quarter that follows the canal past Jan Van Eyckplein, northeast of the Markt. Just walking out here is a treat, as it gets you away from the tourists. **Café Terrastje** is a cozy pub serving light meals and Belgian specialties such as *waterzooi*. Enjoy the subdued ambience inside, or relax on the front terrace overlooking the canal and heart of the district (Fri-Mon 12:00-23:30 but food service stops earlier, Tue until 18:00, closed Wed-Thu; corner of Genthof and Langerei, tel. 050-330-919, Ian and Patricia). **Herberg Vlissinghe** is the oldest pub in town (1515). Bruno keeps things basic and laid-back, serving simple plates (lasagna, grilled cheese, and angel-hair spaghetti) and great beer in the best old-time tavern atmosphere in town. This must have been the Dutch Masters' rec room. The garden outside comes with a *boules* court—free for guests to watch or play (Wed-Sat 11:00-22:00, Sun until 19:00, closed Mon-Tue, Blekersstraat 2, tel. 050-343-737). **Pub 't Gezelleke** lacks the mystique of the Vlissinghe, but it's a true neighborhood pub offering spaghetti and a few basic plates and a good chance to drink with locals (if you sit at the bar). Its name is an appropriate play on the word for "cozy" and the name of a great local poet (Mon-Tue and Thu-Sat 16:00-24:00, closed Wed and Sun, no outdoor seating, Carmersstraat 15, tel. 470-122-183, Jean de Bruges).

**Beer Cellar North of the Markt:** Filling a warm, welcoming cellar, **Comptoir des Arts** has 90 types of Belgian beer, a fine selection of whisky, knowledgeable barkeeps, a big fireplace, and occasional live music (typically on Sunday evenings, but not in the peak of summer). It's a short walk from the Markt, away from the worst tourist crowds (not much in the way of food, Wed-Mon

19:00-late, closed Tue, also closed Mon May-Sept, Vlamingstraat 53, tel. 0494-387-961, www.comptoirdesarts.be).

**Beer with a View:** I wouldn't bother eating at these places—they're all about the beer and the views.

The bar at **2Be,** though tucked in back of a tacky tourist shop (see listing under "Shopping in Bruges," later), serves several local beers on tap and boasts a fine scenic terrace over a canal. **Duvelorium Grand Beer Café** is pricey but picturesque. It's located upstairs from the Historium, with a spiny Gothic terrace overlooking the bustle on the Markt. Choices are more limited than some local watering holes (eight beers on tap, plus lots of bottles), and the prices are high—but it's worth paying extra for the view (same hours as Historium—see listing on page 24, you can enter the pub without paying for the museum, last orders at 18:00, may be open later in summer).

## SWEETS AND QUICK EATS
### Belgian Fries

Belgian French fries *(frieten)* are a treat. Proud and traditional *frituur*s serve tubs of fries and various local-style shish kebabs.

Belgians dip their *frieten* in mayonnaise or other flavored sauces, but ketchup is there for the Yankees. I encourage you to skip the ketchup and try a sauce adventure.

For a quick, cheap, and scenic snack on the **Markt,** hit a *frituur* and sit on the steps or benches overlooking the square. Twin takeaway fry carts are at the base of the bell tower (daily 10:00-24:00). I find the cart on the left better quality and more user-friendly.

**$ Chez Vincent,** with pleasant outdoor tables on a terrace facing St. Salvator's Cathedral along the lively Steenstraat shopping drag, is a cut above. They use fresh, local ingredients to turn out tasty fries and all manner of other fried and grilled Belgian tasties: burgers, sausages, meatballs, croquettes, and so on. Join the mob at the counter inside to order and pay, then find a table and wait for your pager to buzz (Tue-Sun 11:30-20:00, closed Mon, Sint-Salvatorskerkhof 1, tel. 050-684-395).

At **$$ 't Brugsch Friethuys,** a block off the Markt, you can sit down while enjoying your fries, but you must also buy a drink. Their "Big Hunger menu" of greasy, deep-fried foods comes with all the traditional gut bombs (daily 11:00-late, at the corner of

Geldmuntstraat and Sint Jakobsstraat, Luc will explain your options).

## Picnics
A handy location for groceries is the **Carrefour Express** mini supermarket, just off the Markt on Vlamingstraat (daily 8:00-19:00); for a slightly wider selection, **Delhaize-Proxy** is just up Geldmuntstraat (Mon-Sat 9:00-19:00, closed Sun, Noordzandstraat 4). For midnight snacks, you'll find Indian-run corner grocery stores scattered around town.

## Belgian Waffles and Ice Cream
You'll see waffles sold at restaurants and takeaway stands around town. One of Bruges' best is also one of its most obvious: **Chez Albert,** on Breidelstraat connecting the Markt and Burg Square, is pricey, but the quality is good and—thanks to the tourist crowds—turnover is quick, so the waffles are fresh (daily 10:00-18:30, at #18, tel. 050-950-009). Another popular spot is **Lizze's Wafels,** which makes them extra-large—try some drizzled in chocolate (Wed-Sun 11:00-17:00, closed Mon-Tue, Sint-Jakobsstraat 16, tel. 050-348-769).

    **Gelateria Da Vinci,** the local favorite for homemade ice cream, has creative flavors and a lively atmosphere. As you approach, you'll see a line of happy lickers. Before ordering, ask to sample the Ferrero Rocher (chocolate, nuts, and crunchy cookie) and plain yogurt (daily 11:00-22:00, Geldmuntstraat 34, tel. 050-333-650, run by Sylvia from Austria).

# Shopping in Bruges

Touristy Bruges isn't the place to shop for authenticity or bargains (Brussels, Antwerp, and Ghent are more satisfying). But souvenir shoppers find plenty of options. Shops are generally open from 10:00 to 18:00 and closed Sundays.

## WHAT TO BUY
**Chocolate:** A box of Belgian pralines is at the top of most souvenir shoppers' lists; see my tips and recommended chocolate shops on page 34.

    **Beer:** Another consumable souvenir is Belgian beer—either a bottle (or three) for later in your trip, or a prized brew checked carefully in your luggage home. In addition to the pubs listed earlier—a few of which sell bottles to go—the streets of Bruges are lined with bottle shops. At some, you can buy the glass that's designed to go with each type of beer (it's a fragile item to pack, but purists insist). Options include the touristy souvenir store **2Be** (described later) or **The Bottle Shop,** which sells 600 different beers and has a staff that enjoys helping visitors navigate the many choices (daily 10:00-18:30, just south of the Markt at Wollestraat 13, tel. 050-349-980).

**Lace:** This is a popular item, but very expensive; **'t Apostelientje,** described on page 32, is one good option (and conveniently located across the street from the Lace Center).

## WHERE TO SHOP

Souvenir shops abound on the streets that fan out from the Markt and the ones heading southwest, toward the Church of Our Lady. **2Be,** in a classic old brick mansion overlooking a canal a block south of the Markt, is huge, obvious, and grotesquely touristy... but filled with a wide variety of tacky and not-so-tacky Belgian souvenirs: Tintin, Smurfs, beer, and chocolates. The "beerwall" at the entrance shows off over a thousand types of Belgian brew; their cellar bottle shop is remarkably well-stocked; and their pub has several rotating draft beers you can enjoy on a relaxing terrace floating over a perfect canal (daily 10:00-19:00, Wollestraat 53, tel. 050-611-222, www.2-be.biz).

Two parallel streets, running southwest between the Markt and 't Zand squares, are lined with shops that cater to both tourists and workaday Bruggians. **Steenstraat,** which becomes **Zuidzandstraat** closer to 't Zand, has lots of affordable clothing chains (H&M, Zara), department stores (Hema), and mobile phone shops. At the Markt end of the street, a few tourist/souvenir shops are mixed in, but the farther you go, the more local it becomes.

More colorful are the shops a block to the north, along **Geldmuntstraat** (which becomes **Noordzandstraat**). Along this atmospheric drag—with perhaps Bruges' most enjoyable window-shopping—are smaller, more expensive chains and upscale boutiques (including L'Héroïne, highlighting Belgian designers with Antwerp cred at Noordzandstraat 32); housewares shops (such as Cook & Serve, a fun kitchen gadgets shop, at Geldmuntstraat 16); and the popular Da Vinci gelato shop (described earlier).

The **old fish market** (Vismarkt) just over the bridge from Burg Square still sells fresh fish most mornings, while souvenir stands fill some of its arcades all day long and into the evening. It's a central place to browse toys, jewelry, accessories, starving artists' depictions of Bruges, and more.

For the highest concentration of tourists (and, consequently, the highest concentration of souvenir, chocolate, lace, and *wafel* shops), head down **Katelijnestraat,** which runs south from the Church of Our Lady and Sint-Janshospitaal. While you'll find no great values here, it's convenient for souvenir shopping.

# Nightlife in Bruges

After dark, Bruges is sleepy but enchanting. While there's entertainment to be found, perhaps the city's most rewarding nighttime experience is strolling its floodlit cobbles and monuments. My favorite way to spend a late-summer evening in Bruges is in the twilight on a rental bike, savoring its back streets, far from the touristic commotion. Another good option is to settle into a characteristic pub (or hop between a few) to enjoy some beer; of the several pubs listed earlier (under "Eating in Bruges"), **Herberg Vlissinghe** and **De Garre** are particularly memorable places for a drink.

I've suggested some other options for entertainment below (for locations, see the "Bruges Beer Halls and Nightlife" map, earlier). For live music, also check www.agendabrugge.be.

## CONCERTS

The tiny courtyard behind the bell tower has a few benches where people can enjoy free evening **carillon concerts** (generally mid-June-mid-Sept Mon and Wed at 21:00; also Wed, Sat, and Sun at 11:00—schedule posted on courtyard wall).

Otherwise, see what's on at one of the city's main venues: The **Concertgebouw,** a performance hall on the spacious square called 't Zand, features esoteric dance, classy orchestral music, and other high culture (tel. 050-476-999, www.concertgebouw.be). The **Municipal Theater** (Brugse Stadsschouwburg), two blocks north of the Markt on Vlamingstraat, features an eclectic lineup of classical and modern presentations, from ballet to contemporary dance to musical theater to big-name jazz performers (www.ccbrugge.be; check location carefully—some performances take place in smaller venues around town). The TI can give you information for any of these; the booking office inside the TI also sells tickets for most events in town.

Luc Vanlaere presents 40-minute **harp concerts** most days in summer at Old St. John's Church (Oud Sint Jan), across from the Church of Our Lady and tucked behind Sint-Janshospitaal (free but donations appreciated, generally Tue-Sat 15:00, 17:00, and 18:30, no concerts Sun-Mon, fewer concerts off-season, Mariastraat 38, www.lucvanlaere-harp.be).

Other churches sometimes host concerts, including **St. Salvator's Cathedral** (organ concerts many Friday and some Tuesday evenings in summer, just southwest of the Markt along the busy Steenstraat shopping drag, www.kathedraalconcerten.be), **St. Walburga** (Jesuit church on Sint-Maartensplein east of the Markt), or **St. James** (on Sint-Jakobsplein, just northwest of the Markt).

**BRUGES SLEEPING, EATING & MORE**

## LIVELY AFTER-HOURS STREETS

Check out the following areas for lively bars, many of which have loud music or DJs late at night:

**Eiermarkt** ("Egg Market"), a tiny, table-clogged lane a few steps off the Markt (follow Geernaartstraat, straight across the square from the bell tower), is a rollicking scene that gets younger as the night gets older; Café Pick anchors the scene with frequent live DJs.

Just to the north, **Kupiersstraat** runs behind the City Theater (Stadsschouwburg), with a smattering of bars that cater to various demographics—from funky dives for teens to elegant cellars with well-dressed retirees. Along here, 't **Zwart Huis** is the elegant trendsetter, with a classy bar/restaurant upstairs and 't **Under Ground** cellar bar below (described later).

Farther out to the west, the long, broad square called 't **Zand** (dominated by the Concertgebouw) is packed with outdoor tables. The bar at the north end of the square, around **Ma Rica Rokk,** is the most youthful scene.

East of the Markt, **Langestraat** is lined with young, borderline-rowdy bars and clubs.

## BARS WITH LIVE MUSIC

In addition to the general areas noted earlier, these places have occasional live music.

**Wijnbar Est,** a classy and cozy little wine bar right in the middle of the tourist zone, has live music most Sundays at 20:00 (jazz and mellow covers, no cover charge, closed Tue-Wed, Braambergstraat 7, www.wijnbarest.be).

't **Zwart Huis** ("The Black House") is a vast, atmospheric space with an upscale vibe. You can get a good meal here, but the main appeal is the chance to enjoy live jazz and blues in a fine setting (performances every other Sun at 21:00, usually €5 cover for music, closed Mon-Tue, Kuipersstraat 23, tel. 050-691-140, www.bistrozwarthuis.be). 't **Under Ground,** in the cellar, is a casual and cozy place for drinks, but has no live music; they sometimes have dance music late.

**Comptoir des Arts,** a cozy recommended beer cellar, offers live music on many Sunday evenings (described earlier, under "Eating in Bruges").

**Charlie Rockets** is an American-style bar—lively and central—with foosball, darts, and five pool tables in the inviting back room (a block off the Markt at Hoogstraat 19). Because they run a youth hostel upstairs, it's filled with a young, international crowd who take full advantage of the guest-only happy hour prices. It's open nightly with nonstop rock 'n' roll (mostly recorded, sometimes live).

# Bruges Connections

## BY TRAIN

For information on rail travel in Belgium, see www.belgianrail.be; see also the "Transportation" section in the Practicalities chapter.

From Bruges by Train to: **Brussels** (3/hour, usually at :10, :31, and :58, 1 hour), **Brussels Airport** (3/hour, 1.5 hours, transfer at Brussels Midi), **Ghent** (4/hour, 30 minutes), **Antwerp** (2/hour, 1.5 hours, half the trains change in Ghent), **Ypres/Ieper** (hourly, 1.5 hours, change in Kortrijk), **Ostend** (3/hour, 15 minutes), **Delft** (at least hourly, 2.5 hours, change in Ghent, Antwerp, and Rotterdam), **The Hague** (at least hourly, 2.5 hours, change in Ghent and Antwerp, sometimes also Rotterdam), **Cologne** (8/day, 3 hours, change to fast Thalys train at Brussels Midi or InterCity Express at Brussels Nord), **Paris** (roughly hourly via Brussels, 3 hours on fast Thalys trains—it's best to book the day before), **Amsterdam** (hourly, 4 hours, transfers at Brussels Midi or Ghent and Antwerp; transfer can be tight—check with conductor), **Amsterdam's Schiphol Airport** (at least hourly, 3.5 hours with 3 transfers; faster connection possible with Thalys, 2.5 hours with 1-2 transfers), **Haarlem** (hourly, 4 hours, 2-3 changes).

Trains from London: Bruges is an ideal "Welcome to Europe" stop after London. Take the Eurostar train from London to Brussels (10/day, 3 hours, see page 207 for details), then transfer, backtracking to Bruges (3/hour, 1 hour, entire trip just a few dollars more with Eurostar ticket).

## BY CRUISE SHIP

The tiny town of **Zeebrugge,** just 10 miles north of Bruges, has a gigantic port that welcomes cruise ships. For more details, see my *Rick Steves Northern European Cruise Ports* book.

From the port, most cruise lines offer shuttles to the Blankenberge train station, the jumping-off point for hourly trains to Bruges (15 minutes), Ghent (50 minutes), and Brussels (1.5 hours). Otherwise, you can ride the coastal tram called Kusttram to the station.

# NEAR BRUGES: FLANDERS FIELDS

These World War I battlefields, about 40 miles southwest of Bruges, remain infamous in military history. In Flanders Fields, the second decade of the 20th century saw the invention of modern warfare: machine guns, trenches, poison gas, and a war of attrition. The most intense fighting occurred in the area called the Ypres Salient, a nondescript but hilly—and strategic—bulge of land just east of the medieval trading town of Ypres. (Ypres is pronounced EE-preh, but the Flemish call it Ieper and pronounce it YEE-per.) Over a period of three and a half years, hundreds of thousands of soldiers drew their last breaths here. Fields and forests turned first into trenches and battlefields, and then into desolate, muddy wastelands, entirely devoid of life.

Today, visitors driving through this part of Flanders will pass countless artillery craters, monuments and memorials, stone markers of this advance or that conquest, and war cemeteries alternating with pastureland. Farmers here pull rusty relics of World War I from the earth when they till their fields. Many locals have their own garage collection of "Great War" debris fished out of a field. Human remains are regularly disinterred, with every effort made to identify the fallen soldier and notify any surviving family.

If you're interested in this chapter of history, you can visit several Flanders Fields sights in a one-day side-trip from Bruges (best by car or guided tour). The most important and accessible sights are the pleasant market town of Ypres, with its impressive In Flanders Fields Museum; the town of Passchendaele, with a nearby museum (humble but inter-

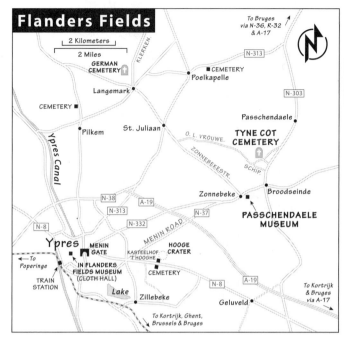

**Flanders Fields**

To Bruges
via N-36, R-32
& A-17

N-313

2 Kilometers
2 Miles

KLERKEN

GERMAN
CEMETERY

■ CEMETERY
Poelkapelle

Langemark

N-303

CEMETERY ■

Passchendaele

Pilkem

St. Juliaan

O. L. VROUWE.

**TYNE COT
CEMETERY**

Ypres Canal

ZONNEBEKESTR.

SCHIP.

N-38

A-19

Zonnebeke

Broodseinde

N-313

N-37

N-332

MENIN ROAD

**PASSCHENDAELE
MUSEUM**

N-8

**Ypres**

MENIN
GATE

HOOGE
CRATER

← To
Poperinge

KASTEELHOF
'T HOOGHE

IN FLANDERS
FIELDS MUSEUM
(CLOTH HALL)

CEMETERY

N-8

A-19

To Kortrijk
& Bruges
via A-17

TRAIN
STATION

Lake

Zillebeke

Geluveld

To Kortrijk, Ghent,
Brussels & Bruges

esting); and Tyne Cot Cemetery, where thousands of enlisted men from the British Commonwealth are buried and honored. Because most of the fighting here involved British Commonwealth troops, the majority of visitors are Brits, Canadians, Australians, and New Zealanders, for whom the stories of Flanders Fields are etched, like names on gravestones, into their national consciousness. You'll notice on maps that many places have English names—often anglicized approximations of the Flemish names (Passiondale for Passchendaele) or evocative new names (Mount Sorrow, Hellfire Corner).

Between the sights, you'll drive through idyllic Belgian countryside, streaked with cornfields, dotted with pudgy cows, and punctuated by the occasional

artillery crater—now overgrown with grass or trees, or serving as a little pond.

## GETTING THERE

It's very difficult to see the scattered sights around Ypres using public transportation: Taking a tour (from Ypres or Bruges) or renting

## In Flanders Fields

In Flanders fields the poppies blow
Between the crosses, row on row,
That mark our place; and in the sky
The larks, still bravely singing, fly
Scarce heard amid the guns below.

We are the Dead. Short days ago
We lived, felt dawn, saw sunset glow,
Loved and were loved, and now we lie,
In Flanders fields.

Take up our quarrel with the foe:
To you from failing hands we throw
The torch; be yours to hold it high.
If ye break faith with us who die
We shall not sleep, though poppies grow
In Flanders fields.

—John McCrae, Canadian soldier during the Second Battle of Ypres who died on the front lines in 1918

a car is a must. Be aware that road signs and transportation timetables use the Flemish "Ieper," not "Ypres."

**By Tour:** To delve into Flanders Fields, your best bet is to take a tour. These come with a rolling history lecture, taking you to off-the-beaten-path sights you'd likely not find on your own. Several companies based in Ypres run tours of the area (for information, check with the Ypres TI listed later); if you're coming from Bruges, it's more convenient to take the Quasimodo big-bus tour (described on page 20).

**By Car:** Here's a one-day plan for seeing the sights listed in this chapter. From Bruges, to make a beeline to Ypres, head south on the A-17 expressway all the way to A-19 and head west, following *Ieper Centrum* signs. For a slower, more scenic route that takes you past more sights, exit the A-17 expressway at R-32 and circle around the northern edge of Roeselare, then head west on N-36, then south on N-313. This leads to Langemark and the German cemetery there. From Langemark, take Zonnebekestraat southeast to the village of Zonnebeke and the Passchendaele Museum. From there follow the Menin Road (N-37) into Ypres, crossing under the Menin Gate as you enter town. After touring Ypres' museum, you can explore more countryside sights or head back to Bruges (fastest route between Ypres and Bruges: A-19 expressway east to the A-17 interchange near Kortrijk, then zip north on A-17).

**By Public Transportation to Ypres:** You can get to Ypres by train from Bruges (hourly, 1.5 hours with a transfer in Kortrijk) or from Ghent (direct hourly, 1 hour).

## BACKGROUND

Because American forces played a relatively minor role in the fighting at Flanders Fields, its history is obscure to many visitors from the US. This section will get you up to speed.

From 1830, Belgium was established as an independent and neutral state—an essential buffer zone to protect European peace,

surrounded by four big powers: France, Prussia, the Netherlands, and Britain. After defeating France and unifying in 1870, Germany was on the rise—an upstart powerhouse hungry for overseas colonies to fuel its growing economy. Germany amassed an intimidating army while the rest of Europe worriedly watched. Some European nations scrambled to ally themselves with their neighbors against potential German encroachment; others threw in with Germany. Because many alliances were secret, and often conflicting, no one knew for sure exactly where anyone else stood. As H. G. Wells said, "Every intelligent person in the world knew that disaster was impending and knew no way to avoid it."

On June 28, 1914, while on a visit to Sarajevo, the heir to the Austro-Hungarian throne, Archduke Franz Ferdinand, and his wife were assassinated by a teenage terrorist working for Bosnian Serb separatists. The Austrians held Serbia responsible and declared war. Germany joined Austria, and Russia (allied with France) backed Serbia. Through an intricate web of alliances—which ironically had been created to prevent war—soon most of Europe was drawn into the conflict. On August 4, 1914, Germany sent some 800,000 troops across the border into neutral Belgium en route to France. By August 20, they had already taken Brussels, and four days later they were in western Flanders.

The Germans expected to blow through the country quickly. But the small Belgian army—less than a quarter the size of the German army—pushed back hard, as they waited for British reinforcements to come from across the Channel. In the **Battle of the Yser (Ijzer) River,** the Belgians opened a sea gate to flood a low-lying plain just before a German advance. This diverted the German effort slightly to the south, around Ypres.

Ypres was just an ordinary town. But its surrounding, mostly flat terrain and modern weaponry turned it into a perpetual battlefield. This conflict saw the advent of the machine gun—an invention that, before the war, was called "the peacekeeper" because it was assumed that no sane commander would ever send his boys into its fire. With the machine gun, even the slightest gain in elevation was a strategic advantage. From any ridge, machine guns and artillery could mow down enemy troops—advancing armies were sitting ducks. Consequently, the low-lying ridges just east of Ypres—which came to be known as the **Ypres Salient** (the French term for "bulge")—saw some of the fiercest fighting of World War I.

The **First Battle of Ypres,** in October and November 1914, began when German troops attempted to invade the town. It became a priority of the Allies—Belgians, French, and British Commonwealth troops—to hold the Germans at bay. Both sides sustained huge losses, but the German troops—mostly inexperienced young conscripts who had underestimated the opposition—were devastated; to this day, Germans call the battle *Kindermord,* "Massacre of the Innocents."

Both sides regrouped and prepared for a harsh winter. They dug trenches, as it was human nature for soldiers ducking machine-gun bullets to burrow down. Separated by as little as 50 yards, enemy armies were close enough to offer each other a *Gesundheit!* after each sneeze. It was during this time that the famous "Christmas Truce" took place, in which German soldiers erected little candlelit *Tanenbaum*s beside their trenches and even approached the English trenches with gifts, kind words, and a pick-up soccer game.

During the **Second Battle of Ypres,** in spring 1915, the Germans used poison gas for the first time on a large scale, catching the Allies off guard. Chlorine gas (a.k.a. bertholite) reacts with moisture in the lungs to form hydrochloric acid—choking soldiers from the inside out. It was also one of the first times flamethrowers were used in battle. Still, the Germans were unable to take the town. By May 1915, the opposing forces were deadlocked near the town of Passchendaele, seven miles east of Ypres; for two years, little progress was made in either direction.

Although the Western Front appeared to be "all quiet," each side fortified its positions. The Germans established an elaborate network of five successive trenches, connected to and supplied by one another with perpendicular "switches." They built stout fortresses with flat tops, designed to protect troops from British artillery while allowing them to quickly emerge to man nearby machine-gun nests. These flat-top German fortresses—which you'll see everywhere—were dubbed "pillboxes" (the Germans used the pillbox design again in World War II, but with a rounded top—which better withstood artillery blasts). The British opted for underground wooden tunnels, called "dugouts," and reserved concrete bunkers for more specialized use as command posts and shelters for the wounded.

In the summer of 1917, the Allies attempted their own offensive against the newly strengthened German lines. This was the **Third Battle of Ypres** (a.k.a. the Battle of Passchendaele). After a sustained two-week artillery bombardment of German positions, some four million projectiles turned the countryside into a desolate wasteland. One soldier said that "the earth had been churned and rechurned"; another termed it "as featureless as the Sahara."

The British infantry then took to the battlefield, going over the tops of the trenches—only to face barbed wire, machine-gun fire, dangerously exposed high ground, and liquid mud. The devastation of the shelling, combined with historic rainfall (the most in the history of Flanders), turned the Ypres Salient into a sea of mud. With the ground like quicksand, troops and tanks could barely move, and the British gained only two of the four miles they needed to conquer. This battle was the first time the Germans used mustard gas, which blistered skin on contact.

As fall approached, heavy rains continued to deluge the area, but British soldiers made inroads, bunker by bunker. Their goal was the destroyed village of Passchendaele, perched on a modest ridge with a strategic view over the flat lands below. The village's name literally meant "passing the valley," but the Brits dubbed it "Passiondale"...the valley of suffering. Menin Road, which connected Ypres to Passchendaele (now road N-37), was the focus of much warfare—especially the intersection dubbed "Hellfire Corner."

In the end, British forces never succeeded in taking Passchendaele; Canadian forces finally took it in November 1917. By this point, each side had lost about a quarter of a million men in what had become a battle of attrition.

Two pivotal events took place during the winter of 1917-1918: The United States entered the war on the side of the Allies; and Germany agreed to a separate peace with Russia, allowing it to steer more men and resources to the Ypres Salient. In spring 1918, the **Fourth Battle of Ypres** (a.k.a. the Battle of the Lys) saw German forces trying to push through to the town of Ypres before US troops could arrive. Always innovative on the battlefield, the Germans introduced an elite squad of storm troopers (*Stosstruppen*, literally "shock troops")—lightly armed but well-trained and highly mobile special units tasked with breaking through enemy lines.

But by late April, the German advance stalled for lack of supplies. Meanwhile, American troops had come to the rescue, and by the fall of 1918, in the **Fifth Battle of Ypres,** Allied forces made huge gains. Less than a month later, Armistice Day (November 11, 1918) brought an end to the war to end all wars...until the next war.

World War I claimed the lives of an estimated nine million

## Dulce et Decorum Est

Bent double, like old beggars under sacks,
Knock-kneed, coughing like hags, we cursed
    through sludge,
Till on the haunting flares we turned our backs
And towards our distant rest began to trudge.
Men marched asleep. Many had lost their boots
But limped on, blood-shod. All went lame;
    all blind;
Drunk with fatigue; deaf even to the hoots
Of tired, outstripped Five-Nines that dropped
    behind.

Gas! Gas! Quick, boys!—An ecstasy of fumbling,
Fitting the clumsy helmets just in time;
But someone still was yelling out and stumbling,
And flound'ring like a man in fire or lime...
Dim, through the misty panes and thick green
    light,
As under a green sea, I saw him drowning.

In all my dreams, before my helpless sight,
He plunges at me, guttering, choking, drowning.

If in some smothering dreams you too could
    pace
Behind the wagon that we flung him in,
And watch the white eyes writhing in his face,
His hanging face, like a devil's sick of sin;
If you could hear, at every jolt, the blood
Come gargling from the froth-corrupted lungs,
Obscene as cancer, bitter as the cud
Of vile, incurable sores on innocent tongues, —
My friend, you would not tell with such high zest
To children ardent for some desperate glory,
The old Lie: Dulce et decorum est
Pro patria mori.

> —Wilfred Owen, English soldier who died in
battle in 1918

people; about a million were killed, wounded, or declared missing in action here in the Ypres Salient. In the century since, Flanders Fields has become a compelling destination for the descendants of the victims and survivors of the fighting here. As you tour the place, keep in mind that everything you see—every building, every tree—dates from after 1918.

Poppies were the first flowers to bloom in Ypres' ravaged landscape after the war. And today, this far-western corner of Belgium is blooming once more, having adopted that flower as a symbol of sacrifice and renewal.

## Sights in Flanders Fields

### YPRES TOWN

About 40 miles southwest of Bruges is the town most English speakers call Ypres. By the end of the war, Ypres was so devas-

tated that Winston Churchill advocated keeping it in ruins as a monument to the travesty of warfare. But locals did rebuild, resurrecting its charming main market square (Grote Markt), watched over by the grand and impressive Cloth Hall (which houses the In Flanders Fields Museum). Today's Ypres is a pleasant market town (Saturday morning is market day), with a steady stream of mostly British tourists interested in the WWI sights.

**Tourist Information:** The helpful TI, downstairs in the Cloth Hall, has information on tours (below the museum, daily 9:00-17:00, tel. 057-239-220, www.toerisme-ieper.be).

**Helpful Hints:** There's free **parking** at the train station, and pay parking right on the main market square, next to the giant Cloth Hall that houses the museum (3-hour limit). If you're exploring on your own, get a **local guidebook and map** to point you to the many additional sights beyond what I list (several are available at local bookstores and tourist offices). For practical information about the area, see www.flandersfields.be.

### ▲▲In Flanders Fields Museum

Using artifacts and thoughtful presentations, this excellent museum offers a moving look at the battles fought on the Belgian front near Ypres. The focus is not on strategy and commanders, but on the people who fought and died here, and features personal testimony about life in the trenches.

**Cost and Hours:** €9; daily 10:00-18:00; mid-Nov-March Tue-Sun 10:00-17:00, closed Mon and for three weeks in Jan; last entry one hour before closing, in Ypres' huge Cloth Hall at Grote Markt 34, tel. 057-239-220, www.inflandersfields.be.

**Visiting the Museum:** Upon entering the high-tech displays, you'll receive a bracelet. Once you register it, some of the exhibits are tuned to your age, gender, and country. One display shows aerial photos of the region today, which you can then select and swipe to see what it looked like from the air during the war.

Throughout the museum, large video panels show actors portraying eyewitnesses to the events of the war. One panel has Germans justifying gas attacks, followed by a different German describing the aftermath—"even the insects died." In a small theater is the most moving exhibit in the entire place—doctors and nurses talking about treating the wounded and dying.

**Nearby:** The Cloth Hall's **belfry** (231 steps to the top, €2 extra) offers a panoramic view of the surrounding countryside.

### ▲Menin Gate

This impressive Victorian archway is an easy two-block walk from the museum (past the end of Grote Markt). Built into the old town wall of Ypres, it's etched with the names of British Commonwealth victims who fought here. It marks the Menin Road, where many Brits, Canadians, Aussies, and Kiwis left this town for the battlefields and trenches, never to return. The gate is formally a mausoleum for "the Missing," 54,896 troops who likely perished at Flanders Fields but whose remains were never found.

To honor the hundreds of thousands of British subjects who gave their lives, every night under the arch at 20:00, a Belgian bugle corps plays the "Last Post" to honor the dead. Arrive under the arch at 19:30 to get the best view.

## NEAR YPRES

Most of these sights are on or near the Menin Road between Ypres and Passchendaele (to the northeast), where the most famous battles took place. The German Cemetery is a bit to the north (but still within a few miles).

The sights listed here are just the beginning. You can't drive a mile or two without passing a monument or memorial. Tranquil forests open into clearings with eerily rippled contours—overgrown trenches, pockmarks, and craters. Certain nondescript ponds and lakes are actually flooded artillery craters. Joining a tour helps you find some of the more out-of-the-way remnants of the war. If you're exploring on your own, get a guidebook on the region. If you have a special interest—for example, a nationality or a specific battle an ancestor participated in—just ask around to find related sites.

### ▲Passchendaele Museum

Though a bit old-fashioned, this exhibit supplements the In Flanders Fields Museum nicely, with a focus on strategy and battles.

**Cost and Hours:** €10.50, daily 9:00-18:00, last entry at 16:30, closed mid-Dec-Jan, Ieperstraat 5, in Zonnebeke about 5 miles east of Ypres and 2 miles west of Passchendaele, tel. 051-770-441, www.passchendaele.be.

**Visiting the Museum:** Presented chronologically on the top floor of a chalet-like mansion, this museum details each advance and retreat, from the first German boot on Belgian soil to Armistice Day. You'll see displays of uniforms, medical instruments, and objects illustrating day-to-day life at the front. One exhibit explains—and lets you sniff—the four basic types of poison gas used here.

An exit takes you through a simulation of the wooden underground "dugout" tunnels used by British forces as their headquarters (built after artillery fire had so scorched the ground above that nothing was left). Outside, you'll walk through a reconstruction of the shallow trenches that zigzagged along No Man's Land. Note how later trenches had slotted walkways so that soldiers didn't have to wade through mud.

Finally, back at the museum, you can hear video testimony from WWI veterans—Brits, Aussies, Kiwis, and Canucks—on what it was like at Passchendaele.

### ▲Tyne Cot Cemetery

This evocative cemetery is the final resting place of 11,956 British, Canadian, Australian, New Zealander, South African, and other British Commonwealth soldiers. It was named for a blockhouse on this site that was taken by British forces, who nicknamed it "Tyne Cottage" after the river in North England.

**Cost and Hours:** Free, visitors center open daily 10:00-18:00, closed Dec-Jan, just northeast of Zonnebeke, off of N-37 toward Passchendaele, about 6.5 miles east of Ypres, www.cwgc.org.

**Visiting the Cemetery:** The cemetery grounds hold three German pillbox bunkers and seemingly endless rows of white headstones, marked with a soldier's name and his unit's emblem (such as the maple leaf of Canada). Many graves are marked simply "A soldier of the Great War, known to God."

In the center of the cemetery, near the tallest cross (marking the location of Tyne Cottage), notice the higgledy-piggledy arrangement of graves. During the war, when this cottage was a makeshift medic station, this area became an impromptu burial ground. Any cemetery that's neat and symmetrical—like the surrounding headstones—dates from after the war.

Running along the top of the cemetery is a wall inscribed with the names of 34,857 "officers and men to whom the fortune of war denied the known and honoured burial given to their comrades in death." The visitors center has a few artifacts and exhibits about the fighting here.

## Hooge Crater

This giant flooded crater, about three miles east of Ypres, was created by successive mine explosions detonated in turn by both British and German forces. The strategic high ground around the crater (where a château used for a time as British headquarters once stood) switched hands repeatedly throughout the war.

Today the Hooge Crater area has a large British Commonwealth **cemetery** and the **Hooge Crater Museum,** a touristy exhibit with historic information about the fighting here (€5, Tue-Sat 10:00-18:00, Sun until 21:00, closed Mon, www.hoogecrater.com). Hiding out in the woods just down the road is a hotel/restaurant called **Kasteelhof 't Hooghe,** where you can pay €1 to stroll around the adjacent crater-pond and see some old bunkers and trenches (restaurant closed Sun, www.hotelkasteelhofthooghe.be).

## German Military Cemetery (Deutscher Soldatenfriedhof) at Langemark

A relatively rare site dedicated to the invaders of this region, this is the where 44,324 Central Powers soldiers are buried (along with

two Brits who were originally misidentified). Compared with the gleaming British Commonwealth cemeteries nearby, it's dull and drab. That's because the Treaty of Versailles that concluded World War I forbade German WWI cemeteries from using white stones. Instead, gray basalt and even oak are used to  mark the graves. As you wander the cemetery, you'll notice many Slavic names: Troops were sent to fight here from the far eastern corners of the multiethnic Austro-Hungarian Empire. In the center is a mass grave with 25,000 soldiers (cemetery located on the northern outskirts of Langemark, about five miles north/northeast of Ypres).

# BRUSSELS

# ORIENTATION
# TO BRUSSELS

*Brussel • Bruxelles*

Six hundred years ago, Brussels was just a nice place to stop and buy a waffle on the way to Bruges. With no strategic importance, it grew as a free trading town. Today it's the capital of Belgium, the headquarters of NATO, and the seat of the European Union (EU). It's also a fascinating and vibrant city in its own right, with fun-to-explore neighborhoods, good sightseeing, pleasant pedestrian zones, an impressive selection of restaurants, and a quirky Flemish/French mix.

The Brussels of today reflects its past. The city enjoyed a Golden Age of peace and prosperity (1400-1550) when many of its signature structures were built. In the late 1800s, Brussels had another growth spurt, fueled by industrialization, wealth taken from the Belgian Congo, and the exhilaration of the country's recent independence (1830). The "Builder King" Leopold II erected grand monuments and palaces. Then, in 1992, 12 countries established the European Union by signing the Treaty of Maastricht, and sleepy Brussels was thrust into the spotlight as the unofficial capital of the new Europe. It started a frenzy of renovation, infrastructure projects, foreign visitors, and world attention.

As a tourist destination, Brussels captivates some visitors and exasperates others. At its best, Brussels mingles French class and Belgian spunk. At its worst, it's a crowded, jaded city of demanding tourists, stuffy bureaucrats, and down-and-out immigrants. Its museums are respectable, but not quite befitting its status as a world capital. But if you make an effort to explore some less-traveled neighborhoods, you'll experience another side of Brussels. The more you see, the more you'll like it.

In Brussels, people speak French. Bone up on *bonjour* and *s'il vous plaît* (see the French survival phrases in the appendix). The Bruxellois are cultured and genteel—even a bit snobby compared to their earthier Flemish cousins. The whole feel of the town is urban French, not rural Flemish. And yet there's an impish sparkle and joie de vivre, as evidenced by the Bruxellois love of comic strips (giant comic-strip panels are painted on buildings all over town) and their civic symbol: a statue of a little boy peeing.

Brussels is the cutting edge of modern Europe, but still clothed in its Old World garments. Stroll the Grand Place, snap a selfie with the *Manneken-Pis,* and watch diplomats at work at the EU assembly halls. Then grab some mussels, fries, and a hearty Belgian beer, and watch the sun set behind the Town Hall's lacy steeple.

## BRUSSELS: A VERBAL MAP

Central Brussels is surrounded by a pentagon-shaped ring of roads, which replaced the old city wall. All hotels and nearly all the sights I mention are within this ring (romantics think it looks more like a heart than a pentagon). The epicenter (or *petite ceinture,* literally "little belt") holds the main square (the Grand Place), the TI, and Central/Centraal station (all within three blocks of one another).

What isn't so apparent from maps is that Brussels is a city divided by altitude. A ridgeline splits the town into the Upper Town (east half, elevation 200 feet) and Lower Town (west, at sea level), with Central station in between.

Brussels' bilingual street signs give the French name first, then the Dutch. That, combined with the near-complete lack of a regular grid plan, can make navigating the city confusing. It's easy to get turned around. I rely heavily on a good map when exploring this town. Note that in the Brussels chapters of this book, after introducing a name in French and Dutch, I've used the French names alone to keep things simple.

It's helpful to think of the city as a series of neighborhoods, each with its own character.

**The Lower Town:** This crowded, touristy district—with the Grand Place (in Dutch: Grote Markt, *H*ROH-teh markt), narrow streets, old buildings, modern shops, tourist-trap eateries, and the famous *Manneken-Pis* peeing-boy statue—is squeezed between the Central train station and Boulevard Anspach.

**West of Boulevard Anspach:** This once-bustling but now pedestrianized boulevard, which runs over the city's forgotten river, marks the boundary between Brussels' touristy core and its more characteristic neighborhoods. Just beyond Boulevard Anspach— past a block or two of high-rise ugliness—is the lively and youthful market square called **Place St-Géry** (Sint-Goriksplein). The **Dansaert** district (just above Place St-Géry, along Rue Antoine Dansaert) is emerging as a high-fashion district, with a creative "bobo" *(bourgeois-bohème)* ambience. Just to the north is the **Ste. Catherine** neighborhood, a charming village-within-a-city hud-

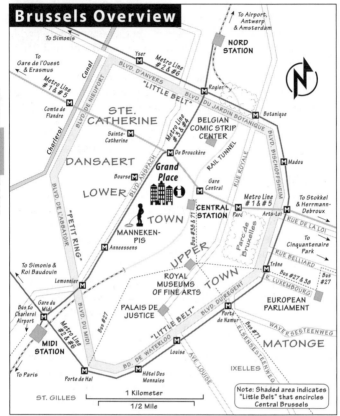

dled around the old fish market, and home to several recommended hotels and restaurants.

**The Upper Town:** This uphill, upper-crust district surrounds the Royal Palace. Traditionally the home of nobility and the rich, this area has big marble palaces, broad boulevards, and the major museums. Compared to other parts of the city, it feels stately and sterile. The zone between the Upper and Lower towns, called **Sablon,** feels French and urbane.

**Beyond the Core:** Everything within the center of town is walkable. Outside that zone, sprawling suburbs and vast green spaces contain attractions that are more easily reached by public transportation or taxi. To the east are the **European Parliament** and, beyond that, the **Park of the Cinquantenaire** (with the Royal Museum of the Armed Forces and Military History, Autoworld, and a lesser art museum). Tucked between the European Parliament and the Upper Town is **Matongé,** an immigrant African neighborhood that has become high-rent. And far to the north is the **1958 World's Fair site,** with the Atomium and Mini-Europe.

## PLANNING YOUR TIME
For a city of its size and prominence, Brussels can be seen quickly: Its main attraction, the Grand Place, is a short walk from the Central train station; several good museums and neighborhoods are also easily walkable. On a quick trip; a day and a night are enough for a good first taste (but if you have more time, Brussels has enjoyable ways to fill it). Or—if you're in a hurry—Brussels can be done as a day trip by train from Bruges, Ghent, or Antwerp (frequent trains, less than an hour from any of these) or a stopover on the Amsterdam-Paris or Amsterdam-Bruges ride.

### Brussels in Three to Five Hours
Toss your bag in a locker at Central station and confirm your departure time and station (note that fast international trains depart from Midi/Zuid station). Then walk about five minutes into town and do this Brussels blitz:

Head directly for the Grand Place and take my Grand Place Walk. To streamline, skip the *Manneken-Pis* until later, and end the walk at the Bourse (stock-exchange building). From there, walk a few blocks to Place de Brouckère, where you can catch a taxi to Place Royale (Koningsplein) in the Upper Town. Enjoy the Royal Museums of Fine Arts. If catching a train, make a beeline to the station; if you have another hour or two, do my Upper Town Walk, which ends near the *Manneken-Pis* and the Grand Place. Buy a box of chocolates and a bottle of Belgian beer, and pop the top as your train pulls out of the station.

### Brussels in One to Two Days
A full day (with one or two overnights) is about right to get a more complete taste of Brussels. With a second day, you can slow down and really delve into the city.

**Day 1**

| | |
|---|---|
| 10:00 | Get your bearings with my Grand Place Walk. |
| 12:00 | Walk up to the Ste. Catherine neighborhood for a quick lunch at one of my recommended eateries. |
| 13:30 | Tour the Musical Instruments Museum on your way to the Upper Town. |
| 15:00 | Tour the Royal Museums of Fine Arts. |
| 17:00 | Follow my Upper Town Walk. |
| Evening | Relax with a predinner drink on the Grand Place. Then explore some of the interesting neighborhoods away from the touristy core, and find a good place |

for dinner: Poke around the fun and colorful streets around Place St-Géry and Ste. Catherine, or venture out to Matongé.

**Day 2**

If staying for two days, you could do the Grand Place Walk on the first day, and save the art museums and Upper Town Walk for the second day. To fill in the remaining time each day, consider the following options.

Historians enjoy the excellent story of Belgium at the BELvue Museum (very near the Royal Museums). Aficionados of the funny pages head for the Belgian Comic Strip Center (in the Lower Town, a 15-minute walk from the Grand Place). And political-science majors visit the European Parliament complex for a lesson in Euro-civics (best on weekdays).

With more time or a special interest, head to the museums at the Park of the Cinquantenaire, or visit the kitschy former fairgrounds at the giant Atomium. Outside of town, see the Mémorial 1815 museum at the site of the Battle of Waterloo, or venture to Tervuren to tour the Royal Museum for Central Africa, set in a big park.

# Overview

## TOURIST INFORMATION

Brussels has two centrally located TIs. The more crowded one is inside the Town Hall on the Grand Place and focuses on just the city of Brussels (daily 9:00-18:00, shorter hours off-season; tel. 02-513-8940, www.visitbrussels.be). The TI at Rue du Marché aux Herbes 63 has a bare-bones staff but can answer questions on Brussels and Flanders (daily 10:00-18:00, shorter hours off-season; three blocks downhill from Central station, tel. 02-504-0390, www.visitflanders.com).

Travelers should pick up a free public transit map and/or €1 city map. The €1.50 *Brussels Guide* booklet—sold only at the Grand Place TI—gives a more complete overview of the city and its many museums, and outlines a series of neighborhood walks. For concerts and entertainment options, look for the free weekly magazine *Bruzz* (in English, French, and Dutch).

**Alternative Tourist Information:** The excellent, welcoming **USE-IT** information office, which is geared toward backpackers, offers in-the-know advice about Brussels and other Belgian destinations, including Bruges, Antwerp, and Ghent (Mon-Sat 10:00-18:00, closed Sun, in the Galeries Ravenstein shopping arcade at Rue Ravenstein/Ravensteinstraat 25, uphill from Central train station, www.brussels.use-it.travel). Their user-friendly maps of Brussels and other Belgian cities are packed with homegrown insight (downloadable from website).

**Sightseeing Pass:** The **Brussels Card,** sold at TIs and museums, includes entrance to nearly all major sights except the Comic Strip Museum (€26/24 hours, €34/48 hours, €42/72 hours, www.brusselscard.be)—but you'll need to do a lot of sightseeing to get your money's worth. You can pay a bit more for a version that includes the City Sightseeing hop-on, hop-off bus.

## ARRIVAL IN BRUSSELS
## By Train

Brussels has three stations (none of which is officially the "main" train station): Central/Centraal (central), Midi/Zuid (south), and Nord/Noord (north). Most Brussels-bound trains (except high-speed international trains) stop at all three stations, but Central station is by far the most convenient for arriving sightseers. The three stations are connected by regular trains (leaving every few minutes).

### Central/Centraal Station

This station, nearest to the sights and my recommended hotels, has handy services: a small grocery store, fast food, waiting rooms, and luggage lockers (between tracks 3 and 4, coins only).

You can walk from the station to the Grand Place in about five minutes: Following signs inside the station for *Marché aux Herbes/Grasmarkt,* you'll be directed through the Galerie Horta shopping mall, where you'll ride an escalator down, pass a Smurf shop, and pop out 50 yards from the little square nicknamed "Agora." At the far end of this square, turn left to reach the Grand Place, or continue straight ahead to find the Brussels and Flanders TI on your left. If you arrive after 20:00 (18:00 on Sun), when the shopping mall is closed, you may have to exit through the station's main door upstairs and head downhill on Rue de l'Infante Isabelle to the square.

Hop-on, hop-off tourist buses depart from Central station—a handy way to get oriented to the city (see "Tours in Brussels," later).

### Midi/Zuid Station

About a mile and a half southwest of the city center, Midi station serves the fastest high-speed international connections, such as Eurostar, Thalys, and TGV, which stop only at this station (for more on these, see "Brussels Connections," on page 207). All other trains that stop at Midi also stop at Central and Nord.

It's a good idea to know both the French and Dutch names for this station (Bruxelles-Midi and Brussel-Zuid), as you may see signs for either one.

Midi's tracks are connected by a long, gloomy, gray-steel concourse with ample computer screens showing upcoming trains.

BRUSSELS ORIENTATION

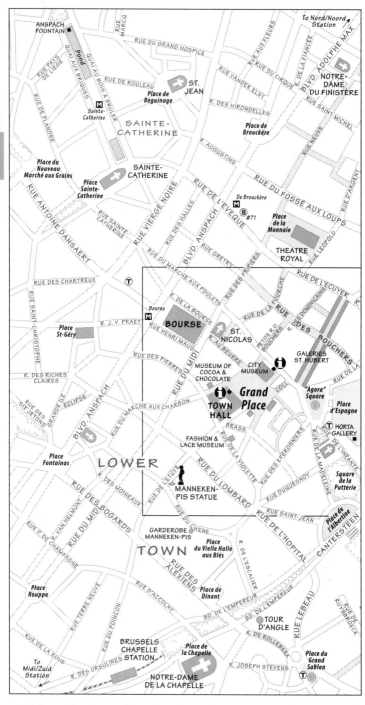

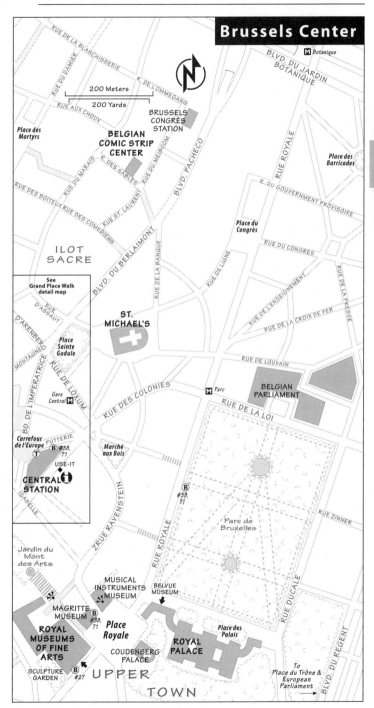

## Brussels Waffles...Linguistically

Brussels is the one part of Belgium that's neither fully French, nor fully Flemish. (It occupies its own bicultural mini province, near the border between Wallonia and Flanders.) While residents spoke mostly Dutch until 1900, today Brussels is officially bilingual and bicultural. In practice, 65 percent of "Bruxellois" speak French as their first language, and only 5 percent speak Dutch (and call themselves "Brusselaar").

The remaining 30 percent aren't Bruxellois, or even Belgian—they're nonnatives who speak their own languages. As the unofficial capital of Europe, Brussels is multicultural. Besides its immigrant population, it hosts politicians and businesspeople from around the globe and features a world of ethnic restaurants. The city is home to 400 embassies (the US has three here, one each to the EU, NATO, and Belgium). Every sizable corporation has a lobbyist in Brussels. Most businesspeople, diplomats, and politicians use English as their default. Some predict that in 20 years, English will be the city's de facto first language.

High-speed trains use tracks 1-6 (1-2 for Eurostar and 3-6 for the others). The station has plenty of luggage lockers (between tracks 6 and 7, coins only), as well as three separate Travel Centre ticket offices (for domestic, international, and international/immediate departures). The area around the station is a rough-and-tumble immigrant neighborhood.

**Getting from Midi Station to the Center:** If you must disembark at Midi station, it's easy to make your way to **Central station** and on to Grand Place. Trains run every few minutes, and the fare is covered by any train ticket into or out of Brussels (or an activated rail pass). Scan the departure boards—even if "Central" isn't listed as a destination, trains headed for many places (the airport, Antwerp, Leuven, Liège, Namur, etc.) will stop there. Note that trains headed in the opposite direction—including those to Ghent and Bruges—have *already* stopped at Central station.

Alternatively, you can take a **taxi** from Midi into the city center. It should cost no more than €10, but cabbies from this station are notorious for taking a roundabout route. So insist on the meter, follow the route on a map, and if the total fare seems too high, enlist the help of your hotel receptionist.

### Nord/Noord Station

Any train that goes through Nord station will also stop at the other two. Don't bother getting off at this station (surrounded by a seedy red light district)—disembark at Central station instead.

## By Plane

Brussels is served by two airports. Most flights use the primary Brussels Airport, a.k.a. Zaventem. No-frills carriers use the Brussels South Charleroi Airport. For details on both, see page 210.

## HELPFUL HINTS

**Theft Alert:** The tourist zone—the area within the pentagon-shaped ring road—is basically safe at any hour of day or night, but as in any big city, low-level street crimes (purse snatching/pickpocketing) do occur. Be aware of your surroundings in the Métro, train stations, or any crowded zone.

**Sightseeing Schedules:** Brussels' most important museums are closed on Monday. Of course, the city's single best sight—the Grand Place—is always open. You can also enjoy a bus tour any day of the week, or visit the more far-flung sights (which are open daily), such as the Atomium/Mini-Europe, the European Parliament's Parlamentarium museum, or the 1815 Mémorial museum commemorating the Battle of Waterloo.

**Travel Bookstore: Anticyclone des Açores** has a wide selection of maps and travel books, including many in English (Mon-Sat 11:00-18:00, closed Sun, Rue Fossé aux Loups 34, tel. 02-217-5246, www.anticyclonedesacores.be).

**Bilingual Brussels:** Because the city is officially bilingual, Brussels' street signs and maps are in both French and Dutch. In this book—due to space constraints—I've generally given only the French name. Because the languages are so different, many places have two names that barely resemble each other (for example, Marché aux Herbes/Grasmarkt, or Place Royale/Koningsplein).

**Laundry: Wash Club** is near the Grand Place, along the shopping street Rue du Marché au Charbon (at #68, daily 7:00-22:00). **Maximousse,** at Rue Flandre 51, is convenient for those sleeping in the Ste. Catherine neighborhood (daily 7:00-22:00, no change machine).

**Car Rental:** All major agencies have offices at Midi/Zuid station and Brussels Airport.

## GETTING AROUND BRUSSELS

Most of central Brussels' sights can be reached on foot. But public transport is handy for connecting the train stations, climbing to the Upper Town, visiting sights outside the central core (the European Parliament, Autoworld, Atomium, or Matongé neighborhood), and getting to Ste. Catherine neighborhood hotels. The city-run Villo system has public bike stations around town.

# Brussels Public Transportation

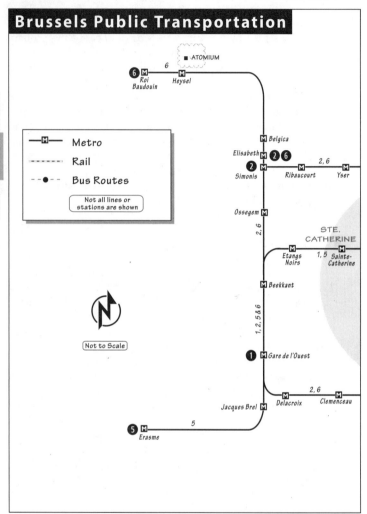

## By Public Transportation

Brussels has an extensive public transport network running the Métro, trams, and buses (www.stib-mivb.be). Transit stops are labeled in both French and Dutch (though sometimes just one name works in both languages). The excellent, free *Métro Tram Bus Plan* is available at either TI or any Métro station.

**Buying and Using Tickets:** A single-fare €2.10 **ticket** is good for one hour on all public transportation—Métro, buses, trams, and even trains shuttling between the city's train stations. An **all-day pass** (Discover Brussels 24H) is €7.50—cheaper than four single tickets—and on Sat-Sun and holidays, this pass covers two people.

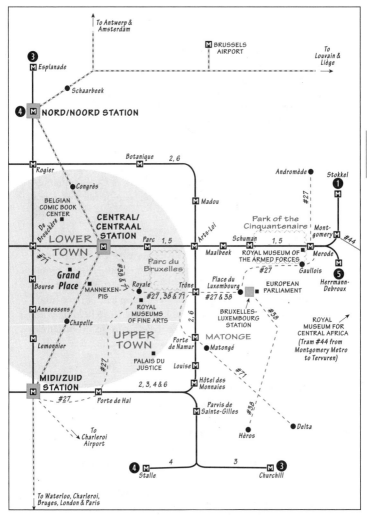

If you're staying more than a few days, you might save a few euros with a **10-ride pass** (€14 plus €5 nonrefundable fee for MOBIB transit card; not efficient for most tourists).

Buy individual tickets from vending machines at Métro stations and many central bus stops, or (for €0.40 extra) from the bus driver. Ticket machines are easy to figure out (select "English" to start) and generally take coins or US credit cards with PIN.

When you enter the Métro, a bus, or a tram, validate your ticket by touching the scanner until you hear the beep.

**Métro:** Lines 1 and 5 travel east-west through the city, with stops at Sainte-Catherine/Sint-Katelijne (recommended hotels),

De Brouckère (hotels near the Bourse and Grand Place), Gare Central/Centraal Station (trains), Parc/Park (Upper Town), and continuing east to Merode (Cinquantenaire). The other Métro lines are less helpful for travelers. Lines 3 and 4 run north and south, with stops at De Brouckère, Bourse/Beurs, and Gare du Midi/Zuidstation. Métro line 6 takes you to sights far north of downtown (Atomium, near Métro stop Heysel/Heizel).

**Buses:** Buses #38 and #71 travel roughly east-west, connecting the Lower Town (near Central station), the Upper Town (Royal Museums), and sights farther east (#38 to the European Parliament, #71 to Matongé). Bus #27 connects the Royal Museums with the European Parliament and the Park of the Cinquantenaire. Hop-on, hop-off buses (described later) can be helpful to get to some outlying sights.

## By Bike

The city of Brussels subsidizes the **Villo** network of cheap rental bikes for short rides within the city. To pick up a bike from a rental station, you must know the PIN for your credit card. After you register at the kiosk (€1.60/day, €7.90/week), you can borrow bikes at will, then drop them off at any other station (a €150 hold on your credit card ensures you return the bike; free for up to 30 minutes, €0.50/30-60 minutes, €1/1-1.5 hours, €2/1.5-2 hours, www.villo.be).

## By Taxi or Uber

Cabbies charge a €4 drop fee, then €1.80 per additional kilometer (€2 surcharge after 22:00). You'll pay about €15 for a ride from the Place de Brouckère to the Royal Museums of Fine Arts, or about €10 from Central station to the Ste. Catherine neighborhood. Figure €12 to ride from the center to the European Parliament. Convenient taxi stands near the Grand Place are at Place de Brouckère and at the "Agora" square (Rue du Marché aux Herbes). In the Upper Town, try Place du Grand Sablon. For short trips within the central core, the tangled one-way streets make taxis inefficient; it's easier to just walk. To call a cab, ring **Taxi Bleu** (tel. 02-268-0000) or **Autolux** (tel. 02-512-3123). If you use **Uber,** it works in Brussels just like it does in the US (UberX service).

# Tours in Brussels

### Hop-On, Hop-Off Bus Tour

**City Sightseeing Brussels** offers two 1.5-hour loops with (mediocre) recorded narration on double-decker buses that go topless on sunny days. One loop serves the far-flung European Parliament and Park of the Cinquantenaire; the other serves the Atomium.

The handiest starting point is at Central station, where you can also transfer between the two loops (€25, or €23 when booked online, ticket valid 24 hours, runs about twice hourly, roughly Mon-Fri 10:00-16:00, longer on Sat-Sun, shorter hours in winter; tel. 02-466-1111, www.citysightseeingbrussel.be).

## Bus Tour

**Brussels City Tour's** three-hour guided bus tour (in up to five languages) provides an easy way to get the grand perspective on Brussels. You start with a walk around the Grand Place, then jump on a tour bus (€30, year-round daily at 10:00, meet at their office a block off Grand Place at Rue du Marché aux Herbes 82; buy tickets there, at TIs, or hotels; tel. 02-513-7744, www.brussels-city-tours.com).

## Local Guides

Erwin Liekens and his knowledgeable team at **Taste the City** offer good walks, including tours focused on Belgian food and drink (€180/3 hours, €350/day, mobile 0495-625-215, www.tastethecity.be, info@tastethecity.be). You can also hire a private guide through **Visit Brussels** (€170/3 hours, tel. 02-548-0448, guides@visitbrussels.be; I enjoyed the guiding of Didier Rochette).

# SIGHTS IN BRUSSELS

The Grand Place may be Brussels' top sight, but the city offers a variety of museums, big and small, to fill your time here. I've divided the sights between the Lower Town, the Upper Town, and the outskirts.

## LOWER TOWN
### On the Grand Place
The Grand Place and some of the sights fronting it, including the Town Hall, City Museum, and chocolate shops, are described in more detail in the 📖 Grand Place Walk chapter.

### ▲▲▲Grand Place
Brussels' aptly named Grand Place (grahn plahs; in Dutch: Grote Markt, *H*ROH-teh markt), is the heart of the old town and the city's greatest sight. Any time of day, it's worth swinging by to see what's going on. Concerts, flower markets, sound-and-light shows, endless people-watching—it entertains (as do the streets around it).

### Town Hall (Hôtel de Ville)
With the Grand Place's tallest spire, this is the square's centerpiece, but its interior is no big deal. Admission is only possible with a 45-minute English tour, which also covers city history and the building's tapestries and architecture.

**Cost and Hours:** €6, English tours offered Wed at 14:00, Sun at 11:00, 15:00, and 16:00; tickets available day of tour in the TI shop on Grand Place; 25-person limit—assure a spot by buying tickets when the TI opens at 9:00.

### ▲City Museum (Musée de la Ville de Bruxelles)
Inside the King's House (Maison du Roi) building on the Grand Place, this mildly interesting museum has city history exhibits, the

original *Manneken-Pis* statue, models of old Brussels, and some old tapestries, altarpieces, and paintings. Posted information is in Dutch and French only, but there are English info sheets throughout. (Note that the BELvue Museum in the Upper Town is better for Belgian history).

**Cost and Hours:** €8, ticket also valid for GardeRobe Manneken-Pis—described later; Tue-Sun 10:00-17:00, closed Mon; Grand Place, tel. 02-279-4350, www.museedelavilledebruxelles. be.

**Visiting the Museum:** Begin your visit on the ground floor and work your way up.

**Ground Floor:** Here you'll see the original statues that once adorned the Town Hall. The limestone is no match for the corrosive acidic air, so they were brought inside for protection. Also on this floor are a few old paintings (one may be by Jan Brueghel the Elder), fine carved altarpieces, and porcelain. Spend some time with a Brussels specialty—tapestries. With access to great materials (via the thriving cloth trade) and great artists (like Peter Paul Rubens), Brussels cranked out these wall hangings that adorned Europe's homes as both functional insulators and artistic masterpieces.

**Middle Floor:** Watch the 20-minute video (in English) for a bite-sized introduction to Brussels history. Find the model of the

city in the 13th century. (Get oriented: Uphill is east.) The largest structure back then was St. Michael's Cathedral. At the top of the model is the Upper Town—which, at this point, hasn't even a hint of its monumental future. At the bottom of the hill is the (former) River Senne, which was the city's trading lifeline. In between stands the fledgling Grand Place—only a small clearing amid a cluster of houses.

The city was a port town—see the crane unloading barges—since it was at this point that the shallow Senne became navigable. Grain from the area was processed in the watermills, then shipped downstream to Antwerp and on to the North Sea.

By the 1200s, Brussels—though tiny by today's standards—was an important commercial center, and St. Michael's was the region's religious hub. Still, most of the area inside the 2.5-mile-long city wall was farmland, dotted with a few churches, towers, markets, and convents (such as the Carmelite convent hugging the south wall).

Another model (at the far end of the room) shows the city a

# Brussels at a Glance

▲▲▲**Grand Place** Main square and spirited heart of the Lower Town. See page 122.

▲▲▲**Royal Museums of Fine Arts of Belgium** Museums displaying Old Masters, turn-of-the-century art, and works by Belgian Surrealist René Magritte. **Hours:** Old Masters and Fin-de-Siècle museums—Tue-Sun 10:00-17:00, closed Mon; Magritte Museum—daily 10:00-17:00. See page 131.

▲▲*Manneken-Pis* World-famous statue of a leaky little boy. **Hours:** Always peeing. See page 125.

▲▲**BELvue Museum** Belgian history with a focus on the popular royal family. **Hours:** Tue-Fri 9:30-17:00 (July-Aug until 18:00), Sat-Sun 10:00-18:00, closed Mon. See page 132.

▲▲**European Parliament** Soaring home of Europe's governing body. **Hours:** Parlamentarium and House of European History—Tue-Fri 9:00-18:00, Sat-Sun from 10:00, Mon from 13:00; Parliament tours offered Mon-Fri. See page 134.

▲▲**Mémorial 1815** State-of-the-art museum at the site of the Battle of Waterloo. **Hours:** Daily 9:30-18:30, Oct-March 10:00-17:30. See page 147.

▲**City Museum** Models and exhibits of Brussels' history, plus the original *Manneken-Pis* statue. **Hours:** Tue-Sun 10:00-17:00, closed Mon. See page 122.

▲**Fashion and Lace Museum** World-famous Brussels lace and embroidery. **Hours:** Tue-Sun 10:00-17:00, closed Mon. See page 126.

▲**St. Michael's Cathedral** White-stone Gothic church where Belgian royals are married and buried. **Hours:** Mon-Fri 7:00-18:00, Sat-Sun from 8:30. See page 127.

▲**Belgian Comic Strip Center** Homage to the Smurfs, Tintin, Lucky Luke, and more. **Hours:** Daily 10:00-18:00. See page 128.

▲**Musical Instruments Museum** Exhibits with more than 1,500 instruments, complete with audio. **Hours:** Tue-Fri 9:30-17:00, Sat-Sun from 10:00, closed Mon. See page 131.

▲**Autoworld** Hundreds of historic vehicles. **Hours:** Daily 10:00-18:00, shorter hours off-season. See page 140.

▲**Royal Museum of the Armed Forces and Military History** Vast collection of weaponry and uniforms. **Hours:** Tue-Sun 9:00-17:00, closed Mon. See page 141.

couple of centuries later—much bigger, but still within the same wall. By this time, the Upper and Lower Towns are clearly defined. In the Upper Town, the huge palace of the dukes of Burgundy marks the site of today's Royal Palace.

**Top Floor:** The main hall—under an interesting wood-carved roof—showcases the original *Manneken-Pis* statue. The exhibit explains that Brussels has had a tradition of fountains that spurted through various body parts perhaps dating back a thousand years. This floor also generally has temporary exhibits highlighting the city's history.

### Brewery Museum

This little basement-level, bar-like place has one room of old brewing paraphernalia and one room of new (beer video in English). It's pretty lame...skip it unless you're really thirsty.

**Cost and Hours:** €5 includes an unnamed local beer, daily 10:00-17:00, Grand Place 10, tel. 02-511-4987, www.belgianbrewers.be.

### ▲Chocolate Shops on the Grand Place

For many, the best thing about the Grand Place is the chocolate sold at its venerable chocolate shops: Godiva, Neuhaus, Mary, Galler, and Leonidas (shops generally open daily until 22:00). It takes a lot of sampling to judge. For more, see the sidebar on page 154.

### Museum of Cocoa and Chocolate

This touristy exhibit, just off the Grand Place to the right of Town Hall, is a delightful concept and tries hard, but it's overpriced. Its three floors feature meager displays, a ho-hum video, a look at a "chocolate master" at work (live demos 2/hour), and a choco-sample.

**Cost and Hours:** €6, daily 10:00-17:00, Rue de la Tête d'Or 9, tel. 02-514-2048, www.choco-story-brussels.be.

## South of the Grand Place
### ▲▲*Manneken-Pis*

Brussels is a great city with a cheesy mascot: a 17th-century statue of a little boy urinating (apparently symbolizing the city's irreverence and love of the good life). Read up on his story at any postcard stand. His facsimile is three short blocks off the Grand Place: For directions, take my Grand Place Walk; look for small, white *Manneken-Pis* signs; or just ask a local, *"Où est le Manneken-Pis?"* (oo ay luh man-ay-kehn peese). The little squirt may be wearing some clever outfit, as costumes are sent for him from around the world. (For more about his fashion statements, visit the museum described later.) The tourist hubbub and frantic selfie derby on this street corner is as much of a sight as the statue itself.

## GardeRobe Manneken-Pis

That little bronze boy with the bladder control problem is also a clothes horse, so if you really want to see his wardrobe, this is the place.

For three centuries, it's been a tradition for the statue to be outfitted in clothing—the little guy pees through several costume changes each week. Many of the outfits you see here were donated by other countries. There are some 1,000 costumes in the archives, including a Civil War Union soldier, an El Salvadorian farmer, a Polish hussar, a Japanese samurai, an Indian maharajah, a Spanish bullfighter, a Russian cosmonaut, and a Fiji islander.

**Cost and Hours:** €8, ticket also covers the City Museum on Grand Place; Tue-Sun 10:00-17:00, closed Mon; about half a block from the little squirt at Rue du Chêne 19, tel. 02-514-5397, www.mannekenpis.brussels.

## ▲Fashion and Lace Museum (Musée Mode et de la Dentelle)

This fine little museum showcases rotating exhibits of historic fashion as well as the art of lace. You'll enjoy exquisite costumes, feathery fans, and baby baptismal gowns. As the lace is fragile, much of it is stored in drawers—be sure to pull them out. At the entry, borrow the necessary English booklet that describes each showpiece.

**Cost and Hours:** €8, Tue-Sun 10:00-17:00, closed Mon, Rue de la Violette 12, a block off the Grand Place, tel. 02-213-4450, www.fashionandlacemuseum.brussels.

## West of the Grand Place

These two fun-to-explore spots, just across the busy Boulevard Anspach from the Bourse and minutes apart on foot, offer some of Brussels' most appealing restaurants (far less touristy than those near the Grand Place). Ste. Catherine is also a fine place to sleep. If you're looking for a bustling nighttime neighborhood full of inviting eateries and bars, you'll enjoy strolling these two areas.

## Ste. Catherine and the Old Fish Market (Vieux Marché aux Poissons)

Two blocks northwest of the Bourse is the ragtag Church of Ste. Catherine, which marks an inviting "village in the city" area with great eating options. The church itself is falling apart—during its construction, the architect got the commission for the Place of Justice in the Upper Town and rushed to complete this church so he could begin the more lucrative new job as quickly as possible. In front of the church stretches the long, skinny former fish market, lined with a range of upscale fish restaurants. Alongside the church is Place Ste. Catherine (Sint-Katelijneplein), with more restaurants, bars, and the city's best cheap-and-fast lunch options (see page 202 for recommended eateries).

### Place St-Géry

This square—called Sint-Goriksplein in Dutch—was actually once an island in the now covered-up Senne River, Brussels' former trad-

ing lifeline. The market hall in the middle of the square evokes a time when goods were offloaded a few blocks away, at the old fish market, and brought here for sale. Today the hall houses a café and special exhibits. On Sunday mornings, the square is filled with a comics market.

Across from the southwest corner of the hall, at #23 (next to the *Ô Lion d'Or* information board), duck through the little gateway to find a relaxing oasis of a courtyard—you might see businesspeople dozing on their lunch breaks here. At the far end of the courtyard, there's even a small exposed stretch of the Senne.

## East of the Grand Place
### ▲St. Michael's Cathedral

One of Europe's classic Gothic churches, built between roughly 1200 and 1500, Brussels' cathedral is made from white stone and topped by twin towers. For nearly

1,000 years, it's been the most important church in this largely Catholic country. (Whereas the Netherlands went in a Protestant direction in the 1500s, Belgium remains 80 percent Catholic—although only about 20 percent attend Mass.)

**Cost and Hours:** Free, but small fees to visit the underwhelming crypt and treasury; Mon-Fri 7:00-18:00, Sat-Sun from 8:30; www. cathedralisbruxellensis.be.

**Visiting the Cathedral:** The white-themed nave is bare but impressive, with a few nice stained-glass windows and a marvelous carved pulpit of Adam and Eve supporting the preacher. On top, St. Michael stabs Satan in serpent form.

This church is where royal weddings and funerals take place.

Photographs (to the right of the entrance) show the funeral of the popular King Baudouin, who died in 1993. He was succeeded by his younger brother, Albert II, who abdicated in 2014 to allow his son, Philippe, to become king. (Belgium's newest euro coins show Philippe, but older ones with Albert will stay in circulation for years.) Traditionally, the ruler was always a male, but in 1992 the constitution was changed to allow the oldest child of either gender to take the throne. King Philippe and Queen Mathilde's first child, Elisabeth, born in 2001, is next in line for the throne.

Before leaving, pause on the outer porch to enjoy the great view of the Town Hall spire with its gold statue of St. Michael.

### ▲Belgian Comic Strip Center (Centre Belge de la Bande Dessinée)

Belgians are as proud of their comics as they are of their beer, lace, and chocolates. Something about the comic medium resonates with the wry and artistic-yet-unpretentious Belgian sensibility. Belgium has produced some of the world's most popular comic characters, including the Smurfs, Tintin, and Lucky Luke. You'll find these, and many less famous local comics, at the Comic Strip Center. It's not a wacky, lighthearted place, but a serious museum about a legitimate artistic medium.

Even if you don't have the time or interest to visit the museum's collection, pop into the lobby to see the groundbreaking Art Nouveau building (a former department store designed in 1903 by Belgian architect Victor Horta), browse through comics in the bookshop, and snap a photo with a three-foot-tall Smurf. That's enough for many people—especially for kids, who might find the museum itself boring. But those who appreciate art in general will enjoy this sometimes humorous,  sometimes probing, often beautiful medium. Most of the cartoons are in French and Dutch, but descriptions come in English. Borrow the free, English guidebooklet to read short bios of famous cartoonists.

**Cost and Hours:** €10, daily 10:00-18:00, 10-minute walk from the Grand Place to Rue des Sables 20, tel. 02-219-1980, www.comicscenter.net.

**Getting There:** From Central station, walk north along the big boulevard, then turn left down the stairs at the giant comic character (Gaston Lagaffe).

**Visiting the Museum:** The collection changes often, but no matter what's on you'll see how comics are made and watch early

# Tintin 101

The Belgian comic character Tintin is beloved to several generations of Europeans. He's increasingly known in the US, thanks to translations of his adventures and Steven Spielberg's 2011 animated Tintin film.

In 1929, Brussels cartoonist Georges Rémi (1907-1983),  using the pseudonym Hergé, created a dedicated young reporter with a shock of blond hair who's constantly getting into and out of misadventures. A precise artist, Hergé used a simple, uncluttered style with clear lines and appealing color.

Combining fantasy, mystery, and sci-fi with a dash of humor, the Tintin stories quickly found an appreciative audience. *The Adventures of Tintin* spanned 47 years and 24 books (selling some 200 million copies—and counting—in 50 languages). Tintin's popularity continues even today, as nostalgic parents buy the comics they grew up on for their own kids.

Tintin is the smart, upbeat, inquisitive, brave-but-not-foolhardy young man whose adventures propel the plot. His newspaper sends him on assignments all over the world. Snowy, Tintin's loyal fox terrier, is his constant companion—and often saves the day. The grizzled, grouchy, heavy-drinking Captain Haddock is as cynical as Tintin is optimistic, with a penchant for colorful curses ("Blistering barnacles!"). Professor Calculus is as brilliant as he is absentminded and hard of hearing, and comic relief is provided by the bumbling, nearly identical detectives called Thomson and Thompson.

Throughout his swashbuckling adventures, Tintin travels far and wide to exotic destinations. Hergé has been acclaimed for his meticulous research—he studied up on the places he portrayed and tried to avoid basing his stories on assumptions or stereotypes (though by today's standards, some of the comics still betray an ugly Eurocentrism—one of the earliest, *Tintin in the Congo,* Hergé himself later acknowledged was regrettably racist).

And though the supporting characters are dynamic and colorful, Tintin himself has a rather bland personality. His expressions are usually indistinct (Hergé wanted the young reader to project his or her own emotions onto Tintin's blank-canvas face). While presumably a teenager, Tintin's age is unclear—at times we imagine him to be a young boy, while at others he's seen drinking a beer, piloting a plane, or living in his own apartment (we never meet his family, if he has one). All of this is intentional: Hergé's style subconsciously encourages readers to put themselves in Tintin's everyman shoes.

animated films. The heart of the collection is the golden age of comics in the 1950s and 1960s. You'll likely see a sprawling exhibit on Tintin, the intrepid young reporter with the button eyes and wavy shock of hair, launched in 1929 by Hergé and much loved by older Europeans. Brussels' own Peyo (a.k.a. Pierre Culliford, 1928-1992) invented the Smurfs—the little blue forest creatures that stand "three apples high." First popular across much of Europe, especially in Belgium (where they're known as Les Schtroumpfs), the Smurfs became well-known to a generation of Americans after they starred in Hanna-Barbera's 1980s televised cartoons. In this century, they've won over a new generation with a series of major movies. The cowboy Lucky Luke (by Morris, a.k.a. Maurice De Bevere, 1923-2001) exemplifies Belgians' fascination with exotic locales, especially America's Wild West.

The top floor's temporary exhibits are often dedicated to "serious" comics, where more adult themes and high-quality drawing aspire to turn kids' stuff into that "Ninth Art" (*neuvième art*—the French term for comics as fine art). These works can be grimly realistic, openly erotic or graphic, or darker in tone, often featuring flawed antiheroes. The museum's bookstore is nearly as interesting, giving you the chance to page through reproductions of classic comics.

**Nearby:** The related **Marc Sleen Museum,** across the street, is dedicated to the oh-so-typically Belgian cartoonist whose big-nosed, caricatured drawings are recognizable even to many Americans. Sleen's *Adventures of Nero and Co.,* which he churned out in two strips a day for a staggering 55 years, holds the record for the longest-running comic by a single artist. Still, the collection is worth a visit only to his fans (€1 extra with Comic Strip Center entry, or €2.50 alone; daily 11:00-13:00 & 14:00-18:00; tel. 02-219-1980, www.marc-sleen.be).

**Other Comic Sights:** If you're a Belgian comics completist, consider visiting the **Museum of Original Figurines** (MOOF), at the entrance to the Horta Gallery at the lower end of Central station (a few steps from "Agora" square). They feature changing exhibits of colorful figurines of your favorite Belgian characters (closed Mon-Wed, www.moofmuseum.be). A handy **Smurf Store** is next door.

## UPPER TOWN

Brussels' grandiose Upper Town, with its huge palace, is described in the ▢ Upper Town Walk chapter. Along that walk, you'll pass the following sights (for locations, see the map in that chapter).

### ▲▲▲Royal Museums of Fine Arts of Belgium
### (Musées Royaux des Beaux-Arts de Belgique)

This sprawling complex houses a trio of museums showing off the country's best all-around art collection. The **Old Masters Muse-**

**um**—featuring Flemish and Belgian art of the 14th through 18th century—is packed with a dazzling collection of masterpieces by Van der Weyden, Bruegel, Bosch, and Rubens. The **Fin-de-Siècle Museum** covers art of the late 19th and early 20th centuries, including an extensive Art Nouveau collection. The **Magritte Museum** contains more than 200 works by the Surrealist painter René Magritte. Although you won't see many of Magritte's most famous pieces, you will get an unusually intimate look at the life and work of one of Belgium's top artists.

**Cost and Hours:** €10 for each individual museum, €15 combo-ticket covers all three, free first Wed of month after 13:00; Old Masters and Fin-de-Siècle museums—Tue-Sun 10:00-17:00, closed Mon; Magritte Museum—daily 10:00-17:00; audioguides-€4 each, tour booklet-€2.50, Rue de la Régence 3, tel. 02-508-3211, www.fine-arts-museum.be or www.musee-magritte-museum.be.

### ▲Musical Instruments Museum
### (Musée des Instruments de Musique)

One of Europe's best music museums (nicknamed "MIM") is housed in one of Brussels' most impressive Art Nouveau build-

ings, the beautifully renovated Old England department store. This museum has more than 1,500 instruments—from Egyptian harps, to medieval lutes, to groundbreaking harpsichords, to the saxophone (invented by Belgium's own Adolphe Sax).

**Cost and Hours:** €10, includes audioguide; Tue-Fri 9:30-17:00, Sat-Sun from 10:00, closed Mon, last entry 45 minutes before closing; mandatory free bag check, Rue Montagne de la Cour 2, just downhill and toward Grand Place from the Royal Museums, tel. 02-545-0133, www.mim.be.

**Visiting the Museum:** With your included audioguide, you're free to wander through exhibits on several levels. These include musical mechanisms like radios and organs on the lower floor, folk instruments from around the world on the first floor, a history of Western musical instruments on the second, and rotating special exhibits on the fourth. As you approach an instrument, you hear it playing on your headphones. On the fifth floor is an exhibit about the history of the building and Brussels Art Nouveau in general.

The displays lack complete English descriptions, but the music you'll hear is an international language. Don't miss the great city views from the corner alcoves on each level.

**Eating with City Views:** The 10th floor has a restaurant, a terrace, and a great view of Brussels (no charge to enter—tell the staff at museum entrance you want to go only to the restaurant).

## ▲▲BELvue Museum

This 21st-century museum is the best introduction to modern Belgian history (1830-2015) that you'll find in Brussels. It's well described in English, organized by modern themes, and spiced up with iPads and interactive technology. But it's also Belgian history— so it is what it is. The museum sits over the (skippable) archaeological remains of the 12th-century Coudenberg Palace. If you do tour the palace ruins, see the BELvue Museum first, because you'll exit the Coudenberg downhill, near the Musical Instruments Museum.

**Cost and Hours:** Museum-€7, palace remains-€7, €12 combo-ticket covers both; Tue-Fri 9:30-17:00 (July-Aug until 18:00), Sat-Sun 10:00-18:00, closed Mon; adjacent to the Royal Palace at Place des Palais 7, tel. 02-500-4554, www.belvue.be.

**Visiting the Museum:** Start in the first floor hallway, where you'll get a brief overview of how Belgium achieved independence from the Netherlands in 1830. From there, each room explores a theme of Belgian history through artifacts, exhibits, and even commentary from everyday Belgians (via video screens).

**First Floor:** In Room 1 you'll explore "Democracy" (women didn't get the vote until 1948) and see a timeline of the Belgian royal family. It's clear the dynasty is generally appreciated, even loved. Since these imported German monarchs arrived in 1830, each of the seven "Kings of the Belgians" (as they're officially known) has had his own style and claim to fame. Leopold I was the visionary who united the young nation. Leopold II was the "Builder King" and Congo exploiter. Albert I guided Belgium through World War I—only 30,000 Belgian troops died. Controversial World War II-era Leopold III was tainted after his attempt to negotiate with Hitler, and later abdicated in disgrace. He was followed by Baudouin, who restored respect for the monarchy. His equally popular brother became King Albert II. Albert II's son Philippe now reigns as king; the royal family includes his wife Mathilde, two princes (Gabriel and Emmanuel), and two princesses (Elisabeth and Eléonore).

Next comes "Prosperity" (Room 2), which covers how Belgium welcomed the Industrial Revolution (it had the first railroad on the Continent), thrived by exploiting its colony in Africa, and embraced the idea of a united Europe after World War II. The following room explores "Solidarity" and the rise of the labor movement (look for quotes from Vincent van Gogh and Karl Marx, both of whom lived in Brussels for a time). One of the major battles inside Belgium was over religion and who would run the schools: The "Pluralism" exhibit (Room 4) explores the "school wars" over two centuries.

**Second Floor:** The "Migration" exhibit covers both the departure of Belgians for better lives (more than 200,000 emigrated to the US) as well as the tide of immigration into Belgium after World War II. Perhaps the most fascinating issues are examined in "Language" (Room 6). An excellent video tries to explain the back story of the festering Flemish-Walloon conflict and the bitter struggle to prevent Belgium from splitting completely in half. The final room focuses on postwar efforts to launch the European Union.

**Coudenberg Palace:** Below the museum, long, vaulted cellars are all that's left of this 12th-century royal palace. Although well-lit and explained, the archaeological remains require too much imagination to make them meaningful. A small exhibit explains artifacts from the palace. The best part is the free orientation video you see before descending underground.

### Notre-Dame du Sablon Church

This 15th-century church in the Flamboyant Gothic style retains some of its original stained-glass windows (prettily illuminated from inside at night). It also holds a little statue of the Virgin Mary that's been venerated by Bruxellois since the 1300s.

**Cost and Hours:** Free, daily 9:00-18:30, Rue de la Régence 3, tel. 02-511-5741.

## EAST OF DOWNTOWN

Two clusters of sights lie just east of the city center: the European Parliament (museums about the European Union and European history plus tours of the parliament complex) and the Park of the Cinquantenaire (with three museums: cars, the military, and art). Between these sights and central Brussels is the Matongé neighborhood—a fascinating blend of Congolese influences and Belgian *bohème,* and a fun place to grab a bite to eat.

East Brussels

## Planning Your Time

Because the areas are connected by a quick bus ride, it's easy to visit both in a single half-day excursion. The best days to visit are Tuesdays through Fridays, as some Cinquantenaire museums are closed on Mondays, and the European Parliament is pretty dead on weekends. Here's a suggested itinerary:

Start with the **Park of the Cinquantenaire** (details on getting to the park are later).

After visiting the museums, take a bus to the **European Parliament.** To get there, catch bus #27 behind the Autoworld building on Avenue des Gaulois (bus stop: Gaulois/Galliërs, direction: Gare du Midi/Zuidstation, 4/hour Mon-Fri, 2/hour Sat-Sun) to the Luxembourg stop. Arriving at Place du Luxembourg, you immediately see the modern gray-and-glass buildings that make up the EU complex.

After your European Parliament visit, catch bus #38 to the city center (or walk to the **Matongé** district).

## ▲▲European Parliament

Europe's governing body welcomes visitors with an exhibit about the European Union and its parliament. You can also follow an

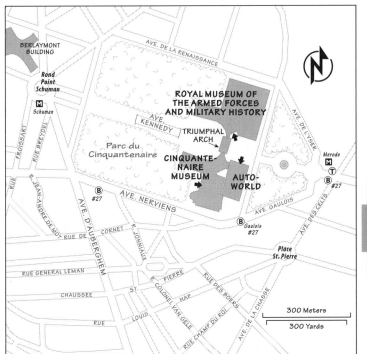

audioguide tour of the actual parliament chamber—the Hemicy-

cle. The parliament's sprawling complex of modern glass build-ings is a babel of black-suited politicians speaking 24 differ-ent Euro-languages. It's exciting just to be here—a fly on the wall of a place that aspires to chart the future of Europe "with re-spect for all political thinking... consolidating democracy in the spirit of peace and solidarity."

**Getting There:** The European Parliament is next to Place du Luxembourg (a skippable information office called "Station Eu-rope" is in the Neoclassical former train station). Bus #38 heads here from Central station or the Royal Museums; bus #27 comes from the Royal Museums or the museums at the Park of the Cinquantenaire. Place du Luxembourg is a seven-minute walk from the Trône/Troon Métro stop (straight ahead up Luxembourg street—Europe's "K" Street, teeming with lobbyists). From Place du Luxembourg, signs direct you to the complex's main visitor sights: the Parlamentarium, the House of European History, and

# The European Union

Brussels is the capital of one of the biggest, most powerful, and most idealistic states in the world (and, argu-ably, in history): the European Union (EU). In just one generation, more than two dozen European countries have gone from being bitter rivals to compatriots. This union of such a diverse collection of separate na-tions—with different languages, cultures, and soccer teams—is almost unprecedented. And it all started in the rubble of a war.

World War II left 40 million dead and a continent in ruins, and it convinced Europe-ans that they had to work together to main-tain peace. Poised between competing su-perpowers (the US and the USSR), they also needed to cooperate economically to survive in an increasingly globalized economy. Just after the war ended, visionary "Eurocrats" began the task of convincing reluctant Eu-ropean nations to relinquish elements of their sovereignty and merge into a united body.

The transition happened gradually, in fits and starts. It began in 1948, when Belgium, the Netherlands, and Luxembourg—joint-ly called "BeNeLux"—established a free-trade zone. That evolved into an ever-broadening alliance of states (the European Coal and Steel Union, then the European Economic Community, or "Com-mon Market"). In 1992, with the Treaty of Maastricht, the 12 mem-ber countries of the Common Market made a leap of faith: They created a "European Union" that would eventually allow for free movement of capital, goods, services, and labor.

In 2002, most EU members adopted a single currency (the euro), and for all practical purposes, economic unity was a reality. As of 2019 there will be 27 member states—encompassing nearly all of Western Europe, and much of Eastern Europe and Scandina-via. Almost all EU members have joined the open-borders Schen-gen Agreement, making passport checkpoints obsolete. This makes the EU the world's seventh-largest "country" (1.6 million square miles), with the third-largest population (around 450 mil-lion people), and an economy slightly smaller than the US (around

the Hemicycle tour. To return to the city center, catch bus #38 from Place du Luxembourg.

### Parlamentarium

This high-tech, informative museum is designed to let you meet the European Union and understand how it works. Pick up your free audioguide headset and wander through its many exhibits. You'll learn about how the EU came to be and the many challenges it has faced; "meet" virtual EU parliamentarians; find out about some of

$16 trillion GDP).

The EU is governed from Brussels. While it has a parliament, the EU is primarily led by the European Commission (with commissioners appointed by individual member governments and approved by its parliament) and the Council of Ministers. Daily business is conducted by an army of bureaucrats and policy wonks.

Unlike America's federation of 50 states, Europe's member states retain the right to opt out of some EU policies. Denmark, for example, belongs to the EU but hasn't adopted the euro as its currency. While the 2009 Lisbon Treaty streamlines EU responses to conflicts and issues, there's no unified foreign or economic policy among the member countries. The EU also lacks a powerful chief executive—the president of the European Council, appointed for a two-and-a-half-year term, is much weaker than the US president, as EU laws require consensus on taxes, foreign policy, defense, and social programs.

The goal is to create a competitive, sustainable, environmentally friendly economy that improves the quality of life for all Europeans. Still, many "Euroskeptics" remain unconvinced that the EU is a good thing. There's no clearer evidence than Britain's stunning 2016 vote to leave the EU ("Brexit"). It rattled Brussels. No one knows exactly how Britain's move will play out once it leaves. Other EU countries are debating similar referendums, and leaders in Hungary and Poland have become unabashed Euroskeptics. These EU critics chafe at the highly regulated business environment and high taxes. They complain about the bureaucracy and worry that their national cultures will be swallowed up and Eurofied. As Europe faces immigration and refugee issues, some countries want to control their own borders rather than leave decisions to Brussels. And wealthier member countries (mostly in the north) are reluctant to bail out their economically unsound compatriots (mostly in the south) to prop up the euro, while troubled countries resent the cuts demanded by the richer ones.

Still, despite these problems, Europeans don't want to go back to the days of division and strife. Even with the "Brexit" vote, most agree that a strong, unified Europe is necessary to keep the peace and compete in a global economy.

BRUSSELS SIGHTS

Europe's most powerful political parties and movements; cast your own vote regarding recent hot-button EU issues; and get a rundown of each EU country's culture, commerce, and contemporary challenges. The interactive exhibits are rather dry, and the pro-EU propaganda, while expected, can be heavy-handed. Nothing addresses the recent trends toward nationalism, and the UK vote to leave the EU ("Brexit") is barely mentioned. Still, it's good introduction to the EU; it's smart to visit before your parliament tour.

**Cost and Hours:** Free; Tue-Fri 9:00-18:00, Sat-Sun from 10:00, Mon from 13:00; www.europarl.europa.eu/visiting.

### Parliament Tours

The only way to get inside the European Parliament itself is to join a free 30-minute audioguide tour. You'll learn about the world's largest transnational parliament, and get a look at the Hemicycle, the semicircular chamber where EU members debate issues and cast votes. While you can't make an advance reservation, drop by the starting point about 10 to 15 minutes before the tour to register (bring ID—passport or driver's license).

**Cost and Hours:** Free; tours offered on the hour Sept-June Mon-Thu 9:00-16:00, Fri until 11:00; July-Aug continuous access Mon-Thu 9:00-12:00 & 14:00-16:00, Fri 9:00-12:00. No tours Sat-Sun.

**Getting There:** The Parliament building is behind the main complex, a five-minute walk from the circular main square—follow *Visit Hemicycle* signs. You'll walk through an arcade and down a long set of stairs. When you see the statue of the woman holding a euro sign, turn left and follow along the building. The parliament tour entrance will be on your right—near a piece of the Berlin Wall.

**Visiting the Parliament:** When you check in, you'll be sent through security and given an audioguide. Head up the stairs and wait for your tour to begin in the atrium, with exhibits and a gift shop. At the appointed time, your escort leads you to various viewpoints in the complex where you'll be instructed to listen to the related audioguide commentary. You'll learn how early visionary utopians (like Churchill, who in 1946 called for a "United States of Europe" to avoid future wars) led the way as Europe gradually evolved into the European Union (1992).

From the balcony overlooking the building's lobby, you can see the giant *Confluence* sculpture with moving metal-wire pieces—representing people coming together for a common purpose. The building itself is in line with EU idealism: It's functional, transparent, and very "green."

The grand finale is the vast "Hemicycle," where the members of the European Parliament sit. Here you'll listen to a political-science lesson about the all-Europe system of governance. The parliamentarians who hash out pan-European issues in this hall represent 160 different national political parties and are organized into seven different voting blocs—based on political ideals rather than nationality.

With the president facing them, they're seated from left to right—both literally and politically—which means that from their perspective, they sit on the "wrong" side of the hall. This is done to foster empathy. Although most parliamentarians can speak English, in this setting they are encouraged to talk in their mother tongues—ensuring they will be fully comfortable in expressing their thoughts. That makes this the largest multilingual operation on the planet, with a very busy army of translators, who simultaneously translate every word into all 24 official languages.

## House of European History

This high-tech museum does its part in the grander project to foster European unity. Its main theme is how history has shaped Europeans' memories and daily lives from the 19th century to today. It works hard to show how fundamental characteristics of European culture—such as cooking, leisure activities, and politics—are distinctive in each country but also broadly similar. While well intentioned, it's a little underwhelming, though still worth visiting for history buffs.

**Cost and Hours:** Free, includes audioguide; Tue-Fri 9:00-18:00, Sat-Sun from 10:00, Mon from 13:00; in Léopold Park behind the main EU buildings at Rue Belliard 135, tel. 02-283-1220, www.historia-europa.ep.eu.

**Visiting the Museum:** As at other EU sights, you'll have to pass through security, then leave bags in lockers on the ground floor. Head one floor up to pick up the audioguide, which comes on a tablet (essential, as most exhibits are not labeled). The initial floors skim big-picture topics such as Europe as a global power and a geographical entity; as you go up the floors, the museum focuses on history.

Exhibits explore European unification efforts post-World War II, as visionary leaders tried to overcome the continent's many divisions. The Cold War's brutal severing of Europe into eastern and western halves receives a lot of attention, as well as the dramatic fall of communist regimes in 1989 that stitched the halves back together. All of this is thoughtfully illustrated with historical objects, such as the cap worn by the "Irish liberator" Daniel O'Connell or a wall of class photos from the 1950s, '60s, and '70s from both sides of the Iron Curtain.

**Nearby:** The worthwhile **Royal Belgian Institute of Natural Sciences** (Institut Royal des Sciences Naturelles de Belgique) sits practically next door to the European Parliament. Dinosaur enthusiasts come here for the world's largest collection of iguanodon skeletons (€7, Tue-Fri 9:30-17:00, Sat-Sun 10:00-18:00, closed Mon, Rue Vautier 29, tel. 02-627-4211, www.naturalsciences.be).

## Park of the Cinquantenaire Museums

Standing proudly in a big park in eastern Brussels is a trio of sprawling museums housed in cavernous halls: the Royal Museum of the Armed Forces and Military History, Autoworld, and the Cinquantenaire Museum. These attractions thrill specialists but bore most others.

The complex itself is interesting to see. There's a huge Neo-classical triumphal arch, and the place is surrounded by a spacious park (Parc du Cinquantenaire). It has a grandiose history: The ambitious 19th-century Belgian king Leopold II wanted Brussels to rival Paris. In 1880, he celebrated the 50th anniversary *(cinquantenaire)* of Belgian independence by building the arch flanked by massive exhibition halls, which today house the museums.

**Getting There:** Take Métro line 1 or 5 from the city center to Métro stop Merode. Exit the Métro station following signs to *Yser/IJzer,* then cross the street toward the big arch. Other options: Take bus #27 from the Upper Town (Royale/Koning) to the Gaulois/Galliërs stop or consider a hop-on-hop-off bus (see page 120).

## ▲Autoworld

A cavernous hall filled with 400 historic cars shows the vast array of motorized vehicles built over the last century-plus. The place is made for browsing—each car is clearly labeled. Besides historic cars, Autoworld always features some of the latest and hottest designs. Vroom.

There's an audioguide and some English descriptions, but for much of it, you're left to either bring your own knowledge or simply admire the high-polish gleam.

**Cost and Hours:** €10, daily 10:00-18:00, shorter hours off-season, audioguide-€2, in Palais Mondial, Parc du Cinquantenaire 11, tel. 02-736-4165, www.autoworld.be.

**Visiting the Museum:** Start by tracing the history of automobiles, decade-by-decade, along the right wall. (But first up, admire the humongous green 1929 Minerva sedan at the entrance—a rarity by Belgium's best-known automaker, which went defunct in the 1950s.)

As you work your way counterclockwise through the ground floor, you'll see the first handmade cars—basically converted horse carriages. Then comes mass production (introduced by America's Henry Ford) and the big luxury cars of the 1920s. During the Great Depression, small economy cars were in vogue—France's Citroën and Hitler's brainchild, the Volkswagen. It was Hitler and Mussolini who built the first freeways to quickly mobilize troops in wartime. The postwar years produced monstrous gas-guzzling cars for the suburban masses—particularly in America.

Head upstairs to the sporty '60s, the fuel-efficient '70s (after the Arab oil embargo of 1973), and the international brands of the '80s and '90s. Then just browse the rest of this vast collection.

### ▲Royal Museum of the Armed Forces and Military History (Musée Royal de l'Armée et d'Histoire Militaire)

Wander through this enormous collection of weaponry, uniforms, tanks, warplanes, and endless exhibits about military history, fo-

cusing on the 19th and 20th centuries. The museum is filled with real, tangible history. This impressively complete museum is nirvana for fans of military history and aviation (but skippable for those who think a "panzer" is a pretty flower).

**Cost and Hours:** €5, credit card only; Tue-Sun 9:00-17:00, closed Mon; au-

dioguide-€3, Parc du Cinquantenaire 3, tel. 02/737-7811, www.klm-mra.be.

**Visiting the Museum:** Exploring the whole place is exhausting, so be selective. Each item is labeled in French and Dutch, but some good English descriptions are available; to get the most out of your visit, renting the audioguide is essential.

Here's how I'd tour the place. From the entrance, go straight ahead, through the Belgian military history section—seeing Belgian flags, cannons, uniforms, and Leopold II's tricycle (midway along). This leads to exhibits on World War I and World War II (which, naturally, are strong on the role of Belgium). The grand finale is the vast (and I mean vast) aviation hall filled with warplanes. You'll see WWI biplanes and WWII fighters, plus a Soviet MiG fighter (with camouflage paint) that crashed in Belgium in 1989 (one of the last airspace violations of the Cold War). Some of these planes are one-of-a-kind relics—including a French Nieuport fighter, a Schreck seaplane, and two German observation planes from World War I. There's much more to the museum, including the arms and armor section (access it through the gift shop near the entrance).

Finish your visit at the Panorama—the stunning viewpoint atop the Cinquantenaire arch (free, open in summer only). The elevator is near the museum's entrance lobby and gift shop—follow signs to *Arcades* and *Panorama*. You'll enjoy Napoleonic views over the park complex and the Brussels skyline—some of the best in the city. Find the distant Atomium and the curved glass arch of the European Parliament.

### Cinquantenaire Museum

This varied, decent (but not spectacular) collection features artifacts from many cultures—both European and non-European—ranging from prehistoric times to the present. As you wander the almost-empty halls, you'll see fine tapestries, exquisite altarpieces, impressive Islamic and antiquities collections, gorgeous Art Nouveau and Art Deco, and a "museum of the heart" (featuring various creative depictions of everyone's favorite organ, donated by a local heart doctor).

**Cost and Hours:** €10; Tue-Fri 9:30-17:00, Sat-Sun from 10:00, closed Mon; audioguide-€3, limited English information; hiding behind Autoworld at Jubelpark 10, Parc du Cinquantenaire, tel. 02-741-7211, www.kmkg-mrah.be.

**Visiting the Museum:** The collection is arranged somewhat haphazardly; pick up the brochure at the entry to figure out which items you'd like to find. As you enter and stand under the rotunda, to the left is the Non-European wing (American Indian, Mayan, Asian), and to the right is European (Gothic-Renaissance-Baroque tapestries, altarpieces, and jewels).

A highlight is the Antiquities wing: From the rotunda, head left, then turn left at the totem pole. Start in Rome, in a spacious hall with a vast floor mosaic of an animal hunt, overseen by a bronze statue of Emperor Septimius Severus. There's a room-sized model of ancient Rome (on the same level as the floor mosaic)—find the Colosseum, the Circus Maximus chariot-race course, and the grand buildings of the Forum in between. (Ask when the next model demonstration takes place.) On other floors, you'll find Greek pottery and a reconstructed Egyptian tomb you can walk inside.

### ▲Matongé Neighborhood

About one of every 10 Brussels residents claims African ancestry. Wedged between the campus of the European Parliament and the royal sights of the Upper Town is the Matongé (mah-tong-gay) district, a mélange of African immigrant culture, fine turn-of-the-century architecture, and young Bruxellois in search of a trendy scene in an "emerging" neighborhood. Consider riding the Métro to Matongé, exploring the neighborhood, and staying for lunch or dinner (for eating recommendations, see page 203).

**Getting There:** Take the Métro to Porte de Namur/Naamse-poort. If you're starting at the European Parliament, it's a 15-minute walk to Porte de Namur.

**Background:** Matongé, part of the Ixelles district of Brussels, had ties to Africa even before any Africans lived here. Back when the Belgian Congo was a colony, many of its administrative offices were located in this part of Brussels. A Congolese choir was invited to perform at the 1958 World's Fair, and soon after, several of the performers decided to return to Belgium to study at the university. A local aristocrat bought them a residential building in this neighborhood. More and more immigrants arrived—from Congo and throughout Africa—and soon the neighborhood was nicknamed Matongé (after a market district in the Congolese capital, Kinshasa). For decades, Matongé was a center of "Belgican" (Belgian African) culture, although more recently it supports large Indian, Pakistani, and Latin American communities. And now, drawn by fine old buildings and a central location near the European Parliament, a younger, richer clientele is easing into the neighborhood, and rents are on the rise.

**Exploring Matongé:** From the Porte de Namur/Naamse-poort Métro station, exit toward *Chaussée d'Ixelles/Elsensesteenweg* and *Chaussée de Wavre/Waversteenweg*. Riding the escalator up into the square, head up Chaussée d'Ixelles (with your back to the giant traffic circle and modern monument), then take the first left down **Chaussée de Wavre.** You'll pass the landmark Cinéma Vendôme art house theater on your left. Soon after, on your right, look for the entrance to the bustling African market. The sign *Souriez, vous êtes à Matongé* means "Smile! You are in Matongé." You can enter the market, or if that's too intense, simply keep strolling down the street—passing exotic taste-of-Africa grocery shops (displaying cassava, plantain, and other ingredients utterly unknown to Belgian chefs), call shops offering cheap rates for phone calls to Africa, boutiques selling colorful batik fabric, and neighborhood-gathering-place barber shops and hair salons.

After two blocks, you reach a little crossroads. Turn right down Rue Ernest Solvay to find a collection of ethnic shops. Soon you'll arrive at the cross-street of **Rue Saint-Boniface.** This energetic café row, which dead-ends at the front door of St. Boniface Church, is one of Matongé's most gentrified drags. It has a decidedly urbane-Bruxellois vibe, with busy brasseries and cafés, and an eclectic range of eateries. Explore a bit, and don't miss the lovely **Art Nouveau facades** at #17 (housing the Comptoir Florian tea house) and #19. They're also around the intersection with Rue Ernest Solvay.

Wander slowly up toward the church—window-shopping for a drink or meal—and just before you reach the door, turn left on **Rue de la Paix.** Halfway down the block on the right is **Inzia** (at #37), a Congolese restaurant.

At the end of the block, you'll run into **Rue Longue Vie.** On a nice evening, this street is the buzzing center of Matongé, with two popular recommended African restaurants (**Au Soleil d'Afrique** and **Cap Africa**).

From here, you can head back to the Métro station (up Rue Longue Vie, which runs into Chaussée de Wavre). Or, to discover

another fun neighborhood with some trendy nightspots, keep going. Turn right down Rue Longue Vie, then immediately right again on Rue Bouré. At the cute little square behind the church, take a left, then a right down "Tulip Street" to find your way to charming **Place Fernand Cocq.** This leafy, triangular square—facing the Town Hall of the district of Ixelles—feels a world away from the African vibe just a few streets away. A dozen cafés, bars, and restaurants compete for your attention, all with inviting sidewalk tables.

When you're ready to head back, you can retrace your steps through the heart of Matongé. Or, for a more direct route, head away from the Town Hall and up Chaussée d'Ixelles all the way back to the Métro.

## NORTH OF DOWNTOWN
### 1958 World's Fair Grounds Sights
These sights are next to each other about four miles north of the Grand Place at Bruparck, a complex of tacky-but-fun attractions at the old 1958 World's Fair grounds. Authorities are planning to redevelop the area—see it before the kitsch police tear down some of the mid-century architecture.

**Getting There:** It's a 20-minute Métro ride from the center to Heysel/Heizel; from there, walk about five minutes toward the can't-miss-it Atomium. You'll come to a little pavilion with a walk-way going over the train tracks; to reach Mini-Europe, take this walkway and enter "The Village," a corny food circus (with a giant cineplex and a water park) done up like a European village. Entering this area, turn left and head down the stairs to reach the Mini-Europe entrance. If you're only going to the Atomium, simply go straight through the pavilion and head for the big silver balls.

## Atomium

This giant, silvery scale model of a steel molecule, with escalators and stairs connecting the various "atoms" and a view from the

top sphere, was the über-optimistic symbol of the 1958 World's Fair. It's Brussels' answer to Paris' Eiffel Tower, Seattle's Space Needle, and St. Louis' Gateway Arch. Reopened after an extensive renovation, the Atomium celebrates its kitschy past with fun space-age videos and displays.

Your ticket includes an elevator ride to the panorama deck, with views over the fair-grounds and Mini-Europe (which looks *really* mini from up here). From there, you'll meander on endless escalators and stairs through five of the nine balls on your way back down. Renting the audioguide provides a good explanation of the building and the 1958 World's Fair, including sound clips from people who attended.

**Cost and Hours:** €13, €25.70 combo-ticket with Mini-Europe, daily 10:00-18:00, free audio-tour app or €2 for an audioguide, overpriced restaurant inside, tel. 02-475-4775, www.atomium.be.

**Nearby:** Your Atomium admission also covers entry into the ADAM: Brussels Design Museum, with changing exhibits on 20th-century style (tel. 02-669-4929, www.adamuseum.be).

## Mini-Europe

This kid-pleasing sight, sharing a park with the Atomium, has 1:25-scale models of 350 famous European landmarks such as Big Ben, the Eiffel Tower, and Venice's canals. The "Spirit of Europe" section is an interactive educational exhibit about the European Union.

**Cost and Hours:** €15.50, €25.70 combo-ticket with Atomium; daily 9:30-18:00, July-Aug until 20:00, shorter hours off-season and closed Jan-mid-March, last entry one hour before closing; tel. 02-474-1313, www.minieurope.com.

BRUSSELS SIGHTS

## OUTSIDE BRUSSELS
### ▲Royal Museum for Central Africa
### (Musée Royal de l'Afrique Centrale)

This worthwhile museum, housed in an immense palace surrounded by a vast park in the town of Tervuren, covers the Congo and much more of Africa, including its ethnography, sculpture, jewelry, flora, and fauna. Besides cataloging the region's abundant natural wonders, the exhibits look openly at Belgium's colonial history in the Congo (the king exploited it much like a private plantation). Note that the museum has been closed for an extensive renovation but should be reopen by the time you visit; ask locally or check their website for visiting information (tel. 02-769-5211, www. africamuseum.be).

**Getting There:** The museum is at Leuvensesteenweg 13 in the town of Tervuren. By public transit, Tervuren is about an hour east of Brussels. Take Métro line 1 (direction: Stockel/Stokkel) to Montgomery, and then catch tram #44 and ride it about 20 minutes to its final stop, Tervuren. From there, walk 300 yards through the park to the palace.

## Battle of Waterloo Sights

For anyone who lived through 9/11, it's clear that history can pivot in just one day. On June 18, 1815, the fate of Europe was decided on farm fields about 10 miles south of Brussels. More than 40,000 men were killed or wounded in a day-long struggle that ended the reign of Napoleon and made Britain the superpower of the 19th century.

**Planning Your Time:** While it's called the Battle of Waterloo, the action really took place about a mile south of the town. If you have time for only one sight, make it the **Mémorial 1815** museum, with spectacular displays and a movie experience not to be missed. Those with more time can consider visiting the ho-hum town of Waterloo and the Duke of Wellington's headquarters (Wellington Museum, of most interest to British military aficionados, www.museewellington.be), or Hougoumont Farm, a decisive battlefield site (described later). Another sight in Waterloo, Napoleon's Last Headquarters, is a sad attempt to give equal time to the emperor—skip it.

**Getting There:** A **car** works best, as the battlefield sites are scattered. The Mémorial 1815 museum is about a 30-minute drive south of Brussels. Leaving central Brussels, take the E-19 motorway toward Charleroi, exit onto the R0 ring road (direction: Waterloo), and get off at exit 25 (signed *Lasne/Braine-l'Alleud*). Turn right at the end of the ramp and park in the lot on the left.

By **public transit,** you can take a train/bus combo to the museum: Ride the train from Brussels to Braine-l'Alleud (2/hour, 20 minutes, direction: Charleroi Sud). Outside the station in Braine-l'Alleud, hop on the W bus (usually 2/hour, leaves at :20 and :50). Get off at the fifth stop, marked *Lion, Route de Nivelles* (look for an Esso gas station across the street). Head for the traffic lights, where signs will point you to the *Butte du Lion;* it's a five-minute walk to the museum.

**Background:** By 1815, the Grand Alliance (England, Prussia, Austria, and Russia) had defeated Napoleon, sending him into exile on Elba, and putting Louis XVI's brother on the French throne. It was as if the French Revolution never happened. But on March 1, 1815, Napoleon escaped and returned to France, driving out the king and restoring his army to its former glory. His rise sent shockwaves throughout Europe, and members of the alliance pledged 150,000 troops to rout him.

Napoleon's best chance was to attack the allied armies separately, before they had a chance to unite. On the day of the Battle of Waterloo, 72,000 French faced off against 68,000 British and Dutch troops under the Duke of Wellington. Within marching distance of the battlefield were 45,000 Prussians under General Gebhard von Blücher.

Wellington, a master of defense, took the high ground and hunkered down atop a ridge. Napoleon advanced, but then paused to let the field dry from the previous night's rainfall. This, some say, was his fatal mistake. Napoleon finally attacked, and Wellington pushed back. Meanwhile, the Prussians attacked the nearby village of Plancenoit.

Napoleon realized he had to act quickly or he'd have to fight both armies on the battlefield. He had no choice but to send in his elite Imperial Guard. But the British surprised the guard by rising up from the cover of a wheat field. As the French corps retreated in chaos, Wellington swooped down from the ridge while Blücher's soldiers punched through. By nightfall, the British and Prussian armies had come together. The Prussians even captured Napoleon's abandoned carriage, chock full of diamonds—the booty later became part of the Prussian crown jewels. Napoleon's reign of glory was over, and Waterloo became a metaphor for a crushing defeat.

## ▲▲Mémorial 1815

Built for the 200th anniversary of the battle, Mémorial 1815 is an ultramodern museum that doles out its history in small doses. With its smart design, you can skim the surface with your audioguide or plunge into the arcane depths of the Napoleonic wars for hours.

**Cost and Hours:** €16 ticket includes audioguide and covers Mémorial 1815, Panorama, Lion's Mound, and Hougoumont Farm; daily 9:30-18:30, Oct-March 10:00-17:30; tel. 02/385-1912, www.waterloo1815.be. Don't bother getting the Pass 1815 (€20), unless you're also visiting the Wellington Museum.

**Visiting the Museum:** Pick up the excellent audioguide and begin your tour with a series of rooms charting the French Revolution, Napoleon's rise to power, and his conquest of most of Europe. Next is a brilliant display of military equipment and uniforms that also serves as a timeline leading up to the battle.

The star of the museum is the "4-D" movie that clearly explains the events of the day. It's really a 3-D movie augmented by special effects. You'll feel the ground tremble during a cavalry charge and smell the smoke of a burning farmhouse. Best of all, you'll clearly understand the major turning points in the battle: Napoleon's delay, relentless cavalry attacks, the siege of a crucial farm complex, the Prussians' arrival, and the final charge of the Imperial Guard—and how the British soldiers surprised them. The concluding scenes of the post-battle carnage send a not-very-subtle message that this must never happen again (movie in French and English, with your audioguide providing the translation; turn your audioguide volume up before the movie begins—the soundtrack is loud).

Your visit ends with exhibits on the aftermath of the battle and how Waterloo is perceived today.

**Panorama:** Your ticket includes this 360-degree painting of the battle. Skip it unless you want to see a static Victorian rendering of what happened here.

**Lion's Mound** (Butte de Lion): This hill on a ridge where Wellington made his stand was also the likely site where the future King William II of the Netherlands was wounded by a musket shot. The Dutch commemorated their contribution to the battle by building a huge mound that ruined the battlefield geography—so most historians hate it. For visitors, it provides a sweeping view of the battlefield (after climbing 226 steep stairs).

### Hougoumont Farm

Included in your Mémorial 1815 ticket, this farm is one of the few relics of the battle to survive to this day—though much of it burned during the fighting (what you see is mostly a restoration). A free shuttle takes you there from Mémorial 1815 at least hourly. It's also possible to walk from the visitors center (about 30 minutes)—battlefield buffs enjoy this chance to see the lay of the land away from crowds.

At the farm, a fine, 20-minute movie in English explains why the farm was key to Wellington's victory. Just prior to the battle, the British fortified its brick buildings. French troops could not make a direct attack on British lines without facing withering fire from the farm. Somehow the British troops and their Hanoverian allies managed to hold it despite repeated French assaults. At one legendary moment, 40 French soldiers started pouring in, but 10 English and Scottish soldiers somehow closed the gates behind them. All the French soldiers inside were killed except for their 10-year-old drummer boy. When the day was over, more than 6,000 soldiers perished at the farm. Wellington later said, "The success of the battle turned upon closing the gates at Hougoumont."

# GRAND PLACE WALK

Like most European cities, Brussels has a main square, but few are as "Grand" as this one. From its medieval origins as a market for a small village, the Grand Place has grown into a vast public space enclosed by Old World buildings with stately gables. Today, the "Place" is the place to see Europe on parade. If Brussels is indeed the "capital of Europe," there's no better evidence than the crowds that flock here from every nation. Visitors come to bask in the ambience, sample chocolate, and relax with a beer at an outdoor café.

This walk allows all that, but also goes a bit beyond. We'll take in the spectacular (if heavily touristed) square, browse an elegant shopping arcade, run the frenetic gauntlet of restaurant row (Rue des Bouchers), stand at the center of modern Brussels at the Bourse, and end at the grand finale (he said with a wink): the one-of-a-kind *Manneken-Pis*.

## Orientation

**Length of This Walk:** Allow two hours.
**Town Hall:** €6, English tours offered Wed at 14:00, Sun at 11:00, 15:00, and 16:00 (get tickets from TI shop on Grand Place).
**City Museum:** €8, Tue-Sun 10:00-17:00, closed Mon.
**Brewery Museum:** €5, daily 10:00-17:00.
**Chocolate Shops on the Grand Place:** Generally open daily until 22:00.

## The Walk Begins

### ❶ Grand Place
This colorful cobblestone square is the heart—historically and geographically—of heart-shaped Brussels. As the town's market

square for 1,000 years, this was where farmers and merchants sold their wares in open-air stalls, enticing travelers from the main east-west highway across Belgium, which ran just north of the square. Today, shops and cafés sell chocolates, *gaufres* (waffles), beer, mussels, fries, *dentelles* (lace), and flowers (for details on cafés and chocolate shops on the Grand Place, see the sidebar).

Brussels was born about 1,000 years ago at a strategic spot on the banks of the Senne (not Seine) River, which today is almost completely bricked over. The main road from Cologne to Bruges crossed the river here.

Pan the square to get oriented. Face the Town Hall with its skyscraping spire. One TI is on your right, under the Town Hall's arches, while another TI is one block behind you; Rue des Bouchers and its restaurants are another block beyond that. To your right, a block away (downhill), is the Bourse building. The Upper Town is to your left, rising up the hill beyond Central/Centraal station. Over your left shoulder a few blocks away is St. Michael's Cathedral. And most important? The *Manneken-Pis* is three blocks ahead, down the street that runs along the left side of the Town Hall.

The **Town Hall** (Hôtel de Ville) dominates the square with its 300-foot-tall tower, topped by a golden statue of St. Michael slaying a devil. Built in the 1400s, this was where the city council met to rule this free trading town. Brussels proudly maintained its self-governing independence while dukes, kings, and clergymen ruled much of Europe. These days, the Town Hall hosts weddings—it's where King Philippe got married in 1999. (The Belgian government demands that all marriages are first performed in simple civil ceremonies.) You can step into the Town Hall courtyard for a little

peace (but the building's interior is only open by tour—see page 122).

Opposite the Town Hall is the impressive, gray **King's House** (Maison du Roi), which now houses the **City Museum**. The structure has gone through several incarnations in its 800-year history. First it was the medieval square's bread market—hence, the building's Dutch name—Broodhuis. Then (early 1500s) it became the regional office for the vast Habsburg empire of Charles V—hence, its French name—Maison du Roi. The lacy, prickly Gothic facade dates from the late 1800s, when it was renovated to be the City Museum (for details on visiting the museum, see page 122.)

The fancy smaller buildings giving the square its uniquely grand medieval character are former **guild halls** (now mostly shops and restaurants). They have impressive gabled roofs topped with statues, and gray stone facades trimmed in gold. Once the home offices for the town's different professions (brewers, bakers, and *Manneken-Pis* corkscrew makers), they all date from shortly after 1695—the year French king Louis XIV's troops took the

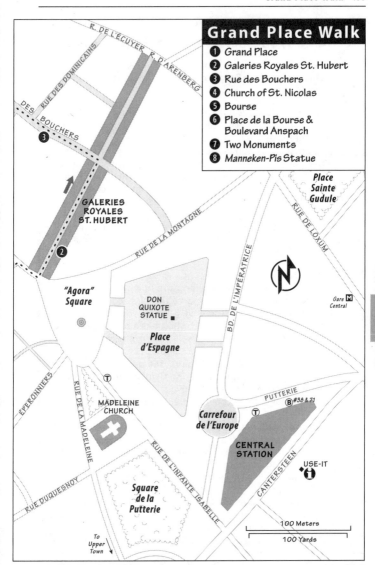

# Grand Place Walk

1. Grand Place
2. Galeries Royales St. Hubert
3. Rue des Bouchers
4. Church of St. Nicolas
5. Bourse
6. Place de la Bourse & Boulevard Anspach
7. Two Monuments
8. Manneken-Pis Statue

R. DE L'ECUYER  R. D'ARENBERG

RUE DES DOMINICAINS

DES

BOUCHERS

3

GALERIES
ROYALES
ST. HUBERT

2

RUE DE LA MONTAGNE

Place
Sainte
Gudule

RUE DE LOXUM

"Agora"
Square

DON
QUIXOTE
STATUE

Place
d'Espagne

BD. DE L'IMPERATRICE

N

Gare M
Central

EPERONNIERS

RUE DE LA MADELEINE

MADELEINE
CHURCH

RUE DE L'INFANTE ISABELLE

Carrefour
de l'Europe

PUTTERIE

B #58 & 71

T

CENTRAL
STATION

CANTERSTEEN

USE-IT
i

RUE DUQUESNOY

Square
de la
Putterie

100 Meters

100 Yards

To
Upper
Town

**GRAND PLACE WALK**

high ground east of the city, sighted their cannons on the Town Hall spire, and managed to level everything around it (4,000 mostly wooden buildings) without ever hitting the spire itself. As a matter of pride, these Brussels businessmen rebuilt their offices better than ever, completing everything within

# Tasty Treats Around the Grand Place

Brussels' grand square (and the surrounding area) offers plenty of places to sample Belgium's culinary specialties.

## Cafés

Mussels in Brussels, Belgian-style fries, yeasty local beers, waffles...if all you do here is plop down at a café on the square, try some of these specialties, and watch the world go by—hey, that's a great afternoon in Brussels.

The outdoor cafés are casual and come with fair prices (a decent Belgian beer costs €4.50, and a really good one is more like €5-7—with no cover or service charge). Have a seat, and a waiter will serve you. The half-dozen or so cafés on the downhill side of the square are all roughly equal in price and quality for simple drinks and foods—check the posted menus. As they are generally owned by breweries, you won't have a big selection of beers.

## Choco-Crawl

The best chocolate shops lie along the north (uphill) side of the square, starting with Godiva at the high end (higher in both altitude and price). The cost goes down slightly as you descend to the other shops. Each shop has a mouth-watering display case of chocolates and sells 100-gram mixes (six or so pieces) for about €5, or individual pieces for about €1 (for more on buying chocolate in Belgium, see page 34).

**Godiva** is synonymous with fine Belgian chocolate. Now owned by a Turkish company, Godiva still has its management and the original factory (built in 1926) in Belgium. This store, at Grand Place 22, was Godiva's first (est. 1937).

**Mary,** at #23, was founded in 1919 by the first woman chocolatier, Mary Delluc. She shot to stardom when the royal family began favoring her chocolates. Today, the store and its treats' packaging are faithful to her original designs.

**Neuhaus,** at #27, has been encouraging chocoholics since 1857 and claims to have invented the praline. Their main store is in the Galeries Royales St. Hubert. Neuhaus publishes a good little pamphlet explaining its products. The "caprice" (toffee with vanilla crème) tastes like Easter.

**Galler,** just off the square at Rue au Beurre 44, is homier and less famous because it doesn't export. Still family-run, it proudly serves less sugary dark chocolate. The top-end choice, 85 percent pure chocolate, is called simply "Black 85"—and worth a sample if you like chocolate without the sweetness. Galler's products are well described in English.

**Leonidas,** four doors down at Rue au Beurre 34, is where cost-conscious Bruxellois get their fix, sacrificing 10 percent in quality to nearly triple their take (machine-made, only €2.20/100 grams). White chocolate is their specialty. If all the chocolate has made you thirsty, wash it down with **250 Beers,** next to Leonidas.

seven years. They're in stone, taller, and with ornamented gables and classical statues. While they were all built at about the same time, the many differences in styles reflect the independent spirit of the people and the many cultural influences that converged in this crossroads trading center. The result is that you're completely surrounded by centuries-old buildings, free from any hint of a modern skyscraper, and immersed in historic ambience.

The **Swan House** (#9, just to the left of the Town Hall) once housed a bar where Karl Marx and Friedrich Engels met in February of 1848 to write their *Communist Manifesto.* Later that year, when the treatise sparked socialist revolution around Europe, Belgium exiled Marx and Engels. Today, the once-proletarian bar is one of the city's most expensive restaurants. Next door (#10) was and still is the brewers' guild, now housing the **Brewery Museum.**

Imagine this already glorious square filled with a carpet of flowers. Every other August, florists create a colorful 19,000-square-foot pattern of tightly packed begonias—that's about three-quarters of a million individual flowers (www.flowercarpet.be). Begun in 1971 by a begonia salesman as a way to promote his wares, this gorgeous display has become a biennial Brussels fixture that makes this grand space even grander. If you're here in August on the off-year, there is a massive floral display inside the Town Hall (see www.floralientime.be).

Each **rooftop statue** comes with its own uninteresting legend, but the Bruxellois have an earthier explanation: "What's that

smell?" say the statues on the roof of the Swan House. "Someone farted." "Yeah," says the golden man riding a horse atop the Brewery Museum next door, "it was that guy over there," and he points north across the square to another statue. "It wasn't me," says that statue, "it was him—way over there." Follow his gaze to the middle of the northwest side of the square, where the statue of a saint with a shepherd's staff hangs his head in shame.

• *Exit the Grand Place next to Godiva (from the northeast, or uphill, corner of the square), and go north one block on Rue de la Colline. Along the way, you'll pass a popular* **Tintin boutique** *(at #9), selling merchandise of the popular Belgian comic-strip hero (see sidebar on page 129). Continue to Rue du Marché aux Herbes, which was once the main east-west highway through Belgium. The little parklike square just to your right—a modest gathering place with market stalls—is nicknamed "Agora" (after the nearby covered shopping area). Looking to the right,* *notice that it's all uphill from here to the Upper Town, another four blocks (and 200-foot elevation gain) beyond. Straight ahead, you enter the arcaded shopping mall called...*

## ❷ Galeries Royales St. Hubert

Built in 1847, Europe's oldest still-operating shopping mall served as the glass-covered model that inspired many other shopping gal-

leries in Paris, London, and beyond. It celebrated the town's new modern attitude (having recently gained its independence from the Netherlands). Built in an age of expansion and industrialization, the mall demonstrated efficient modern living, with elegant apartments upstairs above trendy shops, theaters, and cafés. It was the center of upwardly mobile Brussels—progressive newspapers, French expats (Hugo, Dumas, Baudelaire), and where the first Belgian motion picture was screened. Originally, you had to pay to get in to see its fancy shops, and that elite sensibility still survives. Even today, people live in the upstairs apartments.

Looking down the arcade (233 yards long), you'll notice that it bends halfway down, designed to lure shoppers farther. Its iron-and-glass look is still popular, but the decorative columns, cameos, and pastel colors evoke a more elegant time. It's Neo-Renaissance, like a pastel Florentine palace.

In this shopping mall, there's no Gap, no Foot Locker, no Cinnabon. Instead, you'll find hat, cane, and, umbrella stores that sell...hats, canes, and umbrellas—generally handmade on the premises. **Canterie Italienne** (immediately on the right) has been making ladies' leather gloves since 1890. Since 1857, **Neuhaus** (near the end of the first section, on the right) has sold chocolates from here at its flagship store, where many Brussels natives buy their pralines—invented in this very house in 1912. Across from Neuhaus, the **Taverne du Passage** restaurant serves the same local specialties that hometown singer-songwriter Jacques Brel used to come here for: *croquettes de crevettes* (shrimp croquettes), *tête de veau* (calf's head), *anguilles au vert* (eels with herb sauce), and *fondue au fromage* (cheese croquettes).

• *Midway down the mall, where the two sections bend, turn left and exit the mall onto...*

## ❸ Rue des Bouchers

Yikes! During meal times, this street is absolutely crawling with tourists browsing through wall-to-wall, low-quality restaurants.

Brussels is known worldwide for its food, serving all kinds of cuisine, but specializing in seafood (particularly mussels). You'll have plenty to choose from along this table-clogged restaurant row, where hustlers will try to draw you into their eateries. Don't count on getting a good value here—better restaurants are just a few steps away (for specifics, see page 198).

Many diners here are day-trippers. Colin from London, Marie from Paris, Martje from Holland, and Dietrich from Frankfurt could easily all "do lunch" together in Brussels—just three hours from home.

GRAND PLACE WALK

The first intersection, with Petite Rue des Bouchers, is the heart of the restaurant quarter, which sprawls for several blocks. The street names reveal what sorts of shops used to stand here— butchers *(bouchers),* herbs, chickens, and cheese.

• *At this intersection, turn left onto Petite Rue des Bouchers and walk straight back to the Grand Place. (You'll see the Town Hall tower ahead.) At the Grand Place, turn right (west) on Rue au Beurre. Comparison-shop at the Galler and Leonidas chocolate stores and pass by the little "Is it raining?" fountain. At the intersection with Rue du Midi is the...*

## ❹ Church of St. Nicolas

Since the 12th century, there's been a church here. The outside has been freshly cleaned, so—like a Hollywood actress—it looks a lot younger than it really is. Inside, along the left aisle, see rough stones in some of the arches from the early church. Outside, notice the barnacle-like shops, such as De Witte Jewelers, built right into the church. The church was rebuilt 300 years ago with money provided by the town's jewelers. As thanks, they were given these shops with apartments upstairs. Close to God, this was prime real estate. And jewelers are still here.

• *Just beyond the church, you run into the back entrance of a big Neoclassical building.*

## ❺ The Bourse and Art Nouveau Cafés

The Bourse (stock exchange) was built in the 1870s in the Historicist style—a mix-and-match, Neo-everything architectural movement. Plans are in the works for the former stock exchange to host a big beer museum. The **ruins** under glass on the right side of the

Bourse are from a 13th-century convent; there's a small museum inside.

Several **historic cafés** huddle around the Bourse in a car-free zone. To the right (next to the covered ruins) is the woody **Le Cirio,** with its delightful circa-1900 interior. Around the left side of the Bourse is the **Falstaff Café,** which is worth a peek inside. Some Brussels cafés, like the Falstaff, are still decorated in the early-20th-century Art Nouveau style. Ironwork columns twist and bend like flower stems, and lots of Tiffany-style stained glass and mirrors make them light and spacious. Slender, elegant, willowy Gibson Girls decorate the wallpaper, while waiters in bowties glide by.

• *Circle around to the front of the Bourse, toward Boulevard Anspach.*

## ❻ Place de la Bourse and Boulevard Anspach

Brussels is the political nerve center of Europe (with as many lobbyists as Washington, DC), and the city sees several hundred demonstrations a year. When the local team wins a soccer match or some political group wants to make a statement, Place de la Bourse is where people flock to wave flags and honk horns.

It's also where the old town meets the new. To the right along Boulevard Anspach are two shopping malls and several first-run movie theaters. Rue Neuve, which parallels Anspach, is a bustling pedestrian-only shopping street.

Boulevard Anspach was once the city's main drag, choked with cars. It covers the still-flowing Senne River (which was open until 1870). Remember that Brussels was once a port, with North Sea boats coming as far as this point to unload their goods. But with frequent cholera epidemics killing thousands of its citizens, the city decided to cover up its stinky river.

Since 2015, much of the area has been closed to car traffic, creating the second largest pedestrian zone in Europe. If you see construction here during your visit, it's because they're still transforming concrete pavement into a more parklike setting. Imagine what your town would be like if it followed Brussels' lead.

Beyond Boulevard Anspach—two blocks past the black, blocky skyscraper—is the charming **Ste. Catherine** neighborhood, clustered around the former fish market and the Church of Ste. Catherine. This village-like zone is the easiest escape from the bustle of downtown Brussels, and features two recommended lunch

GRAND PLACE WALK

stops: the Mer du Nord/Nordzee fish bar and the delightful Belgian cheese shop Crèmerie de Linkebeek (both worth a detour; see the Brussels Sleeping, Eating & More chapter).

• *For efficient sightseeing, consider catching bus #71 from Place de Brouckère, a few blocks north on Boulevard Anspach, to the Place Royale, where you can follow my Upper Town Walk (see next chapter), ending near the* Manneken-Pis. *But if you'd rather stay on foot in the Lower Town, return to the Grand Place.*

## From the Grand Place to the *Manneken-Pis*

• *Leave the Grand Place kitty-corner, heading south down the street running along the left side of the Town Hall, Rue Charles Buls (which soon changes its name to Stoofstraat). Just five yards off the square, under the arch, are* ❼ *two monuments honoring illustrious Brussels notables:*

The first monument is a leafy scene on the wall featuring a beautiful young man. It's an Art Nouveau allegory of knowledge and science (which brings illumination, as indicated by the Roman oil lamp) designed by Victor Horta. It honors **Charles Buls,** mayor from 1888 to 1899. If you enjoyed the Grand Place, thank him for saving it. He stopped the "Builder King" Leopold II from blasting a grand esplanade from Grand Place up the hill to his palace.

A few steps farther you'll see tourists and locals rubbing a **brass statue of a reclining man.** This was Alderman Evrard 't Serclaes, who in 1356 bravely refused to surrender the keys of the city to invaders, and so was tortured and killed. Touch him, and his misfortune becomes your good luck. Judging by the reverence with which locals treat this ritual, I figure there must be something to it.

From here, the street serves up a sampler of typical Belgian products. A half-block farther (on the left), the **N. Toebac Lace Shop** shows off some fine lace. Brussels is perhaps the best-known city for traditional lacemaking, and this shop still sells handmade pieces in the old style: lace clothing, doilies, tablecloths, and ornamental pieces. The shop gives travelers with this book a 15 percent discount. For

## Tapestries

In 1500, tapestry workshops in Brussels were famous, cranking out high-quality tapestries for the walls of Europe's palaces. They were functional (as insulation and propaganda for a church, king, or nobleman) and beautiful—an intricate design formed by colored thread. Even great painters, such as Rubens and Raphael, designed tapestries, which rivaled Renaissance canvases. The best Belgian tapestries are in Madrid, because the Golden Age of Belgian tapestries was under Spanish rule in the 16th and 17th centuries. Also impressive are the Brussels-made tapestries of the Sistine Chapel, which some say were so extraordinary that they sparked the Northern Renaissance.

To make a tapestry, neutral-colored threads are stretched vertically over a loom. (In Renaissance Belgium, the threads were made from imported English wool.) The design of the tapestry is created with the horizontal weave, from the colored threads that (mostly) overlay the vertical threads. Tapestry making is much more difficult than basic weaving, as each horizontal thread is only as long as the detail it's meant to create. A single horizontal row can be made up of many individual pieces of thread. Before weaving begins, an artist designs a pattern for the larger picture, called a "cartoon," which weavers follow for guidance as they work.

Flanders and Paris (in the Gobelins workshop) were the two centers of tapestry making until the art died out, mirroring the decline of Europe's noble class.

more on lace, visit the Fashion and Lace Museum (a block away and just around the corner—see page 126).

A block farther down the street is the recommended, always-popular **Waffle Factory,** where a few euros gets you a freshly made takeaway "Belgian" waffle.

Cross busy Rue du Lombard and step into the **Textilux Center** (Rue du Lombard 41, on the left) for a good look at Belgian tapestries—both traditional wall-hangings and modern goods, such as tapestry purses and luggage in traditional designs.

Continuing down the street, notice a **mural** on the wall ahead, depicting that favorite of Belgian comic heroes, Tintin. Tintin, the intrepid boy with the wavy hair, is known and beloved by virtually all Europeans. In this scene, he's fleeing yet another misadventure, scrambling down a fire escape. He's accompanied by his faithful dog

Snowy, and his friend Captain Haddock, who always keeps an eye out for him. Dozens of these building-sized comic-strip panels decorate Brussels, celebrating the Belgians' favorite medium (if interested in tracking them down, buy a map from the TI). Just as Ireland has its writers, Italy its painters, and France its chefs, Belgium has a knack for turning out world-class comic artists.

• *Follow the crowds, noticing the excitement build, because in another block you reach the...*

### ❽ *Manneken-Pis*

Even with low expectations, this bronze statue is smaller than you'd think—the little squirt's under two feet tall, practically the size of a newborn. Still, the little peeing boy is an appropriately low-key symbol for the unpretentious Bruxellois. The statue was made in 1619 to provide drinking water for the neighborhood. Notice that the baby, sculpted in Renaissance style, actually has the musculature of a man instead of the pudgy limbs of a child. The statue was knighted by the occupying King Louis XV—so French soldiers had

to salute the eternally pissing lad when they passed.

It's tradition for visiting VIPs to bring the statue an outfit—and he also dresses up for special occasions—so you can often see the *Manneken* peeing through a colorful costume. A sign on the fence lists the month's festival days and how he'll be dressed. For example, on January 8, Elvis Presley's birthday, he's an Elvis impersonator; on Prostate Awareness Day, his flow is down to a slow drip. He can also be hooked up to a keg to pee wine or beer. The collection of costumes he's worn for three centuries—GardeRobe Manneken-Pis—is just around the corner on Rue du Chêne.

There are several different legends about the story behind *Manneken*—take your pick: He was a naughty boy who peed inside a witch's house, so she froze him. A rich man lost his son

and declared, "Find my son, and we'll make a statue of him doing what he did when found." Or—the locals' favorite version—the little tyke loved his beer, which came in handy when a fire threatened the wooden city: He bravely put it out. Want the truth? The city commissioned the *Manneken* to show the

*GRAND PLACE WALK*

freedom and joie de vivre of living in Brussels—where happy people eat, drink...and drink...and then pee.

The gathering crowds make the scene more interesting. Hang out for a while and watch the commotion this little guy makes as tour groups come and go. When I was there, a Russian man marveled at the statue, shook his head, and said, "He never stop!"

GRAND PLACE WALK

# UPPER TOWN WALK

The Upper Town has always had a more aristocratic feel than the medieval, commercial streets of the Lower Town. It's the Brussels of the late 1800s, when it was a cosmopolitan European city and capital of a colonial empire. With broad boulevards, big marble buildings, palaces, museums, and so many things called "royal," it also seems much newer and a bit more sterile. But the Upper Town has plenty to offer and even a bit of personality poking out from behind its stuffy veneer.

Use this walk to get acquainted with this less-touristed part of town, sample some world-class museums, see the palace, explore art galleries, and get the lay of the land from a panoramic viewpoint. The tour starts at Place Royale, a half-block from the one essential art sight in town, the Royal Museums of Fine Arts of Belgium—consider a visit while you're here (see the next chapter). The Musical Instruments Museum is also in the neighborhood.

From Place Royale, we'll walk south along the ridge, pop into a stained-glass-filled Gothic church, continue on to the towering Palace of Justice (next to the best view of the city), descend through the well-worn tapestry of the Sablon quarter's antique stores, art galleries, and cafés, and end at a homey little square right near the *Manneken-Pis*, the pride and joy of Brussels.

## Orientation

**Length of This Walk:** Allow 1.5 hours.

**Getting There:** The walk begins at Place Royale in the Upper Town. You have several ways to get there: From the Grand Place, **walk uphill** for 15 minutes; catch a **taxi** (about €15 from Rue Orts, near Place de la Bourse); ride frequent **bus** #38 or #71 two stops to Royale/Koning (catch from Putterie street just north of Central/Centraal station, direction: Héros/Helden or Delta); or take a **hop-on, hop-off** bus tour (hop off at Place Royale).

**Royal Museums of Fine Arts of Belgium:** €10 for one museum, €15 combo-ticket covers all three; Old Masters and Fin-de-Siècle museums—Tue-Sun 10:00-17:00, closed Mon; Magritte Museum—daily 10:00-17:00.

**Musical Instruments Museum:** €10, Tue-Fri 9:30-17:00, Sat-Sun from 10:00, closed Mon, last entry 45 minutes before closing.

**BELvue Museum:** €7, Tue-Fri 9:30-17:00 (July-Aug until 18:00), Sat-Sun 10:00-18:00, closed Mon.

**Notre-Dame du Sablon Church:** Free, daily 9:00-18:30.

## The Walk Begins

### ❶ Place Royale

At the crest of the hill sits Place Royale (Koningsplein), encircled by cars and trams and enclosed by white Neoclassical buildings forming a mirror image across a cobblestone square. A big, green statue of a horseman stands in the center.

The **statue** depicts local hero Godfrey de Bouillon, one of the leaders of the First Crusade (in 1096). The ultimate Catholic knight, he rides forward with his flag, gazing down on the Town Hall spire. Godfrey, a patriarch of the House of Flanders, established his family's rule over what would become Belgium. This hilltop in Brussels became home to the region's rulers. In the 12th century, a castle called the Coudenberg Palace was built (located over God-

frey's right shoulder, just outside the square). Today, it's the Royal Palace, where modern Belgium's king still lives.

Behind Godfrey is the **Church of St. Jacques-sur-Coudenberg,** with its imposing cupola, dominating the square's ring of buildings. This building (from 1787) stands on the spot of the original church built here next to the 12th-century castle. Locals remember that it was on the porch of the Church of St. Jacques, on July 21, 1831, that their first king took the oath that established modern Belgium.

In the 1870s, as Belgium industrialized and modernized, this tight ensemble of buildings and squares was given a makeover. It signaled that Brussels had arrived as a world capital. Old buildings were refurbished and new ones built to create a planned neighborhood on a grand scale. If Godfrey turned and looked left down

Rue de la Régence, he'd see the domed Palace of Justice at the end of the boulevard. This Neoclassical look—broad vistas down wide boulevards, ending at gleaming white, Greek-columned monuments—was all the rage, seen not only here, but in Paris, London, and Washington, DC.

The square has several worthwhile museums. The main entrance to the **Royal Museums of Fine Arts of Belgium** is a half-block to the right (see the next chapter). The **Musical Instruments Museum** is straight downhill from the square—if Godfrey spurred his horse straight ahead, he'd pass it on his right. Housed in an early-20th-century iron-and-glass former department store, its Art Nouveau facade was a deliberate attempt to get beyond the retro Greek columns and domes of the Place Royale. (Even if you don't visit the Musical Instruments Museum, you can ride the elevator up to the museum café for a superb Lower Town view—see listing on page 131.)

• *Before heading south, exit Place Royale on the north side, which opens up to the large, tree-lined...*

## ❼ Parc de Bruxelles

Copying Versailles, the Habsburg empress Maria Theresa of Austria (Marie-Antoinette's mom) had this symmetrical park laid out

in 1776 (she ruled, but never visited, the city). This is just one of many large parks in Brussels, which started with an awareness of the importance of city planning.

At the far (north) end of the park (directly opposite the Royal Palace, no need to actually walk there) is the Parliament building. Which parliament? The city hosts several: the European Parliament, the Belgian Parliament, and several local, city-council-type parliaments. This is the Belgian Parliament, seen on nightly newscasts as a backdrop for talking heads and politicians.

In 1830, Belgian patriots rose up and converged on the park, where they attacked the troops of the Dutch king. This was the first blow in a short, almost bloodless revolution that drove out the foreign-born king and gave the Belgians independence...and a different foreign-born king.

• *The long building facing the park is the...*

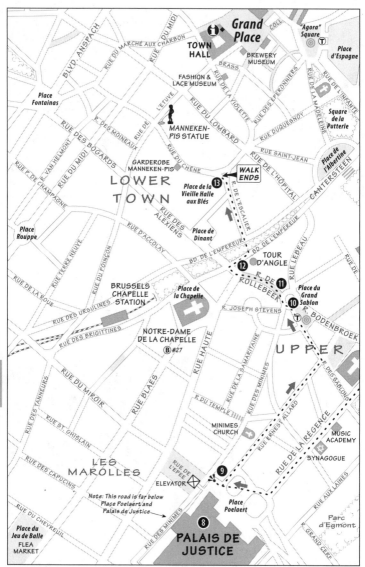

### ❸ Royal Palace (Palais Royale)

Belgium struck out twice trying to convince someone to be its new king. Finally, Leopold I (r. 1831-1865), a nobleman from Germany, agreed to become "King of the Belgians." Leopold was a steadying influence as the country modernized. His son rebuilt this palace—near the site of earlier palaces, dating back to the 10th century—

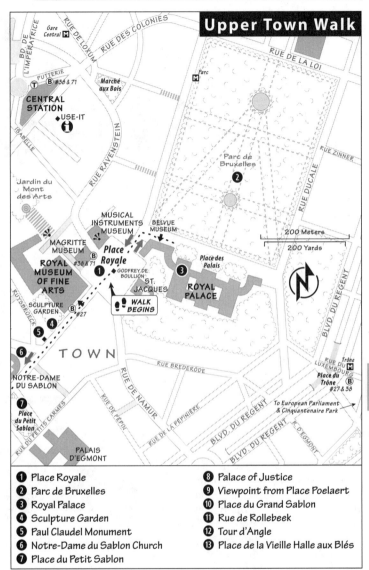

**① Place Royale**
**② Parc de Bruxelles**
**③ Royal Palace**
**④ Sculpture Garden**
**⑤ Paul Claudel Monument**
**⑥ Notre-Dame du Sablon Church**
**⑦ Place du Petit Sablon**
**⑧ Palace of Justice**
**⑨ Viewpoint from Place Poelaert**
**⑩ Place du Grand Sablon**
**⑪ Rue de Rollebeek**
**⑫ Tour d'Angle**
**⑬ Place de la Vieille Halle aux Blés**

by linking a row of townhouse mansions with a unifying facade (around 1870).

Leopold's great-great-great-great-grandnephew, King Philippe (b. 1960), today uses the palace as an office. (His head is on Belgium's euro coins.) Philippe and his wife, Queen Mathilde, live in a palace north of here (near the Atomium), at several country estates, and on the French Riviera. If the Belgian flag (black-yellow-red) is flying from the palace, the king is somewhere in Belgium.

Philippe is a figurehead king, as in many European democracies, but he serves an important function as a common bond between bickering Flemish and Walloon citizens. The king—regarded by some as awkward and standoffish—is not as

popular as Queen Mathilde, also a Belgian native. Their daughter, Elisabeth, born in 2001, is first in line to become the next Belgian monarch.

The palace is off-limits to tourists except from late July through early September (see www.opt.be for the latest schedule; gardens open April-May). The adjacent **BELvue Museum** has a well-presented exhibit on Belgian history (see listing on page 132).

• *Return to Place Royale, then continue south along Rue de la Régence, passing the main entrance to the Royal Museums of Fine Arts of Belgium complex. Just past the museums, on the right, you'll see a...*

UPPER TOWN WALK

## ❹ Sculpture Garden (Jardin de Sculpture)

This pleasant public garden features a statue by Aristide Maillol, a master of the female form and a contemporary of Rodin. In *The River* (1938-1943), the moving water is personified as a woman sprawled on her side (and looking terrified, or at least stressed—the statue was originally conceived to represent a victim of war). The wave-like figure teeters on the edge of a pool of water, about to pour in. Is she a symbol of the mystery of water, the trauma of war...or is she just washing her hair?

Another copy of this bronze statue sprawls near a pool in the courtyard of New York's Museum of Modern Art.

The garden looks like a great way to descend into the Sablon quarter, but the gates at the bottom are often locked.

• *Continue a few steps farther along Rue de la Régence. Pause at the small monument to...*

## ❺ Paul Claudel

Consider the cosmopolitan world of Brussels around the turn of the 20th century. Frenchmen like the poet Claudel traveled easily back and forth between Paris and Brussels. The French sculptor Rodin also found inspiration in Brussels. Both Rodin and his great rival, Maillol (whose works we just saw), were inspired by the female form. And Rodin's personal muse and mistress was none other than Camille Claudel, the sister of the poet Paul. It was a small world.

• *Continue down the street to...*

## ❻ Notre-Dame du Sablon Church

The round, rose, stained-glass windows in the clerestory of this 14th-century Flamboyant Gothic church are nice by day, but are thrilling at night, when the church is lit from inside and glows like a lantern, enjoyed by locals at the cafés in the surrounding square. It's worth a stop inside.

**Visiting the Church:** The church is made of simple gray stone lit by the warm light of the **stained-glass windows.** The windows

in the nave (which date from the 19th and 20th centuries) are notable for their symmetry—rows of saints in Gothic niches topped by coats of arms. The glorious apse behind the altar—bathed in colorful light from some original 15th-century windows—is what Gothic is all about.

Midway up the nave is an artistically **carved pulpit,** supported by an angel and animals, the symbols of the Evangelists. Next to the pulpit, a plaque mentions that none other than Paul Claudel worshiped here. The left transept has relics of the last Habsburg emperor, Karl I (1887-1922). Karl's legendary Catholic devotion inspires many devoted people to pray here, and he was beatified in 2004.

The church's claim to fame is next to the altar—a small wooden **statue of Mary** dressed in white with a lace veil. The statue is near and dear to the hearts of the people of Brussels. This is a copy, but the original statue was thought to have had miraculous powers that saved the town from plagues. In 1348, the statue spoke to a godly woman named Beatrix, prompting her to steal the statue away from Antwerp on a boat. (That's why the church is decorated with several images of boats, including the small **wooden boat** high up in the right transept.) When the citizens of Antwerp tried to stop Beatrix, the Mary statue froze them in their tracks.

When Beatrix and the statue arrived here, the Bruxellois welcomed Mary with a joyous parade—the Ommegang. Now, every summer, the citizens re-create the procession by dressing up in tights and flamboyant costumes and parading the streets with colorful banners and large puppets. The Ommegang begins here, threads downhill, and culminates in a climax on the Grand Place.

• *We'll return to the colorful Place du Grand Sablon (below the church) later in the walk. For now, head to the other side of Rue de la Régence from the church, where you'll find a leafy, fenced-off garden called the...*

### ❼ Place du Petit Sablon

Step into this charming little park, a pleasant refuge from the busy street and part of why this neighborhood is considered so livable.

Its central fountain, a fine example of 19th-century Romanticism, honors two local nobles who were executed because they promoted tolerance during the Inquisition. Good friends, one Catholic and the other Protestant, they were beheaded on the Grand Place in 1568.

Check out the other statues. The 48 small figures atop the wrought-iron fence represent the craftsman guilds—weavers, brewers, and butchers—of 16th-century Brussels. And inside the garden, the 10 large statues represent hometown thinkers of the 16th century—a time of great intellectual accomplishments in Brussels. Gerardus Mercator (1512-1594), the Belgian mapmaker who devised a way to more accurately show the spherical earth on a flat surface, holds a globe.

This collection of statues is a reminder that, even though Belgium was never a great power, Belgians have much to be proud of as a people. From here, look back at the church and enjoy its flamboyant late Gothic lines.

• *Continue along Rue de la Régence. You'll pass (on the left) the Music Academy and Brussels' main synagogue, and an ugly, prefab, concrete Lego-style building from the 1960s (on the right). Soon you'll reach the long-scaffolded...*

### ❽ Palace of Justice (Palais de Justice)

This domed mountain of marble sits on the edge of the Upper

Town ridge, dominating the Brussels skyline. Built in wedding-cake layers of Greek columns, it's topped with a dome taller than St. Peter's in Rome, rising 340 feet. Covering more than six acres, it's the size of a baseball stadium. Extending seven floors underground, it's so big it has its own postal code.

The palace dates from the late 19th century, when tiny Belgium was a global power. It was built under King Leopold II (son of Leo I, r. 1865-1909) and epitomizes the brassy, showy grandeur of his reign. Leopold became obscenely wealthy by turning Africa's Congo region—80 times the size of Belgium—into his personal colony. Whip-wielding Belgian masters forced Congolese slaves to tend lucrative rubber plantations, exploiting the new craze for car tires. Leopold spent much of this wealth expanding and beautifying the city of Brussels.

Today the building (which stands on the historic site of the town gallows) serves as a Hall of Justice, where major court cases are tried. If you pop in to the lobby, you may see lawyers in black robes buzzing about. The building is perennially scaffolded. At the end of World War II, the Nazis set fire to it as they left town, compromising the cupola's structure, and the palace has never quite recovered.

Notice the rack of city bikes. Like many other European cities, Brussels subsidizes a public-bike system. The program, called "Villo," is designed for riders to pick up a bike in one part of town and drop it off anywhere else. But the scheme doesn't always work as well as intended: These bike racks are often empty, since this is a popular place to grab a bike for the easy ride back down to the Lower Town.

• *One of the best views of Brussels is immediately to the right of the Palace of Justice.*

### ❾ Viewpoint from Place Poelaert

You're standing 200 feet above the former Senne River Valley. Gazing west over the Lower Town, pan the valley from right (north) to left:

Near you is the stubby **clock tower** of the Minimes Church. To the left of that, in the distance past a tall square skyscraper, is the lacy, white Town Hall **spire** (marking the Grand Place).

Twinkling in the far distance, six miles away, you can see one of the city's landmarks, the **Atomium.** (No doubt, someone atop it is looking back at you.) The Atomium's nine shiny steel balls form the shape of an iron molecule that's the size of the Palace of Justice behind you. Built for the 1958 World's Fair, it's now a middle-aged symbol of the dawn of the Atomic Era.

Next (closer to you) rises the **black clock tower** of the Notre-Dame de la Chapelle church, the city's oldest (from 1134, with a tower that starts Gothic and ends Baroque). On the distant horizon, see **four boxy sky-scrapers,** part of the residential sprawl of this city of over a million, which now covers 62 square miles. Breaking the horizon to the left is a **green dome,** which belongs to the Basilica of Koekelberg (fourth-biggest in the world). And finally (panning quickly to the left), you see a **black glass skyscraper** marking the Midi/Zuid train station, where you can catch high-speed train lines, such as the Eurostar to London.

At your feet lies the **Marolles neighborhood.** Once a funky, poor place where locals developed their own quirky dialogue, today it can be either seedy or colorful, depending on the time of day and your perception. The area is famous for its sprawling flea market (daily 7:00-14:00, best on weekends). Two of the streets just below you—Rue Haute and Rue Blaes—are lined with secondhand shops. A free **elevator** connects Place Poelaert with the Marolles neighborhood, which is worth a 10-minute detour to its café-lined square. People who brake for garage sales may want to cut out of this walk early and head to the Marolles from here.

Gazing off into the distance to the far left (south), you can't quite see the suburb of **Waterloo,** 10 miles away. It was there that the tide of 19th-century European history turned: Napoleon suffered a crushing defeat on the Waterloo battlefield, his rule of Europe ended, and Belgium was placed under a Dutch king—until the Belgians won their independence in the 1830 revolution.

Behind you, in Place Poelaert, is a memorial to the two world wars. Both conflicts slashed through Belgium with deadly force.

• *Backtrack east, descending to Place du Grand Sablon by walking down Rue Ernest Allard. Passing lots of antique shops and galleries, you'll eventually reach a square below the Notre-Dame du Sablon Church. (For a light meal, $$ Le Pain Quotidien—on the square at Rue des Sablons 11—offers a fine value with delightful seating and baked goods right out of the oven.)*

## ⑩ Place du Grand Sablon

The Sablon neighborhood that surrounds this square and its church features cafés and restaurants, antique stores, and art galleries.

Every weekend, there's an antique market on the square. On warm summer evenings, the square sparks magic, as sophisticated locals sip aperitifs at the café tables, admiring the church's glowing stained glass. **Chocolatier Wittamer** (on the far side of the square, at #6) often has elaborate window displays. And at the bottom of the square is the shop of the innovative **Pierre Marcolini**—one of the world's top chocolatiers—with a tempting buffet upstairs.

• *Sloping Place du Grand Sablon funnels downhill into the pedestrian-only street called...*

## ⑪ Rue de Rollebeek

With a few surviving brick buildings, this street gives you a taste of the city before its 1695 bombardment by France's Louis XIV (during the Nine Years' War—fought between France and just about all the rest of Europe). Today it's a delightful traffic-free lane lined with sidewalk cafés, art galleries, shops, midrange restaurants, and boutiques—a pleasant place to press "Pause" before returning to the bustle of Brussels. This is an easy place to comparison-shop for a drink or meal. **Toscana 21** (at #21) feels like a slice of Italy, with fine pizzas and pastas. **Peï & Meï** (at #15) serves creative fare in a bright interior. A block south of Rue de Rollebeek is the more workaday Rue Joseph Stevens—home to the appealing sandwich shop **Pistolet Original** (at #24) and the hip, split-level bar **Skievelat Sablon** (at #16).

• *Rue de Rollebeek leads down to the busy Boulevard de l'Empereur. To the right on the boulevard, just past the bowling alley, is the...*

## ⑫ Tour d'Angle

The "Corner Tower" is a rare surviving section of Brussels' medieval city wall. It stood over one of seven gates along the 2.5-mile-long wall that enclosed

13th-century Brussels. Notice the slash through the city here that marks where underground trains connect Central station (to your right) and Midi station (to your left). Six tracks under you are kept busy with about a thousand trains a day. This ambitious bit of city infrastructure was a project started in 1902 and not finished until 1952—two occupations by Germany slowed things down.

• *Cross the street, head right, and take the first left at Rue de l'Escalier, which leads downhill to a pleasant square at the T-intersection.*

## ⑱ Place de la Vieille Halle aux Blés

Do a 360-degree sweep from the center of this little square—circled by nice apartments and lined with cafés that hum (on a sunny day). Imagine what a delight it would be to call this neighborhood home. Twenty years ago, this was a derelict slum—a good reason why Brussels was famous as a fine place to work but a lousy place to live. People were moving out, leaving the down-and-out downtown. But in 1989 Brussels became its own political region and got its own government. Since then, its policy has been to revitalize the center of town; tearing down homes to build office space is no longer allowed. Consequently, new construction is reserved for residences, and people are moving into the area again. As in so many European cities, government policies are spurring the revitalization of old town centers.

• *Your walk is finished. From here, the* Manneken-Pis *is about a five-minute walk and his costume collection at GardeRobe Manneken-Pis is along the way (both described in the Sights in Brussels chapter). Grand Place is about a 10-minute walk. If you're hungry or thirsty, return to Rue de Rollebeek, with several options for a meal, or try the nearby recommended La Fleur en Papier Doré, a classic Belgian café (see listing on page 195).*

# ROYAL MUSEUMS OF FINE ARTS TOUR

*Musées Royaux des Beaux-Arts de Belgique*

This museum complex, spread throughout three large buildings, covers much of the history of Western painting. We'll visit a trio of interconnected museums: the Old Masters Museum (pre-1850); the Fin-de-Siècle Museum (1850-1910); and the Magritte Museum, which celebrates the work of the popular Belgian Surrealist painter. The collections, while enjoyable, can be overwhelming, so this chapter highlights the museums' strengths: Flemish and Belgian artists. But don't limit your visit to these works—let the museums surprise you.

## Orientation

**Cost:** €10 for each individual museum, €15 combo-ticket covers all three. All are free the first Wed of the month after 13:00.

**Hours:** The Old Masters and Fin-de-Siècle museums are open Tue-Sun 10:00-17:00, closed Mon. The Magritte Museum is open daily 10:00-17:00.

**Getting There:** The main entrance, with access to all three museums, is at Rue de la Régence 3 in the Upper Town, a five-minute walk uphill from Central/Centraal station, or take bus #38 or #71 from Putterie street. Bus #38 or #27 connects this area with the European Parliament, with #27 continuing to the Park of the Cinquantenaire.

**Keep Your Magrittes Straight:** Don't confuse this Magritte Museum with the much smaller René Magritte Museum, located in the artist's former home on the outskirts of Brussels. This is clearly the place to enjoy his art.

**Information:** Tel. 02-508-3211, www.fine-arts-museum.be or www.musee-magritte-museum.be.

**Tours:** Consider the €4 audioguides for the Old Masters Museum or Magritte Museum (it's helpful here), the €4 videoguide for the Fin-de-Siècle Museum, or the €2.50 *Twenty Masterpieces* tour booklet sold in the museum shop.

**Length of This Tour:** Allow one hour for the Old Masters and Fin-de-Siècle museums, and another hour for the Magritte Museum.

**Cuisine Art:** There's a **$$** café and a fancy **$$$** brasserie on site. The Musical Instruments Museum, a block away, has a much-appreciated rooftop restaurant.

**Starring:** Bruegel's *Census at Bethlehem;* Post-Impressionist works by Seurat, Gauguin, and Ensor; and Magritte's *The Treachery of Images.*

## The Tour Begins

Enter at Rue de la Régence 3 and buy your ticket. It's smart to get a combo-ticket to see all three museums. Continue into the large entrance hall and get oriented.

The Old Masters Museum is on level 1 (in the galleries you can see above you); reach it through the doorway directly ahead. The Fin-de-Siècle Museum is through the passageway to the right, down several levels. The Magritte Museum is also to the right, through the same passageway.

Pause at the information desk to pick up a free map and consider renting an audioguide. Now let's dive in.

## Old Masters Museum

• *Go up to level 1 and start with the Flemish masters. The art is displayed in (roughly) chronological order, working counterclockwise around the central gallery. So, turn right, and enter the corner room (70), and find a small canvas with a portrait.*

### ❶ Rogier van der Weyden, *Portrait of Anthony of Burgundy,* c. 1456-1465

Anthony and his cultured family—the dukes of Burgundy—are largely responsible for the art we're about to see in this first museum.

In this sensitive portrait, young Prince Anthony of Burgundy wears a black cloak, a bowl-cut hairdo, and a dark-red cap, with his pale face and hand emerging from a dark background. Anthony

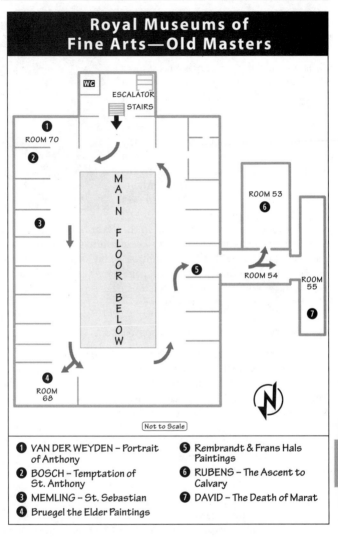

## Royal Museums of Fine Arts—Old Masters

WC
ESCALATOR
STAIRS

**1** ROOM 70
**2**
**3**
**4** ROOM 68

MAIN FLOOR BELOW

ROOM 53
**6**
ROOM 54
**5**
ROOM 55
**7**

Not to Scale

**1** VAN DER WEYDEN – Portrait of Anthony
**2** BOSCH – Temptation of St. Anthony
**3** MEMLING – St. Sebastian
**4** Bruegel the Elder Paintings
**5** Rembrandt & Frans Hals Paintings
**6** RUBENS – The Ascent to Calvary
**7** DAVID – The Death of Marat

ROYAL MUSEUMS

was a well-known Renaissance Man—soldier, scholar, and patron of the arts—whose sense of style impressed other European princes, like Florence's young Lorenzo the Magnificent.

In the 1400s, Anthony and the dukes of Burgundy helped make Brussels one of the richest and most progressive cities in Europe, rivaling Florence and Venice. They built the Coudenberg Palace (100 yards from here), the magnificent City Hall (on Grand Place), and turned a gangly collection of French-speaking and Dutch-speaking provinces into the nation we know today as Belgium. The Burgundian court attracted Europe's greatest artists, who chronicled this aristocratic family so famous across Europe.

Van der Weyden (c. 1399-1464), Brussels' official portrait painter, captures the prince in all his glory. Anthony fingers an arrow like a bowstring, indicating his renown as a great archer. From his gold necklace dangles a Golden Fleece, one of Europe's more prestigious knightly honors. You can even see the wrinkles in Anthony's neck and the faint shadow his chin casts on his Adam's apple. Anthony gazes into the distance, his clear, sad eyes lit with a speckle of white paint.

Anthony was known in his day as the Great Bastard, the brave and distinguished (but illegitimate) son of Philip the Good. Compare this portrait with that of Philip's, whom Van der Weyden had also painted—see the photo on page 64. The two men's long, elegant faces and full lips are a mirror image—pretty convincing DNA evidence in a paternity suit.

• *Continue counterclockwise around the central gallery. As you head up the long right side, stop in the first section and find...*

### ❷ Hieronymus Bosch, *Triptych of the Temptations of St. Anthony,* c. 1501

The explosion of art in the Low Countries produced the eccentric and visionary artist named Hieronymus Bosch. He added a fanciful strain to the sober realism of Flemish art.

In the center panel, find the central figure of St. Anthony—the Christian hermit who withdrew to the desert where he was haunted by demonic apparitions. Anthony (in gray robe and beard) looks out with an expression that says, "What have I gotten myself into?"

All around are bizarre supernatural creatures who try to divert Anthony from his faith. There are humans with animal heads, animals with human heads, boats that look like fish, and birds that look like boats. In the right panel, a haggard-looking Anthony tries to block the visions out by reading his Bible. In the left panel, he's carried off by airborne devils (above) and tended to by friends (below). According to legend, Anthony persevered through it all to become an inspiration to others plagued by demons of the mind.

• *Continue up the long right side to the third section.*

### ❸ Hans Memling, *Martyrdom of St. Sebastian (Le Martyre de Saint Sébastien),* c. 1475

Memling's Sebastian is as placid as Bosch's Anthony is turbulent. Sebastian—an early Christian killed by pagans—looks peaceful as he's punctured with arrows by a serene firing squad in a serene landscape. (In fact, Sebastian miraculously survived, so they clubbed him to death.)

Hans Memling (c. 1430-1494) was a student of Rogier van der Weyden and his "Flemish Primitive" style (for more, see the sidebar on page 63). Memling purposely

disregarded the 3-D realism so admired in Italy at the time. For example, Sebastian's arm is tied to a branch that's not arching overhead, as it should be, but instead is behind him. And an archer aims slightly behind, not at, Sebastian. The other archer strings his bow in a stilted pose.

Nevertheless, Memling is clearly a master of detail. He freezes this dramatic scene so we can admire the colorful costumes, expressive faces, hazy landscape, and the cityscape in the background. Altogether it creates a meditative mood appropriate to where the painting originally stood—in a church in Bruges.

• *Next, head for the far-right corner of the gallery and find Room 68, where paintings by Pieter Bruegel the Elder are displayed.*

### ❹ Pieter Bruegel the Elder, *The Census at Bethlehem (Le Dénombrement de Bethléem),* 1566

Bruegel sets a Bible scene—the birth of Jesus—in a typical snow-covered village near Brussels. Perched at treetop level, you have a

bird's-eye view over the action. Kids throw snowballs and sled across the frozen canals. A crowd gathers at the inn (lower left), where a woman holds a pan to catch blood while a man slaughters a pig. Most everyone has their back to us or head covered, so the figures speak through poses and motions.

Into the scene rides a woman on a donkey led by a man—it's Mary and husband Joseph. They're hoping to find a room at the inn (or at least a manger), because they didn't reserve ahead and now Mary's going into labor.

The year is 1566—the same year that Protestant extremists throughout the Low Countries were vandalizing Catholic church-

ROYAL MUSEUMS

es and tearing down "idolatrous" depictions of the Virgin Mary. In a similar vein, Bruegel brings Mary down to earth—she's in the humble here and now. The busy villagers put their heads down and work, oblivious to the future Mother of God and the wondrous birth about to take place.

This room may also contain other works by Bruegel I (c. 1527-1569). He's famous for his crowds of everyday peasants going about their daily lives. He also dabbled in flights of bizarre fancy and obscure symbolism in the style of Bosch. You may also see works by his less famous sons—Pieter Brueghel the Younger (who copied his dad's style and even some exact paintings), and Jan the Elder (who did glossy still lifes of flowers).

• *Continue your counterclockwise circuit around the gallery of the Old Masters collection. As you round the corner and head up the other long side, pause midway along, in the fourth alcove, with a few works by* ❺ *Rembrandt and Frans Hals. From here, enter the big adjoining Room 54, and then left into Room 53, full of large paintings by Rubens, including the massive...*

## ❻ Peter Paul Rubens, *The Ascent to Calvary* (*La Montée au Calvaire*), c. 1636

Life-size figures scale this 18-foot-tall canvas on the way to Christ's Crucifixion. The scene ripples with motion, from the windblown clothes to steroid-enhanced muscles to billowing flags and a troubled sky. Christ stumbles—he might get trampled by the surging crowd. Veronica kneels to gently wipe his bloody head.

This 200-square-foot canvas was manufactured at Rubens' studio in Antwerp. Hiring top-notch assistants, Rubens (1577-1640) could crank out large altarpieces for the area's Catholic churches. First, Rubens himself did small-scale sketches and studies in oil (like the studies you may see in Room 53). His assistants would reproduce them on the large canvas, and Rubens would then add the final touches.

This work is from late in Rubens' long and very successful career. He got a second wind in his fifties, when he married 16-year-old Hélène Fourment. She was the model for Veronica, who consoles the faltering Christ in this painting.

• *Backtrack to Room 54, turn left, and enter Room 55, where you'll find...*

### ❼ Jacques-Louis David, *The Death of Marat (Marat Assassiné)*, 1793

In a scene ripped from the day's headlines, Jean-Paul Marat—a well-known crusading French journalist—has been stabbed to

death in his bathtub by Charlotte Corday, a conservative fanatic. Marat's life drains out of him, turning the bathwater red. With his last strength, he pens a final, patriotic, *"Vive la Révolution"* message to his fellow patriots. Corday, a young noblewoman angered by Marat's campaign to behead the French king, was arrested and guillotined three days later.

Jacques-Louis David (1748-1825), one of Marat's fellow revolutionaries, set to work painting a tribute to his fallen comrade right after the 1793 assassination. (He signed the painting: *"À Marat"*—"To Marat.")

David makes it a secular pietà, with the brave writer portrayed as a martyred Christ in a classic dangling-arm pose. Still, the deathly pallor and harsh lighting pull no punches, creating in-your-face realism.

David, the official art director of the French Revolution, supervised propaganda and the costumes worn for patriotic parades. A year after finishing this painting, in 1794, his extreme brand of revolution (which included guillotining thousands of supposed enemies) was squelched by moderates, and David was jailed. He emerged later as Napoleon's court painter. When Napoleon was exiled in 1815, so was David, spending his last years in Brussels.

• *To get to the Fin-de-Siècle Museum, return to the ground floor and the large main entrance hall of the Old Masters Museum, where a passageway leads to the Fin-de-Siècle and Magritte museums. Immediately after entering the passageway, you'll pass by the tiny Modern Museum (included in the combo-ticket). Go down the escalators and through the passageway (noting the entrance to the Magritte Museum), then continue down into the Fin-de-Siècle wing.*

## Fin-de-Siècle Museum

Brussels likes to think of itself as the capital of Art Nouveau and the crossroads of Europe, and this space presents a convincing case. Around the year 1900—the "turn of the century," or *fin-de-siècle*—many cultural trends converged in Brussels to create great art. The collection features a handful of high-powered paintings by notable

Impressionists, Post-Impressionists, Realists, and Symbolists. It also houses a dazzling assemblage of Art Nouveau glassware, jewelry, and furniture. And it's all placed in the historical context of the dynamic city of Brussels.

• *You enter on level -3. On your visit, you'll go down, down, down through several levels. (Pray the elevator is working for the trip back up.) Keep the big picture. I've pointed out a few specific paintings, but don't worry so much about finding them all. Enlist the help of nearby guards if you must find a particular piece.*

## Welcome to the Fin-de-Siècle (Level -5)

Paintings of distinguished men in suits and ladies in gowns introduce you to the elegance of the era. Nearby, black-and-white photographs of Brussels show that it was also a time of great technological progress—the train, camera, and telegraph. As you browse the rest of the museum, keep in mind that the art was paid for and consumed by these wealthy industrialists and their trophy wives.

• *Continue down to the next level, which often displays the museum's best-known masterpieces.*

## Impressionism and Post-Impressionism (Level -6)

In the late 1800s, there was a revolution in painting—Impressionism. The displays start with traditional Academic paintings of the usual subjects—serene landscapes, Greek gods, and stuffy aristocrats. But as the next rooms show, painters burst out of the studio to paint the "real" world. They captured the harsh reality of peasant life and factory workers. They hung out in cafés, sketchbook in hand, capturing the bustle of modern life, or set up their canvases in the open air to paint a landscape. Here you'll find some classic examples.

**Georges Seurat** (1859-1891) painted a Sunday-in-the-park view from his favorite Parisian island in *The Seine at Grande-Jatte (La Seine à la Grande-Jatte)*. Taking Impressionism to its extreme, he builds the scene out of small points of primary colors that blend at a distance to form objects. The bright colors capture the dazzling, sunlit atmosphere of this hazy day.

**Paul Gauguin** (1848–1903), though schooled in Impressionism, soon developed his own unique style. In *Breton Calvary (Calvaire Breton; a.k.a. The Green Christ/Le Christ Vert)*, he returned to the bold, black, coloring-book outlines of more Primitive (pre-

3-D) art. The Christian statue and countryside look less like Brittany and more
like primitive Tahiti, where Gauguin
would soon settle.

Finally, find paintings by Belgium's
own **James Ensor** (1860-1949). At 22,
Ensor, an acclaimed child prodigy,
proudly presented his lively Impression-
ist-style works to the Brussels Salon for
exhibition. They were flatly rejected.

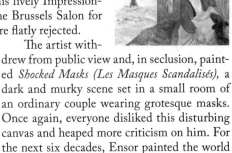

The artist with-
drew from public view and, in seclusion, painted *Shocked Masks (Les Masques Scandalisés)*, a
dark and murky scene set in a small room of
an ordinary couple wearing grotesque masks.
Once again, everyone disliked this disturbing
canvas and heaped more criticism on him. For
the next six decades, Ensor painted the world
as he saw it—full of bizarre, carnival-masked,
stupid-looking crowds of cruel strangers who mock the viewer.
• *Descend to the next floor, enjoying exhibits on...*

## Opera (Level -7)

Opera played a central role in turn-of-the-century life. Painters
collaborated with writers, composers, and directors to create lavish
sets, costumes, and art design.

Among the paintings, it's hard not to notice *The Caress of the
Sphinx (Des Caresses)*, where a young man cozies up to a cheetah-
girl. The painter, **Fernand Khnopff** (1858-1921), was James Ensor's college buddy. Khnopff championed the Symbolist movement,
presenting arresting images (often of women as femme fatales) intended to provoke primeval emotions.
• *Now head for the bottom floor.*

## Art Nouveau (Level -8)

The collection's final paintings show how turn-of-the-century Post-
Impressionism led the way to more abstract styles of Modernism.

The Gillion Crowet Collection is a stunning assemblage of
Art Nouveau paintings, jewelry, woodwork furniture, and flowery
vases (by the likes of Emile Gallé). You'll also see pieces by Brussels' own Victor Horta, whose influential architecture (such as the
Belgian Comic Strip Center—see listing in the Sights in Brussels
chapter) steered the curvaceous Art Nouveau style toward simpler
Art Deco and Modernism.
• *Which is the perfect segue to Magritte. Return to the Fin-de-Siècle
entrance on level -3, then go up the stairs to find the entrance to the...*

# Magritte Museum

Bowler hats, clouds, birds...these are the iconic images that have become associated with Belgium's great Surrealist, René Magritte.

Magritte's puzzling works are perhaps best described in his own words: "My paintings are visible images which conceal nothing. They evoke mystery, and indeed, when one sees one of my pictures, one asks oneself this simple question: 'What does that mean'? It does not mean anything, because mystery means nothing either, it is unknowable." If that brainteaser titillates you, you'll love this museum.

The exhibits take you on a chronological route through Magritte's life and art. Each of the three floors is devoted to a period of his life. Timelines (in English) put the art in its historical context. Fascinating quotes from Magritte are posted around the museum (but only in French and Dutch, so pick up the English translation as you enter). The audioguide is helpful.

The following tour follows the layout of the museum, but it's not really intended as a room-by-room analysis. It's best to read this tour ahead of time for background, then enter the darkened rooms and let Magritte transport you to his world.

• *From the entrance, you'll take an elevator up to level +3.*

## The Struggling Artist, 1898-1929 (Level +3)

Born to a middle-class Belgian family, Magritte moved to Brussels at age 17. He studied at the Academy, where he learned to draw meticulously and got a broad liberal arts education. In the 1920s, he eked out a living designing advertisements, posters, and sheet music. Meanwhile, he wrote for the avant-garde *7 Arts* **magazine** (you'll see samples posted). He dabbled in **various styles**—Post-Impressionism, Futurism, Cubism—in search of his own voice.

In 1922, he married his childhood sweetheart, **Georgette,** who became his lifelong companion, artist's model, and muse. It's said that all the women he would paint were versions of Georgette. (It's touching to think that he found a soul mate who could truly understand and encourage his weirdness.)

Influenced by the Dada and Surrealist movements coming out of Paris (Salvador Dalí, Marcel Duchamp, Giorgio de Chirico), Magritte became intrigued with the idea of painting dreamscapes that capture an air of mystery.

For Magritte, 1927 was a watershed year, when he painted his first truly Surrealist work—*The Man from the Sea*. It featured a man on a beach with a wood-block head, pulling a lever.

Together, René and Georgette mingled in sophisticated, bohemian circles. He and his friends took **photographs,** striking wacky tableaux and distorted poses.

## The Art of René Magritte

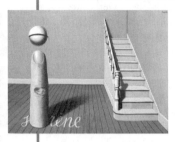

René Magritte (1898-1967) is Belgium's most famous 20th-century artist. He trained and worked in Brussels, but also lived for a time in Paris, where he connected with other Surrealist painters. Though he's well-known now, it took decades before his peculiar brand of Surrealism caught on. He painted real objects with photographic clarity, and then jumbled them together provocatively. Or he confounded the viewer's expectations by presenting ordinary items as something altogether different (as in his iconic painting of a smoker's pipe, which he labeled "This is not a pipe").

Magritte had his own private reserve of symbolic images. You'll see clouds, blue sky, open windows, the female torso, men in bowler hats, rocks, tobacco pipes, spheres with slits (sleigh bells), birds, castles, and turtles. All of these are placed side by side as if the arrangement means something. He heightens the mystery by making objects unnaturally large or small. People morph into animals or inanimate objects. The juxtaposition short-circuits your brain only when you try to make sense of it. Magritte's works are at once playful and disorienting...and, at times, disturbing.

Magritte began writing words on paintings. This culminated in his most famous work, of a **tobacco pipe** (in the Los Angeles County Museum of Art, though there's a similar version here). On the picture, Magritte wrote (in French) "This is not a pipe." Of course it's not a pipe, Magritte always insisted—it's a *painting* of a pipe. It forces the viewer to ponder the relationship between the object and its name—between the "signified" and the "signifier," to quote the deconstructionist philosophy that Magritte's paradoxical paintings inspired. Some credit this work for planting the seeds of Postmodernism. By the way, two decades later, Magritte did another version with the message: "This is still not a pipe."

• *Head downstairs to the next phase of Magritte's life.*

## Recognition—and the War, 1930-1950 (Level +2)

After a time in Paris, Magritte returned to Brussels, where he struggled through the Depression years by doing ad work and portraits.

He now had his **signature style:** combining two arresting images to disrupt rational thought and produce an emotion of mystery. The paintings have his now-familiar motifs such as clouds and bowler hats. The background and foreground seem to shift.

The paintings' **weird titles**—*Forbidden Literature, God is No Saint*—added another layer of disruption. These were intentional non sequiturs, which he and his Surrealist friends made up during regular Sunday-night get-togethers.

Then came World War II, and Brussels was under Nazi occupation. Magritte began using **birds,** as a metaphor for the longing to be free.

He also dabbled in a **variety of styles:** Impressionistic colors and rough brushwork, tongue-in-cheek "portraits" of animals, a Technicolor nude of Georgette. He went through a childlike period of comic-book-inspired paintings (like the green man with a long nose), which are quite different from his normal photorealistic style.

• *Continuing to the final floor, note that it has two different sections, with two different entrances from the landing.*

## Mature Years, 1951-1967 (Level +1)

These two rooms are like a victory lap for all of the symbols and styles we've seen. Nearing the end of his prolific life, Magritte had a quiver full of artistic arrows to shoot at the canvas. He mixed his **trademark symbols**—doves, clouds, balls, open windows, forlorn landscapes—in recombinant ways.

The collection culminates at his *Empire of Lights.* This painting of a typical bourgeois home at twilight suggests that even well-scrubbed suburbia can possess an ominous air of mystery. Magritte loved night-sky tones. He often created several versions of the same work, which explains why there are several *Empire of Lights* canvases in the world.

By the end of his life, Magritte was well-known, especially in America. His use of everyday objects and poster-art style inspired Pop Art. His mix of words and images inspired Postmodernist philosophers. His bizarre imagery inspired the psychedelia of the '60s. And the mystery his canvases evoke is timeless.

• *Exit to the bookshop and an appropriately perplexing 50-minute film about Magritte (plays constantly, English subtitles). From here you can find your way either back to the other museums, or to the exit...and reality.*

ROYAL MUSEUMS

# BRUSSELS SLEEPING, EATING & MORE

As the capital of Belgium—and of the European Union—Brussels is a great place to spend some time. This chapter provides suggestions for the best places to sleep and eat; tips for shopping and after-hours fun; and a rundown of the connections to points throughout Belgium, the Netherlands, and beyond, as well as tips for getting to and from the city's two airports.

## Sleeping in Brussels

Hotel prices are high in central Brussels. This popular business destination tends to be busiest and most expensive on weekdays, especially in spring and fall. Brussels' fancy business-class hotels can be desperately empty most of July and August and on most Friday and Saturday nights. During these slow times, rates drop. You may be able to rent a double room at a three-star hotel in the center with enough comforts to keep a diplomat happy, including a fancy breakfast, for about €90.

Conversely, Bruges—a pleasure destination—has higher demand on weekends. If your trip is flexible, consider arranging your overnights in these two towns with these patterns in mind.

### NEAR THE GRAND PLACE

$$$ Hotel Le Dixseptième, with sleek, 21st-century rooms behind its luxurious lounges and entryway, is ideally located a block

below Central station. Prim, proper, and peaceful, with chandeliers and squeaky hardwood floors, the hotel's 37 rooms are each themed after a different painter (summer discounts, air-con, elevator, Rue de la Madeleine 25, tel. 02-517-1717, www.ledixseptieme.be, info@ ledixseptieme.be).

**$$$ Art de Séjour** is a classy splurge B&B a few blocks from the Grand Place (farther than the others listed here...but worth it). Well-run by Mario, it fills a gorgeously restored building with five thoughtfully appointed rooms that are an engaging mix of new (Macs in every room) and old (original woodwork). Mario's training as an engineer shows in all the special touches (air-con, elevator and a few stairs, Rue des Bogards 12, tel. 02-513-9755, www. artdesejour.com, concierge@artdesejour.com).

**$$$ Hotel Ibis off Grand Place,** well-situated halfway between Central station and the Grand Place, is the best of several Ibis locations around Brussels. It's a big, modern hotel offering 184 simple, industrial-strength-yet-comfy rooms (breakfast extra, air-con, elevator, Marché aux Herbes 100, tel. 02-514-4040, www. ibishotel.com, h1046@accor.com).

**$$ Hotel Opéra,** on a people-filled street near the Grand Place, is professional but standardized, with lots of street noise and 49 well-worn rooms (RS%, family rooms, request a quieter courtyard room, elevator, Rue Grétry 53, tel. 02-219-4343, www.hotel-opera.be, reception@hotel-opera.be).

**$$ Hotel La Madeleine,** on the small "Agora" square between Central station and the Grand Place, rents 42 plain, dimly lit rooms, plus 14 budget rooms with shared bathrooms. It has a great location and a friendly staff (RS%—free breakfast with this book, request a quieter back room when you reserve, air-con in some rooms, elevator, Rue de la Montagne 22, tel. 02-513-2973, www. hotel-la-madeleine.be, info@hotel-la-madeleine.be, Philippe).

**$$ Hotel La Légende** rents 26 small, straightforward rooms a block from the *Manneken-Pis* statue. Although it's on a busy road, its classic lobby sits back on a pleasant courtyard. The furnishings are basic, but the location and price are right, and the rooms are modern and comfortable (request a quieter courtyard room, elevator, Rue du Lombard 35, tel. 02-512-8290, www.hotellalegende. com, info@hotellalegende.com).

**Sleeping in Brussels** runs two cozy **$$** B&Bs, **Les Clarisses** and **La Petite Éclipse,** with a total of 12 straightforward, slightly scruffy rooms a few blocks from the Grand Place, just far enough from the Place St-Géry liveliness. Arrange a meeting time in advance, and check in at the Winehouse Osteria on the corner (apartments available, breakfast extra for apartments, Rue de la Grande Ile 42, tel. 02-350-0921, mobile 0488-920-093, www. sleepinginbrussels.com, sleepinginbrussels@gmail.com).

BRUSSELS SLEEPING, EATING & MORE

**$ Hotel the Moon** is an efficient budget option, with 17 bare-bones rooms and no public spaces. Ask for one of the renovated rooms, which go for the same price but are in much better shape than older units. It's noisy (thin walls and on a square), but it's just steps from the Grand Place—and it's the cheapest centrally located hotel this side of a youth hostel (RS%, ask for a quieter room in the back, stairs but no elevator, on the small "Agora" square at Rue de la Montagne 4, tel. 02-508-1580, www.hotelthemoon.com, info@hotelthemoon.com).

## STE. CATHERINE, NEAR THE OLD FISH MARKET

The following listings are a 10-minute walk from the intensity of the old center, near the Sainte-Catherine/Sint-Katelijne Métro stop (two stops from Central station). This charming neighborhood, "the village in Brussels," faces the canalside fish market and has many of the town's best restaurants.

**$$$ Hotel Welcome,** run by an energetic bundle of hospitality named Michel Smeesters and his wife Sophie, offers outrageous-

ly creative rooms, exuberantly decorated with artifacts they've picked up in their world travels. Each of the 17 rooms has a different geographic theme, from India to Japan to Bali: It's worth the extra euros to spend a night in such exotic settings (RS%, family rooms, suites have whirlpool baths, includes breakfast if you book through their website, air-con in most rooms, elevator, reasonably priced laundry service, pay parking, Quai au Bois à Brûler 23, tel. 02-219-9546, www.hotelwelcome.com, info@hotelwelcome.com).

**$$$ Be in Brussels B&B** is on a quiet backstreet excellently located near Place Ste. Catherine. Run by cordial Taxiari—a Belgian by way of Greece—the three rooms are tastefully though simply decorated (Rue du Chien Marin 10, mobile 0496-550-687, www.bb-beinbrussels.com, b.bbeinbrussels@yahoo.com).

**$$$ Citadines Sainte-Catherine Apart'hotel,** part of a Europe-wide chain, is a huge apartment-style hotel with modern, shipshape rooms. Choose from efficiency studios with foldout double beds or two-room apartments with a bedroom and a foldout couch in the living room. All 169 units come with a kitchen, stocked cupboards, stereo, and dishwasher. This is a good option for families staying several nights (breakfast extra, pay parking, Quai au Bois à Brûler 51, tel. 02-221-1411, www.citadines.com, stecatherine@citadines.com).

**$$$ Hotel Ibis Brussels City Centre** is a big, impersonal,

BRUSSELS SLEEPING, EATING & MORE

ANSPACH FOUNTAIN

RUE MARCQ
RUE DU GRAND HOSPICE
RUE AUX FLEURS
To Nord/Noord Station
RUE DE LA FIANCÉE
BLVD. ADOLPHE MAX
NOTRE-DAME DU FINISTÈRE

RUE PAYS DE LIÈGE
QUAI AUX BRIQUES
Pond
RUE DU CIRQUE
RUE VANDER ELST
R. DES HIRONDELLES
RUE SAINT-MICHEL

QUAI AU BOIS À BRULER
RUE DE ROULEAU
Place de Beguinage
ST. JEAN
RUE AUGUSTINS

Sainte-Catherine
SAINTE-CATHERINE
Place de Brouckère

RUE DE FLANDRE
RUE VIERGE NOIRE
SAINTE-CATHERINE
Place Sainte-Catherine
RUE DE L'ÉVEQUE
De Brouckère
#71
Place de la Monnaie
RUE NEUVE
RUE D'ARGENT
RUE D'OR

Place du Nouveau Marché aux Grains
RUE DES HALLES
BLVD. ANSPACH
RUE GRETRY
THEATRE ROYAL
RUE LEOPOLD

RUE ANTOINE DANSAERT
RUE SAINTE CATHERINE
RUE DU FOSSÉ AUX LOUPS

RUE DES CHARTREUX
RUE DU MARCHÉ AUX POULETS
RUE DE L'ÉCUYER

RUE SAINT-CHRISTOPHE
Place St-Géry
Bourse
R. DE LA BOURSE
BOURSE
RUE DE LA RUE
RUE DES DOMINICAINS

R. J. V. PRAET
RUE HENRI MAUS
ST. NICOLAS
PETITE R.D. BOUCHERS
GALERIES ST. HUBERT
RUE DES BOUCHERS

R. DES RICHES CLAIRES
RUE DES PIERRES
MUSEUM OF COCOA & CHOCOLATE
CITY MUSEUM
'Agora' Square
Place d'Espagne

RUE DES GRANDS
Grand Place
TOWN HALL
BREWERY MUSEUM
HORTA GALLERY

RUE DES SIX JETONS
BLVD. ANSPACH
RUE DU MARCHÉ AUX CHARBON
FASHION & LACE MUSEUM
RUE DE LA VIOLETTE
RUE DE L'INFANTE

Place Fontainas
LOWER
RUE DU LOMBARD
Square de la Putterie

RUE DES MOINEAUX
MANNEKEN-PIS STATUE
RUE DUQUESNOY
RUE SAINT-JEAN
Place de l'Albertine

RUE F. DE CHAMPAGNE
RUE DU CHENE
GARDEROBE MANNEKEN-PIS
Place du Vielle Halle aux Blés
RUE DE L'HOPITAL

TOWN
RUE DES ALEXIENS
Place du Dinant
R. DE L'ESCALIER
CANTERSTEEN

Place Rouppe
RUE D'ACCOLAY
BD. DE L'EMPEREUR
TOUR D'ANGLE
R. DE RUYSBROECK

To Midi/Zuid Station
RUE DE LA ROUE
BRUSSELS CHAPELLE STATION
Place de la Chapelle
R. DE ROLLEBEEK
Place du Grand Sablon

RUE DES URSULINES
NOTRE-DAME DE LA CHAPELLE
R. JOSEPH STEVENS

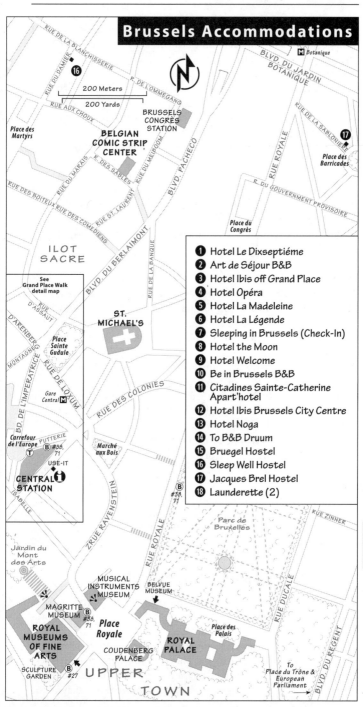

# Brussels Accommodations

1. Hotel Le Dixseptiéme
2. Art de Séjour B&B
3. Hotel Ibis off Grand Place
4. Hotel Opéra
5. Hotel La Madeleine
6. Hotel La Légende
7. Sleeping in Brussels (Check-In)
8. Hotel the Moon
9. Hotel Welcome
10. Be in Brussels B&B
11. Citadines Sainte-Catherine Apart'hotel
12. Hotel Ibis Brussels City Centre
13. Hotel Noga
14. To B&B Druum
15. Bruegel Hostel
16. Sleep Well Hostel
17. Jacques Brel Hostel
18. Launderette (2)

BRUSSELS SLEEPING, EATING & MORE

perfectly comfortable place with 236 rooms in a great location that offers discounts during slow times (breakfast extra, air-con, elevator, Rue Joseph Plateau 2 at Place Ste. Catherine, tel. 02-513-7620, www.ibishotel.com, h1454@accor.com).

**$$ Hotel Noga** feels very homey, with 19 rooms, a welcoming game room, and old photos of Belgian royalty lining the hallways. It's carefully run by Frederich Faucher and his son, Mourad (family rooms, very quiet, pay garage parking, Rue du Beguinage 38, tel. 02-218-6763, www.nogahotel.com, info@nogahotel.com).

**$$ B&B Druum** is artsy and cool, with six rooms, each designed by a different artist. Some have wild and creative light fixtures, while others feel more sedate, with original photography on the walls—but all come with a contemporary, minimalist flair. It's comfortable and not as pretentious as it sounds (pay parking, Rue du Houblon 63, mobile 0472-054-240, www.druum.be, sleep@druum.be).

## HOSTELS

Three classy and modern hostels—in buildings that could double as small, state-of-the-art, minimum-security prisons—are within a 10-minute walk of Central station. Each accepts people of all ages, serves cheap and hot meals, and includes sheets, breakfast, and showers down the hall.

**¢ Bruegel Hostel,** an "official" hostel and a fortress of cleanliness, is handiest and most comfortable (private rooms available, open 7:00-13:15 & 14:00-1:00 in the morning, midway between Midi and Central stations, behind Chapelle church at Rue de St. Esprit 2, tel. 02-511-0436, www.youthhostels.be, brussel@vjh.be).

**¢ Sleep Well Hostel,** surrounded by high-rise parking structures, is also comfortable (private rooms available, no curfew, Rue de Damier 23, tel. 02-218-5050, www.sleepwell.be, info@sleepwell.be).

**¢ Jacques Brel Hostel** is a little farther out, but it's still a reasonable walk from everything (private rooms available, no curfew, Rue de la Sablonnière 30, tel. 02-218-0187, www.laj.be, brussels.brel@hostelbrussels.be).

# Eating in Brussels

Brussels is known for both its high-quality, French-style cuisine and for multicultural variety. Seafood—fish, eel, shrimp, and oysters—is especially well-prepared here.

When it comes to choosing a restaurant, many tourists congregate on the Grand Place or at Rue des Bouchers, the city's restaurant row. While the Grand Place is undeniably magnificent for enjoying dessert or a drink, go elsewhere to eat well, such as the ethnic and trendy zone past the Bourse near Place St-Géry; the area around Place Ste. Catherine; or the colorful Matongé neighborhood.

## OLD CENTER
## Dining on the Grand Place

My vote for northern Europe's grandest medieval square is lined with hardworking eateries that serve predictable dishes to tourist crowds. Of course, you won't get the best quality or prices—but, after all, it's the Grand Place.

For an atmospheric cellar or a table right on the Grand Place, two traditional standbys have the same formula, with tables outside overlooking the action. **$$$$ L'Estaminet du Kelderke**—with its one steamy vault under the square packed with both natives and tourists—is a real Brussels fixture. It serves local specialties, including mussels (daily 12:00-24:00, no reservations taken, Grand Place 15, tel. 02-513-7344). **$$$$ Brasserie L'Ommegang,** with a fancier restaurant upstairs, once offered perhaps the classiest seating and best food on the square, but under new ownership, it can be hit or miss (Grand Place 9, tel. 02-511-8244).

### Lunches near the Grand Place

The super-central square dubbed the "Agora" (officially Marché aux Herbes, just between the Grand Place and Central station) is lined with low-end eateries—Quick, Subway, Panos sandwich shop, Exki health-food store—and is especially fun on sunny days. On the other side of the Grand Place is Rue du Marché aux Fromages, jammed with mostly Greek and gyros places, with diners sitting elbow-to-elbow at cramped tables out front. For something fresher and more interesting, stroll a few blocks to one of the following alternatives, or consider the nearby Ste. Catherine neighborhood (see listings, later).

**$$ Bia Mara** ("Sea Food" in Irish Gaelic) offers five different styles of fish-and-chips made with sustainable ingredients (plus a chicken option and a rotating special). Considering Belgium's affinity for fried food and its proximity to the sea, it's a wonder that it took an Irishman—gregarious owner Barry—to introduce this innovative concept, which started as a food cart in Dublin. The industrial-mod interior is small, so lines can be long at peak times (daily 12:00-22:30, closes between 14:30 and 17:30 Mon-Thu, around the corner from the Grand Place at Rue du Marché aux Poulets 41, tel. 02-502-0061).

**$$ Peck 47** is a mod café with artistic decor and white subway

## Mussels in Brussels

Mussels *(moules)* are available all over town. Mostly harvested from aqua farms along the North Sea, they are available for most of the year (except from about May through mid-July, when they're brought in from Denmark). The classic Belgian preparation is *à la marinière,* cooked in white wine, onions, celery, parsley, and butter. Or, instead of wine, cooks use light Belgian beer for the stock. For a high-calorie version, try *moules à la crème,* where the stock is thickened with heavy cream.

You order by the kilo (just more than 2 pounds), which is a pretty big bucket. While restaurants don't promote these as splittable, they certainly are. Your mussels come with Belgian fries (what we think of as "French fries"—dip them in mayo). To accompany your mussels, try a French white wine such as Muscadet or Chablis, or a Belgian blonde ale such as Duvel or La Chouffe. When eating mussels, you can feel a little more local by nonchalantly using an empty mussel shell as a pincher to pull the meat out of other shells. It actually works quite nicely.

tile. They offer brunch all day and an American dinner menu in the evening with fresh and innovative style—and veggie options. If you have a hankering for eggs Benedict, come here (daily 9:00-22:00, Rue du Marché aux Poulets 47, tel. 02-513-0287).

**Groceries:** Minimarkets dot the city. Marked "night shop" and often run by Pakistani and Indian immigrants, they're often open late. A convenient **Carrefour Express** is along the street between the Grand Place and the Bourse, near a public drinking fountain (Rue au Beurre 27). Another Carrefour is near Central station on Rue de l'Infante Isabelle. **AD Delhaize** is major supermarket, at the intersection of Rue du Marché aux Poulets and Boulevard Anspach (Boulevard Anspach 63).

### More Eateries near the Grand Place
These restaurants are good for a sit-down meal day or night.

**$$ Arcadi Café** is a delightful little eatery serving daily plates, salads, and a selection of quiche-like tortes. The interior comes with a fun, circa-1900 ambience; grab a table there, on the street, or at the end of Galeries St. Hubert (daily 9:00-23:30, 1 Rue d'Arenberg, tel. 02-511-3343).

**$$ Le Mokafé** is inexpensive but feels splurgy. They dish up light café fare at the quiet end of the elegant Galeries St. Hubert, with great people-watching outdoor tables. This is also a good spot to try a Brussels waffle or to order a *café-filtre*—an old-fashioned method where the coffee drips directly into your cup (Tue-Sun 9:00-23:45, closed Mon, Galerie du Roi 9, tel. 02-511-7870).

**$ La Maison des Crêpes,** a little eatery a half-block south of the Bourse, looks underwhelming but serves delicious crêpes (both savory and sweet varieties) and salads. Even though it's just a few steps away from the tourist bustle, it feels laid-back and local (good beers, fresh mint tea, sidewalk seating, daily 12:00-23:00, Rue du Midi 13, mobile 0475-957-368).

**$$ Yaki** is a tempting Vietnamese and Thai noodle bar in a stately old flatiron building tucked between the Grand Place and the Rue du Marché au Charbon café/nightlife zone. Choose between the tight interior and the outdoor tables (daily 12:00-23:00, Rue du Midi 52, tel. 02-503-3409).

**$$$ Osteria a l'Ombra,** a true Italian joint, is good for a quality bowl of pasta with a glass of fine Italian wine. A block off the Grand Place, it's pricey, but the woody bistro ambience and tasty food make it a good value. The ground-floor seating on high stools is fine, but also consider sitting upstairs (Mon-Sat 12:00-14:30 & 18:30-23:30, closed Sun, Rue des Harengs 2, tel. 02-511-6710).

**$$ La Fleur en Papier Doré** is a homey café covered in old-fashioned paintings and memorabilia that looks a bit like your eccentric great-aunt's house. René Magritte was a regular and held his wedding reception here (see the big picture of him in the back). A selection of *stoemp* specialties—mashed potatoes with vegetables—makes this a good spot for a casual meal (Tue-Sat 11:00-24:00, Sun until 19:00, closed Mon, Rue des Alexiens 55, tel. 02-511-1659).

## Waffles near the Grand Place

Dozens of waffle windows clog the streets surrounding the Grand Place. Most of them are suspiciously cheap (€2)—but the big stack of stale waffles in the window clues you in that these are far from top-quality. Below I've listed a couple of good options that sell both Liège-style and Brussels-style waffles (for details on both types, see page 338).

**$ Maison Dandoy,** which has been making waffles since the 19th century, is the pricey, elegant choice. You can take the waffles to go or enjoy them at a table in an upscale Parisian atmosphere (Mon-Sat 9:30-19:00, Sun from 10:30, just off the Grand Place at Rue Charles Buls 14, tel. 02-512-6588).

**$ Waffle Factory,** near the *Manneken-Pis,* is cheaper but still good. While it has an American fast-food ambience, it's efficient and popular—and thanks to the high turnover, you'll usually get a waffle that's grilled while you wait. Get your waffle to go, or sit

ANSPACH
FOUNTAIN
24

18
20
17
16

RUE MARCQ
RUE DU GRAND HOSPICE
RUE AUX FLEURS
QUAI AU BOIS À BRÛLER
Pond
ST.
JEAN
Place de
Beguinage
RUE DE ROULEAU
R. DES HIRONDELLES
RUE VANDER ELST
RUE DU CIRQUE
R. DE LA FIANCÉE
BLVD. ADOLPHE MAX
NOTRE-
DAME
DU FINISTÈRE
RUE SAINT-MICHEL

Sainte-
Catherine
SAINTE-
CATHERINE
Place de
Brouckère
RUE NEUVE

Place du
Nouveau Marché aux Grains
SAINTE-
CATHERINE
Place
Sainte-
Catherine
19
21
23
22

RUE ANTOINE DANSAERT
RUE VIERGE NOIRE
RUE DES HALLES
RUE SAINTE-CATHERINE
RUE DE L'ÉVÊQUE
RUE AUGUSTINS
RUE DU FOSSÉ AUX LOUPS
De Brouckère
B #71
Place de
la Monnaie
THÉÂTRE
ROYAL
RUE D'ARGENT
15
RUE LEOPOLD

25
28
26

RUE DES CHARTREUX
RUE SAINT-CHRISTOPHE
3
RUE DU MARCHÉ AUX POULETS
27
30
31
RUE DE LA BOURSE
BOURSE
RUE HENRI MAUS
BLVD. ANSPACH
RUE GRÉTRY
RUE DES FRIPIERS
34
36
ST.
NICOLAS
RUE DE L'ECUYER
RUE DE LA FOURCHE
35
11
12
RUE DES DOMINICAINS
13
14
RUE DES BOUCHERS
PETITE R.D.
BOUCHERS
R. D'ARENBERG
4

Place
St-Géry
R. J. V. PRAET
Bourse
RUE DES PIERRES
5
27
RUE AU BEURRE
MUSEUM OF
COCOA &
CHOCOLATE
6
GALERIES
ST. HUBERT
CITY
MUSEUM
7
RUE DE LA

R. DES RICHES
CLAIRES
RUE DES SIX JETONS
GRANDE ÎLE
ÉCLIPSE
RUE DU MIDI
RUE DU MARCHÉ AUX CHARBON
TOWN
HALL
Grand
Place
1
COLL.
'Agora'
Square
Place
d'Espagne
HORTA
GALLERY

BLVD. ANSPACH
9
2
BRASS.
FASHION
& LACE MUSEUM
10
RUE DE LA VIOLETTE
RUE DES ÉPERONNIERS
RUE DUQUESNOY
Square
de la
Putterie

Place
Fontainas
33
LOWER
R. DES MOINEAUX
RUE NEUVE
MANNEKEN-
PIS STATUE
32
RUE DU LOMBARD
RUE SAINT-JEAN
RUE DE L'HOPITAL
Place de
l'Albertine

RUE DES BOGARDS
RUE DU MIDI
RUE VAN HELMONT
RUE P. DE CHAMPAGNE
GARDEROBE
MANNEKEN-PIS
RUE DU CHÊNE
Place
du Vielle Halle
aux Blés
R. DE L'ESCALIER
CANTERSTEEN

TOWN

Place
Rouppe
RUE TERRE NEUVE
RUE DU POINÇON
RUE D'ACCOLAY
RUE DES
ALEXIENS
8
Place de
Dinant
BD. DE L'EMPEREUR
TOUR
D'ANGLE
R. DE ROLLEBEEK
RUE LEBEAU
RUE RUYSBROECK

To
Midi/Zuid
Station
RUE DE LA ROUE
R. DES URSULINES
BRUSSELS
CHAPELLE
STATION
Place de
la Chapelle
R. JOSEPH STEVENS
NOTRE-DAME
DE LA CHAPELLE
Place du
Grand Sablon

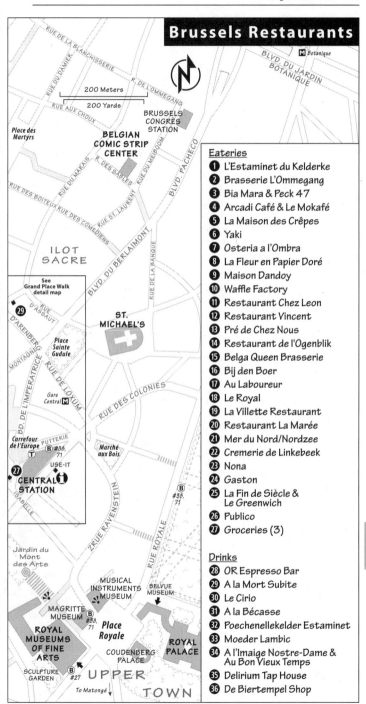

# Brussels Restaurants

## Eateries

1 L'Estaminet du Kelderke
2 Brasserie L'Ommegang
3 Bia Mara & Peck 47
4 Arcadi Café & Le Mokafé
5 La Maison des Crêpes
6 Yaki
7 Osteria a l'Ombra
8 La Fleur en Papier Doré
9 Maison Dandoy
10 Waffle Factory
11 Restaurant Chez Leon
12 Restaurant Vincent
13 Pré de Chez Nous
14 Restaurant de l'Ogenblik
15 Belga Queen Brasserie
16 Bij den Boer
17 Au Laboureur
18 Le Royal
19 La Villette Restaurant
20 Restaurant La Marée
21 Mer du Nord/Nordzee
22 Cremerie de Linkebeek
23 Nona
24 Gaston
25 La Fin de Siècle & Le Greenwich
26 Publico
27 Groceries (3)

## Drinks

28 OR Espresso Bar
29 A la Mort Subite
30 Le Cirio
31 A la Bécasse
32 Poechenellekelder Estaminet
33 Moeder Lambic
34 A l'Imaige Nostre-Dame & Au Bon Vieux Temps
35 Delirium Tap House
36 De Biertempel Shop

**BRUSSELS SLEEPING, EATING & MORE**

---

## Saving Brussels' Fry Shacks

The *frietkot*—local lingo for a "fry shack"—was once a Brussels landmark. These streetside takeout stands were where locals traditionally came for cheap and tasty fries, brochettes, seafood, and burgers. But in recent years their numbers have dwindled. Owners were retiring, so the shacks were closing.

Fortunately, interest in preserving this Belgian institution has grown, culminating in a campaign to create new, architecturally distinctive *frietkots.* Just as Paris has its Art Nouveau Métro stations and London has its red telephone boxes, by 2020 Brussels will have 10 iconic fry shacks. With an overall look designed by a Ghent architectural studio, each will have its own individual sign and distinctive tiled walls.

Preserving the *frietkot* is not only about tradition and style, however. These stands are practical, too, as grease from deep-frying will seep into any building's walls. That's enough of a reason to make sure that these stand-alone shacks stick around.

---

upstairs to enjoy some peace and quiet. Besides the standard waffle styles, they also serve their own innovations: the *waffine* (thin and filled with Nutella or jam) or a *lunchwaf* (with savory fillings). For a very Belgian taste treat, top your waffle with *speculoos*—a decadent spread of ground-up gingerbread cookies with the consistency of peanut butter (long hours daily, look for green-and-red-striped awning at corner of Rue du Lombard and Rue de l'Etuve).

### Rue des Bouchers (Restaurant Row)

Brussels' restaurant streets, two blocks north of the Grand Place, are touristy and notorious for touts who aggressively suck you in and predatory servers who greedily rip you off. It's hard to justify dining here when far better options sit just a block or two away (see later listings). If you are seduced into a meal here, order carefully, understand the prices thoroughly, and watch your wallet.

**$$ Restaurant Chez Leon** is a legendary, if touristy, mussels factory, slamming out piles of cheap buckets since 1893. The €16 "Formula Leon" is a light meal consisting of a small bucket of mussels, fries, and a beer (daily 12:00-23:00, kids under 12 eat free, Rue des Bouchers 18, tel. 02-511-1415, www.chezleon. be).

**$$$$ Restaurant Vincent** has you enter through the kitchen to enjoy their 1905-era ambience. This place is better for meat dishes than for seafood (daily 12:00-14:30 & 18:30-23:30, Rue des Dominicains 8, tel. 02-511-2607, www.restaurantvincent.be, Julien).

## Finer Dining near Rue des Bouchers

These options, though just steps away from those listed earlier, are more authentic and a better value.

**$$$ Pré de Chez Nous** may be only a few storefronts from the Rue des Bouchers frenzy, but it's light years away in quality and price. Its €33 three-course *menu* is a remarkable deal for this touristic neighborhood—local, organic, and inventive food that changes every week depending on what's fresh. There's usually a meat, fish, and veggie option for the main dish, and Frédéric is happy to suggest an organic wine or beer to pair with your selection (Tue-Sat 12:00-14:30 & 19:00-23:00, closed Sun-Mon, 19 Rue des Dominicains, tel. 02-833-3737, www.predecheznous.be).

**$$$$ Restaurant de l'Ogenblik,** a remarkably peaceful eddy just off the raging restaurant row, fills an early-20th-century space in the corner of an arcade. The waiters serve well-presented, near-gourmet French cuisine. This mussels-free zone has a great, split-table rack of lamb with 10 vegetables. Their sea bass with risotto and truffle oil is a hit with return eaters. Reservations are smart (Mon-Sat 12:00-14:30 & 19:00-24:00, closed Sun, across from Restaurant Vincent—listed earlier—at Galerie des Princes 1, tel. 02-511-6151, www.ogenblik.be, Yves).

**$$$$ Belga Queen Brasserie,** a huge, dressy brasserie filling a palatial former bank building, is crowded with Brussels' beautiful people and visiting European diplomats. It's expensive, but the cuisine is creative, the service is sharp, and the experience is memorable—from the fries served in silver cones, to the double-decker platters of iced shellfish (€65/person for the Belga Queen platter), to the transparent toilet stalls, which become opaque only after you nervously lock the door (daily 12:00-14:30 & 18:30-23:00 but no lunch on Sat, reservations smart, Rue Fosse-aux-Loups 32, tel. 02-217-2187, www.belgaqueen.be). The vault downstairs is a plush cigar and cocktail lounge.

## STE. CATHERINE, NEAR THE OLD FISH MARKET

A 10-minute walk from the old center puts you in "the village within the city" area of Ste. Catherine (Métro: Sainte-Catherine/Sint-Katelijne). The historic fish market here has spawned a tradition of fine restaurants specializing mostly in seafood. The old fish canal survives, and if you walk around it, you'll see plenty of enticing places to eat, including these very good, yet very different, options.

## Sampling Belgian Beer in Brussels

Brussels is full of atmospheric cafés to savor the local brew. The places lining the Grand Place are touristy, but the setting—plush, old medieval guildhalls fronting all that cobbled wonder—is hard to beat.

All varieties of Belgian beer are available, but Brussels' most distinctive beers are *lambic*-based. Look for *lambic doux, lambic blanche, gueuze* (pronounced "kurrs"), and *faro,* as well as fruit-flavored *lambics,* such as *kriek* (cherry) and *framboise* (raspberry—*frambozen* in Dutch). These beers look and taste more like a dry, somewhat bitter cider. The brewer doesn't add yeast—the beer ferments naturally from wild yeast floating in the marshy air around Brussels. For more on Belgian beer, see the "Eating" section of the Practicalities chapter.

The following places are generally open daily from about 11:00 until late but aren't really good for a full meal—though you can usually get lighter fare, such as a cold-meat plate, a *tartine* (open-face sandwich), or a salad.

**A la Mort Subite,** a few steps above the top end of the Galeries St. Hubert, is a classic old bar that has retained its 1928 decor... and its loyal customers seem to go back just about as far. Named after the "sudden death" playoff that laborers used to end their lunchtime dice games, it still has an unpretentious, working-class feel. The decor is simple, with wood tables, grimy yellow wallpaper, and some-other-era garland trim. Tiny metal plates on the walls mark spots where gas-powered flames once flickered—  used by patrons to light their cigars. A typical lunch or snack here is an omelet with a salad or a *tartine* spread with *fromage blanc* (cream cheese) or pressed meat. Eat it with one of the home-brewed, *lambic*-based beers. This is a good place to try the *kriek* beer (Rue Montagne aux Herbes Potagères 7, tel. 02-513-1318).

**Le Cirio,** across from the Bourse, feels a bit more upscale,

**$$$$ Bij den Boer,** a fun, noisy eatery popular with locals and tourists, has inviting tables out on the esplanade and feels like a traditional and very successful brasserie. Their specialty: fish (Mon-Sat 12:00-14:30 & 18:00-22:30, closed Sun, Quai aux Briques 60, tel. 02-512-6122, www.bijdenboer.com).

**$$ Au Laboureur,** where charming Dimitri churns out hand-made shrimp croquettes from a stand attached to the café, attracts a wide cross-section of Bruxellois—from posh lawyers to laborers to young alternative types. For €10 you get two croquettes worthy

with a faded yet still luxurious gilded-wood interior, booths with velvet padding, and dark tables that bear the skid marks of over a century's worth of beer glasses. The service is jaded—perhaps understandably given its touristy location (Rue de la Bourse 18, tel. 02-512-1395).

**A la Bécasse** keeps a lower profile than Le Cirio, with a simple wood-panel and wood-table decor that appeals to both poor students and lunching businessmen. The *lambic doux* has been served in clay jars since 1825. It's just around the corner from Le Cirio, toward the Grand Place, hidden away at the end of a tight lane (Tabora 11, tel. 02-511-0006).

**Poechenellekelder Estaminet** is a great bar with lots of real character located right across the street from the *Manneken-Pis*. As the word *estaminet* (tavern) indicates, it's not brewery-owned, so they have a great selection of beers. Inside tables are immersed in *Pis* kitsch and puppets. Outside tables offer some fine people-watching (Rue du Chêne 5, tel. 02-511-9262).

**Moeder Lambic** has a modern industrial feel, with owners who are maniacs about craft beer and sell only traditional brews from independent producers. With a knowledgeable staff, this is an excellent place to start exploring the acquired tastes of *lambic, gueuze,* and *kriek.* For a snack, try the toast with *pottekaas,* a spread made with local white cheese and beer (on a square off Boulevard Anspach at Place Fontainas 8, tel. 02-503-6068).

Two tiny and extremely characteristic bars are tucked away down long entry corridors just off Rue du Marché aux Herbes. **A l'Imaige Nostre-Dame** (closed Sun, at #8) and **Au Bon Vieux Temps** (at #12) both treat fine beer with great reverence and seem to have extremely local clientele, whom you're bound to meet if you grab a stool. Au Bon Vieux Temps stocks the legendary Trappist brew Westvleteren 12, which is hard to find outside Belgium.

**Delirium Tap House** is a sloppy frat party nightly with no ambience, a noisy young crowd, beer-soaked wooden floors, rock 'n' roll, and a famous variety of great Belgian beers on tap (near Rue des Bouchers, not far from Chez Leon at Impasse de la Fidélité 4).

of a light lunch or a shared snack. Look out for rotating alternatives: calamari, haddock, or some other fried ocean dweller plus cheesy options. Order and pay for food at the stand, then grab a seat at any table. The bar staff will come around for drink orders (Wed-Sun 11:00-20:00, later on weekends, closed Mon-Tue, Rue de Flandre 108).

**$$$ Le Royal** is a cool-feeling brasserie serving tasty and elegantly presented food that's worth the splurge. They offer traditional Belgian staples and modern fusion dishes—some with a hint of Asian influence. Sit in the trendy interior, or choose a sidewalk table. Reservations are smart (Wed-Sun 12:00-15:00 & 18:00-23:00, closed Mon-Tue, Rue de Flandre 103, tel. 02-217-8500, www.royalbrasseriebrussels.be).

**$$$ La Villette Restaurant** ("The Slaughterhouse") is a romantic, subdued alternative, serving traditional Belgian cuisine: meaty stews, eels, *stoemp* (mashed potatoes and vegetables), and dishes with beer. The chef proudly makes the sauces from scratch, and Agata can match your order to the right beer. The restaurant has a charming red-and-white-tablecloth interior and good outdoor seating facing a small square (Mon-Sat 12:00-14:30 & 18:30-22:30, closed Sun, Rue du Vieux Marché-aux-Grains 3, tel. 02-512-7550).

**$$$ Restaurant La Marée** is a classic local spot a couple of blocks away from the trendy places on the square. With an older clientele, an open kitchen, and an inviting menu, this untouristy bistro specializes in mussels and seafood—their only pretense is their insistence that it's fresh (Tue-Sat 12:00-14:00 & 18:30-22:00, closed Sun-Mon, near Rue du Marché-aux-Porcs at Rue de Flandre 99, tel. 02-511-0040).

## Cheap, Fast, and Tasty Lunches in Ste. Catherine

Place Ste. Catherine, which branches off from the side of Ste. Catherine Church, is lined with enjoyable cafés with outdoor seating.

**$$ Mer du Nord/Nordzee** is as delicious as it is inexpensive. This seafood bar—basically a grill attached to a fresh fish shop—cooks up whatever it catches and serves it on small tapas-like plates with glasses of wine to an appreciative local crowd. Just belly up to the counter and place your order, then eat standing at the tables. The *scampi à la plancha* (grilled shrimp) is exquisite (Tue-Thu 11:00-17:00, Fri-Sat until 18:00, Sun until 20:00, closed Mon, Rue Ste. Catherine 45, at corner with Place Ste. Catherine, tel. 02-513-1192). The similar **Poissonerie/Vishandel ABC,** across the street, has a comparable operation.

**$ Crèmerie de Linkebeek,** owned by charming Laurence, is the best place in town to shop for Belgian cheeses—rubbed and flavored with beer rather than wine or alcohol. The English-speaking staff is happy to help you choose the perfect cheese for your picnic (they also sell baguettes, wine, and crackers—you could assemble a light meal or a snack right here). At midday, they sell delicious €5 baguette sandwiches to go—grab one before they sell out (Mon-Sat

9:00-18:30, Sun 9:30-17:00, Rue du Vieux Marché-aux-Grains 4, tel. 02-512-3510).

**$ Nona** makes traditional Neapolitan pizza using only ingredients from local farms. You might find Brussels sprouts or kale on your pizza—or opt for the seasonal special (daily 12:00-23:00, Rue Ste. Catherine 17, www.nonalife.com).

**$ Gaston** is the choice for waffles, artisan ice cream, and coffee away from the tourist crush around Grand Place. Taking your sugar or caffeine injection here is civilized and delicious (daily 11:00-22:00, shorter hours in winter, Quai aux Briques 86, tel. 02-223-4306).

## ON OR NEAR PLACE ST-GÉRY

For a trendier and youthful scene, head to Place St-Géry (a.k.a. Sint-Goriksplein). The epicenter is at the intersection of Pont de la Carpe and Plétinckx street. This area is more about drinking than about dining, but mixed in among the bars are several eateries: sushi, Italian, Thai, Vietnamese, Indian, and so on. Rue Jules van Praet is lined mostly with interchangeable Asian and Indian restaurants.

**On Rue des Chartreux:** Just across Rue Van Artevelde from the Place St-Géry action, this street has several enticing options. **$$ La Fin de Siècle** is a bohemian place serving basic, unpretentious Belgian/French fare. With appropriately turn-of-the-century atmosphere, mismatched secondhand furniture, and long, shared tables, it has a youthful energy (food served daily 12:00-24:00, at #9, tel. 02-512-5123). Next door at #7, **$$$ Le Greenwich** has an even more exquisite Art Nouveau facade. Just up the street, **$$$ Publico** is hip but accessible, with a black-subway-tile interior and well-priced Belgian and Mediterranean fare. Reservations are smart on weekends (daily 12:00-23:00, at #32, tel. 02-503-0430, www.publicobxl.be).

**Caffeine:** For excellent coffee, drop by **OR Espresso Bar,** the first specialty coffee roaster in Brussels (daily until 18:00, Rue Auguste Orts 9, tel. 02-511-7400).

## MATONGÉ

The neighborhood of Matongé—just past the royal sights of the Upper Town—is a fun-to-explore mix of vivid African immigrant culture and Belgian trend seekers. If you have time, ride the Métro to Porte de Namur/Naamsepoort and explore the neighborhood (see page 142), then hang around for a meal.

**On and near Rue Saint-Boniface:** This broad street, leading up to St. Boniface Church, has some great trendy options—Belgian, French, Italian, Japanese, Greek, and more. Two inviting spots are just in front of the church: **$$$ Le Clan des Belges** is a high-energy hit, with a rustic, cozy interior and a lively, leafy outdoor dining zone with tables in the shadow of the church steeple (Belgian classics, lots of burgers, brunch on Sundays, daily roughly 12:00-14:30 & 19:00-23:00, Rue de la Paix 20, tel. 02-511-1121, www.leclandesbelges.com). A few steps away from the middle of this drag, **$ Eccome No!** is a handy spot for pizza by the slice (daily 12:00-23:00, Rue Ernest Solvay 10, tel. 02-502-1611).

**On Rue Longue Vie:** Around the corner from the church, you'll find a pair of **$** eateries—**Au Soleil d'Afrique** and **Cap Africa**—dishing up similar menus of African classics (long hours daily).

**Place Fernand Cocq:** A few blocks from the heart of Matongé, this grassy square boasts a cluster of inviting bars and **$** eateries with sidewalk tables (all open daily). **Il Nobile** is a popular pizzeria (at #24); **Volle Gas** is a classic, energetic brasserie with old-fashioned woody ambience and crank-'em-out Belgian classics (at #21); and—across the square—**L'Amour Fou** is a painfully hip, artsy bar proud of its burgers (Chaussée d'Ixelles 185).

# Shopping in Brussels

The obvious temptations—available absolutely everywhere—are chocolate and lace. Other popular Brussels souvenirs include EU gear with the gold circle of stars on a blue background (flags, T-shirts, mugs, bottle openers, hats, pens, and so on) and miniature reproductions of the *Manneken*-Pis or the Atomium. Belgian beers are a fun, imbibable souvenir that you can either enjoy at a picnic while traveling, or pack (carefully) in your checked luggage to take home.

### Souvenirs near the Grand Place

The streets immediately surrounding the Grand Place are jammed with Belgium's tackiest souvenir stands, with a few good shops mixed in. In my Grand Place Walk, I've listed some good places to pick up chocolates (page 154) and to browse for tapestries and lace (page 159).

**De Biertempel,** facing the TI on the street that runs below the Grand Place, not only stocks hundreds of types of Belgian beer, but an entire wall of beer glasses—each one designed to highlight the qualities of a specific beer (Rue du Marché aux Herbes 56, tel. 02-502-1906).

### Fashion on Rue Antoine Dansaert

While Antwerp is the epicenter of Belgian design, Brussels has worked hard in recent years to catch up. To browse the best selection of Belgian boutiques, start by heading up Rue Antoine Dansaert (from the big Bourse building, cross Boulevard Anspach and continue straight up Rue Auguste Orts, which becomes Rue Antoine Dansaert). Along here, you'll see an eclectic array of both Belgian and international apparel. While specific designers seem to come and go, the genteel vibe persists. Window-shopping this street, you'll pass fine parks. After Place du Nouveau Marché aux Grains, the high-fashion focus downshifts, and the rest of the street feels like an emerging neighborhood with some funkier, lower-rent shops. You could return the way you came, or

cut a few blocks northeast to the long fish market square at Ste. Catherine, which runs roughly parallel to Rue Antoine Dansaert.

### Funky Design Shops near Place St-Géry

Brussels has its own term for what we might call "hipsters": *bobo,* short for *bourgeois-bohème*...bohemian middle-class kids with enough money and free time for creative endeavors. You'll find *bobo* pockets around town, but these two streets are a good place to start.

**Rue des Chartreux,** which angles off of Rue Antoine Dansaert, has a decidedly lower-rent aura and a lineup of creative shops, such as **Blender 01** (style and gadgets, at #18). A bit closer to the Grand Place, the lively, café-lined **Rue du Marché au Charbon** and the streets nearby (especially Plattesteen) are another good browsing area.

### Big Chains on Rue Neuve

This street, a few blocks north of the Grand Place, is where you'll find big department stores and other international shops. The giant City2 complex on this street is the downtown's primary modern shopping mall.

### Secondhand Shops in Marolles

This somewhat seedy neighborhood is well-known for its second-hand shops. Rue Blaes and Rue Haute, which run southwest from near the old Tour d'Angle (described in the Upper Town Walk chapter) to the Midi train station, are lined with several characteristic stores. There's a lively flea market each morning (7:00-14:00, best on weekends) on Place du Jeu de Balle, just off of Rue Blaes.

### A Taste of Africa in Matongé

Browse the neighborhood of Matongé (described in the Sights in Brussels chapter) for colorful fabrics and exotic ingredients at the many African grocery stores (you'll find the highest concentration along Chaussée de Wavre).

# Nightlife in Brussels

Pick up the free *Bruzz* weekly magazines from the TI, which list events including opera, symphony, and ballet. Make a point to savor the Grand Place at night, when it becomes even more magical—as day-tripping tourists are gone and the Town Hall spire is floodlit.

### Films

At one time, Brussels had a wide range of characteristic little cinemas. These days, most Bruxellois flock to the multiplexes; a handy one is the **UGC** cinema on De Brouckère square (look for *v.o.* for the original version; *v.f.* means it's dubbed in French). A small art-house cinema in the Galeries St. Hubert plays international films in their original language (generally not English), with Dutch and French subtitles.

### Music

The **Ancienne Belgique** concert hall, right by the Bourse, is a major venue for up-and-coming international pop, folk, and singer-songwriter acts (Anspachlaan 110, www.abconcerts.be).

### After-Dark Neighborhoods

Just a few steps west of the Grand Place, **Rue du Marché au Charbon** (Kolenmarkt) is the center of Brussels' gay scene, with many lively cafés and restaurants with outdoor seating. The trendy eateries, shops, and businesses along here change so fast, the locals can't keep track.

Across Boulevard Anspach is **Place St-Géry,** where you'll find a raucous collection of lively bars with rollicking interiors and a sea of outdoor tables. Mappa Mundo anchors the area, with two levels of scenic tables. Zebra Bar, across the street by the market hall, is another fun scene. And inside the market hall is the Café des Halles, with chichi cocktails in an elegantly airy, open-feeling, steel-beamed space, and DJs on the weekends.

A five-minute walk northeast is the pleasant **Ste. Catherine** district, with lively local restaurants and hotels huddled around the Church of Ste. Catherine and the old fish market. On Place Ste. Catherine, the little red wagon with the brightly painted macaw sells tropical drinks to an appreciative local crowd; in warm weather, young people sip mojitos while socializing on the square.

Farther from the center, the **Matongé** African immigrant neighborhood is lively after dark. Rue Saint-Boniface, leading up to the front door of the neighborhood church, is "café row"—with plenty of choices for an al fresco drink. The widest selection of bars and cafés clusters around Place Fernand Cocq.

# Brussels Connections

## BY TRAIN

Brussels has three train stations: Central/Centraal, Midi/Zuid, and Nord/Noord. Most trains stop at all three stations, but high-speed international trains serve only the Midi station. Any train ticket to any Brussels station includes a transfer to any other Brussels train station (but not the airport). For more details on the three stations—and tips on connecting between them—see page 113. For schedules, see www.belgianrail.be or www.bahn.com. For general information on rail travel in Belgium, see the "Transportation" section of the Practicalities chapter.

### Within Belgium and the Netherlands

**From All Brussels Stations by Train to: Bruges** (3/hour, 1 hour, catch InterCity train—direction: Ostend or Knokke-Blankenberge), **Antwerp** (3/hour, 40-50 minutes), **Ghent** (3/hour, 35 minutes), **Ypres/Ieper** (hourly, 2 hours, change in Gent St. Pieters). The following destinations are in the Netherlands: **Haarlem** (hourly, 3 hours, change in The Hague), **Delft** (almost hourly, 2.5 hours, change in Rotterdam), **The Hague** (almost hourly, 2.5 hours).

**Getting Between Brussels and Amsterdam:** Slower, regional trains leave about hourly for Amsterdam and Amsterdam's Schiphol Airport from all three Brussels stations (3 hours to Schiphol, 3.5 hours to Amsterdam's Centraal station). For a faster (but more expensive) connection, the high-speed Thalys train goes direct from Brussels' Midi station to Amsterdam's Centraal station and Schiphol Airport (about hourly, 2 hours).

### Outside Belgium and the Netherlands

The following special, high-speed train lines depart only from Midi station, tracks 1-6. Rail-pass holders must book a seat reservation for Thalys and TGV trains. For schedules, see www.bahn.com or www.b-europe.com (the Belgian rail website for cross-border trains).

**From Brussels by Thalys Train to: Paris** (almost hourly, 1.5 hours), **Cologne** (8/day, 2 hours). Thalys also operates the slower

**BRUSSELS SLEEPING, EATING & MORE**

# Greater Brussels

OUTER RING FREEWAY

To Antwerp & Amsterdam

A-12  R-0  A-1

BRUSSELS AIRPORT

HEYSEL

ATOMIUM ■

Canal

DIEGEM

N-22

To Ghent & Bruges

A-10

Charleroi

KOEKELBERG BASILICA

SCHAERBEEK

A-3

To Liège & Cologne

KOEKELBERG

R-0

NORD STATION

See detail maps

ANDERLECHT

*Grand Place* ■

CENTRAL STATION

Cinquantenaire Park

MIDI STATION

EUROPEAN PARLIAMENT

"LITTLE BELT"

MATONGE

ST. GILLES

N-5

To Ghent & Bruges

To Royal Museum for Central Africa

A-7

To Namur

N-275

CHAUSSÉE D'ALSEMBERG

N-5  R-0

E-19

Note: Shaded area indicates Central Brussels within the "Little Belt"

Waterloo ●

N-253

CHAUSSÉE DE TUBIZE

N

3 Kilometers

Braine-l'Alleud ●

MEMORIAL 1815 ■

N-5

2 Miles

N-2

HOUGOUMONT FARM ■

N-271

To Charleroi & Paris

R-0

but cheaper IZY train on this route (2-3/day, 2.5 hours, rail passes not accepted, www.izy.com). Train info: Toll tel. 07-066-7788, www.thalys.com.

**By TGV Train to France:** French TGV trains connect to **Paris' Charles de Gaulle Airport** (8/day, 1.5 hours, www.tgv-europe.com) and then continue to various destinations in France; to reach downtown Paris you must transfer at the airport.

**By ICE Train to Germany:** Germany's InterCity Express trains zip to **Cologne** (3/day, 2 hours) and **Frankfurt** (3/day, 3 hours), with onward connections to the rest of the country. Reservations are not required except for advance-ticket discounts (besides Midi, these trains make a quick stop at Brussels' Nord station).

**By Eurostar to/from London:** Brussels and London are about 3 hours apart by Eurostar train (10/day). Trains to London leave

**Thalys and Eurostar**

from tracks 1 and 2 at Brussels' Midi station. Arrive early to go through security and passport control (must be completed at least 30 minutes before departure).

Fares are covered by a Eurail Global Pass, or a Eurail Three-Country or Four-Country Select Pass that includes Belgium. Single ticket prices vary depending on how far ahead you reserve (up to 9 months out) and whether you're eligible for other discounts (children, youths, and round-trip travelers all qualify). Typically a **one-way, full-fare ticket** runs about $280 (Standard), $350 (Standard Premier), and $400 (Business Premier—no discounts for this service level). Tickets for Standard and Standard Premier classes are nonrefundable (but can be exchanged one time before departure, with restrictions and fees). Cheaper **advance rates** can sell out quickly. Buy tickets ahead at www.ricksteves.com/rail or at www.eurostar.com (Belgian tel. 02-528-2828).

**Discounts on Connecting Trains:** A Thalys ticket between Brussels and Paris or a Eurostar ticket between Brussels and London can also cover a regional train connection to/from any Belgian station for a few dollars more, if you choose the "ABS option" (or specify your end point) at the time of purchase. Show your ticket when boarding the connecting train(s) within 24 hours of the reserved Brussels arrival or departure (as long as the connecting train is not a Thalys).

**BRUSSELS SLEEPING, EATING & MORE**

## BY BUS

You can save money—but not time—by traveling by Eurolines bus to Paris or London or Flixbus to Paris (Eurolines—tel. 02-274-1350, www.eurolines.eu; Flixbus—UK tel. 44-178-829-8784, www.flixbus.com).

**From Brussels by Bus to: Paris** (around €20-35 one-way, 11/day, 4 hours), **London** (around €30 one-way, 2/day, 9 hours).

## BY PLANE
## Brussels Airport (a.k.a. Zaventem)

Brussels' main airport is nine miles north of downtown. Terminals A and B are connected by an underground walkway; the train station is in the basement at level -1 (airport code: BRU, tel. 0900-70000, www.brusselsairport.be).

Brussels Airport has strengthened security measures, especially for those arriving by private car or taxi. Plan to arrive three hours before your flight.

The clear winner for getting to and from the airport is the **train** that runs between the airport and all three Brussels train stations (€9, 4/hour, 25 minutes, daily 6:00-23:00). If you're connecting the airport with Bruges, take this shuttle train and transfer at Brussels' Nord station (about 1.5 hours total). For a **taxi,** figure on spending around €45 between downtown Brussels and the airport.

Thrifty Brussels Airlines flies between Brussels and several European cities, including Athens, London, Milan, Florence, Zürich, Nice, Lisbon, Barcelona, Madrid, and more (Belgian tel. 07-035-1111, www.brusselsairlines.com).

## Brussels South Charleroi Airport

Discount airlines Ryanair (www.ryanair.com) and Wizz Air (www.wizzair.com) use this smaller airport, located about 30 miles from downtown Brussels in the town of Gosselies, on the outskirts of the city of Charleroi (airport code: CRL, tel. 09-020-2490, www.brussels-charleroi-airport.com).

The easiest way to connect to downtown Brussels is to take the **shuttle bus** to Brussels' Midi station (€14-17, 2/hour, about 1 hour, runs 4:00-22:30; stops right in front of airport terminal; if you're taking the bus from Brussels' Midi station, look for it at the corner of Rue de France and Rue de l'Instruction—the bus stop is not clearly marked, www.brussels-city-shuttle.com). You can also take a **bus-plus-train** connection: Bus #A connects Charleroi Airport and Charleroi station (2/hour, 20 minutes), where you can take the train into Brussels (2/hour, 40 minutes). A **taxi** from the airport into the city center is costly (figure around €90 and 45-90 minutes travel time), but from Brussels to Charleroi you can catch a cheap taxi from Midi station—taxis compete with the airport shuttle and are willing to go as low as €12/person if you're willing to share.

## BY CRUISE SHIP

The cruise port of Zeebrugge—near Bruges—is often billed by cruise lines as "Brussels." While Bruges is the easier choice for an excursion from that port, Brussels is also doable. For more on Zeebrugge, see page 95.

# ANTWERP

# ORIENTATION TO ANTWERP

*Antwerpen • Anvers*

Antwerp (Antwerpen in Dutch, Anvers in French) is Belgium's up-and-coming "second city" after Brussels, with a half-million people. Where Brussels dominates French-speaking Wallonia, Antwerp is the biggest city and de facto (if not official) capital of Dutch-speaking Flanders.

Antwerp has enjoyed an illustrious history. Once Europe's most important trading city, it later was the hometown of accomplished painter Peter Paul Rubens. It was partially destroyed during World War II and then rebuilt. The drab air of heavy industry has been supplanted by an edgy, creative spirit. Like Barcelona, Liverpool, and Rotterdam, it's been reborn as a city of tech and European fashion.

Antwerpenaars (as locals are called) have a love of life, and the city has a funky urbanity. Antwerp's big-city bustle is the yang to Bruges' cutesy-village yin. And while Brussels has become international, Antwerp has retained more of a local identity—it's an honest, what-you-see-is-what-you-get place that feels more Flemish.

The sights here are easily on par with the best in Belgium. Antwerp is renowned for the art of Rubens (and fellow Flemish artists Anthony van Dyck and Pieter Bruegel), a soaring cathedral, several other interesting churches packed with great art, and a red light district that boxes puritan ears. Historians enjoy the Museum Plantin-Moretus, art lovers savor the Snijders-Rockox House, fashionistas love the window shopping, children of immigrants are moved by the Red Star Line Museum, bling junkies adore the DIVA diamond museum, and architecture fans drool over the building housing the Museum aan de Stroom (Museum on the River, or MAS for short). And yet, Antwerp is equally enjoyable without a sightseeing agenda, offering fun-to-explore neighborhoods, abundant al fresco café tables, and an inviting main market square with a carillon that jingles the hour.

## PLANNING YOUR TIME

While Antwerp could easily fill a day or two, it's worth at least a few hours. You could even see it as a day trip from Bruges or Brussels—less than 90 minutes away by train—or on the way between Brussels and Amsterdam. With a few hours, take Parts 1 and 2 of my Antwerp City Walk from the train station to the Old Town (by way of the Rubens House), tour the cathedral, ogle the Grote Markt, and pay a quick visit to other sights that intrigue you (if you're really short on time, skip straight to Part 2). Then zip back to the train station on underground trams known as the "Metro." If you have more time, Antwerp's diverse restaurant scene and lively nightlife make it well worth considering for an overnight. With a variety of quirky boutiques and cafés on each street, it's a delightful place to linger. As in most of Belgium, be aware that many Antwerp museums are closed on Mondays.

# Overview

Antwerp sits along the east bank of the Scheldt River (Schelde in Dutch). The main tourist area is fairly compact. On a quick trip, narrow your focus to these main zones: the Old Town along the river; the train station area and Diamond Quarter to the east, and the Meir shopping district between the Old Town and train station; the newly rejuvenated Little Island (Eilandje) zone and the red light district to the north; and, to the south, the Sint-Andries fashion district and, beyond that, the happening nightlife zone aptly called 't Zuid ("The South"). All these areas are within about a 30-minute walk (or a quick tram or taxi ride) of one another.

## TOURIST INFORMATION

Antwerp's TI has two branches: in the train station (at the head of the tracks, on level 0) and right on the Grote Markt (train station TI Mon-Sat 9:00-17:45, Grote Markt TI opens an hour later, both Sun until 16:45; tel. 03-232-0103, phone answered Mon-Fri only; www.visitantwerp.be). Peruse their racks of fliers and pick up a free town map.

The **Antwerp City Card** covers entry to most museums and churches (plus discounts on special exhibits), includes a public transit pass, and also covers the Citytour Shuttle hop-on, hop-off bus. It can be a good deal, even for those here for a single day. If you visit about four sights (which you easily might by taking my city walk), it could pay for itself—plus you get transportation (€27/24

# Antwerp's History

Owning a prime location where the major Scheldt River meets the North Sea, Antwerp established itself in Roman times as a river-trade town. In the late 15th century, as Bruges' harbor silted up, Antwerp became a major trading center and the Low Countries' top city. As the Age of Exploration dawned, Portuguese and Spanish ships returning from the New World laden with exotic goods docked here in Antwerp, making it a center of world trade. During Antwerp's 16th-century Golden Age, it became Europe's wealthiest city, with a population of about 100,000.

In the mid-16th century, Antwerp was pulled into the Eighty Years' War between the Dutch rebel Protestants and the ruling Spanish Catholics. In 1576, after growing impatience at not being paid by Habsburg King Philip II, Spanish troops relentlessly sacked Antwerp for three days—massacring thousands of its residents and destroying hundreds of homes. The outraged public response to this so-called "Spanish Fury" elevated Antwerp to the capital of the Dutch Revolt. (The event also irrevocably damaged Antwerp's trade ties with partners who wanted no business with a war zone.) But the crushing, Spanish-led Siege of Antwerp (July 1584 through August 1585) wore down the independence movement, and the city fell under Spanish/Catholic control. In a postwar "brain drain," more than half of the city's population fled to Amsterdam... and took the Golden Age with them.

Seeking to rehabilitate its image in the aftermath of the bloody warfare, the Catholic Church invested mightily in building and decorating churches in Antwerp. A local artist named Peter Paul Rubens (1577-1640)—while arguably less talented than some of his contemporaries—found himself in the right place at the right time, and was a brilliant salesman who allied himself with the Church to win big commission after big commission. Rubens' style epitomized exactly what the Church was looking for: bold, bombastic images trumpeting the glory of God (and his Church on earth).

The treaty that ended the Eighty Years' War in 1648 imposed rigid regulations on shipping on the Scheldt River, restricting Antwerp's outlet to the North Sea. The city devolved from an international port to a regional one. Antwerp's industry, led by an elite group of pro-Catholic traders, began to specialize in luxury goods—cabinets, paintings, tapestries, and so on. The city would languish as a Catholic backwater and second-rate shipping city for centuries, although its industry was kept alive by Napoleon, then by Belgian independence, and later by Belgium's colonization of the Congo. By the 20th century, Antwerp ranked as Europe's second-busiest port (just after Dutch rival Rotterdam). Damaged in both world wars, Antwerp has recently begun to enjoy a new gentrification that's making it one of Europe's most exciting young cities.

hours, €35/48 hours, sold only at TI, clock starts running when you visit your first sight or hop on your first bus, tram, or Metro).

## ARRIVAL IN ANTWERP

**By Train:** Antwerp's Central Station (Antwerpen Centraal)—with a grand century-old shell recently refurbished and expanded with a modern underground zone—is one of Europe's most impressive. It's easy to navigate, with three well-signed levels of tracks connected by escalators and elevators.

Level 0 is the hub of activity, where you'll find a large TI and pay luggage lockers tucked under the stairs (exact change only, swipe the printout when you're ready to open the locker, lockers occasionally all in use). As you exit to the street, you pass through the great hall—a gorgeously restored temple of travel—with the ticket windows. Exiting out the front door puts you in the vast and somewhat seedy Koningin Astridplein, with the city's zoo on your immediate right.

To get to the Old Town and most sights, you can **walk** (about 20 minutes to Grote Markt—see my Antwerp City Walk) or ride the **Metro** (actually an underground tram line). From next to the TI, take the escalator marked *Metro* down to the tracks (the train station's Metro stop is named Diamant). Under Antwerp's quirky system, you buy your ticket from the machines on the platform—they accept coins and bills. Take tram #9 or #15 in direction: Linkeroever. Be sure to validate your ticket in the yellow machine when you board. Get off at the Groenplaats stop for the Grote Markt and the historical center.

## HELPFUL HINTS

**Sightseeing Strategies:** Most sights are closed on Mondays, and many sights are free the last Wednesday of the month. Busy sightseers can save money with the Antwerp City Card (described earlier).

**Markets:** At the charming Vrijdagmarkt—"Friday Market"—antiques and other secondhand items are auctioned off in Dutch. The Saturday "Exotic Market" (8:00-16:00 at Oudevaartplaats) features Mediterranean and North African food, clothing, and souvenirs.

**Bookstore: Alta Via,** the town's main travel bookstore, is located a short distance from the center, close to MAS (Mon-Wed and Fri-Sat 10:00-17:30, Thu 10:00-13:00 and 14:00-19:30, closed Sun; Nassaustraat 29, tel. 03-293-8733).

**Laundry:** The most central launderette is **Wassalon Oase** (cash only, 7:00-21:00 at Oever 6, mobile 0477-693-434).

**City Views:** Museum aan de Stroom (MAS) has a free rooftop panorama with sprawling views of the city. A less impressive view of the harbor is available from the panorama tower of the Red Star Line Museum.

## GETTING AROUND ANTWERP

**By Public Transportation:** Sprawling Antwerp is walkable, but using the city's public transit network saves time and sweat. For visitors, the main downtown corridor, where underground tram (Metro) lines #9 and #15 connect, matters the most. You'll most likely use these four stops: Diamant (train station; so named for the surrounding Diamond Quarter), Opera (at east end of Meir shopping street; may be closed due to construction), Meir (at west end of Meir shopping street; Rubens House), and Groenplaats (with a handy underground grocery store; near the cathedral and Grote Markt). Other tram lines can be confusing, as lines going in a similar direction can be marked by different end stations: If you're heading from the train station to the Old Town, look for *Linkeroever;* in the opposite direction, from the Old Town to the train station, look for *Eksterlaar/Boechout.*

A **single ticket** costs €3 and is good for an hour (including a transfer). If you are riding the Metro, it's easy to buy tickets at machines on the platform (select the "Zone 1-2" ticket). On trams and buses pay on board (exact change only). If you're going to Bruges and/or Ghent and plan to use public transportation there as well, consider the shareable **10-ride ticket** for €16. You can use it in all three cities (and anywhere else in Flanders). Other options are a **day pass** (€6) and a **three-day pass** (€12). Validate your ticket when you board—day passes need validation only once. Smart travelers buy their return ticket at the same time to avoid later hassles. Information: Toll tel. 070-220-200, www.delijn.be.

**By Hop-On, Hop-Off Bus:** A simpler alternative on a short visit could be the hop-on, hop-off buses. **Citytour Shuttle** uses an old-fashioned trolley bus to make a loop connecting several harder-to-reach destinations; the 50-minute route includes the train station, the Grote Markt, the MAS museum, and the Red Star Line Museum (€12.50 for all-day ticket; runs April-Oct, generally starting at 12:00 and ending around 16:00; mobile 0479-113-974, www.touristram.be). **Cabrio Sightseeing** runs a similar route but offers a two-day pass for €13 (mobile 0470-999-352, www.antwerp-citytourbus.be).

# Tours in Antwerp

## Walking Tours
The **TI** organizes a two-hour historical walking tour through town combining English and French (€10—or €8 if you book at least a day in advance, July-Aug daily at 14:00, Sept-June Sat-Sun only, departs from TI on Grote Markt).

## Local Guide
The TI can arrange a private guide for an affordable city tour (€75/2 hours, tel. 03-232-0103, info@visitantwerpen.be). One of their excellent guides, **Ariane van Duytekom,** tells Antwerp's story well, with a knack for psychoanalyzing its complicated history. Erwin Liekens and his team from **Taste the City** lead tours in Antwerp as well as Brussels (€180/3 hours, €350/day, mobile 0495-625-215, info@tastethecity.be, www.tastethecity.be).

# SIGHTS IN ANTWERP

Antwerp offers visitors an eclectic array of sightseeing. If you have just one day (or less), you'll need to be selective: art, churches, history, fashion, and so on. Most of these sights are stops on the city walk described in the next chapter. And every sight is either in the old center or within walking distance.

## IN THE OLD TOWN

### ▲▲Rubens House (Rubenshuis)

Here's Europe's best look at the artist Peter Paul Rubens. By touring the house he lived and worked in, you get a sense of both the man and his art. The house is much remodeled and is more a replica than the real thing. There are better places in Antwerp to see old houses (such as the Snijders-Rockox House and Museum Plantin-Moretus). And there are better places to see Rubens' paintings (like Antwerp's cathedral). Still, this is an excellent exhibit that shows how Rubens lived and worked.

**Cost and Hours:** €8, Tue-Sun 10:00-17:00, closed Mon, Wapper 9, tel. 03-201-1555, www.rubenshuis.be.

📖 See the Rubens House Tour chapter.

### ▲▲Cathedral of Our Lady
### (Onze-Lieve-Vrouwekathedraal)

Antwerp's biggest church has a spire that shoots like a Gothic rocket 400 feet up from the middle of the Old Town. Its cavernous interior is packed with fine artwork, including several major paintings by Rubens. While the Museum of Fine Arts is closed for renovation (at least until 2019), you'll see these fine original canvases in the setting for which they were intended here in the cathedral.

**Cost and Hours:** €6, cash only, Mon-Fri 10:00-17:00, Sat

# Antwerp at a Glance

**▲▲Rubens House** The richly decorated home, studio, and garden of Peter Paul Rubens, with a few of his paintings to boot. **Hours:** Tue-Sun 10:00-17:00, closed Mon. See page 220.

**▲▲Cathedral of Our Lady** Cavernous church packed with fine artwork, including paintings by Rubens. **Hours:** Mon-Fri 10:00-17:00, Sat until 15:00, Sun 13:00-16:00. See page 220.

**▲▲Museum Plantin-Moretus** Early printing presses, workshops, and memorabilia from Antwerp's Golden Age. **Hours:** Tue-Sun 10:00-17:00, closed Mon. See page 227.

**▲Red Star Line Museum** Illustrates the "other end" of the Ellis Island experience, where emigrants were processed on their way to the New World. **Hours:** Tue-Sun 10:00-17:00, Easter-Oct Sat-Sun until 18:00, closed Mon. See page 231.

**▲Snijders-Rockox House Museum** Aristocratic 17th-century home with impressive art, furniture, and delightful garden courtyard. **Hours:** Tue-Sun 10:00-17:00, closed Mon. See page 226.

**▲Museum aan de Stroom (MAS)** Displays focusing on Antwerp's and Belgium's history of trade and cultural exchange—plus a rooftop viewpoint. **Hours:** Exhibits open Tue-Sun 10:00-17:00, closed Mon; building open Tue-Sun 9:30-24:00, off-season until 22:30, closed Mon. See page 230.

until 15:00, Sun 13:00-16:00, Handschoenmarkt, tel. 03-213-9951, www.dekathedraal.be.

**Tours:** Free English tours are offered most days when guides are available—ask. Some English info is located near Rubens' paintings. A rack of free pamphlets focuses on the church's three-paneled paintings that hang in their original positions, creating a private little garden of worship space at the base of each column.

**Visiting the Church:** Stepping inside, notice how remarkably wide the cathedral is (250 feet), with three aisles on either side of the nave. Looking up, you'll see that the Gothic design is also dramatically vertical—everything stretches upward (90 feet) toward heaven. The stained-glass windows (some

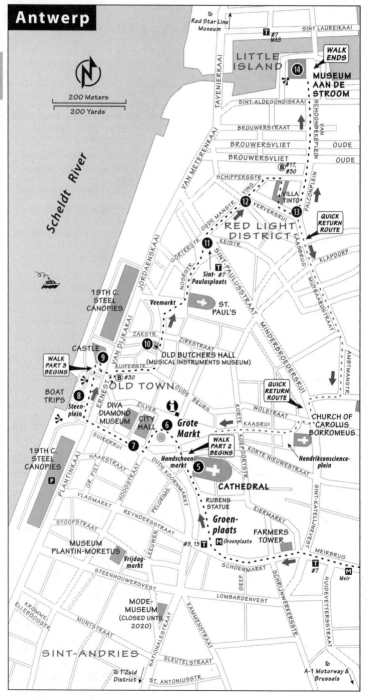

# Antwerp

200 Meters
200 Yards

Scheldt River

To
Red Star Line
Museum

SINT LAUREIKAAI

**T** #7
MAS

LITTLE
ISLAND

⑭

**WALK
ENDS**

**MUSEUM
AAN DE
STROOM**

SINT-ALDEGONDISKAAI

BROUWERSTRAAT

BROUWERSVLIET

BROUWERSVLIET

**B** #17,
#30

OUDE

OUDE

SCHIPPERSSTR.

VILLA
TINTO

**QUICK
RETURN
ROUTE**

⑫

⑬

VERVERSRUI

VING.

KEISTR.

**RED LIGHT
DISTRICT**

KLAPDORP

⑪

Sint-
Paulusplaats

**T** #7

Sint-PAULUSSTRAAT

GORTERSTR.

OUDE MANSTR.

NOSESTR.

JORDAENSKAAI

VAN METERENKAAI

TAVERNIEKKAAI

SCHOONBEKEPLEIN

VAN

FALCONRUI

RASBRUG

MUTSAARDSTRAAT

MINDERBROEDERSRUI

AMBTMANSTR.

**19TH C.
STEEL
CANOPIES**

Veemarkt

ST.
PAUL'S

⑩

ZAKSTR.

ZIRKSTRAAT

**OLD BUTCHERS HALL**
(MUSICAL INSTRUMENTS MUSEUM)

**QUICK
RETURN
ROUTE**

**CASTLE**

**WALK
PART 3
BEGINS**

⑨

VAN DIJKKAAI

KUIPERSTR.

**B** #30

**OLD TOWN**

OUDE BEURS

WOLSTRAAT

**CHURCH OF
CAROLUS
BORROMEUS**

**BOAT
TRIPS**

⑧

Steen-
plein

ERNEST

**DIVA
DIAMOND
MUSEUM**

ZILVER

**CITY
HALL**

ⓘ

**Grote
Markt**

⑥

KAASRUI

KORTE

KOEPOORTSTR.

Hendrikconscience-
plein

**19TH C.
STEEL
CANOPIES**

**P**

SUIKERRUI

⑦

Handschoen-
markt

⑤

**CATHEDRAL**

**WALK
PART 2
BEGINS**

KORTE NIEUWESTRAAT

SINT-KATELIJNEVEST

PLANTINKAAI

HAARSTRAAT

GR. PIET

HOOGSTR.

OUDE KOORNMARKT

RUBENS
STATUE

EIERMARKT

VLASMARKT

REYNDERSSTRAAT

PELGRIMS

LEEUWEN

**Groen-
plaats**

**FARMERS
TOWER**

MEIRBRUG

**T** #7

**M**
Meir

STOOFSTRAAT

**MUSEUM
PLANTIN-MORETUS**

Vrijdag-
markt

#9, 15 **T**

**M** Groenplaats

MEIR

SCHOENMARKT

HUIDEVETTERSSTRAAT

SCHRIJNWERKERSSTR.

STEENHOUWERSVEST

GEEF.

LOMBARDENVEST

KRONME-
ELLEBOOGSTR.

MUNTSTRAAT

**MODE-
MUSEUM**
(CLOSED UNTIL
2020)

NATIONALESTRAAT

KAMMENSTRAAT

SLEUTELSTRAAT

To
A-1 Motorway &
Brussels

**SINT-ANDRIES**

To 't Zuid
District

ST. ANTONIUSSTR.

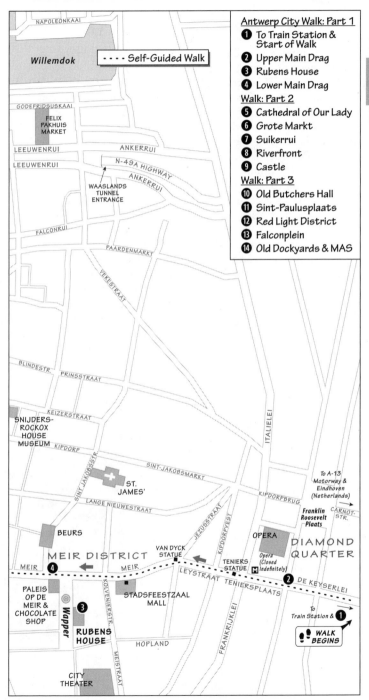

Antwerp City Walk: Part 1
1 To Train Station & Start of Walk
2 Upper Main Drag
3 Rubens House
4 Lower Main Drag

Walk: Part 2
5 Cathedral of Our Lady
6 Grote Markt
7 Suikerrui
8 Riverfront
9 Castle

Walk: Part 3
10 Old Butchers Hall
11 Sint-Paulusplaats
12 Red Light District
13 Falconplein
14 Old Dockyards & MAS

of them still original) colorized the light emanating from inside, drawing worshippers like moths to a flame. After dark, in medieval times, the interior was filled with countless candles, and this was the only place to find bright light.

The cathedral has a troubled history: It was gutted by the fire of 1533, then stripped of its medieval decoration (1566) by iconoclastic Protestants. (A few fragments of colorful murals remain on the underside of the vaults, where the iconoclasts couldn't reach.) After the Catholics came to power (1585), they redecorated the church in bubbly Baroque, including several pieces by Rubens. Napoleon's troops (late 18th century) turned the church into a stable and carried off several Rubens paintings (only returned from Paris later). Church leaders redecorated with a hodgepodge of ecclesiastical art brought here from elsewhere. Most impressive of these is the Rococo pulpit (1713), a riot of birds, foliage, and cupids symbolizing the spread of the faith and the word. All that amazing carving is supported by four figures: allegories of the four main continents, with Europe in front and Africa around back...in the dark.

Large paintings are placed around the nave. These altarpieces—now standing alone—once decorated private altars. Each local guild had its own private area, where members celebrated baptisms, weddings, and funerals—this was truly a community church. The most noteworthy of the paintings is just past the pulpit—a gruesome *Lamentation* by Quentin Matsys, who founded the Antwerp School of painters that eventually produced the genius Peter Paul Rubens.

The church's collection includes three huge Rubens paintings.

In the **Raising of the Cross** (left transept, 1610-1611), biblical bodybuilders strain to upright the cross, which is heavy with the swooning body of Christ. The painting is emotive, sumptuous, and almost sensual. Having just returned from eight years in Italy, the influence is obvious—Michelangelo's twisting poses and bulky musculature and Caravaggio's light-dark contrast. Notice how lifelike Jesus' skin appears—a Rubens forte. The bold diagonal composition, thickly muscled bodies in motion, bright (almost garish) colors, and illusion of movement are vintage Rubens. The painting is the inner panel of a hinged altarpiece; it was normally kept closed, and opened to reveal this scene only on special occasions—when its color and

motion must have been even more striking to churchgoers unaccustomed to this sort of spectacle.

**The Assumption** (choir area, over the main altar, 1626) shows the moment that Mary—the cathedral's namesake—was brought up to heaven. Beneath Mary are the 12 apostles (after the Resurrection, the faithful disciple Matthias replaced Judas) and the three women who were present at her death. The role of Mary in church doctrine was one of the major dividing lines between Catholics and Protestants; whereas the Catholic Church considered her a saint to be venerated, the Protestants embraced the notion that she was an ordinary woman called to do God's work. The gauzy heroine-worship of this canvas makes it clear who finally controlled the turf here.

Rubens' diagonal composition in **Descent from the Cross** (right transept, 1612-1614) is the mirror image of *Raising of the Cross,* the

painting across the nave. It's a freeze-frame of an action-packed moment... just as workers strained to erect the cross with Christ's limp body, now they struggle to lower him from it. But at this somber moment, everyone seems to be moving more slowly, methodically. Notice the pallor of Christ's dead skin—a strong contrast to the lifelike luster of the other painting. The details make the poignancy of this moment come to life: the man in the top-right corner who's holding on to the shroud with his teeth; Mary's outstretched arm, in a tender matronly effort to comfort her son even in death; and, in the lower-right section, a blood-filled bronze basin holding the crown of thorns and the nails. This main canvas is flanked by side panels showing people "carrying" Christ in two very different ways: on the left, a pregnant Mary, and on the right, presenting the young Jesus at the temple. You may see Japanese tourists admiring this painting, as it figured into a novel that's popular in Japan.

Explore the rest of the church. To the right of the altar, the sacristy has historic portraits of the church's 21 local bishops. Nearby, you can descend to the crypt to see foundations of earlier structures, as well as five old tombs painted with red crosses, uncovered during excavation. There's a fourth Rubens painting to the right of the altar: **Resurrection.** A radiant Christ strides vigorously out of the tomb, offering hope of revival to the deceased. Rubens painted it for some prominent Antwerpenaars buried here. Note the names on the plaque: Plantin and Moretus, of the well-known printer families. Finally, before you leave, return to the center of the church and gaze up to the painted dome of the cupola high above the center (which looks domed yet is flat) for one last image of the saint to whom the church is dedicated...Mary.

## Musical Instruments Museum at the Old Butchers Hall (Museum Vleeshuis)

This restored brick palace, home to Antwerp's butchers during the city's glory days, now houses a collection of musical instruments.

The Klank van de Stad ("Sound of the City") exhibition presents two floors of instruments and old music manuscripts (don't miss the cellar). The collection is decent and well presented. You'll stroll from medieval bagpipes, hurdy-gurdies, drums, and sackbuts, to church bells and carillons, to weird early versions of modern instruments, to some classic harpsichords, pianos, and even a "glass organ." The downstairs shows how music fit in with dance and theater. English information is limited, but a free app brings the exhibits to life. Even without a ticket, you can step into the (free) entry area for a peek at the impressive brick vaults (or to use the WC).

**Cost and Hours:** €5, Thu-Sun 10:00-17:00, closed Mon-Wed, ticket includes audioguide (mostly in Dutch), €3.50 booklet with English descriptions, Vleeshouwersstraat 38, tel. 03-292-6100, www.museumvleeshuis.be. To get here from the Grote Markt, face the City Hall and turn right up Braderijstraat, take the first left on Kuipersstraat, then look right.

## ▲Snijders-Rockox House Museum (Snijders&Rockoxhuis)

Nicolaas Rockox (1560-1640) was a mayor of Antwerp and a friend of Peter Paul Rubens. His neighbor was Frans Snijders, a painter of still lifes and also a friend of Rubens. Today their adjoining houses—buried amid a residential zone a 10-minute walk northeast of the cathedral and Grote Markt—have been transformed into a lovely museum.

Here you can get a truly authentic look at aristocratic homes from the period (unlike the Rubens House, which was rebuilt), while viewing impressive artwork, furniture, and a beautiful garden courtyard. Exhibits draw from the men's vast personal art collections and include works by Rubens, Van Dyck, and Breughel.

**Cost and Hours:** €8, Tue-Sun 10:00-17:00, closed Mon, Keizerstraat 10, tel. 03-201-9250, www.rockoxhuis.be.

**Visiting the Museum:** Unlike most museums, there are no labels at all on the paintings and no descriptions. To make your way, you can use either their free videoguide or the full-color English booklet with all the details. Hopefully, my description will give you the general lay of the land and point you to a few paintings worth seeking out.

**Room 1:** You're introduced to the world of Antwerp in the 1600s by several portraits. Rockox is shown from the ruff-collar up. Nearby, a portrait by Rubens shows two more ruff-wearers: Albert and Isabella, the rulers of the Low Countries. And a portrait of Antwerp's bishop is by Anthony Van Dyck.

**Room 2:** Appreciate Rockox's fine fireplace and beautiful art cabinets, where he kept his collection of curios. He would bring these objects out at dinner parties as conversation pieces. Van Dyck's *Study of a Man* demonstrates his skill in bringing ordinary people to life.

Pass through **Room 3,** then cross the courtyard to...

**Room 4:** Spend some time with Pieter Brueghel the Younger's fun *The Proverbs.* This is one of 20 copies he made of his father's famous work. The painting makes literal more than a hundred Flemish sayings and figures of speech. There's your basic "banging your head against a wall" (lower left). Find other well-known proverbs: "armed to the teeth" (lower left), "the die is cast" (in the window, upper left), "don't cry over spilled milk" (lower right), "the blind leading the blind" (upper right), and "casting pearls (roses) before swine" (lower middle). Others don't make literal sense but you get the drift: "He's so rich he tiles his roof with pies" (upper left) or, "He's so poor he's stretched between two bread loaves" (lower right). Many more make no literal sense at all, like the unfaithful wife (lower middle) who cuckolds her husband by "putting on the blue cloak." And, "Who knows why the geese go barefoot"?

**Room 5** has an old rifle, and **Room 6** has a small but insightful portrait by Rubens of an old woman. **Room 7** has several large-scale still lifes, including one of an impressive hanging dead deer. This is the work of Frans Snijders, whose still lifes are noted for their realistic animals. Don't overlook **Room 8** (which is back by the ticket desk) with its portrait of Snijders and his wife, done by none other than their friend Van Dyck. It's amazing to think of the interplay of personalities and ideas in 17th-century Antwerp.

Finally, go **upstairs** for a look at the music room and a collection of period instruments. Here Rockox, Snijders, Rubens, and Van Dyck might have gathered to enjoy good music and the fruits of the Golden Age.

## ▲▲Museum Plantin-Moretus

In the digital age, it's easy to forget how revolutionary printing books once was. Antwerp of the 1500s was a wide-open city, disseminating ideas from its newfangled presses. The museum is named for two influential Antwerp printers: Frenchman Christoffel Plantin, who began a printing business here in 1546; and his son-in-law Jan Moretus, who carried on the family business. (Eventually, they were the official court printer for the Spanish monarchs of the Low Countries.) If you love books, this place is worth ▲▲▲.

This building was both the family's home and their workshop. It's a remarkably well-preserved look at 16th- and 17th-century aristocratic life. It also shows several aspects of Antwerp's Golden Age. You'll see early printing presses, the printer's historic workshop and house, old books (including a Gutenberg Bible), and art and memorabilia owned by the prominent printing family. Every Flemish kid comes here on a field trip to understand their enlightened heritage.

**Cost and Hours:** €8, Tue-Sun 10:00-17:00, closed Mon, audioguide-€2, Vrijdagmarkt 22, tel. 03-221-1450, www.museumplantinmoretus.be.

**Visiting the Museum:** There's a lot to see in this meandering maze of rooms. I'd suggest following my tour to hit the highlights, then using the excellent—and humorous—audioguide for the whole story. Allow at least one hour to appreciate the place. Though the building is large and sprawling, you follow an easy, one-way route.

**Ground Floor:** This floor tries to re-create the house as it looked in the 16th and 17th centuries. Even the lighting is low to simulate a candlelit glow. In Room 2, a large and elaborately decorated hall, find Rubens' portrait of Plantin. In Room 3, find portraits from nine generations of the family—each generation represented by a book on the table.

In the courtyard, find Room 4, a reconstructed bookshop. On the wall is a list of books forbidden by the Catholic Church—the list was printed by, and includes books sold by, Christoffel Plantin. Room 6 offers a chance to look at paper similar to the type used when printing was young. Room 7 has a printing press and displays on how it worked—one man inking it up, another lowering a blank paper onto it, then rinsing and repeating every 20 seconds. If you're lucky, a volunteer will be running the press during your visit—ask if you can help. In the proofreaders' room (Room 9), you can imagine diligent editors huddled around the enormous shared oak desk, debating the 17th-century equivalent of whether "email" takes a hyphen. The publisher's private leather-bound office (Room 10) is classy and surprisingly small.

Finally you reach the actual workshop (Rooms 13-14). Here you'll see several presses, type cases, and other printer's tools. At the far end stand some of the oldest printing presses in the world (c. 1600). Neatly stacked in the entry room are some 10 tons of lead letters, with racks of complete sets of fonts and different type sizes.

**Upstairs:** Exhibits here represent the impact Plantin's books had on the world, organized around the themes of language, science, society, and religion. Look for the vertical red labels by some of the books—these mark what curators feel are the top 10 books in the collection, such as the first Dutch dictionary and the world's first atlas. Room 31 displays a (possible) Bible by the founder of modern printing, Johannes Gutenberg (c. 1461). Room 32 has a highlight of the entire collection: a polyglot Bible, with five languages on one page, printed by Christoffel Plantin. It took five years to compile the text in Latin, Greek, Hebrew, Chaldean (Aramaic), and Syriac. The result is a masterpiece in eight volumes: four for the Old Testament, one for the New Testament, and three of commentary—weighing a total of 106 pounds.

**Nearby:** The museum is on a charming square called Vrijdagmarkt, where there really is a "Friday market."

### DIVA (Diamond and Silver Museum)

The city of Antwerp closed its old-fashioned diamond museum about five years ago, and after some political haggling it's opened a new one behind the City Hall. This high-tech experience showcases both a diamond and silver collection (including examples of some exquisite and over-the-top jewelry) with demonstrations of diamond cutting and silversmithing.

**Cost and Hours:** €10—credit card only, Thu-Tue 10:00-18:00, closed Wed, Suikerrui 17, tel. 03-360-5252, www.divaantwerp.be.

## AT THE OLD DOCKYARDS, NORTH OF DOWNTOWN

The dockyards—an easy 15-minute walk north from the Grote Markt—have been boldly redeveloped and now house a pair of fine museums: the Museum aan de Stroom (MAS) and the Red Star Line Museum. For the most interesting approach here, through Antwerp's red light district, see Part 3 of my Antwerp City Walk (next chapter). Otherwise, from the train station, take Metro lines #3, #5, #9, or #15 (direction: Linkeroever) to the Meir stop. Go above ground there and take tram #7 (direction: Eilandje); get off at MAS, which is the final stop. If you're short on time, the Red Star Line Museum is more worthwhile than the Museum aan de Stroom.

### ▲Museum aan de Stroom (MAS)

The Museum aan de Stroom (Museum on the River)—housed in a strikingly modern building—hosts an eclectic collection that's fitting for this global-crossroads city. In addition to exhibits on Antwerp, you'll also see pre-Columbian stone heads (world-class, but probably not what you came to Antwerp to see), African masks, Polynesian fertility statues, weapons, and an array of temporary exhibits. In this city of excellent museums, this collection is nothing special, but the building itself and its roof terrace—which are free to enter—make it worth the trip.

**Cost and Hours:** Building free to enter and explore, Tue-Sun 9:30-24:00, off-season until 22:30, closed Mon; €10 for entry to permanent collection and any temporary exhibits, €15 combo-ticket with Red Star Line Museum; open Tue-Sun 10:00-17:00, closed Mon; informative English booklets in most rooms; top-floor top-class restaurant (by reservation only), 15-minute walk north of Groenplaats at Hanzestedenplaats 1, tel. 03-338-4400, www.mas.be.

**Visiting the Museum:** In the lobby, buy your ticket (if you want to enter the exhibits) and pick up information brochures, then ride the escalators up, up, up through 10 levels. The escalators and hallways often feature free exhibits such as poems celebrating Antwerp or photographs of the city's people and history.

The museum's **permanent exhibits** are on floors 5-8. Two floors are dedicated to Antwerp (floors 5 and 6). In "Food in Antwerp" (floor 5), you learn the story of food in this busy port town. "World Port" (floor 6) displays models of the many kinds of ships that docked here and traces the evolution of the port through videos and photos. From there, the museum goes global. "Life or Death" (floor 7) considers how world cultures wrestle with these big  questions—from Egyptian mummies to a roomful of Buddhas to Catholic symbols. And finally, floor 8 is an excuse to show off the museum's exquisite collection of pre-Columbian artifacts.

Finish your visit by ascending to the **rooftop panorama.** Find the soaring spire of the Cathedral of Our Lady. To the left of that is the unmistakable Farmers Tower skyscraper (see page 238). To the right of the cathedral is the Scheldt River. And around you is the harbor—the huge cranes, barges, container ships, tugs, and vast warehouses. It stretches into the distance and is one of the busiest ports in the world.

**Nearby:** The low-lying, long building just in front of the MAS houses a small, free exhibit on the **Port of Antwerp,** where you can walk across a blown-up aerial view of the sprawling port area for a sense of its astonishing scale (Tue-Sun 9:30-17:30, closed Mon).

### ▲Red Star Line Museum

Is there anything more poignant than a person willing to sacrifice everything in pursuit of a better life? That's the story of hardscrabble

Europeans heading off to dreamed-of opportunities in far-off America. This cutting-edge museum tells the story of the Red Star shipping line that brought European emigrants to the Americas from 1873 to 1935. The route passed through the port of Ant-
werp, and many emigrants were processed in the very hall where the exhibits now stand. The museum combines personal stories with high-tech presentation to detail the "other end" of the Ellis Island experience. This sight is rated ▲▲ for North Americans descended from immigrants (read: almost all of us), and is worth the 10- to 15-minute walk beyond the MAS.

**Cost and Hours:** €8, €15 combo-ticket with MAS; Tue-Sun 10:00-17:00, Easter-Oct Sat-Sun until 18:00, closed Mon, café, Montevideostraat 3, tel. 03-298-2770, www.redstarline.be.

**Getting There:** From the MAS, cross the drawbridge and head up Nassaustraat, past the two-tone green skyscrapers. Just after those buildings, turn left down Montevideostraat. This part of Antwerp's docklands is still being redeveloped, so it's not easily accessible by public transportation.

**Background:** In the late 19th century, Europe was changing. The Industrial Revolution, the end of traditional peasant lifestyles, and a tremendous population boom led to political instability and difficult lives. Across the Atlantic, the United States and Canada symbolized a hope for a better life. And during the great migration between 1873 and 1935, the Red Star shipping line brought some two million emigrants from Antwerp to New York City. This was the point of exit not only for Belgians but also for people from all over Europe—especially Germany and Eastern Europe—who rode in rickety trains all the way across the Continent to get here. (By the 1930s, many of the emigrants were Jews fleeing the Nazi regime in Germany.) The 10-day steamer journey transported cargo, luxury travelers, and "steerage-class" peasants alike. In these red-brick warehouses, emigrants underwent humiliating health exams and nervously waited while clerks processed their paperwork. (Because arriving passengers who were ill were immediately deported at the shipping line's expense, screening procedures were stringent.)

**Visiting the Museum:** The displays have good English information, there's a free info booklet, and you can log on to the free Wi-Fi to view more on your smartphone (www.rslm.be). Your visit is a one-way route: ground floor, upstairs, and then the elevator to the view terrace.

First up is a powerful exhibit—using wraparound video screens—that drives home the point that immigration is as common today as it was in the heyday of Ellis Island. Displays profile different kinds of immigrants through history—from the first humans who left Africa in 40,000 BC to Ellis Island to the migrant workers of today.

Next, you follow in the footsteps of individuals who passed through this very building to board ships for the prospect of a new start in the New World. A 10-minute video introduces you to some of the Red Star Line's passengers, and touchscreens let you zoom in on stories in the emigrants' own words. You'll see the (deceptively) glossy brochures that the shipping lines used to lure customers. There's a map of Europe demonstrating how far many immigrants had to travel by train even before stepping on the ship. And there are period photos of Antwerp—the last European city many of these soon-to-be-former-Europeans would ever see.

The next section details the invasive processing procedures for passengers before they were allowed on board: They were stripped of their baggage and clothes—which were disinfected—then forced to shower and be inspected for lice and disease.

Upstairs, you'll learn about the actual voyage. With steam power replacing sails, the trip to America went from 40 days down to 10. You'll see models of various Red Star Line ships through the years. Some were floating cities of 2,500 passengers. You'll also see the harsh contrast between life in first class and the miserable world in steerage.

The museum culminates with the stirring moment when immigrants first saw the Statue of Liberty. The final room emphasizes that Antwerp today is a city not of emigrants but of immigrants—people from other countries flocking here to pursue their dreams.

Before leaving, you can ride the elevator (and avoid the seemingly endless stairs) up to the **panorama tower** for a glimpse at the last view many Europeans enjoyed of their home continent before leaving forever.

# ANTWERP CITY WALK

With this single walk, you can say you've "seen" Antwerp, as it laces together many of the city's main sights. It's ideal for day-trippers who want to see it all in a few hours' blitz from the train station.

Another option is to slice and dice Antwerp into savory bites, which you can enjoy at your leisure, and in any order: Part 1 of the walk is an easy stroll from the train station down a modern, pedestrian-friendly shopping street to the heart of town. Part 2 covers the historic core—the towering cathedral, the Grote Markt, and the riverfront where the city was born. Part 3 takes you where fewer tourists go—through a residential neighborhood, the red light district, and to the modern dockyards.

Along the way, you'll see the city's historic architecture, youthful citizens, trendy restaurants, and a high-tech brothel. You can also take this opportunity to stop in and tour several sights, including the Rubens House, the cathedral, or the Museum aan de Stroom (MAS). The walk ends with a view back over the towers, steeples, cranes, and skyscrapers of this teeming city.

## Orientation

**Length of This Walk:** The whole walk covers two miles. Allow at least 30 minutes for each of the three segments, plus another 20-30 minutes for getting back. Budget still more time if you go inside any sights along the way. With limited time, focus on Part 2.

**Rubens House:** €8, Tue-Sun 10:00-17:00, closed Mon.

**Cathedral of Our Lady:** €6, cash only, Mon-Fri 10:00-17:00, Sat until 15:00, Sun 13:00-16:00.

**Musical Instruments Museum at the Old Butchers Hall:** €5, Thu-Sun 10:00-17:00, closed Mon-Wed.

**Museum aan de Stroom (MAS):** Building free to enter, Tue-Sun 9:30-24:00, off-season until 22:30, closed Mon; €10 for entry to permanent collection and temporary exhibits, Tue-Sun 10:00-17:00, closed Mon.

# The Walk Begins

This L-shaped walk starts at the train station, turns right at the Old Town, and ends at the harbor to the north. For a map of the route, see page 222. If you're short on time, skip to Part 2 by riding the Metro directly from the train station to the Old Town (see page 217). You could also skip Part 3 (with the in-your-face red light district) and visit the MAS separately.

## PART 1: FROM THE TRAIN STATION TO THE OLD TOWN

### ❶ Antwerp's Train Station

• *Start on level +1—the highest level of tracks (under the 19th-century steel and glass arch). They dead-end under the ornate old-timey clock.*

The city's central train station is not merely a convenient transportation hub, it's a work of art and a loud-and-clear comment on a

confident new age. Built around the turn of the 20th century, it's an eclectic mix of historical art styles: Industrial Age meets Art Nouveau, giddy with steel and glass.

Look down through the center of the station to see the various levels of train tracks. The original station was all on one level—you'd walk from your wheezing steam train directly to the place you're standing now. But dead-end stations are just too slow for today's express trains, so they've excavated these several layers of tracks. Today's fastest trains, on the lowest level, pass straight through a tunnel beneath the station—connecting Antwerp with Amsterdam or Paris in just an hour or two.

Look up at the vintage clock in the center of the hall. Set into a facade of gray marble and gold trim, towering high above the tracks, this is a temple of time. Timekeeping was crucial in the age of train schedules. Belgium was a busy new colonial power, speeding into the modern age fueled by ivory and rubber from its colony in the Congo. The station is the work of the "builder king" Leopold II. You'll see his *L* monogram everywhere.

The Royal Café, to the left of the big clock, is first-class, yet

## Antwerp's Diamond Quarter

The area around the train station is known as the Diamond Quarter—one of the world's top centers for commerce in these gems. Although the industry is highly secretive, experts guess that four out of every five of the world's rough diamonds pass through Antwerp at some point. The diamond industry is located in the train-station neighborhood for good reason: If you're carrying millions of dollars' worth of precious jewels in your briefcase through a strange city, you don't want to have to venture too far to reach a trader or diamond cutter.

Beginning in the 16th century, the diamond industry in Antwerp was dominated by Sephardic Jews from Spain, but under Catholic rule, they fled to Amsterdam. Then, in the late 19th century, Hasidic Orthodox Jews fleeing the pogroms in Russia settled here and took up the industry. In the streets around the train station, you'll likely see men wearing tall hats and black coats, with long beards and curly locks at their temples, and women with long dresses and hair covers. More recently, the diamond trade here has been increasingly dominated by Indians.

The history of the diamond trade focuses on Africa, where diamond seekers dug the world's biggest man-made hole, the Kimberley Crater in South Africa. In some parts of Africa, the exploitative conditions for finding these gems haven't improved much since the early days of Belgian colonialism. A strict diamond-certification process, introduced in Antwerp in 2000, attempts to block the sale of so-called "blood diamonds"—stones sold by rebels fighting governments in war zones in central and western Africa.

economical and elegant...a fine place for a quiet cup of coffee or light bite.

• *Let's start walking. Pass underneath the big clock, into the main lobby with even more grandiose architecture. Antwerpen Centraal may be the best-decorated train station in Europe.*

*Exit the station: Facing the train ticket office, turn left, exiting under the sign that reads* Keyserlei/Meir/Centrum. *Once in the open air, you can see our route. From here, we'll walk basically straight ahead on the Keyserlei pedestrian mall, past the ugly gold skyscraper, all the way to the Old Town. Your destination is in the distance—the lacy spire of the cathedral.*

## ❷ Upper Main Drag: Train Station to Rubens House

Stroll three blocks gradually downhill on the bustling, sand-colored boulevard called **De Keyserlei,** lined with chain restaurants and shops. Following European trends, this boulevard is becoming a bike-and-pedestrian zone.

You'll pass by a few diamond and jewelry stores. This area is known as the **Diamond Quarter**—one of the world's top centers where diamonds are sold wholesale and cleaved into smaller pieces to prepare them for cutting. While you could explore more of the "Diamond Square Mile" (stretching to the left, in the old Jewish Quarter), it's mostly just more diamond shops and

extremely casual-looking people with briefcases handcuffed to their wrists.

De Keyserlei leads to a noble bronze **statue of David Teniers,** one of several big Antwerp painters. He stands near a lofty, ugly 1960s-era skyscraper, amid a commotion of construction activity. The city is sending traffic underground, creating a people-friendly square, and giving the once-glorious opera house (to the right) the prominence it deserves.

Continue past the Teniers statue, cross the Frankrijklei boulevard (marking the former town wall), and stroll between **towering twin facades,** built in the late-19th-century style called Historicism. This style cobbled together all the best, most bombastic bits and pieces from past styles to wow the viewer.

Passing the **statue of Anthony van Dyck** (1599-1641)—another talented Antwerp artist who worked with Rubens and whose

works appear in many local museums—you reach the pleasant pedestrian shopping street (and neighborhood) called **the Meir** (pronounced "mare"). This showcase shopping zone was built, like the train station, in the boom times around 1900. Ahead on the left is the grand **Stadsfeestzaal shopping mall**

(with the gold niche over the door). Venture inside for a glimpse at its astonishing interior.

The Meir is great for people-watching. Antwerp is diverse, including lots of Muslim citizens (the trendiest of whom are nicknamed "Mipsters"). Along with the biggest Jain temple outside India and a sizable Buddhist community, about 40 mosques call Antwerp home.

One block later, look left down Wapper Square, featuring (a block down) one of the city's top sights, the ❸ **Rubens House.** This former home of Peter Paul Rubens introduces visitors to the artist's work and lifestyle. ☐ See the Rubens House Tour chapter.

## ❹ Lower Main Drag: Rubens House to Cathedral

Just past Wapper Square is an ornate gray building on the left—the **Paleis op de Meir.** This gorgeous Rococo palace, built in 1745, was later purchased by Napoleon, who decorated it in Empire Style. With Belgium's independence in 1830, this became one of the official residences of the king of the Belgians.

But what really matters is chocolate. At the Paleis entrance, step into the **Chocolate Line** shop. Notice the *grisailles*—the monochrome paintings that look like 3-D carved reliefs but are actually flat paintings. Here, you can see the creative work of the crazy "shock-o-latier" Dominique Persoone (€4 for your choice of three wacky flavors, daily until 18:30).

Pass the Meir Metro stop and a rack of city loaner bikes. Then cross the tram tracks and continue straight toward the Art Deco, Gotham City-style skyscraper called the **Farmers Tower** (or Boerentoren, though it's officially named after its current occupant, KBC—a bank). Completed in 1932, this was considered the first American-style skyscraper in Europe, and held the title of Europe's tallest skyscraper for 20 years.

At the Farmers Tower, bear left on Schoenmarkt. This leads to the square called **Groenplaats.** Here

you'll find a handy Metro stop, a statue of Rubens—the third Antwerp artist we've seen on this walk—and the cathedral spire hovering just beyond. The high-fashion district is to your left, and the Old Town is beyond the cathedral.

• *Stroll through the square toward the cathedral. Bear left up a narrow street of restaurants (Jan Blomstraat) known as "Little Italy Lane." It spills out at Handschoenmarkt in front of the cathedral. You've arrived at the historic center of Antwerp.*

## PART 2: FROM THE CATHEDRAL TO THE RIVERFRONT
### ❺ Cathedral of Our Lady

Antwerp's biggest church, with its lacy 400-foot-tall spire—still the tallest structure in the city—dominates the Old Town. Its

mismatched towers tell Antwerp's story in a nutshell. The church was begun in 1352 and consecrated in 1521, when Antwerp was at its peak, and there were grandiose plans to make the already huge church even bigger—the biggest on earth. But then a 1533 fire gutted the church, and in 1576, the Spanish Catholics sacked the city, causing Protestants to flee (mostly to Amsterdam) and Antwerp's fortunes to plummet. The church was left with only one completed tower—once the tallest in the Low Countries; the other is a stump of thwarted dreams.

Though much of the facade was left undecorated, the tympanum (archway) over the main door is remarkable. It's the Last Judgment, and Christ raises his hand to divide the righteous from the wicked. Below him, St. Michael weighs souls. One naughty lady is led away by a gleeful demon to be sexu-

ally harassed for eternity. Farther down (between the doors) is a statue of Mary— "Our Lady"—who smiles, willing to save us from that grim fate.

The church's richly ornamented interior is packed with fine art, including several huge masterpieces painted by Peter Paul Rubens (for details on visiting the church interior, see page 220).

• *Now, as you face the church, turn left and exit the square by walking up Maalderijstraat. You'll emerge in the...*

### ❻ Grote Markt

Antwerp's main square is dominated by the stately **City Hall** (Stadhuis). Dating from Antwerp's Golden Age (16th century), it's adorned with flags from many different countries—representing the importance of international trade to the city. The central tower sports the golden coats of arms of great medieval powers that shaped the city: the lion of the Duchy of Brabant, the gilded coat of arms of the city's Spanish rulers, and the two-headed eagle of the Habsburgs.

The other buildings fronting the square are **guild houses,** celebrating the trade associations of each of the city's industries. Each one is topped with a golden statue, which usually represents that guild's patron saint. There's a man on a rearing horse, a cat (or is it a wolf?), and (between those) a saint with a migraine. Some of these are over-the-top, exaggerated rebuilt versions from the Romantic period in the 19th century. The many ground-

floor cafés (especially the venerable Den Engel and Den Bengel, which catch the most sun) are inviting places for a drink with a view. Locals say that when the outdoor terraces open up, they know summer has arrived in Antwerp.

The unusual **fountain** in the middle of Grote Markt illustrates a gruesome story from Flemish folklore. Supposedly, a giant

named Druon Antigoon collected tolls along the Scheldt River. If someone was unable or unwilling to pay, the giant would sever their hand. His reign of terror finally ended when a brave young Roman soldier named Silvius Brabo defeated Antigoon, then cut off the giant's hand. Here we see Brabo in his wind-up, ready to toss Antigoon's blood-spouting hand into the river. (You can circle around behind to see the giant's bloody stump.) Tour guides love to explain that *hand werpen* ("to throw a hand") evolved into

"Antwerpen"...though scholars prefer less glamorous alternatives: "Antwerp" probably comes from *an 't werf,* "on the wharf"; or *ando verpis,* "where land is thrown up against land" (because the river deposits sludge along the bank here).

Behind the City Hall is a new diamond and silver museum called DIVA (see the Sights in Antwerp chapter).

• *From the Grote Markt, exit the square along the left side of the City Hall. Now head toward the river up the big street called...*

## ❼ Suikerrui

Along Suikerrui you get your first sense of Antwerp's origins as a river-trading port town. Today's paved street was once an open

canal that flowed to the river.
You'll pass the much-loved
statue to the unknown dock-
worker, whose insolent pose is
both carefree and defiant. Created in 1890 (by Constantin
Meunier), it was put here after
World War II to symbolize the
heroic workers who kept the

harbors open during the war. It instantly became a symbol of the
city. Farther along, the building at #5 is adorned with big green
statues. This is the former Hansahuis, where the German guild of
traders had their regional headquarters.

• *Suikerrui street leads to the river. The best place to view the water is up the ramp to the promenade.*

## ❽ Riverfront

Antwerp was born on the Scheldt River. The river flows north-
ward 200 miles, from France to Belgium, where it begins bearing
northwest to the North Sea. The city began right along the riverbank back in Roman times. Antwerp's location was perfect for
commerce: where the river trade to the interior met the oceangoing
trade to the North Sea. The port was fortified with a castle, which,
as you can see, still stands nearby.

During Antwerp's Golden Age (early 1500s), the Scheldt
brought more than a hundred ships a day, carrying goods from all
over the world—sugar and silver from America, pepper and cin-
namon from Asia. The city was completely cosmopolitan, full of
international businessmen. But when Antwerp fell to the Spanish
in 1585, everything changed suddenly. The Dutch gained control
of the Scheldt's river trade, and Antwerp declined. It wasn't until
Belgium gained its independence in the 19th century that sea trade
recovered.

Today, the port of Antwerp is Europe's second largest—but
you'd hardly know it standing here, because the main docks have
moved to the north (see the forest of cranes in the distance to the
right), and the focus of the city has shifted away from the river to
the train station. Now the original riverfront is dingy and drab—
tucked behind a busy boulevard and basically ignored by the city.
The steel canopies nearby are former warehouses, now used for covered parking or to shelter old boats (and a WC below). Cruise ships
dock right here (along the canopies) to disgorge their passengers
into town.

• *From the promenade, backtrack down the ramp, turn left, and head north along the riverfront, through the park 100 yards, to the forlorn and empty* ❾ *castle. It was once part of a city wall that fortified the heart of town, and is all that's left from the medieval era. Billed as "Antwerp's oldest building," it was begun in the 800s, and parts of today's structure date from the 1200s.*

*Enjoy the photogenic anchor out front and the statue of the legendary giant intimidating two poor traders.*

Notice the waist-high concrete **retaining wall** that runs along the busy street. Because the Scheldt is a tidal river, there's a huge risk of flooding—made more serious by rising sea levels. This retaining wall is equipped with orange steel doors that can roll along railroad tracks to open or close. Antwerp's new vision is to control flooding by building raised parklike dikes and revitalizing the entire riverfront.

• *Part 2 of our walk is finished. If you're short on time and want to do some sightseeing in the Old Town, feel free to bail out now. Or, to return to the train station, make your way back to the cathedral and Groenplaats, and hop on tram line #9 or #15.*

*If you stick with Part 3, you'll wander through Antwerp's generally safe and well-patrolled red light district before reaching the rejuvenated old dockyards, with super-modern buildings. (If you'd like to see the dockyards, but not the red lights, you can walk north along the riverbank for about 15 minutes, then turn right at the harbor.)*

## PART 3: FROM THE RIVERFRONT TO THE RED LIGHT DISTRICT AND OLD DOCKYARDS

• *From the castle, find the modest little staircase that takes you up and over the concrete retaining wall. Cross the busy street at the crosswalk, and climb the stairs. At the top of the stairs, make a U-turn left, walk 20 yards, then turn right on Kuipersstraat. Follow Kuipersstraat as it curves through brick row houses. After two blocks, turn left on Vleeshouwersstraat to find a big old building.*

## ⑩ Old Butchers Hall

This hall was built in 1504 to house one of Antwerp's guilds—the butchers. The impressive red-and-white stone structure (which locals say reminds them of bacon) was the neighborhood meat market. It now houses the Musical Instruments Museum (see page 226).

Notice that the building stands

on something quite rare in Antwerp—a small hill. As the hill was always a desirable place to live, this is one of the oldest neighborhoods. But the area today is mostly modern, sterile brick buildings. It was bombed heavily by Nazi V-2 rockets in World War II. Only the Old Butchers Hall survived. Then in the 1970s, whatever remained was replaced by these modern brick "projects"—subsidized housing. Notice there are no pubs or shops in this poor neighborhood. But if you poke around you'll discover pleasant public court-

yards tucked back inside many of these buildings, with benches that are inviting on a sunny day (and sinister on a cold, dark night).

• *From the Old Butchers Hall, head downhill on Vleeshouwersstraat. Walk two blocks. At a pleasant residential square (Veemarkt), cut diagonally across the* basketball court and continue up Nosestraat, passing a church. You'll end up at the square called...

## ⓫ Sint-Paulusplaats

This used to be a medieval harbor, then a bustling sailors' quarter with red lights in the windows. The area now has its share of trendy, youth-oriented restaurants.

At this point, you could cut this walk short and opt out of the red light district. Follow the tram tracks to the Sint-Paulusplaats stop, where tram #7 (direction: Mortsel) can take you back to the Old Town.

Prepare to enter the red light district. In fact, you may want to read ahead (especially the directions) before tucking your book away and walking boldly through.

• *The route through the red light district is simple: It's basically a straight shot—two long blocks. So, start walking past the big anchor and over the tram tracks, up the pedestrian street Oudemanstraat, which becomes Vingerlingstraat, and into the heart of the red light district. Follow the road as it curves to the right (through another block of the red light district) and eventually spills out on peaceful Falconplein. See you there.*

## ⓬ Red Light District

Enter Antwerp's red light district—Belgium's biggest hub of legalized prostitution. There are sex shops, sleazy bars, peep shows, and the main attraction: ladies shimmying in windows. City leaders believe that legalizing prostitution and concentrating it here makes things safer both for the sex workers and for city residents at large.

Antwerp's red light district lacks the touristy patina of Amsterdam's...which makes it feel that much creepier. You'll see fewer rowdy "stag parties" making a racket, but lots of lonely men silently prowling the pedestrian zone. It feels more comfortable during the day and more lively after dark.

In the 19th century, Antwerp's red light district was known (or notorious) the world over; these days, it's a much tamer place...but still provocative, particularly so when you realize that about a third of the "girls" are men. Don't be surprised if you're flashed top and bottom by a transvestite.

Near the end, on the right, is an alleyway marked **Villa Tinto**—essentially a shopping mall of ladies in windows. Designed by prominent artist Arne Quinze, it's a state-of-the-art brothel. It has a high-tech system of "panic buttons" that sex workers can use to call for help and a police station right in the middle. If a prostitute needs help, it's better that a policeman answers the call than a pimp.

• *You'll pop out on a long, narrow square called...*

## ⓭ Falconplein

Falconplein is a nice landing spot after the sleaze of the red light district. It used to be pretty seedy—dubbed "Red Square," for its Russian mafia-style thugs—but city leaders cracked down and gentrified the square.

• *At Falconplein, turn left. Cross busy Brouwersvliet (a former canal where cargo ships unloaded their goods). Continue straight ahead, through Van Schoonbekeplein, toward the red buildings with our final sight: the museum called MAS. Had enough? No MAS? Then you could end the walk now and return immediately to the center of town (for details, see the end of the walk).*

## ⓮ Old Dockyards and MAS (Museum aan de Stroom)

You've reached Antwerp's old industrial port area—once thriving, then dreary, and now revitalized. The port was built by Napoleon in the early 1800s and became the world's first Industrial Age harbor. It was a bustling area of brick warehouses and towering cranes. But by the 1950s and 1960s, the city's shipping industry relocated to larger ports farther north, and it fell into decline. In the mid-1980s, city leaders decided to reclaim and gentrify this prime real estate.

Today it's home to a tidy little yacht marina, a row of desirable condos, some trendy restaurants, and a state-of-the-art museum housed in an eye-catching tower. A few masted ships and old floating cranes keep alive the memory of this harbor's 19th-century heyday.

The **Museum aan de Stroom** (Museum on the River), or **MAS** for short, is housed in a 210-foot-tall blocky tower, encased in

hand-cut red stone and speckled with silver hands (the symbol of Antwerp). Designed to resemble the spiraling stacks of goods in an old maritime warehouse, the museum emphasizes the way Antwerp's status as a shipping center has made it a crossroads for people from around the world. Since you've made it this far, it would be a shame not to check it out. The building itself is free to enter and wander around in (but you need to buy a ticket if you want to enter the exhibition rooms). Take the (free) escalators up 10 stories to the museum's rooftop. It takes a while (and the elevators are restricted to visitors with disabilities), but the view is good. After this long walk, you've earned a look back over all you've traversed. (For a description of the view, the building, and the museum exhibits inside, see page 230.)

The museum's global focus is a fitting end to this walk through Antwerp—a city built on global trade.

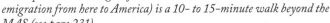

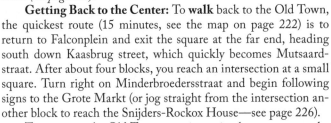

• *You're done. The **Red Star Line Museum** (with its impressive coverage of emigration from here to America) is a 10- to 15-minute walk beyond the MAS (see page 231).*

**Getting Back to the Center:** To **walk** back to the Old Town, the quickest route (15 minutes, see the map on page 222) is to return to Falconplein and exit the square at the far end, heading south down Kaasbrug street, which quickly becomes Mutsaardstraat. After about four blocks, you reach an intersection at a small square. Turn right on Minderbroedersstraat and begin following signs to the Grote Markt (or jog straight from the intersection another block to reach the Snijders-Rockox House—see page 226).

To return to the Old Town or train station by **tram,** cross the water on the pedestrian bridge north of the MAS and turn left, where you'll find the MAS stop for tram #7. Hop on and get off five stops later at Meirbrug, where you can transfer to tram #9 or #15.

To return to the train station by **bus,** backtrack from the MAS to the wide Brouwersvliet, cross it, and look for the bus stop on your right. From here you can catch bus #17 (direction: UZA) to the train station.

# RUBENS
# HOUSE TOUR

*Rubenshuis*

One of the world's most famous artists called this place home. He transformed a traditional Flemish house into an architectural showpiece. Here he worked (in his spacious studio); enjoyed family life (with his young trophy wife); tinkered with his collection of curiosities; and entertained fellow artists, geniuses, and aristocrats.

Your visit has two layers: the house itself and the art decorating it. The historic (if heavily restored) house has impressive wood-paneled and richly furnished rooms as well as a garden courtyard. There's enough fine art here to put this sight on the map as a gallery. Along with many paintings by other artists from Rubens' personal collection, you'll find a half-dozen high-quality paintings by Rubens, plus a few by his talented student, Anthony van Dyck. By seeing the kitchen where Rubens' meals were cooked, the dining room where he ate, the bedroom where he slept, and the studio where he worked, you may walk out seeing this Old Master as a flesh-and-blood human being.

## Orientation

**Cost:** €8.

**Hours:** Tue-Sun 10:00-17:00, closed Mon.

**Getting There:** The house is at Wapper 9, between the train station and the Old Town—to walk here, follow my Antwerp City Walk. Or, ride the Metro to the Meir stop, then walk one long block east (back toward the train station).

**Information:** Tel. 03-201-1555, www.rubenshuis.be.

**Optional Add-On:** An extra €2 gets you admission to the nearby Museum Mayer van den Bergh, whose highlight is Pieter Bruegel the Elder's enigmatic 1562 battle scene starring "Mad

Meg." The museum is pleasant but is located several blocks away, and is skippable for most.

**Warning:** There are lots of stairs and generally no air-con.

**Length of This Tour:** One hour.

**Starring:** His dining room (with portraits of Rubens and wife Hélène) and his studio, with a handful of Rubens paintings.

# The Tour Begins

Buy your ticket at the glass pavilion in the middle of the square in front of the house, then head inside. Here are the highlights.

• *The visit begins in the open air...*

## Courtyard

In 1610, Rubens—age 33 and just hired as the country's official court painter—bought this house and moved in with his wife. Ru-

bens would live here the rest of his long life. In the courtyard, you can see the original Flemish-style 16th-century house (on the left), the Italian palazzo-style studio that Rubens added on to the complex (on the right), the elaborate Michelangelo-flavored portico that connects them, and the Italian-style garden (directly ahead). An architect as well as a painter, Rubens designed the additions himself. The influence of his time in Italy is evident: Notice the dramatic contrast between the traditional Flemish home and the flamboyant Italian palazzo-style studio. By combining these two differing strains—Flemish and Italian—Rubens created his own personal style of art.

• *Now go inside the house and follow the one-way route through the various rooms.*

## Ground Floor

Pass quickly through the parlor (with its fireplace) and kitchen (with rich decorative tile work from Spain). Many of the paintings are not by Rubens but by artists he admired; in fact, his personal art collection was the biggest in the Low Countries.

In the dining room, you get a real sense of Rubens' opulent lifestyle. Admire the rich period furniture, leather-tooled walls, carved mantel, and wood ceiling. On the right is a rare self-portrait of Rubens in his fifties—one of only four known Rubens self-portraits. Facing him from across the room is a portrait (not by Rubens) of his second wife, Hélène Fourment. After his first wife

## Peter Paul Rubens (1577-1640)

Born in Germany in 1577, Rubens at age 12 moved with his family to Antwerp, where he was apprenticed to a local painter. During his twenties, he studied in Rome, where he picked up the Italian fad of painting giant compositions on huge canvases. He returned to Antwerp in 1608, married, and settled down, buying today's Rubens House in 1610. He would live and work there for the remainder of his life, churning out painting after painting.

Rubens' paintings run the gamut, from realistic portraits to lounging nudes, Greek myths to Catholic altarpieces, pious devotion to rough sex. Rubens painted anything that would raise your pulse: battles, miracles, hunts, rapes, and especially, fleshy "Rubenesque" women with dimples on all four cheeks. An expert of composition, Rubens could arrange a pig pile of many figures into a harmonious unit. Each painting was powered with an energy that people called his "fury of the brush."

Everything is on a larger-than-life scale in Rubens' work. Many canvases almost fill entire walls—you can see the seams

died, Rubens married 16-year-old Hélène for love instead of entering into a strategic marriage with a noblewoman.

Next is Rubens' "art room," displaying some of his personal painting collection. Bigshots in Rubens' day often had such a room filled with paintings, statues, and curios dedicated to showing off. In fact, the biggest canvas here actually depicts the "art room" of one of Rubens' Antwerp friends. (Find Rubens himself in the scene—lower left, with brown hair and beard, standing directly above the dog.) Now step into Rubens' rotunda. An ancient bust that Rubens believed to be the Roman philosopher Seneca is the centerpiece of his mini Pantheon rotunda. The world of ancient Rome was Rubens' starting point in art.

### Upstairs

Upstairs you'll pass through several more personal rooms. A well-worn chair has the artist's name ("PET PAVL RUBENS") on its backrest. The short bed is typical of the day when people

where the cloth pieces were stitched together—and approximately 2,500 canvases bear his name. How could he paint so many enormous canvases in one lifetime? He didn't. His house was an art factory, designed to mass-produce masterpieces. As was standard at the time, his assistants did much of the work: After he laid out a painting, his apprentices painted the background and filled in minor details. Rubens orchestrated the production from a balcony, and before a painting was carried out his tall, narrow door, he would put on the finishing touches, whipping each figure to life with a flick of his furious brush.

Rubens' fascination with plus-size models, and his skill at capturing their rippling folds of fat, are the reasons we now describe certain figures as "Rubenesque." The sweet faces and ample proportions of the damsels he painted were inspired by Hélène Fourment, 37 years Rubens' junior, whom the artist married after his first wife died.

Rubens distinguished himself as a smart businessman who knew how to provide wealthy benefactors with exactly what they wanted. In his long career, he was rich, famous, well traveled, and the friend of kings and princes. A true Renaissance Man in the Baroque Age, Rubens was even an accomplished diplomat—he helped to negotiate peace between England and Spain (and was knighted by the kings of both countries in appreciation).

believed it was healthier to sleep sitting up. And don't miss the touching oil sketch nearby (not by Rubens) of a dying infant boy.

• *Continue through a couple more rooms, then across the skyway and downstairs to the air-conditioned studio. You'll find the following paintings in either the large studio or the small adjoining room by the entrance.*

## Studio

If you're an art lover, you'll appreciate the historic nature of this room. Here Rubens and his students produced thousands of paintings. Lingering over the selection of canvases here, appreciate how they were made. For an important commission, Rubens would paint the entire work himself. If it was successful, he'd have his school make copies to sell on a wide scale. Once the copy was 99 percent completed, Rubens would step in to add a few finishing touches...only Rubens himself could create just the perfect twinkle in an eye or glimmer of light on that cellulite. Other times, Rubens would simply do a rough oil sketch of what he wanted, then enlist experts in certain areas (such as flowers or portraits) to fill in the blanks. Then he'd sweep through at the end to finalize the work.

**Rubens' Paintings:** Though the displays change, this room always has a few classic Rubens canvases: large scale and dramatic, with bright colors, rippling flesh, wind-whipped robes, and strong emotions. In good Baroque style, each painting captures an emo-

tional moment. Browse the room, and you'll likely see some of these paintings (or others of equal interest):

Rubens painted twin portraits of the Spanish monarchs of the Netherlands, **Archduke Albert** and **Infanta Isabella,** in their elaborate ruffed collars. Rubens was this couple's official court painter, and these original works were copied in large numbers by his assistants. The monarchs' time was valuable, so Rubens worked quickly. To pose for her portrait, Isabella reportedly came to Antwerp for only one night; Rubens sketched her face quickly, just enough to capture her likeness, then filled in the details later.

**RUBENS HOUSE**

*Adam and Eve* is an early (pre-Italy) work, done when Rubens was barely 21. The poses are a bit stiff, the colors subdued, and

the bodies lack the rippling muscles and folds of fat that would later become Rubens' trademark.

*St. Sebastian* is an early Rubens take on a common Italian subject. In his version, the angel tries to delicately pluck an arrow from the martyr's supple flesh.

*The Annunciation* shows the angel barging into Mary's home (notice the sleeping kitten) to bring the news of Jesus' impending birth. Rubens was frantically soaking up Italian-style dynamism, but here he crams a bit too much action into a tiny apartment.

*The Feast of St. Martin*—with its bonfire in the midst of revelers—is not by Rubens, so why is it here? Rubens had a hobby of buying paintings like this so he could add touches to make it his own. He'd add whitener to the teeth, paint a sparkle in the eyes, and transform a peasant into a society lady. Find his addition to this piece—the woman with the sparkling tiara—in the center.

**Van Dyck Paintings:** You may see a couple of paintings by Anthony van Dyck in this room: a portrait of a Brussels alderman and a self-portrait. Each shows the genius of Rubens' most talented pupil. Van Dyck's ability to capture a personality on canvas made him invaluable to Rubens (whose forte was not faces). While Rubens got the lion's share of the fame, some of his students were even more talented than he was—and Van Dyck was a verifiable genius, who prodded Rubens to become a better painter. And yet Van Dyck was just a painter...whereas Rubens was also an architect, an aristocrat, and a diplomat—a true jack-of-all-trades who carved a large legacy.

It was in this room that Rubens, for decades with his talented team of assistants and students, turned up the wind machine on painted images that brought the artistic gusto of the Baroque era to great churches, palaces, and mansions throughout Europe.

RUBENS HOUSE

# ANTWERP SLEEPING, EATING & MORE

## Sleeping in Antwerp

Because it's a commercial center and a major European port, Antwerp has an abundance of business-class hotels—keep in mind that you can often get a deal there on weekends. Most of my recommended lodgings are more homey establishments concentrated in the Old Town and the high-fashion Sint-Andries district. If you want to look elsewhere, consider 't Zuid and avoid the somewhat seedy train station neighborhood.

**$$$$ Hotel Julien,** an extremely chic boutique hotel, is Antwerp's most enticing splurge. Located in a renovated 16th-century building on a drab street just outside the Old Town, its 21 rooms are a perfectly executed combination of old and new. The public areas, with high ceilings and lots of unfinished wood, feel like an art gallery. If you want to pretend you're royalty—or a rock star— rent the "experience plus" suite (breakfast extra, air-con, elevator, spa in basement, Korte Nieuwstraat 24, tel. 03-229-0600, www. hotel-julien.com, info@hotel-julien.com).

**$$$ APlace B&B** offers two stylish suites and two apartments overlooking charming Vrijdagmarkt and the Museum Plantin-Moretus. Expertly decorated with a lifetime's worth of vintage finds, the spacious suites have a shared kitchenette; the apartments offer full-size kitchens (minimum 3 nights in apartments, Vrijdagmarkt 1, mobile 0473-735-650, www.aplaceantwerp.be, sleep@ aplace.be, knowledgeable Karin makes you feel at home).

**$$$ Rosier 10 B&B,** in the Sint-Andries fashion district, fits its mod neighborhood well. Four spacious rooms each have their own design details that reflect the times of the day (the "night" room has a few naughty extras). Roxanne adds homey touches such as an honor bar and coffee and tea fixings (apartments also available, Rosier 10, mobile 0489-279-999, www.rosier10.be, info@ rosier10.be).

**$$$ Hotel O Kathedral** is an ultramodern boutique hotel with a swanky wine bar and 33 rooms on the small square facing the Cathedral of Our Lady. Superior rooms are plastered with oversized Rubens prints and have sexy—but not exactly private— see-through showers (elevator, breakfast extra, Handschoen-markt 3, tel. 03-500-8950, www.hotelokathedral.com, info@ hotelokathedral.com).

**$$ Matelote Hotel** ("Sailor") enjoys an extremely central location on a characteristic street deep in the Old Town, just a few steps from...everything. Its 10 rooms mix heavy old beams with sleek, sometimes boldly modern flourishes. While getting a bit worn—especially in the budget rooms—the place still feels stylish and has some nice features, such as minifridges with free mineral water and electric kettles for making coffee or tea (breakfast extra, Haarstraat 11a, tel. 03-201-8800, www.hotel-matelote.be, info@ matelote.be).

**$$ At B&B Sablon,** Gea rents three rooms above a café near the river. Two rooms have a private bath across the hall, and one has the bath en suite. While the rooms are a bit plain, the price is right, and the location is handy (cash only, breakfast served in café, Zand 25, mobile 0468-104-917, www.sablonbbb.be, gea@ sablonbbb.be).

**$$ Ibis Antwerpen Centrum,** the cookie-cutter standby, has 150 predictable rooms sharing the big Oudevaartplaats square with the modern City Theater, just south of the Meir and the Rubens House between the train station and Old Town (breakfast extra, air-con, elevator, Meistraat 39, tel. 03-231-8830, www.ibishotel. com, h1453@accor.com).

**$ Hotel Scheldezicht** is getting run down, but it has a homey vibe with friendly service and a budget price. The owners plan to renovate, but until then expect tattered carpet in the hallways and well-worn furniture. The 20 airy rooms are clean; the best are the view rooms with high ceilings on a tree-lined square. Bathrooms are pint-sized (cheaper "simple" rooms have shared WCs, Sint-Jansvliet 12, tel. 03-231-6602, www.hotelscheldezicht.eu, info@ hotelscheldezicht.be).

**¢ Pulcinella Youth Hostel** is Antwerp's newest and best of-

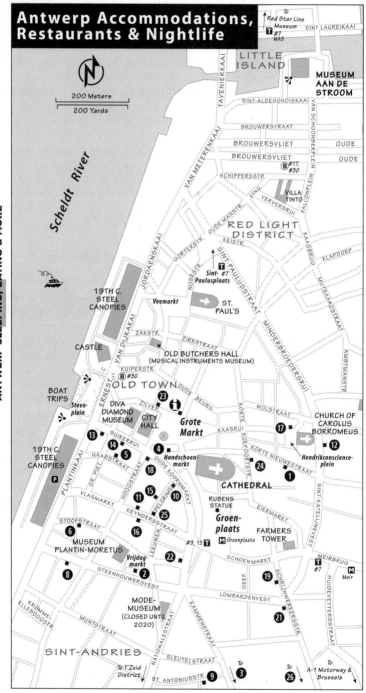

# Antwerp Accommodations, Restaurants & Nightlife

200 Meters
200 Yards

Scheldt River

LITTLE ISLAND

MUSEUM AAN DE STROOM

To Red Star Line Museum
#7 MAS
SINT LAUREIKAAI

SINT-ALDEGONDISKAAI

BROUWERSTRAAT

BROUWERSVLIET

BROUWERSVLIET

SCHIPPERSSTR.

VILLA TINTO

RED LIGHT DISTRICT

19TH C. STEEL CANOPIES

Veemarkt

Sint-Paulusplaats

ST. PAUL'S

CASTLE

OLD BUTCHERS HALL (MUSICAL INSTRUMENTS MUSEUM)

BOAT TRIPS

Steenplein

DIVA DIAMOND MUSEUM

CITY HALL

Grote Markt

OLD TOWN

CHURCH OF CAROLUS BORROMEUS

Hendrikconscience-plein

19TH C. STEEL CANOPIES

Handschoen-markt

CATHEDRAL

RUBENS STATUE

Groen-plaats

FARMERS TOWER

Groenplaats

MUSEUM PLANTIN-MORETUS

Vrijdag-markt

MEIRBRUG

Meir

MODE-MUSEUM (CLOSED UNTIL 2020)

SINT-ANDRIES

To T'Zuid District

To A-1 Motorway & Brussels

## Hotels
1. Hotel Julien
2. APlace B&B
3. To Rosier 10 B&B
4. Hotel O Kathedral
5. Matelote Hotel
6. B&B Sablon
7. Ibis Antwerpen Centrum
8. Hotel Scheldezicht
9. Pulcinella Youth Hostel

## Eateries
10. Pasta Hippo
11. Bij Lam & Yin
12. De Godevaart
13. Maritime
14. Restaurant de Bomma
15. Lollapalooza Restaurant
16. De Groote Witte Arend
17. Brasserie 't Brantyser
18. Frituur No. 1
19. Désiré de Lille
20. Supermarket
21. Lombardia
22. Billie's Bier Kafétaria

## Nightlife
23. Den Engel
24. De Muze Jazzcafé
25. De Vagant
26. To Kapitein Zeppos

ANTWERP SLEEPING, EATING & MORE

ficial hostel. With 23 doubles, it offers privacy and bargain prices (private rooms available, fee for nonmembers, no curfew, in the fashion district at Bogaardeplein 1, tel. 03-234-0314, www.vjh.be, antwerpen@vjh.be).

# Eating in Antwerp

This trendy, youthful city is changing all the time, and the range of options is impressive. What's good one year is old news the next. I recommend a few places below, but it's also smart to just poke around the neighborhoods described here and choose the menu and ambience that appeal. Exploring this evolving scene is enjoyable—a fun part of the Antwerp experience.

If you're dining in the Old Town area, simply accept that anywhere you go will cater at least partly to tourists. But since Antwerp isn't overrun by visitors, these places also entertain their share of locals. For a more authentic Antwerp experience, head south to 't Zuid.

## IN AND NEAR THE OLD TOWN

It seems that 95 percent of Antwerp's tourists dine on a handful of streets in the old center. Touristy restaurants with outdoor seating abound on the **Grote Markt, Handschoenmarkt,** and the square in front of the cathedral. Nearby streets are lined with mostly Italian and Greek/Turkish eateries. On these squares you can choose your view and overpay for mediocre food. **Pelgrimstraat,** a block south of the cathedral, is lined with a tempting variety of options ranging from tapas bars and rustic taverns to sushi, Thai, and Italian restaurants (**Pasta Hippo** is very good).

The following recommendations, all within a few minutes' walk of each other in the Old Town, are less tacky, popular with locals as well as tourists, and offer a quality dining experience.

### Fine Dining

**$$$$ Bij Lam & Yin** Chinese restaurant has a tiny dining room, a small menu, great service, and wonderful traditional Cantonese food served by Hong Kong immigrants. They have two seatings (18:00 and 20:30), and you'll choose from four starters and five main dishes. This is a rare place, with a Michelin star and no pretense—but you'll need to reserve well in advance to snare one of its 36 seats (Wed-Sun only, closed Mon-Tue, Reyndersstraat 17, tel. 03-232-8838, www.lam-en-yin.be).

**$$$$ De Godevaart** is another foodie splurge that's gaining international attention for chef Dave de Belder's innovative, molecular-gastronomy take on Belgian cuisine. The dining room is stately but not pretentious, and the peaceful courtyard in back is good for hot evenings (several enticing many-course tasting menus, reservations smart, Tue-Sat 12:00-15:00 & 18:00-22:00, closed Sun-Mon, Sint-Katelijnevest 23, tel. 03-231-8994, www. degodevaart.be).

**$$$$ Maritime** fish restaurant is a fixture among locals for quality seafood. While the interior is dressy, the outside tables are plain (Fri-Tue 12:00-14:00 & 18:30-21:00, slightly longer hours Sat-Sun, closed Wed-Thu, Suikerrui 4, tel. 03-233-0758).

## Characteristic, Casual Places

**$$$ Restaurant de Bomma,** as the name indicates, is like eating at Grandma's. The family-friendly menu is fun and accessible, with small plates designed for sharing. They serve old-fashioned favorites, stews, and salads, and have fine seating inside and out (daily 12:00-22:00, Suikerrui 16, tel. 03-227-4926).

**$$$ Lollapalooza Restaurant** has a fun, eclectic menu including Thai, fish, and vegetarian dishes, creative salads, and a charming brick grotto facing a pedestrian street (Thu-Mon from 18:30, closed Tue-Wed, Pelgrimstraat 28, tel. 03-227-4142).

**$$$ De Groote Witte Arend,** across from the far end of Pelgrimstraat, is a good place to try well-executed, stick-to-your-ribs Belgian classics. To wash things down, pick from an enticing list of 90 Belgian beers. Explore the sprawling complex, which was originally a merchant's house and then a monastery—see their 500-year-old chapel. You can sit in the cozy cobbled courtyard or in the high-ceilinged interior on two floors (€14.50 three-course menu until 18:00, daily 11:30-22:00, Reyndersstraat 18, tel. 03-233-5033).

**$$$ Brasserie 't Brantyser** is a pub-turned-restaurant facing a delightful Italian-feeling cobbled square dominated by a towering Baroque Jesuit church. They serve standard Flemish fare and creative salads in their characteristic interior or on the square (Thu-Sun and Tue 11:00-22:00, closed Mon and Wed, Hendrik Conscienceplein 7, tel. 03-233-1833). There's a fun assortment of little restaurants in a line beyond this place.

**$ Frituur No. 1** is the place for a cone of *frieten*, or fries. They offer the full array of fried meaty gut-bombs and lots of sauces. While most of their business is takeaway, they have lots of seating (open long hours daily, Hoogstraat 1; for tips on Flemish fast food, see "Belgian Cuisine" in the Practicalities chapter).

**$$ Désiré de Lille** is the local favorite for waffles. If you want a Belgian waffle cooked to order or an old-fashioned decadent dessert, this historic waffle house is your best bet. It has been keeping people happy for a century (daily 10:00-20:00, Schrijnwerkersstraat 16, tel. 03-233-6226).

**Groceries:** A large **Delhaize** supermarket is in the Stadsfeestzaal shopping mall at Meir 78 (Mon-Sat 8:00-20:00, closed Sun).

## JUST SOUTH AND EAST OF THE OLD TOWN

Just a few blocks south of Groenplaats and the Farmers Tower, you'll find charming **Lombardenvest** and other pedestrian streets spinning off from a leafy little no-name square. These streets are filled with a variety of enticing cafés and lunch places.

**$$$ Lombardia** vegetarian restaurant has been serving hippies good organic meals since 1972. It's a flowery place offering a fun fiesta of healthy food and drink to trendy locals. They have fine tables on a peaceful square facing a little playground (a bit pricey, Wed-Sat 9:00-18:00, closed Sun-Tue, Lombardenvest 78, tel. 03-233-6819).

**$$$ Billie's Bier Kafétaria** is a tiny gastropub popular with locals for its good food and even better beer. The small menu covers Flemish basics like pork cheeks, plus a few other hearty helpings such as chili. You might just meet Billie—who isn't the owner but the dog (Wed-Sun 16:00-24:00, Mon 18:00-24:00, closed Tue, Kammenstraat 12, tel. 03-226-3183).

## IN 'T ZUID

Literally "The South," this zone is Antwerp's top restaurant and nightlife zone. Frequented mostly by urbanites, this is where you'll find many of the city's hot new restaurants. Options are scattered around a several-block area, with one or two tempting eateries on each block. It is about a 15-minute walk south of the Grote Markt (along entertaining Kloosterstraat, lined with antique and home-decor shops). Or, from Groenplaats, catch the #4 tram.

Check out the area around **Marnixplaats.** The confluence of eight streets facing a dramatic column dedicated to Neptune creates a circle of corner buildings made-to-order for al fresco drinking and dining. While many of these places are drinks-only (sometimes with light snacks), a few are suitable for a full meal.

**$$$$ Fiskebar** is one of the top picks in this area—and in all of Antwerp—and is worth reserving ahead. Focusing on seafood, it's done up like a fish market (as its name implies) and lists a wide range of specialties on its chalkboard menu high on the wall (Mon-Thu 12:00-14:00 & 18:00-22:00, Fri-Sun 12:00-22:00; #12, tel. 03-257-1357, www.fiskebar.be).

**$$ Lucy Chang,** part of a small and upscale Belgian chain, serves up tasty Asian noodle and rice dishes (daily 12:00-23:00, cash only, #17, tel. 03-248-9560).

At **$$ Pasta Plezir,** order a pasta dish at the counter, then eat at the upstairs tables or on a rustic picnic bench out on the square. If you want to cocoon in your hotel, they deliver (Thu-Tue 16:00-23:00, closed Wed, #7, tel. 03-295-9404).

# Shopping in Antwerp

As a capital of both fashion and avant-garde culture, Antwerp is a shopper's delight, with a seemingly endless array of creative little corner boutiques selling unique items, as well as outlets for big-name international designers. Serious fashionistas and window shoppers alike find Antwerp's quirky browsing culture one of the most delightful in Europe. Note that most shops open between 9:00 and 10:00 and close by the relatively early hour of 18:30.

## SHOPPING STREETS

As you explore, you'll discover that each street has its own person-ality and specialties. For example, **Schuttershofstraat** and **Hopland** are where you'll find famous-label international couture, while **Kammenstraat** is better for young, trendy, retro-hipster fashions.

I enjoy strolling the starburst of traffic-free streets that spin off from the leafy square along **Lombardenvest** (just south of the Farmers Tower). Each street has a different focus, such as shoe stores on Groendalstraat and clothing on Lombardenvest.

**Kloosterstraat,** which sticks closer to the river as it heads south from the Grote Markt area all the way to 't Zuid, focuses on home furnishings—from antiques to minimalist furniture to home decor and gadgets. You'll wish you had an unlimited budget to fur-nish an avant-garde Belgian flat.

A large department store is on the boulevard called **the Meir,** between the train station and the Old Town. South of the Rubens House, streets like **Leopoldstraat, Sint-Jorispoort,** and **Mechels-esteenweg** are noted for antiques and home decor. Near the train station, the street called **De Keyserlei** is known for its jewelry and diamond stores.

## FASHION DISTRICT

Antwerp's status as a fashion mecca is a relatively recent develop-ment. In 1988, six students from the Royal Academy of Fine Arts' fashion department traveled to a London show, where they got a lot of attention. Because their Flemish names were too challenging to pronounce, the English press simply dubbed them the "Antwerp Six." Each one opened a shop in **Sint-Andries,** which at the time was a very poor neighborhood. They put this area on the map, other designers began to move in, and now it's one of Europe's top fashion zones. The academy is still up and running; it has a small enrollment and a strong focus on creativity (www.antwerp-fashion.be).

Sint-Andries is a few minutes' walk south of the Old Town along National-estraat. While it's a three-star destination for couture lovers, anybody would have fun window shopping here. In the shops along the streets of Sint-Andries, you'll find top-name international designers, funky hole-in-the-wall boutiques, vintage shops, jewelers, and more. The TI offers thoughtfully designed resources for people interested in delving into Antwerp's high fashion scene, including detailed map/guides and an app that leads you on a self-guided tour through this zone.

## Nightlife in Antwerp

### IN THE OLD TOWN

After hours, Antwerp's touristy core (around the Grote Markt and cathedral) hums with activity. Find a café or bar with outdoor tables, order a drink, and people-watch. Below are some favorites; note that most of these serve little or no food—go for the ambience and entertainment, not for dinner.

**Den Engel,** an old-fashioned pub at the corner of the Grote Mark (near the City Hall), is an obvious choice but also a local fixture. The cozy interior oozes authentic charm and feels like it's been the family living room of Antwerpenaars for generations. Outside, it boasts my favorite view in Antwerp, of the dramatic cathedral tower rising up behind a row of fine facades (a few bar snacks, long hours daily, Grote Markt 3, tel. 03-233-1252). **Den Bengel,** next door, has equally fine views but a lesser interior.

**De Muze Jazzcafé** is outrageously atmospheric, with happy drinkers filling antique wooden booths on three levels overlooking the bar. Most come for the live jazz (open long hours daily; jazz free and usually from 21:00 or 22:00 on Mon-Tue and Fri-Sat, plus Sun afternoons at 15:00, check schedule at www.jazzcafedemuze.be; Melkmarkt 10, tel. 03-226-0126).

**De Vagant,** located at the end of Pelgrimstraat, specializes in *jenever* (gin), with 200 different kinds to sample to the sound of classical music. It's a real bar with a simple, high-ceilinged, traditional interior (daily 12:00-24:00, Reyndersstraat 25, tel. 03-233-1538).

**De Groote Witte Arend**—which also serves good food (see "Eating in Antwerp," earlier)—is a fine and central spot to sample a Belgian beer.

**Kapitein Zeppos**, a 10-minute walk from the central square, is a big and inviting beer hall with good basic food (mussels and salads) and a serious appreciation for beer. On hot days, the square is filled with tables. Late in the evening the beer hall is filled with locals (Vleminckveld 78).

### IN 'T ZUID
A 15-minute walk or 5-minute bus or tram ride south of the Grote Markt, this area is the more local, somewhat younger alternative to the old core. Bars with outdoor tables cluster around two areas: Marnixplaats and in front of the art museum, at Leopold de Wael-plaats (for details, see "Eating in Antwerp," earlier). Along this square, **Hopper** feels urbane and untouristy—like you're in on an insider's tip. The interior is stark but dignified, and they have live jazz a few times a week (usually Sun at 16:00 and Mon at 21:00, also Tue at 21:00 in winter; open long hours daily, Leopold de Waelstraat 2, tel. 03-248-4933).

# Antwerp Connections

**From Antwerp by Train to: Brussels** (3/hour, 40-50 minutes), **Ghent** (3/hour, 50 minutes), **Bruges** (2/hour, 1.5 hours, half change in Ghent), **Ypres/Ieper** (hourly, 2.5 hours), **Amsterdam** (hourly by pricey Thalys, 1.5 hours; also hourly by slower IC train, 2.5 hours), Amsterdam's **Schiphol Airport** (hourly, 1 hour by Thalys, 2 hours by IC train), **Delft** (hourly, 1 hour, change in Rotterdam), **Paris** (about hourly direct on Thalys, 2 hours; more possible with a transfer at Brussels Midi/Zuid/South to Thalys, 2.5 hours). For train information, see www.belgianrail.be; see also the "Transportation" section in the Practicalities chapter.

# GHENT

# ORIENTATION TO GHENT

*Gent • Gand*

Made terrifically wealthy by the textile trade, medieval Ghent was a powerhouse, and for a time, it was one of the biggest cities in Europe. It erected grand churches and ornate guild houses to celebrate its resident industry. But, like its rival Bruges, eventually Ghent's fortunes fell, leaving it with a well-preserved historic nucleus surrounded by a fairly drab modern shell.

Ghent doesn't ooze with cobbles and charm, as Bruges does; this is a living place—home to one of Belgium's biggest universities and a vibrant student population. Ghent enjoys just the right amount of urban grittiness, with a welcome splash of creative hipster funkiness. It's also a browser's delight, with a wide range of characteristic little shops that aren't aimed squarely at the tourist crowds.

Explore the historic quarter, ponder the breathtaking Van Eyck altarpiece in the massive cathedral, tour impressive art and design museums, stroll picturesque embankments, bask in finely decorated historic gables, and prowl the revitalized Patershol restaurant quarter. Ghent is the kind of town that you visit for a few hours, and find yourself wishing you had a few days.

## PLANNING YOUR TIME

Ghent, about halfway between Brussels and Bruges and a half-hour from either, is ideally located for day-tripping. It's easy to get the gist of the town in a few hours. Either toss your bag in a locker at Ghent's train station on your way between those two cities, or side-trip here from either one. With limited time, focus on the historical center: Follow my self-guided walk, tour the cathedral, and dip into a museum or two. With more time or a strong interest in art, also visit the art museums in Citadelpark, closer to the train station. Museums are closed either Mondays or Wednesdays (though the cathedral and other churches remain open).

Ghent also makes a handy home base for side-tripping to the other destinations in this book.

### Blitz Tour of Ghent

Day-trippers to Ghent can use my Ghent City Walk to weave together the main sights in as little as three hours. From the train station, take tram #1 to Korenmarkt, where the walk begins. Stop along the way to visit whichever sights interest you: Climb the belfry, tour St. Bavo's with the Ghent Altarpiece, browse the House of Alijn, and scramble up the ramparts of the Castle of the Counts. From the Castle of the Counts, catch tram #1 back to the station.

## Overview

Although it's a midsized city (pop. 250,000), Ghent's historic core is appealingly compact—you can walk from one end to the other in about 15 minutes. The train station (with several museums nearby) is a 15-minute tram ride south of the center. Its Flemish

residents call the town Gent (gutturally: *h*ent), while its French name is Gand (sounds like "gone").

### TOURIST INFORMATION

Ghent's TI is in the Old Fish Market (Oude Vismijn) building next to the Castle of the Counts (daily 10:00-18:00, brochure with good self-guided walk, tel. 09-266-5660, www.visitgent.be).

Busy sightseers might save a few euros with the **CityCard Gent,** but on a day-trip blitz with this book, it's probably not worth it (€30/48 hours, €35/72 hours, includes entrance to all the major museums and public transit).

### ARRIVAL IN GHENT

**By Train:** Ghent's main train station, Gent-Sint-Pieters, is about a mile and a half south of the city center. As the station is undergoing an extensive renovation (through 2020), it might differ from what's described here. In the main hall, be sure to look up at the meticulously restored frescoes celebrating great Flemish cities and regions. **Lockers** are just down the hall from the Travel Center.

It's a dull 30-minute **walk** to the city center. Instead, take the

GHENT ORIENTATION

**tram** (about 15 minutes): Buy your €3 tickets from the **Lijnwinkel** transportation office in the train station (Mon-Fri 7:00-19:00) or at the ticket machines outside at the tram stop. You can also buy them on board (exact change only). Once on board, validate your ticket in the yellow machine. If you're going to Antwerp and/or Bruges and will be using public transportation there as well, consider the 10-ride ticket for €16. It's good in all three cities (and anywhere else in Flanders), and you can share the ticket with others. There's also a €6 day pass. Both of these ticket deals must be purchased at the Lijnwinkel office.

Find the stop for tram #1: It's out the front door and 100 yards to the left, under the big, blocky, modern building on stilts. Board tram #1 in the direction of Wondelgem/Evergem (departs about every 10 minutes, 15-minute ride). Get off at the Korenmarkt stop, and continue one block straight ahead to Korenmarkt, where you can see most of the city's landmark towers (and where my Ghent City Walk begins). Figure €10 for a **taxi** into town.

**By Car:** Exit the E-40 expressway at the Gent Centrum exit, then follow the *P-route* (parking route) to various pay garages in town; the most central include P1 (Vrijdagmarkt) and P5 (Kouter). There's also ample parking at the Gent-Sint-Pieters train station, with its easy tram connection into town (see "By Train," earlier).

## HELPFUL HINTS

**Market Day:** Sunday is the main market day in Ghent, with small markets filling squares around town: a flower market at Kouter, secondhand books along Ajuinlei, clothes and pets on Vrijdagmarkt, and more. There are also smaller markets on Fridays and Saturdays.

**Festivals:** Ghent is proud of its **Gentse Feesten** (Ghent Festivities), which last for 10 days and begin around the city holiday of July 21 (www.gentsefeesten.be). This open-air music festival features everything from jazz to techno in venues around town and lots of boozing. Book hotels during this period well in advance. Other events include a jazz festival (the week before the big festival) and a film festival in mid-October.

**Laundry:** A handy, unstaffed coin-op **launderette** is in the heart of the Patershol restaurant neighborhood (daily 7:00-22:00, corner of Oudburg and Zwaanstraat, mobile 048-460-0185). Another option is **Wascenter Netezon,** a few steps west of Vrijdagmarkt square (daily 6:00-22:00, Sint-Jacobsnieuwstraat 3). For locations, see the map on page 302.

**Bike Rental: Jack's House,** in the town center, is a waffle shop that also rents bicycles (€15/day, daily May-Oct, Pensmarkt 1—see the map on page 302, mobile 046-822-2403).

# Tours in Ghent

### Local Guide
Cheerful **Mieke Thienpont** is devoted to sharing her city's history and charm (€120/3 hours, €240/full day, mobile 049-751-6528, miekethienpont@gmail.com).

### Walking Tours
Guided two-hour tours of Ghent depart from the **TI** (€10, €8 if you book online; May-Sept daily at 14:00, April Sat-Sun only, off-season Sat only). **Ghent Guides** also runs historic city walks and themed tours (€80/2-hour tour, tel. 09-233-0772, www.gentsegidsen.be, info@gentsegidsen.be).

### Boat Tours
Lazy little tour boats, jammed with tourists listening to the spiel in several languages, cruise the waterways. Several companies offer essentially the same tour for the same price; boats line up along the Korenlei or Graslei embankments (€7.50, 40-50 minutes, live guides). On weekends during the high season, a hop-on, hop-off **water tram** connects some of the major sights (€12.50/1 day, €15/2 days, covered by CityCard, April-Nov Sat-Sun 11:00-18:30, www. hoponhopoff.be).

**GHENT ORIENTATION**

# SIGHTS IN GHENT

Most of Ghent's sights cluster in the historic city center (easily accessible on foot) or south of the core, near the train station.

## IN THE HISTORIC CENTER

Some of the following sights are covered in more detail in the 📖 Ghent City Walk chapter, including visiting the interiors of the Church of St. Nicholas and the Belfry.

### ▲▲St. Bavo's Cathedral (Sint-Baafskathedraal) and Ghent Altarpiece

This cathedral, the main church of Ghent, houses three of the city's art treasures: the exquisite Van Eyck *Adoration of the Mystic Lamb* altarpiece—widely known as the Ghent Altarpiece; an elaborately carved pulpit; and an altar painting by Rubens depicting the town's patron saint (and the church's namesake).

**Cost and Hours:** Church free to enter but €4 to see original altarpiece and its facsimile, includes audioguide; Mon-Sat 9:30-17:00, Sun from 13:00; Nov-March Mon-Sat 10:30-16:00, Sun from 13:00; Sint-Baafsplein, tel. 09-225-1626, www.sintbaafskathedraal.be.

📖 See the St. Bavo's Cathedral & Ghent Altarpiece Tour chapter.

## Ghent at a Glance

▲▲**St. Bavo's Cathedral and Ghent Altarpiece** Main church housing treasures by Peter Paul Rubens and Jan van Eyck. **Hours:** Mon-Sat 9:30-17:00, Sun from 13:00, Nov-March Mon-Sat 10:30-16:00, Sun from 13:00. See page 268.

▲**Castle of the Counts** Restored fortress with typical castle ramparts, a dungeon, and good tower views. **Hours:** Daily 10:00-18:00, Nov-March 9:00-17:00. See page 272.

▲**Ghent Design Museum** Enjoyable display of Belgian design from the 17th to 21st century. **Hours:** Mon-Tue and Thu-Fri 9:30-17:30, Sat-Sun 10:00-18:00, closed Wed. See page 274.

▲**Fine Arts Museum** Accessible collection of Northern European art. **Hours:** Tue-Fri 9:30-17:30, Sat-Sun 10:00-18:00, closed Mon. See page 274.

▲**Ghent City Museum** High-tech museum tracing the city's history through multimedia exhibits and historic artifacts. **Hours:** Mon-Tue and Thu-Fri 9:00-17:00, Sat-Sun 10:00-18:00, closed Wed. See page 276.

### Church of St. Nicholas (Sint-Niklaaskerk)

This beautiful church, built of Tournai limestone, is a classic of the Scheldt Gothic style. Ghent's merchants started building the Church of St. Nicholas in the 1100s. Among its art treasures is a massive Baroque altar of painted wood.

**Cost and Hours:** Free, Tue-Sun 10:00-17:00, Mon from 14:00, on Cataloniëstraat at the corner of Korenmarkt, tel. 09-234-2869.

### Belfry (Belfort)

This combination watchtower and carillon has been keeping an eye on Ghent since the 1300s. For centuries, this landmark building safeguarded civic documents. Nowadays, the mostly empty interior displays an exhibit of bells, and an elevator whisks visitors up the 300-foot tower to views over the city.

**Cost and Hours:** €8, daily 10:00-18:00, Sint-Baafsplein, tel. 09-233-3954, www.belfortgent.be.

GHENT SIGHTS

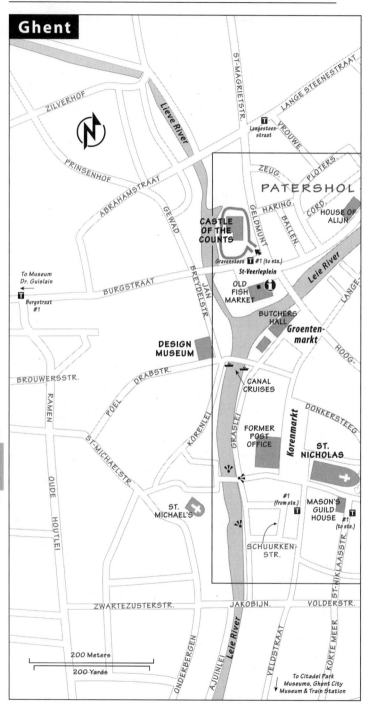

GHENT SIGHTS

Ghent

ZILVERHOF

PRINSENHOF

Lieve River

ST-MAGRIETSTR.

LANGE STEENESTRAAT

VROUWE

Langesteen-straat

ZEUG.

PLOTERS.

PATERSHOL

HARING.

CORD.

HOUSE OF
ALIJN

BALLEN.

GELDMUNT

ABRAHAMSTRAAT

GEWAD

JAN BREYDELSTR.

CASTLE
OF THE
COUNTS

Gravensteen  #1 (to stn.)

St-Veerleplein

Leie River

LANGE

To Museum
Dr. Guislain

Burgstraat
#1

BURGSTRAAT

OLD
FISH
MARKET

BUTCHERS
HALL

Groenten-
markt

HOOG-

DESIGN
MUSEUM

BROUWERSSTR.

RAMEN

POEL

DRABSTR.

CANAL
CRUISES

KORENLEI

GRASLEI

FORMER
POST
OFFICE

Korenmarkt

DONKERSTEEG

ST. NICHOLAS

ST-MICHAELSTR.

OUDE HOUTLEI

ST.
MICHAEL'S

#1
(from stn.)

MASON'S
GUILD
HOUSE

#1
(to stn.)

ST-NIKLAASSTR.

SCHUURKEN-
STR.

ZWARTEZUSTERSTR.

JAKOBIJN.

VOLDERSTR.

ONDERBERGEN

AJUINLEI

Leie River

VELDSTRAAT

KORTE MEER

To Citadel Park
Museums, Ghent City
Museum & Train Station

200 Meters

200 Yards

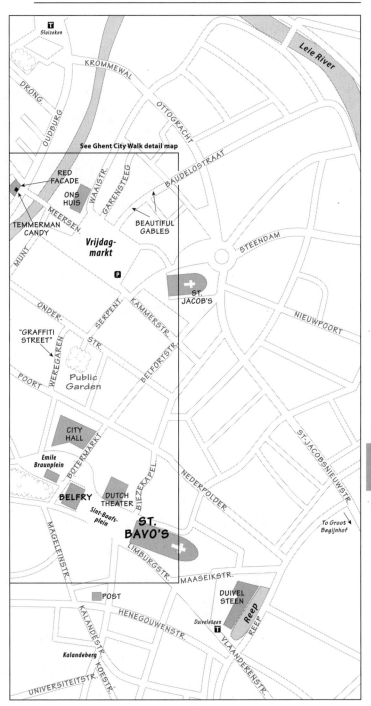

Sluizeken

KROMMEWAL

Leie River

DRONG

OUDBURG

OTTOGRACHT

BAUDELOSTRAAT

See Ghent City Walk detail map

RED
FACADE

WAAISTR.

GARENSTEEG

ONS
HUIS

MEERSEN.

BEAUTIFUL
GABLES

STEENDAM

TEMMERMAN
CANDY

MUNT

*Vrijdag-markt*

P

NIEUWPOORT

ONDER-

SERPENT.

KAMMERSTR.

ST.
JACOB'S

"GRAFFITI
STREET"

WEREGAREN

STR.

BELFORTSTR.

POORT

*Public
Garden*

ST.-JACOBSNIEUWSTR.

CITY
HALL

BOTERMARKT

*Emile
Braunplein*

BIEZEKAPEL

NEDERPOLDER

BELFRY

DUTCH
THEATER

*Sint-Baafs-plein*

ST.
BAVO'S

To Groot
Begijnhof

MAGELEINSTR.

LIMBURGSTR.

MAASEIKSTR.

POST

DUIVEL
STEEN

Reep

HENEGOUWENSTR.

*Duivelsteen*

REEP

VLAANDERENSTR.

KALANDESTR.

KOESTR.

*Kalandeberg*

UNIVERSITEITSTR.

## House of Alijn (Huis van Alijn)

This small museum re-creates scenes from Belgian daily life through the last few centuries. All in all, it's a mildly intriguing collection of bric-a-brac, from dishes, toys, cribs, and kitchen appliances, to a statue of a woman wiping a baby's bum.

**Cost and Hours:** €6; Mon-Tue and Thu-Fri 9:00-17:00, Sat-Sun 10:00-18:00, closed Wed; Kraanlei 65, tel. 09-235-3800, www.huisvanalijn.be.

**Visiting the Museum:** The rooms guide you through a calendar year, showcasing customs, holidays, and rites-of-passage—some universal and some specific to Belgium. You'll see rooms devoted to birth, showing Belgian christening dresses and the "pink box" of childcare products the government distributes to new mothers. One room features teenage memorabilia—cringe at the '70s and '80s fashions. The room on getting older explains how Belgians mourn after the death of a loved one.

You'll see 19th-century antiques like wooden toy soldiers and 20th-century antiques like rotary telephones and Atari consoles. There are few labels or descriptions, but the objects (and their time periods) speak for themselves. The tranquil courtyard of what used to be an almshouse (a refuge for poor elderly people) hosts a little café.

## ▲Castle of the Counts (Gravensteen)

Though it dates from 1180, this fortress has morphed over the centuries, and much of it is rebuilt and restored. It's impressive from

the outside, but mostly bare inside and information is skimpy. Still, it's a fun opportunity to get a feel for the medieval world as you twist through towers and ramble over ramparts. It has all the parts of a typical castle: courtyard and keep, throne room, chapel, 18-foot-deep dungeon, and ramparts. There are displays of authentic swords and suits of armor, along with a reconstructed guillotine that was last used in 1861. For fans of torture museums, this one has real instruments of "persuasion" (see

# Castle of the Counts: A Torturer's Toolbox

In the Middle Ages, torture was used to extract confessions from heretics and criminals, and to punish the convicted prior to execution. Torturers had a huge toolkit with which to practice their art.

One device was the rack, designed to pull the victim's limbs apart. A prisoner's arms and legs were tied to opposite ends of the machine. Then the torturer turned the crank, expanding the rack and leaving the victim with dislocated joints, or even limbless.

Another nasty tool was a finger screw—a set of bars and screws that tightened to crush fingers and toes. Since finger screws were small and portable, they were a favorite of traveling medieval interrogators.

The iron maiden was a spike-filled cabinet, just tall enough to fit a standing human. It had small holes through which torturers inserted sharp objects to stab prisoners, sometimes killing them. A variant was the torture chair, entirely covered in spikes. Victims' wrists were tied to the arms of the chair, and weights were attached to their legs and feet. Sitting in the chair usually resulted in death from blood loss.

For public executions, prisoners would be stretched over a wheel, and the executioner would break their bones with an iron hammer, leaving them to die from shock and dehydration. For less serious crimes, prisoners received the gift of one swift and deadly blow to the neck.

Then there was waterboarding. In medieval times jailers

poured water—and often bodily fluids—down prisoners' throats. To avoid drowning, "suspects" might drink the liquid, which resulted in a sort of intoxication and often death. The modern variation—practiced by the Japanese during World War II, the French in Algeria, and the CIA at Guantanamo Bay—could be described as "slow-motion drowning." Interrogators covered prisoners' faces with cloth or another thin material, then poured water over their nose and mouth, triggering the gag reflex and a sensation of drowning.

Today, although 146 members of the United Nations have ratified an international convention outlawing torture, it remains rampant worldwide. Carl Jung's observation is still relevant: "The healthy man does not torture others—generally it is the tortured who turn into torturers."

sidebar), including an exhibit showing how waterboarding was practiced by the Inquisition centuries before Dick Cheney endorsed its use as "a no-brainer." If you climb to the top of one of the towers (lots of claustrophobic stairs), you'll get good views—and the feeling that you're the ruler of your own castle.

**Cost and Hours:** €10, daily 10:00-18:00, Nov-March 9:00-17:00, last entry 45 minutes before closing, tel. 09-225-9306, Sint-Veerleplein, www.gravensteengent.be.

### ▲Ghent Design Museum (Design Museum Gent)

This collection celebrating the Belgian knack for design is enjoyable for everyone, but worth ▲▲▲ for those interested in 17th-

to 21st-century decorative arts. Furniture, glass, ceramics, and jewelry are displayed in a classic old building with a creaky wood interior, with a bright-white, spacious, and glassy modern hall in the center. You'll cross back and forth between these sections, seeing both old-timey rooms and contemporary design. Don't miss the 18th-century dining room, with a remarkable wood-carved chandelier.

**Cost and Hours:** €8; Mon-Tue and Thu-Fri 9:30-17:30, Sat-Sun 10:00-18:00, closed Wed; Jan Breydelstraat 5, tel. 09-267-9999, www.designmuseumgent.be.

## MUSEUMS NEAR THE TRAIN STATION

Several museums are closer to the train station than to the historical center, which makes them ideal to visit on your way in or out of Ghent. The Fine Arts Museum and the Stedelijk Contemporary Art Museum are located at Citadelpark, while the Ghent City Museum is a bit farther north of the station.

### ▲Fine Arts Museum (Museum voor Schone Kunsten)

This museum offers a good, representative look at Northern European art. It's one of the most user-friendly collections of Low Countries art you'll find in Belgium, with lesser-known yet fun works by artists such as Bosch, Rubens, Van Dyck, and Magritte.

**Cost and Hours:** €8; Tue-Fri 9:30-17:30, Sat-Sun 10:00-18:00, closed Mon; in Citadelpark along Fernand Scribedreef street, tel. 09-323-6700, www.mskgent.be.

**Getting to the Citadelpark Museums:** To reach Citadelpark and its museums from the train station (about a 10-minute walk), exit straight ahead to the modern sculpture in the middle of the plaza. Turn right and walk up the tree- and bike-lined Koningin

Astridlaan about five minutes, then cross the road and enter Cita-delpark. Walk straight ahead, then curl around the left side of the big, modern building at the center of the park; as you round the far side, the Neoclassical entrance to the Fine Arts Museum is across the small street, and the Stedelijk Contemporary Art Museum (with a large *S.M.A.K.* sign over the entrance) is on your right.

**Visiting the Museum:** As you enter, to the right (in num-bered rooms) are older works, and to the left (in lettered rooms) are 19th- and 20th-century works and temporary exhibits. To take a counterclockwise, chronological spin though the collection, turn right from the entrance, and keep an eye out for the fine pieces highlighted below.

**Room 2: Hieronymus Bosch**'s jarring *Christ Carrying the Cross* (1515-1516) features a severe-looking Jesus surrounded by

grotesque faces. Typical of the Middle Ages, Bosch believed that evil was ugly—and all but three faces on this canvas (form-ing a diagonal, from lower left to upper right) are hid-eous. The serene woman to the left of Christ is Veron-ica, who has just wiped his face. In the upper right, with an ashen complex-ion, is the stoic good thief,
flanked by a doctor and a taunting monk. Meanwhile, in the lower right, the orange-tinged unrepentant thief sneers back at his heck-lers. Nearby, Bosch's c. 1505 portrait of St. Jerome—who was his personal patron saint—shows the holy hermit having discarded his clothes. Just above his legs, notice the owl (representing evil) sin-isterly eyeing a titmouse (good). Also in this room, in **Rogier Van der Weyden**'s *The Virgin with a Carnation* (1480), the Baby Jesus makes a benediction gesture with his little hand. This small paint-ing was designed as a focal point for personal meditation.

**Room 4:** This room is devoted to the restoration of **Jan and Hubert van Eyck**'s *Adoration of the Mystic Lamb* altarpiece housed in St. Bavo's Cathedral. You can watch as conservators work on one panel at a time, removing old varnish and retouching damaged sec-tions. The €1.4 million project should be completed in 2020.

**Room 5:** In here you'll find **Peter Paul Rubens**' altarpiece de-picting St. Francis of Assisi receiving the stigmata—the wounds of the crucified Christ—from a six-winged angel, whose own hands and feet are fastened to a cross. Francis' brother Leo stares in amazement from below.

**Room 6:** This room features **Pieter Brueghel II**'s copy of his more famous father's much-loved *Peasant Wedding in a Barn*. The elder painter trained his kids to carry on the family business—and younger Brueghel became a talented painter in his own right. In his *Village Lawyer,*  we see the attorney behind a desk piled with papers, as peasants bring items to barter for his services.

**Room 7:** Rubens' student **Anthony van Dyck** depicts the mythological story of *Jupiter and Antiope*—a horned-and-horny god about to inseminate a sleeping woman.

• *Circle into the modern (lettered) wing.*

**Room A:** You'll find works by homegrown Belgian modernist **René Magritte**. His clever *Perspective II*—part of a larger series—wryly replaces the four subjects on Edouard Manet's famous *Balcony* painting with coffins. Next to this are similar surrealist works by **Max Ernst** and **Paul Delvaux**. A Belgian artist who studied, worked, and taught in Brussels, Delvaux became famous for his surrealistic paintings of nude women, often wandering through weirdly lit landscapes. They cast long shadows, wandering bare-breasted among classical ruins.

**Room D:** Find the *Portrait of Physician Ludwig Adler* by Viennese Secessionist painter **Oskar Kokoschka**. The artist uses dynamic, expressionistic brushstrokes to capture the personality, rather than a precise reproduction, of his subject.

## Stedelijk Contemporary Art Museum (Stedelijk Museum voor Actuele Kunst, a.k.a. SMAK)

This art gallery is constantly changing, both the "permanent" collection and many temporary exhibits. It's worth a visit only for art lovers, and is conveniently located just across the street from the Fine Arts Museum.

**Cost and Hours:** €8; Tue-Fri 9:30-17:30, Sat-Sun 10:00-18:00, closed Mon; tel. 09-240-7601, www.smak.be. For directions on how to reach the museum, see "Getting to the Citadelpark Museums," earlier.

## ▲Ghent City Museum (Stadsmuseum Gent, a.k.a. STAM)

This cutting-edge museum, housed in a beautiful 14th-century Gothic abbey complex called Bijloke, explains the history of Ghent with all the bells and whistles you'd expect in this fashion-forward city. The permanent exhibit traces the city's history in high-tech treatments mixed with historic artifacts. Everything is explained in English, but it's worth paying extra for the excellent audioguide.

GHENT SIGHTS

**Cost and Hours:** €8; Mon-Tue and Thu-Fri 9:00-17:00, Sat-Sun 10:00-18:00, closed Wed, last entry one hour before closing; audioguide-€3, Godshuizenlaan 2, tel. 09-267-1400, www.stamgent.be.

**Getting There:** From the train station, it's a 15- to 20-minute walk: Exit straight ahead, then angle left up the busy, tram-tracks-lined Koning Albertlaan. After the bridge, turn right on Godshuizenlaan. Or, from the station, you could ride tram #1 to the Veergrep stop, backtrack a long block to the first busy road, and turn right.

**Visiting the Museum:** Begin in the modern annex, where you'll buy your ticket on the ground floor, then head upstairs to the first floor. In the Ghent Today room, you can walk across a giant aerial photograph of the modern city sprawl and (in the middle) examine an elevated model of the old center. Then cross over to the old abbey complex, where you'll slowly circle the courtyard for a clockwise, chronological loop that traces the story of Ghent.

Besides viewing the excellent exhibits, you can peer down into the abbey church, nuns' dormitory, and refectory. Mixed between the six rooms of the main collection are some fascinating themed detours; for example, you'll learn about the theft of the still-missing *Just Judges* panel of the Ghent Altarpiece, housed in St. Bavo's Cathedral (see the sidebar on page 297). Your visit ends with a walk through the old church building.

## OUTER GHENT
### Museum Dr. Guislain

Just west of the town center, this museum—set in Belgium's first mental hospital—traces the history of medical achievements in psychiatry. You'll see displays of instruments, research milestones, and art from the time mental illness was considered demonic possession to contemporary treatments.

**Cost and Hours:** €8; Tue-Fri 9:00-17:00, Sat-Sun 13:00-18:00, closed Mon, last entry one hour before closing; Jozeph Guislainstraat 43, tel. 09-398-6950, www.museumdrguislain.be.

**Getting There:** Take tram #1 (direction: Wondelgem/Evergem) to the Guislainstraat stop. Look for the Dr. Guislain Psychiatric Center (with decorative 19th-century brickwork), follow the cloister to the right, and then follow signs to the museum.

### Groot Begijnhof

Begijnhofs were homes for communities of lay women: places to live, pray, and serve society without taking religious vows. Unlike most Flemish cities with just one begijnhof, Ghent has three. Groot Begijnhof is the largest—and its Flemish Gothic Revival architecture differs greatly from the begijnhof in Bruges (described in the Sights in Bruges chapter).

**Cost and Hours:** Free, daily 6:00-23:00, main office at Groot Begijnhof 67, tel. 09-228-2308, www.grootbegijnhof.be.

**Getting There:** From Korenmarkt take bus #18 (direction: Merendree), get off at the Schoolstraat stop, turn right on School-straat, and look for the arched gateway at the end of the next side street.

# GHENT CITY WALK

The heart of Ghent still looks much like it did circa 1500, when this was one of Europe's greatest cities: bristling with skyscraping towers, rich with art, and thronged with upscale citizens.

This self-guided walk starts at the former harbor, where this city of clothmakers plugged into the global economy. Next we pass by the towers for which the city became known. The grandest is the soaring steeple of St. Bavo's, home to the main art sight in town, Van Eyck's famous altarpiece. Then it's down main street (Hoog-poort) through the heart of town, whose many shops make clear that this city of traders lives on. The last part of the walk winds along small lanes, making its way through the trendy residential district. We'll end with the fun-to-tour Castle of the Counts and several photogenic squares.

## Orientation

**Length of This Walk:** Allow 1.5 hours to traverse this mile-long walk, plus more time to go inside sights along the way—you can see it all in about three hours. With limited time, end the walk at the Castle of the Counts, where you can catch tram #1 back to the station.

**Getting There:** Take tram #1 from the train station to Korenmarkt (see page 266 for details).

**Church of St. Nicholas:** Free, Tue-Sun 10:00-17:00, Mon from 14:00.

**Belfry:** €8, daily 10:00-18:00.

**St. Bavo's Cathedral:** Church-free, altarpiece-€4; Mon-Sat 9:30-17:00, Sun from 13:00; Nov-March Mon-Sat 10:30-16:00, Sun from 13:00.

**House of Alijn:** €6, Mon-Tue and Thu-Fri 9:00-17:00, Sat-Sun
10:00-18:00, closed Wed.

**Castle of the Counts:** €10, daily 10:00-18:00, Nov-March 9:00-
17:00, last entry 45 minutes before closing.

# The Walk Begins

• *From the Korenmarkt tram #1 stop, walk straight ahead, turn left at
the gray church, and you'll soon reach the bustling square where our tour
begins.*

## ❶ Korenmarkt Square

You're at the center of historic Ghent. The square is enclosed by
the big gray-stone church, a prickly medieval-looking facade, and
several historic townhouses with
classic gables. The scene captures
the glory of Ghent in its heyday.

The city boomed in the
Middle Ages, when the wool
trade made it wealthy. By the
14th century, Ghent's population was around 65,000—posi-
tively massive in an age when
most of Europe was rural farm-
land (north of the Alps, only Paris was larger). Two-thirds of the
city's population were textile workers, making Ghent arguably Europe's first industrial city. Imagine Ghent at its peak around the
year 1500, flush with guilders from weaving high-fashion cloth
and shipping it around Europe. With its wealth, Ghent became
a proud city of soaring towers. In fact, Ghent was so big that, unlike lesser cities in Belgium, it didn't have just one single "Great
Market" (Grote Markt). It had many squares, each specializing in
a different trade. For instance, this square, the "Grain Market," was
where citizens flocked to buy food.

The big building with prickly steeples (opposite St. Nicholas)
is the **former post office,** now transformed into a ritzy shopping
complex. While it seems medi-
eval, it's actually much newer—
eclectic Neo-Gothic and Neo-
Renaissance, completed in 1910.
Ghent was thriving once again
and used this retro style that
captured the feel of its glory
days. Over the entrance you'll
see symbols glorifying Belgium,
Flanders, Wallonia, and the

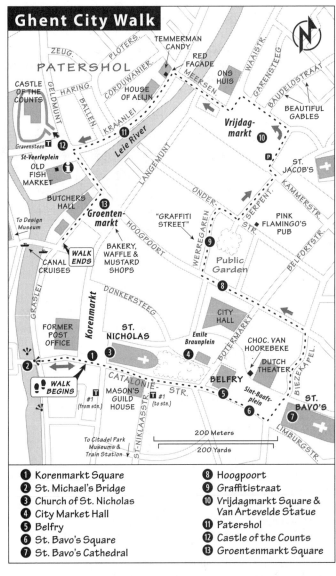

# Ghent City Walk

ZEUG. PLOTERS
PATERSHOL
TEMMERMAN CANDY
RED FAÇADE
ONS HUIS
CASTLE OF THE COUNTS
HARING BALLEN GELDMUNT
CORDUWANIER
HOUSE OF ALIJN
KRAANLEI
MEERSEN
WAAISTR.
GARENSTEEG
BAUDELOSTRAAT
BEAUTIFUL GABLES
Gravensteen
St-Veerleplein
OLD FISH MARKET
Leie River
LANGEMUNT
Vrijdagmarkt
ST. JACOB'S
KAMMERSTR.
BUTCHERS HALL
Groentenmarkt
HOOGPOORT
"GRAFFITI STREET"
ONDER-
WERREGAREN
SERPENT STR.
PINK FLAMINGO'S PUB
BELFORTSTR.
To Design Museum
CANAL CRUISES
WALK ENDS
BAKERY, WAFFLE & MUSTARD SHOPS
Public Garden
GRASLEI
DONKERSTEEG
Korenmarkt
FORMER POST OFFICE
ST. NICHOLAS
CITY HALL
Emile Braunplein
BOTERMARKT
CHOC. VAN HOOREBEKE
DUTCH THEATER
BIEZEKAPEL.
WALK BEGINS
CATALONIE STR.
MASON'S GUILD HOUSE
#1 (from stn.)
#1 (to stn.)
ST.-NIKLAASSTR.
BELFRY
Sint-Baafs-plein
ST. BAVO'S
LIMBURGSTR.
To Citadel Park Museums & Train Station
200 Meters
200 Yards

❶ Korenmarkt Square
❷ St. Michael's Bridge
❸ Church of St. Nicholas
❹ City Market Hall
❺ Belfry
❻ St. Bavo's Square
❼ St. Bavo's Cathedral
❽ Hoogpoort
❾ Graffitistraat
❿ Vrijdagmarkt Square & Van Artevelde Statue
⓫ Patershol
⓬ Castle of the Counts
⓭ Groentenmarkt Square

GHENT CITY WALK

Belgian Congo. In the window friezes you can find the coat of arms of all the Belgian provinces and major cities. The busts over the windows are leaders of all the nations who joined the International Postal Union—a big deal back when the global economy was laced together by letters and mailed documents. On the side of the building, you can find a bust of Florence Nightingale, the famed English nurse of the Victorian era.

*• Circle around the left side of the post office building, and out onto...*

## ❷ St. Michael's Bridge (Sint-Michielsbrug)

The city was founded at the confluence of two rivers: the Lys (Leie in Dutch) and the Scheldt (Schelde in Dutch). The waterway under

your feet—now plied by tourist-laden boats—was the city's busy harbor. Lining the embankment are several ornately decorated guild houses—meeting halls for the town's boatmen, grain traders, and weighers.

This viewpoint offers Ghent's best 360-degree panorama. At one end of the canal, find the imposing tower of the Castle of the Counts, rising above the Old Fish Market. That's where we'll end this tour.

Now turn 90 degrees right and look back down Cataloniëstraat. View the spires of Ghent's three main buildings: the rectangular tower of the Church of St. Nicholas, the belfry (with a dragon rather than a cross on top), and St. Bavo's Cathedral. We'll see all three, then circle around through town to the Castle of the Counts.

*• Return to the Korenmarkt and turn your attention to the big gray church.*

## ❸ Church of St. Nicholas (Sint-Niklaaskerk)

This stout church was built mostly during the 13th century, a boom time for Ghent. It's dedicated to St. Nicholas, the patron saint of sailors, so it was only natural that it became the favorite of the river traders who sold their goods on the Korenmarkt. The church is a textbook example of Scheldt Gothic style, which marks the transition from Romanesque to Dutch Gothic: bluish-gray stone, turrets, and a single tower in the center (rather than twin towers on the facade).

The church's exterior is a microcosm of Ghent's rise and fall. The bluish-gray limestone of its tower tells you it was built before 1400, when Ghent was rolling in wool money and could afford to float the valuable stone down the Scheldt River from the distant city of Tournai. The yellow sandstone of one of the portals along the right side dates this section to between 1400 and 1500, when the economy was slowing, and builders quarried local stone. The red brick along the church's right wall was locally produced after 1500, when competition from Brussels and England, combined with a conservative guild leadership that was slow to adapt to changing markets, caused Ghent's economy to tank. (Proud Ghent natives gleefully point out that their rival, Bruges, is built mostly of brick—indicating that city's lowlier economic status in medieval times.)

**Visiting the Church:** Enter through the side door facing the tram tracks. You can tell the church was built from the front to the back, as the stone transitions from the blue-gray limestone used first to the yellow sandstone used later.

While the building itself is Gothic, the decorations inside—like most in Ghent—are much newer. As this region was at the forefront of the Protestant Reformation in the 16th century, the interior of Ghent's churches suffered at the hands of the iconoclasts—Calvinist Protestants who stripped Catholic churches of all adornments to mark their difference with Catholic "idolatry" and wealth. The church interior was redecorated during the Counter-Reformation with the very Baroque altar of corkscrew columns (painted wood, not marble) and in the 19th century with an impressive organ. Iconoclasts destroyed essentially all the medieval glass in Ghent—the modern stained glass above represents the seven sacraments.

• *Exiting the church, look across the street and notice the statue-topped gable of the* **Masons' Guild House.** *This 15th-century facade was only revealed in 1976, when renovators discovered the old facade behind a brick wall. During the renovation, they added the six statues of twirling dancers.*

Turn left and head down Cataloniëstraat (away from the river). Beyond St. Nicholas stands the big, wooden roof of the...

## ❹ City Market Hall (Stadshal)

Just a few years ago, this space was no more than an ugly parking lot. But city leaders decided to beautify and turn this prime real estate into a 21st-century social hub. Now there's a public square, partially sheltered by a modern twin-gabled timber roof meant to evoke the rooftops of medieval Ghent. While many residents embrace the new market hall, some hate it (especially as it obscures the view of City Hall) and have dubbed it the "Sheep Shed" and the "Hall of Shame." Take a moment to wander beneath the gables, where light filtering in through hundreds of slits scatters in ever-changing patterns. On the lower level is a café, free WCs, and a bicycle parking garage. You'll also see an original 17th-century bell from the adjacent belfry. Nearby cafés, wine bars, and (often) food trucks cater to office workers on their lunch breaks.

• *The next tall building is the...*

## ❺ Belfry (Belfort)

This tower has stood here since the 14th century, built to house and protect the parchment record of Ghent's favored privileges, granted to the city by the counts of Flanders in exchange for financial support. The Neo-Gothic spire (from the gargoyles up) was added when Ghent proudly hosted the World's Fair in 1913. The dragon

at the top symbolizes not the devil (as was typical in the Middle Ages), but a protector who never sleeps as it watches over the city's rights. It was also a fire watchtower, represented by the four sentries positioned at the corners. The carillon in the tower often plays the Ghent town anthem at the top of the hour.

**Visiting the Belfry:** You can ascend the belfry for a decent, if not stunning, view over town. It's just a couple of flights of stairs, then an elevator most of the way. Enter on the side facing the tram tracks, and ogle the gorgeous wall painting of old Ghent in the main hall (borrow the English explanations as you enter). Then walk down through some excavations, and spiral up to level 0, which shows off models of the former spires that topped the tower (including an original dragon, from 1380). From here, you can walk or ride the elevator to different levels with exhibits: on level 1, a bell museum, including a film about how bells are cast; on level 2, the giant bell called "Roland"; and on level 3, a big rotating drum with pegs used to program short carillon melodies.

The long building at the base of (and behind) the belfry is the **Cloth Hall,** which was important to this textile center.

• *The square beyond the belfry is...*

## ❻ St. Bavo's Square (Sint-Baafsplein)

This square became a symbolic battleground between Belgium's Dutch-speaking and French-speaking factions during the 1800s and 1900s. Belgium was dominated by the French-speaking bourgeoisie, even though Dutch speakers were in the majority. So when the ornate **Dutch Theater** (Koninklijke Nederlandse Schouwburg, or NT Gent)

was built in 1899, it finally gave the town's Dutch speakers a place to perform plays of their own. By embracing Dutch as a language worthy of theater, the spunky Flemish were asserting their cultural legitimacy. The golden mosaic depicts Apollo returning to Mount Parnassus, much as the Flemish felt they were coming home to their beloved language.

The **statue** in the middle of the square—of a muscular man and comely woman—also celebrates the resurrection of the Dutch

language here. Notice the lion, a symbol of Flanders, on their flag. The relief on the base (facing the theater) depicts Jan Frans Willems, one of the founders of the Flemish revival.

(By the way, it took a full century before Ghent's prestigious university was allowed to teach courses in Dutch, rather than in French and Latin. To protest the change, the French-speaking industrialist who owned the local electric company spitefully cut power to mourn, in his eyes, the university's rejection of enlightened thinking.) For more on the Flemish-Walloon conflict, see the sidebar in the Belgian History chapter.

To the left of the theater is **Chocolatier Van Hoorebeke,** a producer of fine pralines. To see the chocolate makers hard at work, look through the glass floor inside the shop.

• *At the end of the square is Ghent's top sight.*

### ❼ St. Bavo's Cathedral (Sint-Baafskathedraal)

Ghent's Gothic cathedral can claim plenty of history (Holy Roman Emperor Charles V was baptized here), and it has a beautifully carved pulpit and a Rubens altar painting. But the showstopper here is the monumental *Adoration of the Mystic Lamb* altarpiece by Jan Van Eyck and his brother, Hubert.

For details, see the ▢ St. Bavo's Cathedral & Ghent Altarpiece Tour chapter.

• *Facing the cathedral, turn left and head down the curving street called Biezekapelstraat. You'll pass the medieval turrets and arcades of the back of the Achtersikkel mansion—the former home of a powerful family of patricians, now restored to house a music academy (you may hear students rehearsing). Exiting this street, turn left on Nederpolder. You're now heading up the main street of medieval Ghent.*

### ❽ Hoogpoort

This "High Gate" street connects Ghent's two rivers. As you walk, notice you're on a slight hill; Ghent was founded at a high point between the rivers, which people made ample use of for trade.

Crossing Belfortstraat, you'll see the giant, eclectic, slightly run-down **City Hall** (Stadhuis) on your left. As Ghent in its heyday

had negotiated special privileges from the counts of Flanders, the City Hall was a prestigious symbol, serving as a monument to self-rule. Notice how it's been augmented over the years. The ornate Gothic core (along Hoogpoort) dates from the early 16th century. The blocky, black-and-gold-columned Neoclassi-cal section (down Botermarkt) was added a century later, following the fashion of the time.

• *Continue along Hoogpoort, observing the many facets of this one build-ing—Gothic statues, then banded columns. A few steps beyond the end of City Hall, find the narrow passageway (on the right) called Werregaren-straat. It's better known as...*

## ❾ Graffitistraat

Once used to drain water away from this high ground, this pas-sageway now has a different purpose and an apt nickname: Graffiti

street. Walk down the lane, enjoying the artwork provid-ed by the people of Ghent. This is a typically pragmatic Belgian solution to a social problem: Rather than out-lawing graffiti entirely, the police have designated this one street to give would-be artists a legal, controlled outlet for their impulses.

Halfway down the lane, notice the beautiful fenced-in garden on your right. This restful, city-owned, picnic-perfect space is open to the public. (The entrance is farther ahead, at Onderstraat #22.)

• *Emerging from Graffitistraat, turn right on Onderstraat, then turn left down narrow Serpentstraat. This street is lined with some fun boutiques and colorful secondhand stores (for details, see "Shopping in Ghent," on page 305). At the end, turn left and you'll be in...*

## ❿ Vrijdagmarkt Square

This large square represents Ghent as a city of the common people, and several days a week, it hosts a market. While traditionally the big town market was on Friday (as the square's name—Vrijdag—indicates), these days the primary market day is Sunday, when six different locations around the old center are lively with antiques, secondhand books, and—on this square—chirping birds, among other things. Vrijdagmarkt also hosts a smaller market on Friday mornings and Saturday afternoons. But any day, it's a great place to pause for a beverage at one of the cafés ringing the spacious square.

The statue in the square depicts **Jakob van Artevelde,** a clever businessman who saved the day in the 14th century, when Ghent

was caught between powerful France (which controlled the city) and England (which provided it with wool). Van Artevelde—not an aristocrat, but an ordinary citizen—boldly negotiated directly with the king to keep Ghent neutral in the conflict and keep the wool coming in. Van Artevelde's memory was resurrected during the nationalism of the late 19th and early 20th centuries, as a symbol of the Flemish people of Ghent asserting their independence from the Francophones. Today he's still celebrated by the people of Ghent, who sometimes call their city "Artevelde-Stad."

Directly behind the Van Artevelde statue is **Baudelostraat,** a street worth a peek for some particularly beautiful gables dating to the early 20th century. It's also home to a fun antique mall (see "Shopping in Ghent," page 305).

Towering in a corner of the square is the eclectic **Ons Huis** ("House of the People," with the sign for *Bond Moyson*—a socialist health insurance); it's the headquarters for the region's socialist movement. Not surprisingly for a city with a long industrial heritage, Ghent is a hotbed of left-leaning politics and the birthplace of the original Belgian Labor Party. Above the door, notice the rooster—crowing to wake up the workers.

Directly in front of the Ons Huis is the popular **Frituur Jozef** fry wagon.

• *Exit the square down the narrow street just left of the workers' hall (Meerseniersstraat). In a block you reach a bridge. As you cross the bridge, notice the walkways that line the riverbank, allowing you a scenic and uncrowded stroll just above the water. Now, enter the district called...*

## ⓫ Patershol

Until recently a run-down and dangerous district, today this neighborhood is one of Ghent's trendiest. And though it's predominantly residential, Patershol is also a great place for restaurant-hunting (see the Ghent Sleeping, Eating & More chapter).

As you cross the bridge, you'll see two particularly fine (if well-worn) gabled **facades.** The red facade features panels with figures symbolizing the five senses: monkey = taste; eagle = sight; deer = hearing; dog = smell; and humans = touch (since we have no hair on our hands). The other building

has panels demonstrating six virtuous acts (the seventh—burying the dead—was deemed too gruesome to depict, so it's symbolized by the urn on top). The ground floor of this building houses a favorite old-fashioned candy shop, **Temmerman,** with some unique Ghent treats. Wippers are toffee with a sugar coating, marshmallowy Lieve Vrouwkes are shaped like the Virgin Mary, and cone-shaped Cuberdons—the local favorite—are filled with raspberry syrup.

• *Turn left and walk along Kraanlei, passing the **House of Alijn** (with a tourable interior—see the Sights in Ghent chapter). Continue along the pleasant canal, curving right with the road. You arrive at a square called Sint-Veerleplein, dominated by the imposing...*

## ⓬ Castle of the Counts (Gravensteen)

Built in 1180 by Philip of Alsace, this rough-stone fortress was designed not to protect the people of Ghent, but to intimidate

the city's independence-minded citizens. It was modeled on the Krak des Chevaliers in Syria, which Phillip visited during the Second Crusade. At the time, it was outside the city walls. Today, you can tour the castle (see the Sights in Ghent chapter).

This castle was inhabited only briefly; the counts of Flanders moved to what would later become the (more comfortable) palace of Holy Roman Emperor Charles V. In 1540, Charles V (who was born in Ghent but ruled from Spain) demanded a huge tribute. When the citizens refused, he came here personally to crush the rebellion. The leaders of Ghent had to pay the money, then beg forgiveness, on their knees, with nooses around their necks. Today, you'll see many allusions to the noose around town, in particular the very popular beer called **'t Stropke**—"The Noose." The people of Ghent are often called "noose bearers" *(Stroppedragers).*

Also on the square is the fancy, sculpture-adorned entrance to the **Old Fish Market** (Oude Vismijn), home of the TI and a sprawling brasserie with waterfront seating. Study the facade: That's Neptune on top; below him are Ghent's two rivers: the Scheldt (male) and the Lys (female). It's said that Ghent is the child of these two rivers.

• *If you'd like to end this walk early, you could catch tram #1 to the train station from right in front of the Castle of the Counts (direction: Flanders Expo).*

*Otherwise, to continue to a particularly pleasant square, exit Sint-Veerleplein down Kleine Vismarkt street. Cross the bridge to one final stop.*

## ⓲ Groentenmarkt Square

As you cross the bridge to the Groentenmarkt ("Vegetable Market"), look for the long, medieval **Butchers Hall** (Groot Vlee-shuis) to the right (closed Mon). The hall looks like it's seen better days, but it's worth a peek inside to see its impressive wooden vault (built entirely without nails, and clearly employing ship-builders' expertise). For hygienic reasons, until the 19th

century, this was the only place in town allowed to sell meat. You'll see local cured ham hanging from the rafters. The shop inside sells specialty products from East Flanders.

Outside, the lean-to shacks once sold offal and sausages—giving the adjacent square its name: Pensmarkt ("Sausage market"). For a good snack stop on the square, look for Belgian-fries purveyor **Frituur Filip** (described on page 304). Across the square from the Butchers Hall is a good traditional bakery (Himschoot); next to that, a café sells delicious takeaway waffles, and to the right of that is the **Tierenteyn Verlent mustard shop** (at #3, closed Sun). Made in the cellar, then pumped into a barrel in the back of the shop, the mustard is some of the horseradish-hottest you'll ever sample. They use no preservatives, so you'll need to refrigerate it—or use it for today's picnic.

• *Head to the far end of the Butchers Hall, then the building beyond it. The bridge here affords another good view of Ghent's canals. Just across the bridge and to the right is the good **Ghent Design Museum** (described in the Sights in Ghent chapter). Near this bridge, various companies sell **boat tours** along the canals of Ghent (see the Orientation* to *Ghent chapter). Or you can backtrack (turn right along the river) to the **Castle of the Counts** (where there's a handy tram #1 stop) or the **House of Alijn. Korenmarkt**, where we started our tour, is just a block and a half away. In fact, most of what's worth seeing in Ghent is within a few steps of right here. Enjoy.*

# ST. BAVO'S CATHEDRAL & GHENT ALTARPIECE TOUR

*Sint-Baafskathedraal & Lam Gods*

Ghent's cathedral is a vast Gothic oyster housing the pearl of Flemish painting—the Ghent Altarpiece.

Besides this masterpiece by Jan van Eyck, the church itself has a number of quirky sights: You'll see a heavenly pulpit with down-to-earth angels, a painting in which Rubens and the women in his life appear, and Adam and Eve panels depicting the first couple modeling the first clothes.

But it's Van Eyck's altarpiece—displayed all by itself in a darkened chapel—that invites you to linger. This is where modern oil painting was born. It's where invaders—from kings to conquerors to Nazis—have come to steal this potent symbol of civilization. It's where art pilgrims journey to admire the sensuous detail and provocative symbolism of a work that signals a medieval world awakening to the new age of the Renaissance.

## Orientation

**Cost:** Cathedral-free, Ghent Altarpiece (both original and facsimile)-€4, includes excellent audioguide; tickets sold inside left of the entrance.

**Hours:** Mon-Sat 9:30-17:00, Sun from 13:00; Nov-March Mon-Sat 10:30-16:00, Sun from 13:00. The altarpiece's exterior panels are shut between 12:00 and 13:00 for better viewing.

**Information:** Tel. 09-225-1626, www.sintbaafskathedraal.be.

**Altarpiece Restoration:** Some panels may not be viewable due to ongoing conservation, set to be completed by 2020. (You can watch the restoration process at the Fine Arts Museum—see the listing in the Sights in Ghent chapter.)

**Crowd-Beating Tips:** Though the church is big enough to accommodate even the worst crowds, the small altarpiece room can be packed. Avoid the worst of it by visiting right at opening time or in the late afternoon. An excellent-quality replica of the altarpiece is displayed in a less-crowded chapel.

**Getting There:** The cathedral dominates the central Sint-Baaf-splein square.

**Tours:** During busy times, volunteer guides can show you around. The audioguide included with your altarpiece ticket delivers 50 wonderful minutes of commentary about the painting.

**Length of This Tour:** The church takes 30 minutes. The altarpiece can be seen in a glance or studied for a lifetime.

**Starring:** The altarpiece whose unprecedented realism changed the course of art history.

## The Tour Begins

### ❶ Exterior

Start by taking in the cathedral's sheer bulk, with its jowl-stretching view up the 292-foot tower. The church was erected from about 1350 until 1559 on the site of earlier structures dating back to 942. It's named for St. Bavo, a Ghent-area nobleman who gave up his materialistic existence to help the poor and establish a monastery here.

• *Step inside and look down the...*

### ❷ Nave

Appreciate the sheer volume of this structure, with its spacious 100-foot-high ceiling, Gothic arches, and stained glass. Notice three telltale materials: red brick (the nave walls), yellow stone (the pillars, also the exterior tower), and—for the valuable area around the altar—the gray stone of the choir. As in the Church of St. Nicholas, all the interior decorations and stained glass date from the 19th century (following the iconoclasm of the 16th century, when much of the church's Gothic ornamentation was destroyed).

• *Go for a counterclockwise spin around the cathedral's interior, beginning with the rear pillar (to the right as you enter). You'll see two painted panels showing...*

### ❸ Adam and Eve with Clothes

These are replicas of Van Eyck's famous nude Adam and Eve from the Ghent Altarpiece. The clothes were added to cover Van Eyck's nudes during the puritanical 19th century. It wasn't Adam and Eve's nakedness that was offensive—it was the unflinching realism of Adam's hairy legs, Eve's bulging stomach, and their spindly legs.

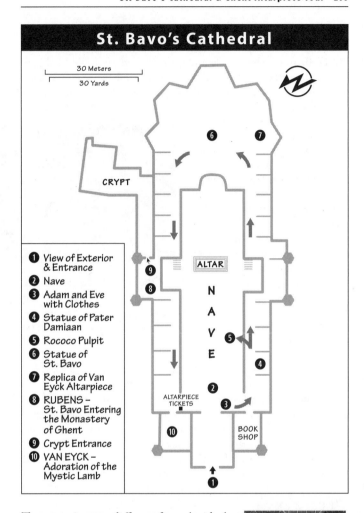

# St. Bavo's Cathedral

30 Meters
30 Yards

CRYPT

❻ ❼

↗ ↖

↓ ↑

**ALTAR**

↓ ↑

**N A V E**

❺ →

❹

❷

ALTARPIECE
TICKETS

❸ ↱

❾
❽

**BOOK
SHOP**

❿

❶ ↑

❶ View of Exterior & Entrance
❷ Nave
❸ Adam and Eve with Clothes
❹ Statue of Pater Damiaan
❺ Rococo Pulpit
❻ Statue of St. Bavo
❼ Replica of Van Eyck Altarpiece
❽ RUBENS – St. Bavo Entering the Monastery of Ghent
❾ Crypt Entrance
❿ VAN EYCK – Adoration of the Mystic Lamb

They were just too different from the ideal-ized nudes of the classical world.

## Right Side

• *Along the right wall (second chapel), find a statue of...*

❹ **Pater Damiaan:** Father Damien (1840-1889) was a Flemish missionary who went to Hawaii to care for lepers, but after 16 years died of leprosy himself. Canonized in 2009, he's a rare saint with a connection to the United States, and an important fig-ure both to Belgians and to Hawaiians.

PATER
DAMIAAN

• *Take a few steps into the nave to admire the remarkable...*

❺ **Rococo Pulpit:** This elaborately carved pulpit was made in the 1740s from white stone and carved wood, with golden highlights. The scene represents the tree of life and the tree of knowledge. The Carrara marble statues just beneath the pulpit drive home a Counter-Reformation message: The woman with the sun on her bosom (representing the power of her faith) wakes up the winged old man on the left (representing time): It's time to wake up to the Catholic faith. The smug frat-boy angels at the bases of the staircases offer a lesson in appropriate worship. The angel on the left watches the pulpit intently, and the one on the right points up to the pulpit

while glancing scoldingly to the back of the church: Hey, you in the back row—pay attention! Up above, notice the two hard-working cupids struggling to raise the cross. Finally, on the very top, notice the golden serpent. Follow its winding body to find the pudgy, winged baby (a sure sign of Rococo) prying the apple of sin from the snake's mouth.

• *In the distance, above the main altar, find the white statue backed by a golden sunburst.*

❻ **Statue of St. Bavo:** The beloved local saint is on his way to heaven. For a better view, circle around the side and step up into the choir area. This seventh-century saint was once a wealthy and rambunctious young soldier, but became a born-again Christian after the death of his wife. Bavo rejected his life of materialism and became a hermit-monk, living for a time in a hollow tree. He is also the patron saint of Haarlem, in the Netherlands.

• *To the right of the main altar is the Vijdt Chapel, which houses the replica of the altarpiece (covered by your original altarpiece ticket).*

❼ **Replica of the Van Eyck Altarpiece:** Van Eyck painted his famous altarpiece specifically for this room. In fact, take note of where the replica altarpiece stands in relation to the chapel's windows. Lit from the right, the altarpiece's figures (such as Adam, upper left) cast shadows to the left.

• *Continue circling the church, rounding the altar to reach the...*

## Left Side

• *In the left transept find a painting by Peter Paul Rubens.*

❽ *St. Bavo Entering the Monastery of Ghent:* This work depicts the moment this bad-boy-turned-saint started on his righteous course. Bavo, in the red cloak, kneels before the abbot to become a monk (Rubens portrayed himself as Bavo). The lower grouping shows Bavo's estate manager distributing his master's belongings to the poor. He's watched, on the left, by Bavo's daughter and her servant. Rubens modeled them after his two wives—his older first wife (in the giant hat) and his much younger, more voluptuous second wife, Hélène Fourment, in the red dress. (The Flemish like to say, with a wink, "An old billy goat loves a young leaf.")

Notice the complex composition. Above, Bavo and the bishop form a diagonal line along the staircase. Below, the women and poor people form another diagonal, perfectly parallel. Compare this dynamic Baroque canvas (1624), pregnant with motion, with the very static composition of Van Eyck's medieval altarpiece (1432). For more about Rubens, see the sidebar on page 248.

• *Across from this canvas is the entrance to the...*

❾ **Crypt:** This area contains some of the building's Romanesque foundations and various chapels decorated with ecclesiastical art both old and modern. Along with tombs of bishops, you'll see faint traces of 15th-century paintings that were whitewashed over by Calvinists, then rediscovered in the 1930s.

• *Circling back to the entrance, you reach the grand finale—the chapel containing the original altarpiece.*

❿ **Ghent Altarpiece:** *Adoration of the Mystic Lamb*

The highlight of the church (and of all Ghent, for art lovers) is Jan and Hubert van Eyck's *Adoration of the Mystic Lamb* (known as the Ghent Altarpiece, and as *"Lam Gods"* in Dutch). It's been called the most influential painting in art history, as it was the first masterpiece done in the new medium of oil, and the first to portray the unidealized realism of the everyday world.

Hubert van Eyck (c. 1385-1426) began the painting, but after his death, his better-known younger brother Jan (c. 1390-1441) picked up the brush and completed his vision. Finished in 1432, this altarpiece represents a monumental stride in Northern European art from medieval stiffness to Renaissance humanism. The first work signed by Jan van Eyck, it's also considered one of the first works of the Flemish Primitives, characterized by a precise dedication to detail (if imperfect mastery of perspective).

The work is monumental: 15 feet wide and 11 feet tall, composed of a dozen separate panels, depicting hundreds of figures,

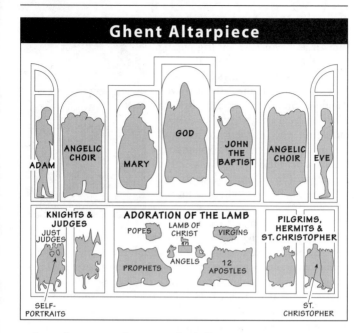

## Ghent Altarpiece

(labels within image) ADAM · ANGELIC CHOIR · MARY · GOD · JOHN THE BAPTIST · ANGELIC CHOIR · EVE · KNIGHTS & JUDGES · JUST JUDGES · ADORATION OF THE LAMB · POPES · LAMB OF CHRIST · VIRGINS · PILGRIMS, HERMITS & ST. CHRISTOPHER · PROPHETS · ANGELS · 12 APOSTLES · SELF-PORTRAITS · ST. CHRISTOPHER

and weighing more than a ton. It challenges visitors with its complex symbolism, multitude of rich details, and sheer scale, but it rewards those willing to invest the time to take it all in.

**Upper Panels:** God—in a rich red robe and three-tiered crown—presides over the scene, raising his hand in a solemn blessing. He's flanked by Mary in her traditional blue and John the Baptist in a green robe over his ascetic camel-hair shirt. Though holy, these figures are obviously modeled on flesh-and-blood people with individualized traits, such as God's jug ears, John's scraggly hair, and Mary's parted lips as she reads along from her book. Ogle the incredible richness of the jewels they wear. The hem of God's robe has an inscription written in pearls, one of the numerous quotes woven into the altarpiece (for instance, "King of Kings" and "Behold the Lamb of God").

Serenading God from either side is a heavenly choir. Unlike earlier altarpieces, these musical angels don't play harps, but rather a 15th-century organ. They have no wings or halos, and each face is unique. Hymnals of the time indicated which face a singer should make when singing a particular note; today's experts can guess which notes the angels are singing from their expressions.

The outermost panels, depicting Adam and Eve, are probably the first Renaissance-era nudes painted north of the Alps. Though Eve still has the big belly and high waistline typical of medieval Eves, Adam steps boldly forward. His toes break the plane of his

# Coveted, Looted, Stolen, Lost

It's a miracle the Ghent Altarpiece has survived for six centuries. It's been the victim of a half-dozen art thefts—perhaps the most stolen painting in existence—and the focus of several international scandals.

In 1566, Protestant iconoclasts stormed St. Bavo's, hell-bent on burning the altarpiece as a symbol of Catholic idolatry. Fortunately, the priests had hidden it safely away at the top of the cathedral tower. In 1794, Napoleon carried off the altarpiece's four central paintings as war trophies and displayed them in the Louvre (1794-1815). In 1821, the king of Prussia smuggled several panels to Germany. Those works were so prized by the world community that the Treaty of Versailles (which ended World War I) specifically ordered Germany to return the panels.

In 1934, someone broke into St. Bavo's and stole the *Just Judges* panel. The thief, possibly a Flemish currency banker, said in his last words that only he knew where the lost panel was.

In World War II, the Ghent Altarpiece got caught up in the battle between Hitler's gang of art looters and the Allies' Monuments Men, a team of art preservationists. Hitler coveted the work as a symbol of the supremacy of Teutonic art. The altar was on its way to safe storage at the Vatican when it had to be hastily squirreled away in the French Pyrenees. The Nazis discovered it and spirited it away to Neuschwanstein Castle in Bavaria, then stored it in a salt mine. At war's end, the Monuments Men tracked it down and returned it to its rightful home—St. Bavo's.

In 2008, some 20 Ghent police officers tore up 225 square feet of a parking garage looking for the missing *Just Judges* panel, following a tip from an amateur sleuth. As late as 2015, another tip drew public attention but was deemed not credible by the authorities.

Today we can enjoy the Ghent Altarpiece in all its restored glory...except for that one pesky piece, the lower left *Just Judges* panel. More than 80 years after it was stolen, the panel has yet to turn up. What you see here is a top-notch copy, and the theft remains Belgium's greatest unsolved art mystery.

niche, a revolutionary example of (still not quite perfect) Italian-inspired perspective. You can actually see each hair on Adam's legs.

**Lower Panels and the Adoration:** The main scene, playing out across five separate panels, depicts the adoration of the Lamb—that is, Jesus, the sacrificial victim who saved the world from sin. The symbolic ungulate poses proudly atop an altar in the middle of a green field. It's the end of days (as described in Revelation 14:1), and everyone has traveled to the New Jerusalem (the towers in the background) to worship the Lamb of God: Angels kneel around the altar, popes wave palm branches (upper left), a legion of virgins gathers (upper right), Old Testament prophets read from their books (lower left), the 12 apostles and Church fathers assemble (lower right), and assorted saints, pagan writers, and Jewish prophets put in an appearance before their savior.

The adoration party spills over into the side panels, as still more worshippers arrive. To the right are groups of pilgrims and hermits, led by the giant St. Christopher. To the left are figures on horseback—knights and judges. Focus in on the bottom-left panel, called the *Just Judges*. It likely has self-portraits of Hubert and Jan van Eyck (the third and fourth figures in), but the painting you see is a copy—the original panel was stolen in 1934 (see the sidebar).

Throughout the lower *Adoration* panels, notice the diversity of the people assembled, wearing all different styles of clothing and headwear—from Asia, India, and the rest of the known world at the time.

Now return to the main panel of the Lamb. A dove (the Holy Spirit) hovers overhead, from which lasers of light stream out over the pristine, shadowless landscape. In the foreground, the Fountain of Life spews water and jewels.

The Lamb of Christ at the center of the work had special meaning here in Ghent, whose wool trade put it on the map. It's too bad that the animal itself—which scholars suspect was later retouched by a lesser artist—isn't particularly well-depicted. He looks more like a fully grown sheep...and is that an extra ear I see?

**Exterior Panels:** On weekdays, the wings of the hinged altarpiece would be folded shut, showing the paintings on the outside panels. You can see these recently restored panels now by circling

around the back side (or visit when the panels are closed). The top panels depict the Annunciation, when an angel (on one panel) came to Mary (on the other) to tell her she would bear God's child. The angel's announcement—"Hail Mary, full of grace"—is written in Latin across the panel. Mary replies, "I am the servant of the Lord." Notice that Mary's words are upside-down—they're intended for God above. Through the windows of Mary's chamber, we get a glimpse of medieval Ghent. Below, kneeling in the lower panels, are the donors who commissioned the work—the mayor of Ghent and his wife. Accompanying them are two St. Johns—the Baptist and the Evangelist.

**A Final Look:** Before leaving, take a moment to review the entire altarpiece and consider what it all means. Scholars mull over the various symbols, the inscriptions, and the cast of saints. The keystone is clearly the venerated lamb at the center of the work. The animal is positioned on a vertical line that descends from God to dove to lamb to the fountain. So—in symbolic terms—God sent the Holy Spirit to Christ on earth who gave his life to bring the faithful the waters of eternal life. John the Baptist is prominently featured on the altarpiece because it was he who proclaimed the arrival of God on earth: *"Ecce Agnus...*Behold the Lamb of God who takes away the sins of the world." At the time the altarpiece was built, the church was dedicated not to St. Bavo but to John the Baptist.

But forget the theology and simply bask in the astonishing level of detail. The countryside scenes are decorated with dozens of different identifiable species of plants and flowers. The feathered wings of the angels around the lamb can be matched to a variety of actual birds (peacocks, pigeons, swallows). And in the jeweled amulet around the neck of the singing angel (in the scene next to Adam), you can see a faint reflection of the window that decorated the chapel where this altarpiece originally stood. All these lush details—faces, robes, jewels, plants, human flesh—reinforced a theological message that was new to Europe: that the hand of God could be found in the beauty of everyday things.

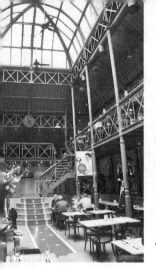

# GHENT SLEEPING, EATING & MORE

## Sleeping in Ghent

A convention town, Ghent is busiest in spring (April-June) and fall (Sept-mid-Dec); things are quieter (and prices lower) in early July (before the Ghent Festivities) and August, and even more so in the winter. These listings are near the town center, a 30-minute walk or a 15-minute tram ride from the train station; see page 265 for details.

**$$$$ Hotel Harmony** is a classy, four-star, family-run boutique hotel with 40 contemporary chic rooms ideally located on the embankment in the town center (air-con, elevator, heated outdoor pool in summer, Kraanlei 37, tel. 09-324-2680, www.hotel-harmony.be, info@hotel-harmony.be).

**$$ Chambreplus** rents four rooms with an impeccable flair for modern design. They say the "plus" is for their personal touch, and this is no exaggeration. With a cozy lounge and an inviting garden, the place oozes class and charm. The garden suite, which costs a little more, includes a private hot tub and fireplace (two-night minimum for weekends, air-con, Hoogpoort 31, tel. 09-226-3181, www.chambreplus.be, chambreplus@telenet.be, Kris and Indira).

**$$ Simon Says** offers two rooms over a colorful café at the far end of Patershol. You're on a small square, so there is some street noise, but you'll feel like a local taking breakfast with the natives in the downstairs café (Sluizeken 8, tel. 09-233-0343, www.simon-says.be, info@simon-says.be, Welshman Simon Turner).

**$$ Erasmus Hotel,** capably run by Peter, has 12 well-maintained rooms around a creaky wooden staircase in a classic 400-year-old building on a boring street, just a short walk from the embankment. A cluttered hallway gives access to a delightful Renaissance garden (no elevator, Poel 25, tel. 09-224-2195, www.erasmushotel.be, info@erasmushotel.be).

**$$ Monasterium PoortAckere,** a monastery until 1998, is now a no-frills hotel with nominally updated rooms that still evoke the aura of monks, seminarians, and visiting clergy. Breakfast, served in the refectory, is extra (Oude Houtlei 56, tel. 09-269-2210, www.monasterium.be, info@monasterium.be).

**$$ Ibis Gent Centrum St-Baafs Kathedraal** offers affordable, cookie-cutter, chain-hotel comfort in 120 rooms right next to the cathedral (breakfast extra, elevator, Limburgstraat 2, tel. 09-233-0000, www.ibishotel.com, h0961@accor.com).

**¢ De Draecke,** Ghent's very institutional hostel, is located in a residential zone a short walk from the castle. Take advantage of the helpful staff (private rooms available, Sint-Widostraat 11, tel. 09-233-7050, www.jeugdherbergen.be, gent@vjh.be).

# Eating in Ghent

## RESTAURANTS IN THE CITY CENTER

**$$$ Pakhuis** is a gorgeously restored, late-19th-century warehouse now filled with a classy, lively brasserie and bar. In this airy, two-story, glassed-in birdhouse of a restaurant, they serve up good traditional Belgian food with an emphasis on locally sourced and organic ingredients. It's tucked down a nondescript brick alley, but worth taking the few steps out of your way (Mon-Sat 12:00-23:00, closed Sun, Schuurkenstraat 4, tel. 09-223-5555).

**$$$ De Acht Zaligheden** (The Eight Beatitudes) prides itself on its regional and seasonal dishes with an always-innovative presentation. Their €38-45 fixed-price dinners are a good value (Tue-Sun 12:00-14:00 & 18:00-22:00, closed Mon, Oudburg 4, tel. 09-224-3197).

**$$$ Marco Polo Trattoria** is a good choice for Italian-style "slow food" (specializing in fish). It fills one long, cozy room with warm, mellow music and tables crowded by locals celebrating special occasions. Reservations are smart (Tue-Sat 18:00-22:00, Fri also 12:00-15:00, closed Sun-Mon, Serpentstraat 11, tel. 09-225-0420).

## EATERIES IN PATERSHOL

This former sailors' quarter is one of Ghent's most inviting—and priciest—neighborhoods for dining. Stroll the streets and simply drop in on any place that looks good. Peek into courtyards, many

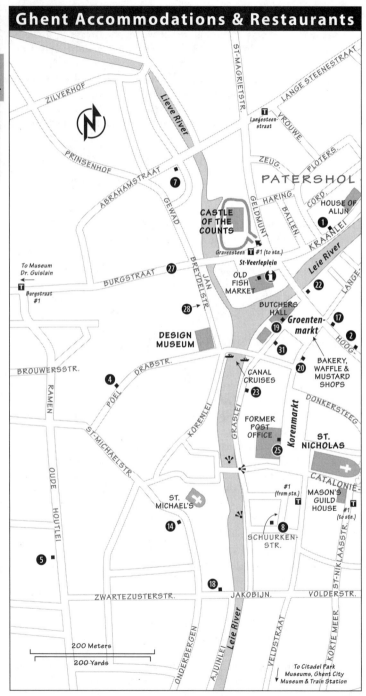

# Ghent Accommodations & Restaurants

ZILVERHOF

Lieve River

ST-MAGRIETSTR.

LANGE STEENESTRAAT

Langesteen-
straat

VROUWE

ZEUG.

PLOTERS.

PRINSENHOF

ABRAHAMSTRAAT

GEWAD

GELDMUNT

HARING.

BALLEN.

PATERSHOL

CORD.

❼

CASTLE
OF THE
COUNTS

HOUSE OF
ALIJN
❶

KRAANLEI

Gravensteen #1 (to stn.)

St-Veerleplein

Leie River

LANGE

To Museum
Dr. Guislain

Burgstraat
#1

BURGSTRAAT

❷❼

JAN BREYDELSTR.

OLD
FISH
MARKET

❶

❷❷

BUTCHERS
HALL

Groenten-
markt

❷❽

DESIGN
MUSEUM

❶❾

❸❶

❷⓿

❶❼

HOOG.

❷

BAKERY,
WAFFLE &
MUSTARD
SHOPS

BROUWERSSTR.

DRABSTR.

❹

POEL

RAMEN

ST-MICHAELSTR.

KORENLEI

GRASLEI

CANAL
CRUISES

❷❸

DONKERSTEEG

FORMER
POST
OFFICE

❷❺

Korenmarkt

ST.
NICHOLAS

OUDE HOUTLEI

ST.
MICHAEL'S

#1
(from stn.)

CATALONIË

MASON'S
GUILD
HOUSE

#1
(to stn.)

❶❹

❽

SCHUURKEN-
STR.

❺

❶❽

ZWARTEZUSTERSTR.

JAKOBIJN.

VOLDERSTR.

ONDERBERGEN

AJUINLEI

Leie River

VELDSTRAAT

KORTE MEER

ST-NIKLAASSTR.

200 Meters

200 Yards

To Citadel Park
Museums, Ghent City
Museum & Train Station

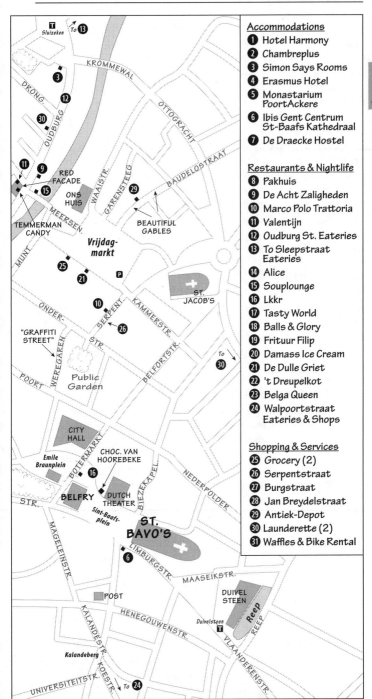

<u>Accommodations</u>
- ❶ Hotel Harmony
- ❷ Chambreplus
- ❸ Simon Says Rooms
- ❹ Erasmus Hotel
- ❺ Monastarium PoortAckere
- ❻ Ibis Gent Centrum St-Baafs Kathedraal
- ❼ De Draecke Hostel

<u>Restaurants & Nightlife</u>
- ❽ Pakhuis
- ❾ De Acht Zaligheden
- ❿ Marco Polo Trattoria
- ⓫ Valentijn
- ⓬ Oudburg St. Eateries
- ⓭ To Sleepstraat Eateries
- ⓮ Alice
- ⓯ Souplounge
- ⓰ Lkkr
- ⓱ Tasty World
- ⓲ Balls & Glory
- ⓳ Frituur Filip
- ⓴ Damass Ice Cream
- ㉑ De Dulle Griet
- ㉒ 't Dreupelkot
- ㉓ Belga Queen
- ㉔ Walpoortstraat Eateries & Shops

<u>Shopping & Services</u>
- ㉕ Grocery (2)
- ㉖ Serpentstraat
- ㉗ Burgstraat
- ㉘ Jan Breydelstraat
- ㉙ Antiek-Depot
- ㉚ Launderette (2)
- ㉛ Waffles & Bike Rental

of which hide restaurant and café tables. It's hard to go wrong in Patershol, but here are some particularly well-regarded favorites:

**$$$$ Valentijn,** in the heart of the district, has a romantic, dressy interior and a no-fuss menu of classics. On Saturday, they serve only a four-course fixed-price dinner (Mon-Wed and Fri-Sat from 18:30, closed Thu, Sun open for lunch only, reservations recommended, Rodekoningstraat 1, tel. 09-225-0429, www.restaurantvalentijn.be).

**Oudburg Street:** You'll find fun, ethnic, youthful **$** and **$$** eateries along this street, including **Ankara,** a good Turkish place (at #44) and the hip, popular, tight, and tasty **Ramen** noodle bar (at #51, open for lunch only, closed Sun-Mon).

**Sleepstraat:** Continue north beyond the end of Oudburg to find Sleepstraat, which is lined with **$** Turkish eateries (locals recommend **Gök,** with three branches along here; **Gök 2** is set in a whimsical 19th-century interior).

## QUICK EATS

**$ Alice,** tucked on a side street near St. Michael's Bridge, serves simple lunches, soups, and sandwiches in a delightful candy-box interior or in the garden (Tue-Sat 8:30-17:30, Sun 9:30-14:30, closed Mon, Onderbergen 6, tel. 09-277-9235).

**$ Souplounge** is basic, but cheap and good. They offer four daily soups, along with salads. Eat in the mod interior, or at the outdoor tables overlooking one of Ghent's most scenic stretches of canal (daily 10:00-19:00, Zuivelbrugstraat 6, tel. 09-223-6203).

**$ Lkkr** ("Yum"), behind the belfry, is a small, modern shop selling sandwiches and salads mostly to businesspeople on lunch breaks. Choose between the cozy interior or outdoor tables (Mon-Sat 10:00-18:00, closed Sun, Botermarkt 6, tel. 09-234-1006).

**$ Tasty World** serves up decent veggie burgers with various toppings, plus a wide range of fresh fruit juices and salads (Mon-Sat 11:00-20:00, closed Sun, Hoogpoort 1, tel. 09-225-7407). They have another branch in the hipster Walpoortstraat neighborhood (described later).

**$$ Balls & Glory,** a small Belgian chain that got its start in Ghent, is about a 10-minute walk from Vrijdagmarkt square. They specialize in gigantic meatballs—two flavors per day are noted on the chalkboard menu. Get yours to go or pay a few euros more to eat in their hip dining room at shared stainless-steel tables. Your meal includes water and fruit (Mon-Sat 10:00-21:00, closed Sun, Jakobijnenstraat 6, mobile 0486-678-776).

**$ Frituur Filip,** a fry shack attached to the Meat Hall on the Pensmarkt, serves real Belgian *frites* cooked twice in ox fat. Try them with Filip's homemade *stoofvleessaus*—the sauce skimmed off his Flemish stew (Thu-Tue 11:30-21:00, closed Wed).

**Dessert:** At the popular **Damass** ice cream shop, you can hang out and people-watch or get a cone and stroll (at the north end of Korenmarkt, #2-C, closed Tue).

**Grocery Stores:** You'll find a well-supplied **Albert Heijn** below the former post office on Korenmarkt (daily until 20:00, Korenmarkt 16). On Vrijdagmarkt, **Carrefour Express** is handy for picnic supplies and basic toiletries (Mon-Sat until 19:30, Sun until 14:30, at #54).

## GHENT'S BAR SCENE

**In the Center:** Two touristy bars in the center are worth considering if you want to sample a wide range of Belgian favorites: beer or gin.

**De Dulle Griet** ("Mad Maggie," named after the large red cannon nearby) on Vrijdagmarkt serves up 249 types of beer in a cozy, sprawling bar with beer glasses hanging from the ceiling (Tue-Sat 12:00-24:00, Sun until 19:30, Mon from 16:30, Vrijdagmarkt 50, tel. 09-244-2455).

**'t Dreupelkot,** guarded by Blackie the white dog, is a cozy little bar along the river offering more than 100 types of Dutch and Flemish gin, or *jenever* (daily from 15:00 until late, Groentenmarkt 12, tel. 0476-750-067).

**Along the Graslei Embankment:** A series of terraces along Graslei, the river embankment near St. Michael's Bridge, offers seating in the picturesque core of Ghent. Many gather at the **Belga Queen,** an outpost of a popular Brussels eatery (described on page 202). Grab a drink on a sunny afternoon to enjoy the view of boats, students, and visitors in the medieval city center (daily 12:00-14:30 & 19:00-22:30, Graslei 10, tel. 09-280-0100).

**Walpoortstraat and Nearby:** On Walpoortstraat and the surrounding streets, you'll find an enticing bunch of restaurants, cafés, and lively street life. This is Ghent's "Little Portlandia," a 10-minute stroll south from the belfry (for the most interesting route here, see the walking directions under "Shopping in Ghent," below).

Along Walpoortstraat are Italian eateries, beer halls, a branch of the Tasty World health-food shop (#38), the good OR Espresso Bar (#26), Yogy frozen yogurt (#2), and a gourmet chocolatier (Yuzu, at #11A, described later).

# Shopping in Ghent

Ghent has an enjoyable real-world feel that makes it a fun place to browse—not for souvenirs, but for interesting, design-oriented items. While not as urbane as Brussels or as cutting-edge as Antwerp, Ghent is creative, yet still accessible. Here are some interesting places to browse:

## Serpentstraat

This little pedestrian street, buried deep between the cathedral and Vrijdagmarkt square (described in my Ghent City Walk), has a fun, funky collection of creative shops. **Roark,** on the corner with Onderstraat at #1B, shows off cutting-edge/retro home decor; next door is the boutique of local clothing designer **Nathalie Engels** (#1A). Zsa, with wildly colorful, smartly designed gadgets and toys (for kids and grown-ups alike), has two branches: **Petit Zsa** for children, at #5, and **Zsa Rogue** at #22. Between them, at #8, sits the **Zoot** shoe shop.

## Streets near the Castle of the Counts

The busy, tram-lined **Burgstraat,** just across the bridge from the castle, isn't particularly charming, but it's an enjoyable place to window-shop at several furniture and home-decor shops and art galleries. The side street **Jan Breydelstraat,** which leads to the Ghent Design Museum, has an eclectic array of clothing, linens, jewelry, design, and chocolate shops.

## Walpoortstraat and Nearby

Walpoortstraat and the adjoining Sint-Pietersnieuwstraat, about a 10-minute stroll southeast of the cathedral, have some of Ghent's most creative and interesting shops.

**Shopping Your Way from the Belfry to Walpoortstraat:** There are several ways to reach Walpoortstraat from the center, but this route, which strings together mostly pedestrianized shopping streets, is especially pleasant. Beginning at the elongated square at the belfry, the middle of Ghent's three big towers, head south along the pedestrianized Mageleinstraat, with restaurants, tearooms, upscale shoe stores, and midrange international clothing shops. After two short blocks, you'll pop out at a fine little square ringed by interesting old buildings. Continue straight ahead down Kalandestraat to the handsome Kalandeberg square—with a gurgling fountain, outdoor seating, and a pair of inviting café/bakeries with sidewalk tables. Angle left at the bottom of the square to continue down Koestraat, which takes you to busier Kortedagsteeg. Here the shops and clientele gradually morph from mainstream middle-aged to creative hipster; cross the bridge (you're now on Walpoortstraat), and the transformation is complete.

**Shops around Walpoortstraat:** The blocks in which Walpoortstraat becomes Sint-Pietersnieuwstraat are fun and picturesque. Wedged between enticing cafés and restaurants are clothing boutiques, vintage and secondhand stores, and some very cool design depots. This area's vibe is exemplified by a couple of stores with bold, creative items for the home: **Piet Moodshop** (at the top of the street, Sint-Pietersnieuwstraat 94) and **Axeswar Design Trendshop** (at #12; both closed Sun).

Closer to the canal, at **Yuzu,** chocolatier Nicolas Vanaise decorates pralines with shiny metallic finishes and infuses them with creative flavors—including Asian elements (closed Sun-Mon, Walpoortstraat 11A). If you want to grab food, coffee, or a beer in this area, see "Ghent's Bar Scene," earlier.

## Antiques near Vrijdagmarkt

**Antiek-Depot** is a sprawling antique mall made for browsing. It sits along a postcard-perfect gabled street just north of Vrijdagmarkt square (closed Tue, Baudelostraat 15).

# Ghent Connections

**From Ghent by Train to: Brussels** (3/hour, 35 minutes), **Bruges** (4/hour, 30 minutes), **Antwerp** (3/hour, 50 minutes), **Ypres/Ieper** (hourly, 1 hour), **Paris** (2/hour, 2.5 hours, change at Brussels Midi/Zuid/South to Thalys train), **Amsterdam** (hourly, 2.5 hours, transfer in Antwerp), **Delft** (2/hour, 2.5 hours, transfer in Antwerp and Rotterdam or Roosendaal). For train information, see www.belgianrail.be; see also the "Transportation" section of the Practicalities chapter.

# BELGIAN HISTORY

Belgium as a nation is less than 200 years old, but its history stretches back to Europe's roots. Located where France, Germany, and the Netherlands meet, it's a unique mix of all three.

## ROMANS AND INVASIONS (AD 1-1300)

Julius Caesar invades (57 BC), conquering the Belgae people who gave the region its name. After Rome's fall (c. 400), the Low Countries shatter into a patchwork of local dukedoms ravaged by invaders, from Franks to Vikings. By AD 1000, several self-governing cities begin to emerge, well located for trade along rivers that flow into the North Sea.

### Sights

- Bruges: Original fort (ruins at Crowne Plaza Hotel) and Basilica of the Holy Blood
- Brussels: St. Michael's Cathedral, model in City Museum, and Tour d'Angle (tower) from city wall
- Ghent: Castle of the Counts

## BOOMING TRADE TOWNS (1300-1500)

Bruges, the midway port between the North Sea and Mediterranean trade routes, becomes Europe's richest and most cosmopolitan city. English-grown wool is woven into cloth in Flanders factories, then shipped abroad by German merchants, all financed by Italian bankers.

As Bruges' harbor silts up, trade shifts to industrious Ghent and to the bustling port city of Antwerp, which then becomes northern Europe's greatest trading city. Meanwhile, the smaller town of Brussels sells waffles and beer to passing travelers along the Germany-Bruges highway.

Politically, the Low Countries are united through marriage with the cultured, French-speaking dukes of Burgundy. Duke Philip the Good (c. 1450) rules an empire stretching from Amsterdam to Switzerland, and his cultured court is a center of art (Van Eyck, Memling, and Van der Weyden), literature, ideas, and pageantry.

But Belgium's medieval Golden Age was threatened by events of the wider world.

## Sights

- Bruges: Bell tower, Gothic Room in the City Hall, and Church of Our Lady; Flemish Primitive art in Groeninge and Sint-Janshospitaal museums
- Brussels: Grand Place, medieval street Rue des Bouchers, and Notre-Dame du Sablon Church; Royal Museums of Fine Arts of Belgium
- Antwerp: Riverfront and Old Town
- Ghent: Cathedral and bell tower; Van Eyck *Adoration* altarpiece at St. Bavo's Cathedral

## PROTESTANTS VS. CATHOLICS AND SPANISH RULERS (1500s)

Belgium's economy stagnates after Columbus' discoveries shift trade to a global market. A much-celebrated royal marriage be-

tween the houses of Burgundy and Habsburg (1477) brings Burgundian Belgium under the rule of the Habsburgs in distant Austria and Spain.

Meanwhile, Protestantism spreads through the Low Countries. In 1566, angry Protestants rise up, vandalizing Catholic churches ("iconoclasm"). Belgium—ruled by the ultra-Catholic Habsburgs—becomes the main battleground, as Spanish troops arrive to brutally punish the heretic Protestants. The thriving city of Antwerp falls to Spanish troops (1585), causing that city's best and brightest to flee to the Netherlands.

Ultimately, while the Netherlands wins independence from Spain, Belgium remains under the Catholic Habsburgs, ruled from their regional capital, Brussels.

## Sights

- Antwerp and Ghent: Church cathedral interiors stripped bare by Protestant iconoclasts and later redecorated in Baroque style
- Brussels: Tapestry designs at Textilux Center

## ELEGANT DECLINE (1600-1800)

Belgium languishes under foreign rule while the world moves on. The Netherlands enjoys a Golden Age of self-rule and global sea trade, and France and England rise to super-power status. The Belgians survive as bankers, small manufacturers, and lacemakers—but on a small scale fitting their geographical size. Antwerp rebounds to become a flourishing cultural center of publishing houses and the flamboyant art of Peter Paul Rubens.

Whenever wars between nearby neighbors break out, tiny Belgium gets caught in the cross fire. Louis XIV of France bombs Brussels (1695) to punish the rest of Europe (his foes in the Nine Years' War). Later, Napoleon invades Belgium and topples the monarchy, ending nearly two centuries of Habsburg rule. When the rest of Europe rallies against Napoleon, where do they send their troops? To Belgium, of course, where they finally defeat Napoleon at Waterloo. Belgium—now little more than a pawn in the game of larger powers—hits rock bottom.

## Sights

- Bruges: Lace Center; Brussels: Fashion and Lace Museum
- Brussels: Grand Place guildhalls; *Manneken-Pis*
- Near Brussels: Mémorial 1815 (museum) at Waterloo
- Antwerp: Rubens House, Rockox House, and Museum Plantin-Moretus; Paleis op de Meir (Napoleon's palace)

## A TINY NATION BECOMES AN EMPIRE (1800s)

Europe's nobles install a king to rule all the Low Countries. Belgians resist this Dutch-controlled government and, in August 1830, take to the streets of Brussels to battle Dutch soldiers. They win their independence and choose their own constitutional mon-

# Typical Church Architecture

History comes to life when you visit a centuries-old church. Even if you wouldn't know your apse from a hole in the ground, learning a few simple terms will enrich your experience. Note that not every church has every feature, and a "cathedral" isn't a type of church architecture, but rather a designation for a church that's a governing center for a local bishop.

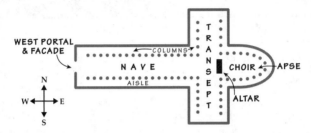

**Aisles:** The long, generally low-ceilinged arcades that flank the nave.

**Altar:** The raised area with a ceremonial table (often adorned with candles or a crucifix), where the priest prepares and serves the bread and wine for Communion.

**Apse:** The space beyond the altar, often bordered with small chapels.

**Barrel Vault:** A continuous round-arched ceiling that resembles an extended upside-down U.

**Choir:** A cozy area, often screened off, located within the church nave and near the high altar where services are sung in a more intimate setting.

**Cloister:** Covered hallways bordering a square or rectangular open-air courtyard, traditionally where monks and nuns got fresh air.

**Facade:** The exterior of the church's main (west) entrance, usually highly decorated.

**Groin Vault:** An arched ceiling formed where two equal barrel vaults meet at right angles. Less common usage: term for a medieval jock strap.

**Narthex:** The area (portico or foyer) between the main entry and the nave.

**Nave:** The long, central section of the church (running west to east, from the entrance to the altar) where the congregation sits or stands through the service.

**Transept:** In a traditional cross-shaped floor plan, the transept is one of the two parts forming the "arms" of the cross. The transept runs north-south, perpendicularly crossing the east-west nave.

**West Portal:** The main entry to the church (on the west end, opposite the main altar).

arch, King Leopold I (the great-great-great-grandfather of today's king).

Under Leopold I, Belgium rapidly becomes Europe's leader in Industrial Revolution technology. Soon coal from Belgian mines is fueling Ghent factories to make cloth, which is shipped on Belgium's state-of-the-art rail system.

Under King Leopold II, tiny Belgium becomes a global empire. Leopold claims Africa's Congo—a region 80 times bigger than Belgium—as his own private colony. The Belgians brutally exploit the Congo's rubber and ivory resources to finance massive building projects. Brussels becomes a world-class capital of broad boulevards and monumental buildings with columns and domes, all frosted with delicate Art Nouveau.

### Sights

- Brussels: Upper Town buildings and Parc du Cinquantenaire; Galeries Royales St. Hubert and BELvue Museum
- Antwerp: Central Station
- Bruges: Choco-Story: The Chocolate Museum; Brussels: Museum of Cocoa and Chocolate

### WORLD WARS, EUROPEAN UNION (1900-2000)

In 1914, prosperous Belgium is suddenly transformed into a horrific battle-scape, as Germany dukes it out with England and France

in World War I. Some of the worst fighting takes place at Flanders Fields near Ypres (Ieper).

As Belgium recovers in the 1920s, a new phenomenon appears—newspaper comics—and Hergé thrills Europeans with his tales of the adventurous young reporter, Tintin.

When World War II breaks out, Nazi Germany easily conquers Belgium, imposing five long years of brutal occupation. Late in the war, Belgium is the site of Germany's last-gasp offensive, the Battle of the Bulge.

After the war, Brussels becomes the center of the budding

# The Battle for Belgium: Flanders vs. Wallonia

Although little, peace-loving Belgium seems like a warm and cozy place, its society is split right down the middle by a surprisingly contentious linguistic divide: the Dutch-speaking people of Flanders (in the north) versus the French speakers of Wallonia (in the south). To travelers, it almost seems as if Flanders and Wallonia are different countries. Each region has its own "national" tourist office, which effectively ignores the other half of the country. One prime minister said that Belgians are united only by the king, a love of beer, and the national soccer team.

From its earliest days, "Belgium" was less a country than a patchwork of dukedoms joined awkwardly together not by language, but by foreign rulers. For centuries, the two language groups coexisted side-by-side as they were successively dominated by Burgundian, Habsburg, Spanish, French, and Dutch overlords.

That changed in 1830, when the modern nation-state of Belgium was born, forcing the two regions together. It was Belgium's French-speaking aristocracy and industrialists that had led the drive for independence from the Netherlands. They said, "Belgium will be French, or it will not be." And so it was: Linguistic and cultural oppression ruled the day, as the Dutch language spoken in Flanders was suppressed. Education at prestigious universities, for example, was only in French. These days, the tables have turned—Flanders today has the healthier, wealthier economy and more inhabitants than Wallonia.

Language issues still dominate Belgium's politics. Some Flemish feel they'd have been better off had Belgium remained part of the Netherlands, which would have respected their native tongue. That's why most Flemish people are not particularly nationalistic about their language—rather than being blinded by Flemish pride, they readily acknowledge that what they speak is a dialect of Dutch.

Whereas a generation ago, virtually every Belgian spoke both Dutch and French, nowadays when Flemish students choose a "second" language to study, many choose English. Meanwhile, in a strange role reversal, Francophones are choosing to learn Dutch, which they realize will open up employment options. On my last visit to Brussels, I saw a sign in a shop window saying, "Bilingual staff wanted."

The Belgian government has taken steps to involve everyone. In 1970, Belgium began decentralizing itself, over time becoming a federal state with three semiautonomous regions: Flanders, Wallonia, and the bilingual city-state of Brussels. But the 21st century has seen the rise of Flemish nationalist parties. As with Catalunya in Spain and Scotland in the United Kingdom, no one knows where a push for independence might lead.

movement toward European unity. It pioneers the Common Market (1957), the BeNeLux economic union (1960), and is a stalwart of NATO. In 1992, Belgium—along with 11 other countries—becomes a founding member of the European Union.

## Sights

- Near Bruges: Flanders Fields (near Ypres)
- Bruges: René Magritte paintings in Groeninge Museum
- Brussels: Atomium and European Parliament quarter; Magritte Museum
- Antwerp: Sint-Andries fashion district, ModeMuseum, "Little Island" area, 't Zuid district
- Ghent: Design Museum

## BELGIUM TODAY

Brussels is the de facto capital of the European Union—a kind of "Washington, DC" for this "United States of Europe."

But ironically, Belgium itself struggles to unite its own diverse population. Since 1970, it's been a nation officially divided into three semi-autonomous regions: Dutch-speaking Flanders, French-speaking Wallonia, and bilingual Brussels (for more on this divide, see the sidebar). It also strives to bring the immigrants from its former African colony into the diverse mix.

The Belgian political landscape is splintered into several different parties, divided largely along language lines. Fortunately, Belgium has a popular (if symbolic) ruler—King Philippe and his charming young family. In 2016, a terrorist attack in Brussels shocked the nation; in the aftermath security has been ramped up, but the country also seems more unified.

Belgium has seen many centuries of turbulence, but that hasn't stopped it from becoming a forward-thinking nation with a long and rich cultural heritage. It welcomes you to come and make your own history.

# PRACTICALITIES

This chapter covers the practical skills of European travel: how to get tourist information, pay for things, sightsee efficiently, find good-value accommodations, eat affordably but well, use technology wisely, and get between destinations smoothly. For more information on these topics, see www.ricksteves.com/travel-tips.

## Tourist Information

National tourist offices **in the US** can be a wealth of information. Before your trip, request or download any specific information you may want, such as city maps and schedules of upcoming festivals.

For Brussels and French-speaking Wallonia, go to www.visitbelgium.com; for Dutch-speaking Flanders, check out www.visitflanders.com. At either website, you can access hotel and city guides, brochures for ABC lovers (antiques, beer, and chocolates), maps, and information on WWI and WWII battlefields.

In **Belgium,** a good first stop is generally the tourist information office (abbreviated **TI** in this book). I make a point to swing by to confirm sightseeing plans, pick up a city map, and get information on public transit, walking tours, special events, and nightlife. Anticipating a harried front-line staffer, prepare a list of questions and a proposed plan to double-check. Some TIs have information on the entire country or at least the region, so try to pick up maps and printed information for destinations you'll be visiting later in your trip. Note that Belgian TIs are state-run, so they're not tainted by a drive for profits.

# Travel Tips

**Emergency and Medical Help:** For any emergency service—ambulance, police, or fire—call **112** from a mobile phone or landline. Operators, who in most countries speak English, will deal with your request or route you to the right emergency service. If you get sick, do as the Belgians do and go to a pharmacist for advice. Or ask at your hotel for help—they'll know the nearest medical and emergency services.

**Theft or Loss:** To replace a passport, you'll need to go in person to the US Consulate and Embassy (see next). If your credit and debit cards disappear, cancel and replace them (see "Damage Control for Lost Cards," later). File a police report, either on the spot or within a day or two; you'll need it to submit an insurance claim for lost or stolen rail passes or travel gear, and it can help with replacing your passport or credit and debit cards. For more information, see www.ricksteves.com/help.

**US Embassy and Consulate:** Brussels—tel. 02-811-4300, after-hours emergency tel. 02-811-4000 (Boulevard du Régent 27, https://be.usembassy.gov).

**Canadian Embassy:** Brussels—tel. 02-741-0611 (Avenue des Arts 58, www.ambassade-canada.be).

**Time Zones:** Belgium, like most of continental Europe, is generally six/nine hours ahead of the East/West Coasts of the US. The exceptions are the beginning and end of Daylight Saving Time: Europe "springs forward" the last Sunday in March (two weeks after most of North America) and "falls back" the last Sunday in October (one week before North America). For a handy time converter, use the world clock app on your mobile phone or download one (see www.timeanddate.com).

**Business Hours:** Most stores throughout Belgium are open from about 9:00 or 10:00 until 18:00-20:00 on weekdays, but close earlier on Saturday and may or may not open on Sunday. Popular destinations are even more crowded on weekends. Many museums and sights are closed on Monday.

**Watt's Up?** Europe's electrical system is 220 volts, instead of North America's 110 volts. Most newer electronics (such as laptops, battery chargers, and hair dryers) convert automatically, so you won't need a converter, but you will need an adapter plug with two round prongs, sold inexpensively at travel stores in the US. Avoid bringing older appliances that don't automatically convert voltage; instead, buy a cheap replacement in Europe.

**Discounts:** Discounts for sights are generally not listed in this book. However, seniors (age 60 and over), youths under 18, and students and teachers with proper identification cards (www.isic. org) can get discounts at many sights—always ask. Some discounts are available only to European citizens.

**Online Translation Tips:** Google's Chrome browser instantly translates websites; Translate.google.com is also handy. The Google Translate app converts spoken English into most European languages (and vice versa) and can also translate text it "reads" with your phone's camera.

# Money

Here's my basic strategy for using money in Europe:

- Upon arrival, head for a cash machine (ATM) at the airport and withdraw some local currency, using a debit card with low international transaction fees.
- Pay for most purchases with your choice of cash or a credit card. You'll save money by minimizing your credit and debit card exchange fees. The trend is for bigger expenses to be paid by credit card, but cash is still the standby for small purchases and tips.
- Keep your cards and cash safe in a money belt.

## PLASTIC VERSUS CASH

Although credit cards are widely accepted in Europe, cash is sometimes the only way to pay for cheap food, taxis, tips, and local guides. Some businesses (especially smaller ones, such as B&Bs and mom-and-pop cafés and shops) may charge you extra for using a credit card—or might not accept credit cards at all. Having cash on hand helps you out of a jam if your card randomly doesn't work.

I use my credit card to book and pay for hotel reservations, to buy advance tickets for events or sights, and to cover most other expenses. It can also be smart to use plastic near the end of your trip, to avoid another visit to the ATM.

## WHAT TO BRING

I pack the following and keep it all safe in my money belt.

**Debit Card:** Use this at ATMs to withdraw local cash.

**Credit Card:** Handy for bigger purchases (at hotels, shops, restaurants, travel agencies, car-rental agencies, and so on), payment machines, and ordering online.

## Exchange Rate

**1 euro (€) = about $1.20**

To convert prices in euros to dollars, add about 20 percent: €20 = about $24, €50 = about $60. (Check www.oanda.com for the latest exchange rates.) Just like the dollar, one euro (€) is broken down into 100 cents. Coins range from €0.01 to €2, and bills from €5 to €200 (bills over €50 are rarely used; €500 bills are being phased out).

**Backup Card:** Some travelers carry a third card (debit or credit; ideally from a different bank), in case one gets lost, demagnetized, eaten by a temperamental machine, or simply doesn't work.

**A Stash of Cash:** I always carry $100-200 as a cash backup. A stash of cash comes in handy for emergencies, such as if your ATM card stops working.

**What NOT to Bring:** Resist the urge to buy **euros** before your trip or you'll pay the price in bad stateside exchange rates. Wait until you arrive to withdraw money. I've yet to see a European airport that didn't have plenty of ATMs.

## BEFORE YOU GO

Use this pre-trip checklist.

**Know your cards.** Debit cards from any major US bank will work in any standard European bank's ATM (ideally, use a debit card with a Visa or MasterCard logo). As for credit cards, Visa and MasterCard are universal, American Express is less common, and Discover is unknown in Europe.

**Know your PIN.** Make sure you know the numeric, four-digit PIN for all of your cards, both debit and credit. Request it if you don't have one and allow time to receive the information by mail.

All credit and debit cards now have chips that authenticate and secure transactions. Europeans insert their chip cards into the payment machine slot, then enter a PIN. American cards should work in most transactions without a PIN—but may not work at self-service machines at train stations, tollbooths, gas pumps, or parking lots. I've been inconvenienced a few times by self-service payment machines in Europe that wouldn't accept my card, but it's never caused me serious trouble.

If you're concerned, a few banks offer a chip-and-PIN card that works in almost all payment machines, including those from Andrews Federal Credit Union (www.andrewsfcu.org) and the State Department Federal Credit Union (www.sdfcu.org).

**Report your travel dates.** Let your bank know that you'll be using your debit and credit cards in Europe, and when and where you're headed.

**Adjust your ATM withdrawal limit.** Find out how much you can take out daily and ask for a higher daily withdrawal limit if you want to get more cash at once. Note that European ATMs will withdraw funds only from checking accounts; you're unlikely to have access to your savings account.

**Ask about fees.** For any purchase or withdrawal made with a card, you may be charged a currency conversion fee (1-3 percent) and/or a Visa or MasterCard international transaction fee (1 percent). If you're getting a bad deal, consider getting a new debit or credit card. Reputable no-fee cards include those from Capital One, as well as Charles Schwab debit cards. Most credit unions and some airline loyalty cards have low-to-no international transaction fees.

## IN EUROPE
### Using Cash Machines

European cash machines have English-language instructions and work just like they do at home—except they spit out local currency instead of dollars, calculated at the day's standard bank-to-bank rate.

In most places, ATMs are easy to locate—in Belgium ask for a *geldautomaat* (Dutch) or a *distributeur* (French). When possible,

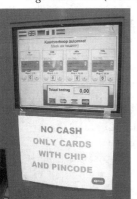

withdraw cash from a bank-run ATM located just outside that bank. Ideally use it during the bank's opening hours so if your card is munched by the machine, you can go inside for help.

If your debit card doesn't work, try a lower amount—your request may have exceeded your withdrawal limit or the ATM's limit. If you still have a problem, try a different ATM or come back later—your bank's network may be temporarily down.

Avoid "independent" ATMs, such as Travelex, Euronet, Moneybox, Cardpoint, and Cashzone. These have high fees, can be less secure than a bank ATM, and may try to trick users with "dynamic currency conversion" (see next page).

### Exchanging Cash

Avoid exchanging money in Europe; it's a big rip-off. In a pinch you can always find exchange desks at major train stations or airports—convenient but with crummy rates. Anything over 5 percent for a transaction is piracy. Banks generally do not exchange money unless you have an account with them.

## Using Credit Cards

US cards no longer require a signature for verification, but don't be surprised if a European card reader generates a receipt for you to sign. Some card readers will accept your card as is; others may prompt you to enter your PIN (so it's important to know the code for each of your cards). If a cashier is present, you should have no problems.

At self-service payment machines (transit-ticket kiosks, parking, etc.), results are mixed, as US cards may not work in unattended transactions. If your card won't work, look for a cashier who can process your card manually—or pay in cash.

**Drivers Beware:** Be aware of potential problems using a US credit card to fill up at an unattended gas station, enter a parking garage, or exit a toll road. Carry cash and be prepared to move on to the next gas station if necessary. When approaching a toll plaza, use the "cash" lane.

## Dynamic Currency Conversion

If merchants offer to convert your purchase price into dollars (called dynamic currency conversion, or DCC), refuse this "service." You'll pay extra for the expensive convenience of seeing your charge in dollars. If an ATM offers to "lock in" or "guarantee" your conversion rate, choose "proceed without conversion." Other prompts might state, "You can be charged in dollars: Press YES for dollars, NO for euros." Always choose the local currency.

## Security Tips

Pickpockets target tourists. Keep your cash, credit cards, and passport secure in your money belt, and carry only a day's spending money in your front pocket or wallet.

Before inserting your card into an ATM, inspect the front. If anything looks crooked, loose, or damaged, it could be a sign of a card-skimming device. When entering your PIN, carefully block other people's view of the keypad.

Don't use a debit card for purchases. Because a debit card pulls funds directly from your bank account, potential charges incurred by a thief will stay on your account while the fraudulent use is investigated by your bank.

To access your accounts online while traveling, be sure to use a secure connection (see the "Tips on Internet Security" sidebar, later).

## Damage Control for Lost Cards

If you lose your credit or debit card, report the loss immediately to the respective global customer-assistance centers. Call these 24-hour US numbers collect: Visa (tel. 303/967-1096), MasterCard (tel. 636/722-7111), and American Express (tel. 336/393-1111). In Belgium, to make a collect call to the US, dial 0800-10010. Press zero or stay on the line for an English-speaking operator. European toll-free numbers can be found at the websites for Visa and MasterCard.

You'll need to provide the primary cardholder's identification-verification details (such as birth date, mother's maiden name, or Social Security number). You can generally receive a temporary card within two or three business days in Europe (see www.ricksteves.com/help for more).

If you report your loss within two days, you typically won't be responsible for any unauthorized transactions on your account, although many banks charge a liability fee of $50.

## TIPPING

Tipping in Belgium isn't as automatic and generous as it is in the US. For special service, tips are appreciated, but not expected. As in the US, the proper amount depends on your resources, tipping philosophy, and the circumstances, but some general guidelines apply.

**Restaurants:** Belgian restaurants include a service charge, although it's common to round up the bill. For details on tipping in restaurants, see "Eating," later.

**Taxis:** For a typical ride, round up your fare a bit (for instance, if the fare is €4.50, pay €5). If the cabbie hauls your bags and zips you to the airport to help you catch your flight, you might want to toss in a little more. But if you feel like you're being driven in circles or otherwise ripped off, skip the tip.

**Services:** In general, if someone in the tourism or service industry does a super job for you, a small tip of a euro or two is appropriate...but not required. If you're not sure whether (or how much) to tip, ask a local for advice.

## GETTING A VAT REFUND

Wrapped into the purchase price of your souvenirs is a Value-Added Tax (VAT) of about 21 percent in Belgium. You're entitled to get most of that tax back if you purchase more than €50 (about $60) worth of goods at a store that participates in the VAT-refund scheme. Typically, you must ring up the minimum at a single retailer—you can't add up your purchases from various shops to reach the required amount. (If the store ships the goods to your US home, VAT is not assessed on your purchase.)

Getting your refund is usually straightforward...and worthwhile if you spend a significant amount on souvenirs.

**Get the paperwork.** Have the merchant completely fill out the necessary refund document. You'll have to present your passport.

Get the paperwork done before you leave the store to ensure you'll have everything you need (including your original sales receipt).

**Get your stamp at the border or airport.** Process your VAT document at your last stop in the European Union (such as at the airport) with the customs agent who deals with VAT refunds. Arrive an additional hour before you need to check in for your flight to allow time to find the customs office—and wait. Some customs desks are positioned before airport security; confirm the location before going through security.

It's best to keep your purchases in your carry-on. If they're not allowed as carry-on (such as knives), pack them in your checked bags and alert the check-in agent. You'll be sent (with your tagged bag) to a customs desk outside security; someone will examine your bag, stamp your paperwork, and put your bag on the belt. You're not supposed to use your purchased goods before you leave. If you show up at customs wearing a Belgian lace wedding veil, officials might look the other way—or deny you a refund.

**Collect your refund.** You can claim your VAT refund from refund companies, such as Global Blue or Premier Tax Free, with offices at major airports, ports, or border crossings (either before or after security, probably strategically located near a duty-free shop). These services (which extract a 4 percent fee) can refund your money in cash immediately or credit your card (within two billing cycles). Otherwise, you'll need to mail the stamped refund documents to the address given by the shop where you made your purchase.

## CUSTOMS FOR AMERICAN SHOPPERS

You are allowed to take home $800 worth of items per person duty-free, once every 31 days. Many processed and packaged foods are allowed, including vacuum-packed cheeses, dried herbs, jams, baked goods, candy, chocolate, oil, vinegar, mustard, and honey. Fresh fruits and vegetables and most meats are not allowed, with exceptions for some canned items. As for alcohol, you can bring in one liter duty-free (it can be packed securely in your checked luggage, along with any other liquid-containing items).

To bring alcohol (or liquid-packed foods) in your carry-on bag on your flight home, buy it at a duty-free shop at the airport. You'll increase your odds of getting it onto a connecting flight if it's packaged in a "STEB"—a secure, tamper-evident bag. But stay away from liquids in opaque, ceramic, or metallic containers, which usually cannot be successfully screened (STEB or no STEB).

For details on allowable goods, customs rules, and duty rates, visit http://help.cbp.gov.

# Sightseeing

Sightseeing can be hard work. Use these tips to make your visits to Belgium's finest sights meaningful, fun, efficient, and painless.

## MAPS AND NAVIGATION TOOLS

A good map is essential for efficient navigation while sightseeing. The maps in this book are concise and simple, designed to help you locate recommended destinations, sights, and local TIs, where you can pick up more in-depth maps.

You can also use a mapping app on your mobile device. Be aware that pulling up maps or looking up turn-by-turn walking directions on the fly requires an internet connection: To use this feature, it's smart to get an international data plan. With Google Maps or City Maps 2Go, it's possible to download a map while online, then go offline and navigate without incurring data-roaming charges, though you can't search for an address or get real-time walking directions. A handful of other apps—including Apple Maps, OffMaps, and Navfree—also allow you to use maps offline.

## PLAN AHEAD

Set up an itinerary that allows you to fit in all your must-see sights. For a one-stop look at opening hours, see the "At a Glance" side-bars for Bruges, Brussels, Antwerp, and Ghent. Most sights keep stable hours, but you can easily confirm the latest by checking with the TI or visiting museum websites.

Don't put off visiting a must-see sight—you never know when a place will close unexpectedly for a holiday, strike, or restoration. Many museums are closed or have reduced hours at least a few days a year, especially on holidays such as Christmas, New Year's, and Labor Day (May 1). A list of holidays is in the appendix; check online for possible museum closures during your trip. In summer, some sights may stay open late; in the off-season, hours may be shorter.

Going at the right time helps avoid crowds. This book offers tips on the best times to see specific sights. Try visiting popular sights very early or very late. Evening visits are usually peaceful, with fewer crowds.

If you plan to hire a local guide, reserve ahead by email. Popular guides can get booked up.

Study up. To get the most out of the self-guided tours and sight descriptions in this book, read them before you visit. The Groeninge Museum is much more entertaining if you've boned up on your Flemish Primitives the night before.

PRACTICALITIES

## AT SIGHTS

Here's what you can typically expect:

**Entering:** Be warned that you may not be allowed to enter if you arrive less than 30 to 60 minutes before closing time. And guards start ushering people out well before the actual closing time, so don't save the best for last.

Many sights have a security check. Allow extra time for these lines. Some sights require you to check daypacks and coats. (If you'd rather not check your daypack, try carrying it tucked under your arm like a purse as you enter.)

**Photography:** If the museum's photo policy isn't clearly posted, ask a guard. Generally, taking photos without a flash or tripod is allowed. Some sights ban selfie sticks; others ban photos altogether.

**Temporary Exhibits:** Museums may show special exhibits in addition to their permanent collection. Some exhibits are included in the entry price, while others come at an extra cost (which you may have to pay even if you don't want to see the exhibit).

**Expect Changes:** Artwork can be on tour, on loan, out sick, or shifted at the whim of the curator. Pick up a floor plan as you enter, and ask museum staff if you can't find a particular item.

**Audioguides and Apps:** Many sights rent audioguides, which generally offer excellent recorded descriptions in English. Many audioguides have a standard output jack, so if you bring your own earbuds, you can often enjoy better sound. To save money, bring a Y-jack and share one audioguide with your travel partner. Museums and sights often offer free apps that you can download to your mobile device (check their websites).

**Services:** Important sights usually have a reasonably priced on-site café or cafeteria (handy places to rejuvenate during a long visit). The WCs at sights are free and generally clean.

**Before Leaving:** At the gift shop, scan the postcard rack or thumb through a guidebook to be sure that you haven't overlooked something that you'd like to see.

Every sight or museum offers more than what is covered in this book. Use the information in this book as an introduction—not the final word.

# Sleeping

Extensive and opinionated listings of good-value rooms are a major feature of this book's Sleeping sections. Rather than list accommodations scattered throughout a town, I choose hotels in my favorite neighborhoods that are convenient to your sightseeing.

My recommendations run the gamut, from dorm beds to fancy rooms with all the comforts. I like places that are clean, central, rel-

atively quiet at night, reasonably priced, friendly, small enough to have a hands-on owner or manager, and run with a respect for Belgian traditions. I'm more impressed by a handy location and fun-loving philosophy than flat-screen TVs and a fancy gym. Most of my recommendations fall short of perfection. But if I can find a place with most of these features, it's a keeper.

Book your accommodations as soon as your itinerary is set, especially if you'll be traveling during busy times. See the appendix for a list of major holidays and festivals in Belgium.

Some people make reservations as they travel, calling ahead a few days to a week before their arrival. It's best to call hotels at about 9:00 or 10:00, when the receptionist knows which rooms will be available. Some apps—such as HotelTonight—specialize in last-minute rooms, often at business-class hotels in big cities. If you encounter a language barrier, ask the fluent receptionist at your current hotel to call for you.

## RATES AND DEALS

I've categorized my recommended accommodations based on price, indicated with a dollar-sign rating (see sidebar). The price ranges suggest an estimated cost for a one-night stay in a standard double room with a private toilet and shower in high season, include breakfast, and assume you're booking directly with the hotel (not through a booking site, which extracts a commission). Room prices can fluctuate significantly with demand and amenities (size, views, room class, and so on), but relative price categories remain constant. Cities in Belgium all charge a hotel tax; it's calculated differently everywhere, but assume you'll pay a few extra euros per person, per night.

Room rates are especially volatile at larger hotels that use "dynamic pricing" to set rates. Prices can skyrocket during festivals and conventions, while business hotels can have deep discounts on weekends when demand plummets. Of the many hotels I recommend, it's difficult to say which will be the best value on a given day—until you do your homework.

**Booking Direct:** Once your dates are set, compare prices at several hotels. You can do this by checking Hotels.com, Booking.com, and hotel websites. To get the best deal, contact family-run hotels directly by phone or email. When you go direct, the owner avoids the commission paid to booking sites, thereby leaving

**PRACTICALITIES**

## Sleep Code

Hotels in this book are categorized according to the average price of a standard double room with breakfast in high season.

| | |
|---|---|
| **$$$$** | **Splurge:** Most rooms over €170 |
| **$$$** | **Pricier:** €130-170 |
| **$$** | **Moderate:** €90-130 |
| **$** | **Budget:** €50-90 |
| **¢** | **Backpacker:** Under €50 |
| **RS%** | **Rick Steves discount** |

Unless otherwise noted, credit cards are accepted, hotel staff speak basic English, and free Wi-Fi is available. Comparison-shop by checking prices at several hotels (on each hotel's own website, on a booking site, or by email). For the best deal, *book directly with the hotel.* Ask for a discount if paying in cash; if the listing includes **RS%**, request a Rick Steves discount.

enough wiggle room to offer you a discount, a nicer room, or a free breakfast (if it's not already included). If you prefer to book online or are considering a hotel chain, it's to your advantage to use the hotel's website.

**Getting a Discount:** Some hotels extend a discount to those who pay cash or stay longer than three nights. And some accommodations offer a special discount for Rick Steves readers, indicated in this guidebook with the abbreviation **"RS%."** Discounts vary: Ask for details when you reserve. Generally, to qualify for this discount, you must book direct (not through a booking site), mention this book when you reserve, show this book upon arrival, and sometimes pay cash or stay a certain number of nights. In some cases, you may need to enter a discount code (which I've provided in the listing) in the booking form on the hotel's website. Rick Steves discounts apply to readers with either printed or digital books. Understandably, discounts do not apply to promotional rates.

## TYPES OF ACCOMMODATIONS
### Hotels

In this book, the price for a double room ranges from $65 (very simple, toilet and shower down the hall) to $250 (maximum plumbing and more), with most clustering at about $130. You'll pay more at Brussels hotels and less at Bruges B&Bs. A hearty breakfast with cereal, meats, local cheeses, fresh bread, yogurt, juice, and coffee or tea is generally included.

Some hotels can add an extra bed (for a small charge) to turn a double into a triple; some offer larger rooms for four or more people (I call these "family rooms" in the listings). If there's space for an extra cot, they'll cram it in for you. In general, a triple room is cheaper than the cost of a double and a single. Three or four people can economize by requesting one big room.

**Arrival and Check-In:** Hotels and B&Bs are sometimes located on the higher floors of a multipurpose building with a secured door. In that case, look for your hotel's name on the buttons by the main entrance. When you ring the bell, you'll be buzzed in.

Hotel elevators are becoming more common, though some older buildings still lack them. You may have to climb a flight of stairs to reach the elevator (if so, you can ask the front desk for help carrying your bags up). Elevators are typically very small—pack light, or you may need to send your bags up without you.

The EU requires that hotels collect your name, nationality, and ID number. When you check in, the receptionist will normally ask for your passport and may keep it for anywhere from a couple of minutes to a couple of hours. (If you're not comfortable leaving your passport at the desk for a long time, ask when you can pick it up.)

If you're arriving early in the morning, your room probably won't be ready. Check your bag safely at the hotel and dive right into sightseeing.

**In Your Room:** Most hotel rooms have a TV, telephone, and free Wi-Fi (although in old buildings with thick walls, the Wi-Fi signal might be available only in the lobby). Simpler places rarely have a room phone.

More pillows and blankets are usually in the closet or available on request. Towels and linens aren't always replaced every day, so hang your towel up to dry.

**Checking Out:** While it's customary to pay for your room upon departure, it can be a good idea to settle your bill the day before, when you're not in a hurry and while the manager's in. That way you'll have time to discuss and address any points of contention.

**Hotelier Help:** Hoteliers can be a good source of advice. Most know their city well, and can assist you with everything from public transit and airport connections to finding a good restaurant, the nearest launderette, or a late-night pharmacy.

**Hotel Hassles:** Even at the best places, mechanical breakdowns occur: Sinks leak, hot water turns cold, toilets may gurgle or smell, the Wi-Fi goes out, or the air-conditioning dies when you need it most. Report your concerns clearly and calmly at the front desk.

If you find that night noise is a problem (if, for instance, your room is over a nightclub), ask for a quieter room in the back or on an upper floor. To guard against theft in your room, keep valuables out of sight. Some rooms come with a safe, and other hotels have safes at the front desk. I've never bothered using one and in a lifetime of travel, I've never had anything stolen from my room.

# Making Hotel Reservations

Reserve your rooms as soon as you've pinned down your travel dates. For busy national holidays, it's wise to reserve far in advance (see page 357).

**Requesting a Reservation:** For family-run hotels, it's generally cheaper to book your room directly via email or a phone call. For business-class hotels, or if you'd rather book online, reserve directly through the hotel's official website (not a booking website). For complicated requests, send an email. Almost all of my recommended hotels take reservations in English.

Here's what the hotelier wants to know:

- Type(s) of rooms you want and size of your party
- Number of nights you'll stay
- Your arrival and departure dates, written European-style as day/month/year (18/06/20 or 18 June 2020)
- Special requests (en suite bathroom, cheapest room, twin beds vs. double bed, quiet room)
- Applicable discounts (such as a Rick Steves reader discount, cash discount, or promotional rate)

**Confirming a Reservation:** Most places will request a credit-card number to hold your room. If you're using an online reservation form, look for the *https* or a lock icon at the top of your browser. If you book direct, you can email, call, or fax this information.

**Canceling a Reservation:** If you must cancel, it's courteous—and smart—to do so with as much notice as possible, especially for smaller family-run places. Cancellation policies can be strict; read

For more complicated problems, don't expect instant results. Above all, keep a positive attitude. Remember, you're on vacation. If your hotel is a disappointment, spend more time out enjoying the place you came to see.

## Bed-and-Breakfasts

B&Bs offer double the cultural intimacy and—often—nicer rooms for a good deal less than most hotel rooms. Hosts usually speak English and are interesting conversationalists.

Especially in Bruges, Belgium has a variety of cozy, funky, affordable B&Bs well-run by gregarious entrepreneurs and typically located up a flight or two of steep, narrow stairs. Local TIs have lists of B&Bs and there's always Booking.com, but you'll save money by booking directly with the B&Bs listed in this book.

## Short-Term Rentals

A short-term rental—whether an apartment, house, or room in a local's home—is an increasingly popular alternative, especially if

| From: | rick@ricksteves.com |
|---|---|
| Sent: | Today |
| To: | info@hotelcentral.com |
| Subject: | Reservation request for 19-22 July |

Dear Hotel Central,

I would like to stay at your hotel. Please let me know if you have a room available and the price for:
• 2 people
• Double bed and en suite bathroom in a quiet room
• Arriving 19 July, departing 22 July (3 nights)

Thank you!
Rick Steves

the fine print before you book. Many discount deals require pre-payment, with no cancellation refunds.

**Reconfirming a Reservation:** Always call or email to reconfirm your room reservation a few days in advance. For B&Bs or very small hotels, I call again on my day of arrival to tell my host what time to expect me (especially important if arriving late—after 17:00).

**Phoning:** For tips on calling hotels overseas, see "Staying Connected," later.

you plan to settle in one location for several nights. For stays longer than a few days, you can usually find a rental that's comparable to—or even cheaper than—a hotel room with similar amenities. Plus, you'll get a behind-the-scenes peek into how locals live.

Many places require a minimum stay and have strict cancellation policies. Also you're generally on your own: There's no hotel reception desk, breakfast, or daily cleaning service.

**Finding Accommodations:** Aggregator websites such as Airbnb, FlipKey, Booking.com, and the HomeAway family of sites (HomeAway, VRBO, and VacationRentals) let you browse properties and correspond directly with European property owners or managers. If you prefer to work from a curated list of accommodations, consider using a rental agency such as InterhomeUSA.com or RentaVilla.com. Agency-represented apartments typically cost more, but this route often offers more help and safeguards than booking direct.

Before you commit, be clear on the location. I like to virtually "explore" the neighborhood using the Street View feature on

# Using Online Services to Your Advantage

From booking services to user reviews, online businesses are playing a greater role in travelers' planning than ever before. Take advantage of their pluses—and be wise to their downsides.

## Booking Sites

Hotel booking websites, including Priceline's Booking.com and Expedia's Hotels.com, offer one-stop shopping for hotels. While convenient for travelers, they present a real problem for small, independent, family-run hotels. Without a presence on these sites, these hotels become almost invisible. But to be listed, a hotel must pay a sizeable commission...and promise that its own website won't undercut the price on the booking-service site.

Here's the work-around: Use the big sites to research what's out there, then book directly with the hotel by email or phone, in which case hotel owners are free to give you whatever price they like. Ask for a room without the commission mark-up (or ask for a free breakfast, if not included, or a free upgrade). If you do book online, be sure to use the hotel's website. The price will likely be the same as via a booking site, but your money goes to the hotel, not agency commissions.

As a savvy consumer, remember: When you book with an online booking service, you're adding a middleman who takes roughly 20 percent. To support small, family-run hotels whose world is more difficult than ever, book direct.

## Short-Term Rental Sites

Rental juggernaut Airbnb (along with other short-term rental sites) allows travelers to rent rooms and apartments directly from locals, often providing more value than a cookie-cutter hotel. Airbnb fans appreciate feeling part of a real neighborhood and getting into a daily routine as "temporary Europeans." Depending on the host, Airbnb can provide an opportunity to get to know a

Google Maps. Also consider the proximity to public transportation and how well connected the property is with the rest of the city. Ask about amenities (elevator, air-conditioning, laundry, Wi-Fi, parking, etc.). Reviews from previous guests can help identify trouble spots.

Think about the kind of experience you want: Just a key and an affordable bed...or a chance to get to know a local? There are typically two kinds of hosts: those who want minimal interaction with their guests, and hosts who are friendly and may want to interact with you. Read the promotional text and online reviews to help shape your decision.

**Confirming and Paying:** Many places require you to pay the

local person, while keeping the money spent on your accommodations in the community.

Critics view Airbnb as a threat to "traditional Europe," saying it creates unfair, unqualified competition for established guesthouse owners. In some places, the lucrative Airbnb market has forced traditional guesthouses out of business and is driving property values out of range for locals. Some cities have cracked down, requiring owners to occupy rental properties part of the year (and staging disruptive "inspections" that inconvenience guests).

As a lover of Europe, I share the worry of those who see residents nudged aside by tourists. But as an advocate for travelers, I appreciate the value and cultural intimacy Airbnb provides.

## User Reviews

User-generated review sites and apps such as Yelp and TripAdvisor can give you a consensus of opinions about everything from hotels and restaurants to sights and nightlife. If you scan reviews of a restaurant or hotel and see several complaints about noise or a rotten location, you've gained insight that can help in your decision-making.

But as a guidebook writer, my sense is that there is a big difference between the uncurated information on a review site and the vetted listings in a guidebook. A user-generated review is based on the limited experience of one person, who stayed at just one hotel in a given city and ate at a few restaurants there. A guidebook is the work of a trained researcher who forms a well-developed basis for comparison by visiting many restaurants and hotels year after year.

Both types of information have their place, and in many ways, they're complementary. If something is well reviewed in a guidebook and also gets good online reviews, it's likely a winner.

entire balance before your trip. It's easiest and safest to pay through the site where you found the listing. Be wary of owners who want to take your transaction offline; this gives you no recourse if things go awry. Never agree to wire money (a key indicator of a fraudulent transaction).

**Apartments or Houses:** If you're staying somewhere for four or more nights, it's worth considering an apartment or rental house (shorter stays aren't worth the hassle of arranging key pickup, buying groceries, etc.). Apartment or house rentals can be especially cost-effective for groups and families. European apartments, like hotel rooms, tend to be small by US standards. But they often come

PRACTICALITIES

---

## Keep Cool

If you're visiting Belgium in the summer, you'll want an air-conditioned room. Most hotel air-conditioners come with a control stick (like a TV remote; the hotel may require a deposit) that generally has similar symbols and features: fan icon (click to toggle through wind power, from light to gale); louver icon (choose steady airflow or waves); snowflake and sunshine icons (cold air or heat, depending on season); clock ("O" setting: run X hours before turning off; "I" setting: wait X hours to start); and the temperature control (20 degrees Celsius is comfortable). When you leave your room for the day, turning off the air-conditioning is good form.

---

with laundry machines and small, equipped kitchens, making it easier and cheaper to dine in.

**Rooms in Private Homes:** Renting a room in someone's home is a good option for those traveling alone, as you're more likely to find true single rooms—with just one single bed, and a price to match. These can range from air-mattress-in-living-room basic to plush-B&B-suite posh. Some places allow you to book for a single night; if staying for several nights, you can buy groceries just as you would in a rental house. While you can't expect your host to also be your tour guide—or even to provide you with much info— some may be interested in getting to know the travelers who come through their home.

**Other Options:** Swapping homes with a local works for people with an appealing place to offer (don't assume where you live is not interesting to Europeans). A good place to start is HomeExchange.

To sleep for free, Couchsurfing.com is a vagabond's alternative to Airbnb. It lists millions of outgoing members who host fellow "surfers" in their homes.

### Hostels

A hostel provides cheap beds in dorms where you sleep alongside strangers for about $30 per night. Travelers of any age are welcome if they don't mind dorm-style accommodations and meeting other travelers. Most hostels offer kitchen facilities, guest computers, Wi-Fi, and a self-service laundry. Hostels almost always provide bedding, but the towel's up to you (though you can usually rent one for a small fee). Family and private rooms are often available.

**Independent hostels** tend to be easygoing, colorful, and informal (no membership required; www.hostelworld.com). You may pay slightly less by booking directly with the hostel. **Official hostels** are part of Hostelling International (HI) and share an online booking site (www.hihostels.com). HI hostels typically require that you be a member or else pay a bit more per night.

# Eating

Belgians brag that they eat as much as the Germans and as well as the French. They are among the world's leading carnivores and beer consumers. Belgium is where France meets northern Europe, and you'll find a good mix of both Germanic and French influences here. The Flemish were ruled by the dukes of Burgundy and absorbed some of the fancy French cuisine and etiquette of their overlords. (The neighboring Dutch, on the other hand, were ruled by the Spanish for 80 years and picked up nothing.) And yet, once Belgian, always Belgian: Instead of cooking with wine, Belgians have perfected the art of cooking with their own unique beers, imbuing the cuisine with a hoppy sweetness.

## RESTAURANT PRICING

I've categorized my recommended eateries based on the average price of a typical main course, indicated with a dollar-sign rating (see sidebar). Obviously, expensive specialties, fine wine, appetizers, and dessert can significantly increase your final bill.

The categories also indicate the personality of a place: **Budget** eateries include street food, takeaway, order-at-the-counter shops, basic cafeterias, and bakeries selling sandwiches. **Moderate** eateries are nice (but not fancy) sit-down restaurants, ideal for a straightforward, fill-the-tank meal. Most of my listings fall in this category—great for getting a good taste of the local cuisine.

**Pricier** eateries are a notch up, with more attention paid to the setting, presentation, and (often inventive) cuisine. **Splurge** eateries are dress-up-for-a-special-occasion-swanky—typically with an elegant setting, polished service, intricate cuisine, and an expansive (and expensive) wine list.

## DINING TIPS

For listings in this guidebook, I look for restaurants that are convenient to your hotel and sightseeing. When restaurant-hunting, choose a spot filled with locals, not the place with the big neon signs boasting, "We Speak English and Accept Credit Cards." Venturing even a block or two off the main drag leads to higher-quality food for a better price.

Belgians eat lunch when we do, but they eat dinner later. If you dine earlier than 19:30 at a restaurant, you'll eat alone (or with other tourists). For cheaper alternatives, consider eating at one of Belgium's affordable chain restaurants, a fry shop, or a bar, café, or brasserie (all described next).

## Restaurant Price Code

Eateries in this book are categorized according to the average cost of a typical main course. Drinks, desserts, and splurge items can raise the price considerably.

| | |
|---|---|
| **$$$$** | **Splurge:** Most main courses over €20 |
| **$$$** | **Pricier:** €15-20 |
| **$$** | **Moderate:** €10-15 |
| **$** | **Budget:** Under €10 |

In Belgium, a *frites* stand or other takeout spot is **$**; a basic café or sit-down eatery is **$$**; a casual but more upscale restaurant is **$$$**; and a swanky splurge is **$$$$**.

Note that there's no free tap water in Belgium. While a glass of water comes with a smile in the Netherlands, France, and Germany, that's not the case in Belgium, where you'll either pay for water, enjoy the beer, or go thirsty. You simply can't get tap water for free; Belgian restaurateurs are emphatic about that.

**Tipping:** At Belgian restaurants that have waitstaff, tax and service are included, although it's common to round up the bill after a good meal (usually 5-10 percent; so, for an €18.50 meal, pay €20). If you order your food at a counter, don't tip.

## Chain Restaurants

While excellent restaurants abound in Belgium, several local chains offer affordable, quick, and predictably good meals. Keep an eye out for these convenient choices.

**Exki** tries hard to be healthy in a country famous for its deep-fried foods and beer-based sauces. Their prepared meals (soups, salads, wraps) emphasize fresh produce, and while the food can be hit-or-miss, it's a handy break from heavy Belgian fare.

**Le Pain Quotidien** ("The Daily Bread") began as an artisanal bakery in Brussels...before its relentless march toward world domination. Although it now has 200 locations in more than a dozen countries, it's still considered a local shop among Belgians. It's a reliable fallback for fresh breads, pastries, and sandwiches.

**Balls & Glory** is a small, fun Flemish chain offering tasty, hand-crafted, softball-sized meatballs. Each day their rotating menu highlights two different flavors of meatball.

## Cafés, Bars, and Brasseries

For a more casual meal, or drinks only, try a bar, café, or brasserie. If you go to one of these places, in general, you can seat yourself, but avoid tables with a sign saying *"reservé"* or *"voorbehouden."* Unlike cafés in Italy or France, the cost of a drink or meal in Belgium is the same at the bar, at a table, or outside on the terrace. If all you want is a drink, you can wait for the server to come around or order directly from the bar. You generally pay for drinks as you go (especially if you're sitting outside), unless you specify you want to open a tab. If you're also ordering food, you pay for everything—drinks and your meal—at the end, as you would at a restaurant.

## Fast Food Fry Shops

Just like every village in England has its "chippy" (for fish-and-chips), and every German burg has its *Wurst* stand (for sausages), every Belgian town has a favored *frituur* (fry shop) or *frietkot* (fry shack). While the pinnacle is the fried potato, there's a wider variety of deep-fried treats than you might expect, such as sausages and meatballs (described later, under "Belgian Cuisine").

Belgian-style fries *(frieten)* taste so good because they're deep-fried twice—once to cook them and once to brown them. The best fries are cooked to a crisp in flavorful ox fat. We call them "French fries" and the Dutch call them *Vlaamse frieten* ("Flemish fries")—but to the Flemish they are plain *frieten*. Traditionally, fries are generously topped with sauces *(sausen)*. These can be mayo, tartar sauce, curry ketchup, *currysaus* (without the ketchup), or another flavored sauce (see list below). Ketchup is sometimes available. You'll generally pay extra (typically less than €1) for any sauce—including mayo.

*Américaine:* Mayo with herbs and a dash of Tabasco

*Joppiesaus:* Sweet yellow curry and onion sauce

*Pickles:* Mayo with pickle relish

*Provencaalse:* Sweet-and-sour tomato flavor

*Samuraisaus/samoeraisaus:* Mayo with spicy chili flavor and a hint of tomato

*Stoofvlees:* Rich Belgian beef stew made with beer; there's also a mayo-based sauce infused with *stoofvlees* flavor.

## BELGIAN CUISINE

Although this book's coverage focuses on the Flemish part of the country, people speak French first in Brussels—so both languages are given below (Dutch/French); if I've listed only one word, it's used nationwide. While the French influence is evident everywhere, it's ratcheted up around Brussels.

## Meat Appetizers and Snacks

These can be served at a *frituur* or *frietkot* (described above) or sometimes at bars or restaurants as appetizers. Many of these meat dishes are fried.

*Ballekes in tomatensaus:* Meatball dish with tomato sauce

**Bicky Burger:** Mystery-meat patty (a combination of pork, chicken, and horse meat) sold at snack stands nationwide; typically

PRACTICALITIES

deep-fried and topped with a sweet ketchup, a brown spicy sauce, and a secret, yellow "Bicky Dressing" (made with mayonnaise, mustard, cabbage, onion, and other vegetables)

**Bitterballen** *(petites croquettes):* Meat croquettes, battered in breadcrumbs and deep-fried; typically served as bar snacks, along with a drink made with bitters

**Boulet, Balleke, Frikadel,** or **Gehaktbal** *(boulette):* Various terms for meatballs, which can be fried, boiled, or grilled. Some meatballs are filled with a surprise; for example, *vogelnestje*—see below

**Frikandel** *(fricandelle):* Minced-meat sausage, usually deep-fried; the basic Belgian wiener

**Frikandel speciaal:** *Frikandel* served with mayo, ketchup, and chopped onions (sometimes called a **curryworst**—not to be confused with a German *Currywurst*)

**Kippenworst:** Chicken sausage; anything that starts with *kip* or includes *de poulet* indicates it's made with chicken

**Viandel:** Variation of *Frikandel*—skinny, deep-fried, often with a crunchy, herbed crust

**Vleeskroketten:** Similar to *Bitterballen* (listed above) but bigger

**Vogelnestje** ("bird's nest"): Meatball stuffed with a hard-boiled egg

## Traditional Dishes

Here are some classic Belgian dishes that may appear on menus. If you see the term *à la flamande,* that means it's cooked in the Flemish style (for instance, made with beer or smothered in a sauce of butter, chopped parsley, and crumbled hard-boiled egg).

**Biersoep/soupe à la bière:** Beer soup

**Filet américain:** Similar to steak tartare, this raw beef dish is named for the American meat grinder it was widely made with after World War II.

**(Gentse) Waterzooi:** Creamy stew made with chicken, eel, or fish; originated in Ghent

**Konijn met pruimen/lapin à la flamande:** Marinated rabbit braised in onions and prunes

**Luikse ballekes/boulettes sauce lapin:** Meatballs made in Liège sauce (a dark syrup from apples, pears, and dates)

**Luikse salade/salade liègeoise:** A warm salad of green beans, potatoes, tomatoes, and bacon

**Stoofvlees/carbonnade:** Rich beef stew flavored with onions, beer, and mustard; similar to French *bœuf bourguignon* but often sweetened with brown sugar or gingerbread

***Vol-au-vent:*** A rich and creamy chicken stew made with meatballs and lots of butter, typically used as the filling for a puff pastry sandwich

## Seafood

Belgium is known for its **mussels** *(mosselen/moules)*. They can be served plain *(natuur/nature)*, with white wine *(witte wijn/vin blanc)*, with shallots or onions *(marinière)*, in a mushroom cream sauce *(à la crème)*, or in a tomato sauce *(provençale)*. You get a big-enough-for-two bucket and a pile of fries. Go local by using one empty shell to tweeze out the rest of the *mosselen*. From about mid-July through April, you'll get the big Dutch mussels (most are from the coastal Zeeland area). Locals take a break from mussels in May and June, when only the puny Danish kind are available.

Here are some other popular seafood dishes:

***Caricoles/escargots (de mer):*** Sea snails. Very local, seasonal, and hard to find—usually sold hot by street vendors

***Grnaalkroket/croquettes de crevettes:*** Minced North Sea shrimp and Béchamel stuffed in a breaded, deep-fried roll

***Noordzee garnalen/crevettes grises:*** Little gray shrimp caught off the North Sea coast

***Paling in het groen/anguilles au vert:*** Eel in green herb sauce. This classic dish isn't always available, as good-quality eel is in short supply.

***Tomaat garnaal/tomattes crevettes:*** North Sea shrimp served inside a carved-out tomato

## Vegetables and Side Dishes

***Asperges:*** White asparagus, available only in spring, and usually served in cream sauce

***Rode kool/chou rouge à la flamande:*** Red cabbage with onions and prunes

***Spruitjes/choux de Bruxelles:*** Brussels sprouts (in cream sauce)

***Stoemp:*** Mashed potatoes and vegetables

***Witloof/chicoree*** or ***chicon:*** Bitter, coarse endive—the classic Belgian vegetable—served both raw and cooked

## Snacks

Popular snacks include fries (*Frieten;* described earlier) and cheese. While the French might use wine or alcohol to rub the rind of their cheese to infuse it with flavor, the Belgians use (surprise, surprise) beer. There are 350 types of Belgian cheeses. From Flanders, look for Vieux Brugge ("Old Bruges") and Chimay (named for the beer they use on it); from Wallonia, Remoudou and Djotte de Nivelles are good. Here are some other popular snacks:

***Croque monsieur:*** Grilled ham-and-cheese sandwich

*Pistolet:* Puffy, round bread-roll sandwich

*Tartine de fromage blanc:* Open-face cream-cheese sandwich, often enjoyed with a *lambic* beer (described later) and found mostly in traditional Brussels bars

## Desserts and Sweets

Belgium is famous for chocolate. The two basic types of Belgian chocolates are **pralines** (what we generally think of as "chocolates"—a hard chocolate shell with a filling) and **truffles** (a softer, crumblier shell with filling). For more on chocolates, see page 34. A *dame blanche* is a chocolate sundae.

Another Belgian specialty is waffles. You'll see little windows, shops, and trucks selling *wafels/gaufres;* either plain (for Belgians and purists) or topped with fruit, jam, chocolate sauce, ice cream, or whipped cream (for tourists). Belgians recognize two general types of waffles. The common takeout version, sold around the clock, is the dense, sugar-crusted, and very sweet **Liège-style waffle** *(Luikse/liègois),* usually served warm. **Brussels-style waffles** *(Brusselse)* are lighter and fluffier, dusted with powdered sugar and sometimes topped with marmalade. Though Americans think of "Belgian" waffles as a breakfast food, Belgians generally have them (or pancakes, *pannenkoeken*) as a late-afternoon snack. Brussels-style waffles are less widely available to go, though you may find them at teahouses or cafés in the afternoon (from about 14:00 until 18:00).

Another popular sweet is *speculoos,* spicy gingerbread biscuits served with coffee. For the Belgian answer to peanut butter or Nutella, look for *speculoos* spread—thick, creamy, and with the flavor of gingerbread cookies. (Trader Joe's sells this in the US with a "Cookie Butter" label.)

## BEVERAGES
### Belgian Beers

Belgium has about 120 varieties of beer and 580 brands, more than any other country—the locals take their beers as seriously as the French do their wines. Even small café menus include six to eight varieties. Connoisseurs and novices alike can be confused by the many choices, and casual drinkers probably won't like every kind offered, since some varieties don't even taste like beer. Belgian beer is generally yeastier and higher in alcohol content than beers in other countries. You must be 16 years old to legally enjoy a good Belgian beer (18 to drink wine and hard liquor).

To bring out their flavor, different beers are served cold, cool, or at room temperature, and each has its own distinctive glass. Whether wide-mouthed, tall, or fluted, with or without a stem, tulip-shaped or straight, the glass is meant to highlight a particular beer's qualities. The choice of glass is so important that if, for some reason, a pub doesn't have the proper glass for a particular beer, they will ask the customer if a different glass will be acceptable—or if they'd like to change their beer order.

To get a basic draft beer in Flanders (Bruges, Antwerp, or Ghent), ask for *een pintje* (ayn pinch-ya; a pint); in Brussels, where French prevails, request *une bière* (oon bee-yair).

But don't insist on beer from the tap. The only way to offer so many excellent beers and keep them fresh is to serve them bottled. In fact, because many specialty beers ferment in the bottle, some of the most famous brews come *only* in bottles. Increasingly, though, bars are adding a few high-end brands to their draft menus.

Belgians pair beer with food, much as the French pair wine. In general, lighter-colored beers (blonde or *Tripel*) go well with chicken or pork; darker beers pair nicely with beef; and wheat beers complement seafood.

## Specialty Beers

Specialty beers can be much more alcoholic than what you're used to back home, and tourists often find themselves overwhelmed by a single pint of Belgian brew. Bottles (and often menus) list the alcohol percentage of each type of beer. For comparison, most mass-market American beers are 4-6 percent alcohol by volume (ABV), while a heavy Belgian ale can run 7-9 percent—and a few powerful beers can be 10-12 percent or even higher.

Monk-run Trappist breweries have given the beer world the terms *Enkel, Dubbel,* and *Tripel* (single, double, triple). While originally these indicated the amount of malt used to gain a higher alcohol content, these days they have more to do with the style of beer: *Enkel* is a very light (nearly "lite") blonde ale; *Dubbel* is a dark, sweet beer; and *Tripel* is a very strong, golden-colored pale ale. The less commonly used term *Quadrupel* is a gimmick to emphasize a beer's alcohol content—usually more than 10 percent.

Some beer producers have returned to their medieval roots, flavoring their beer with a secret mix of spices called *gruit*. This can result in some surprising bouquets that charm and puzzle beer aficionados.

## Beers by Type

Here's a breakdown of types of beer, with some common brand names. This list is just a start, and you'll find many beers that don't fall into these neat categories.

**Ales** (Blonde/Red/Amber/Brown): Easily recognized by their color. Try a blonde or golden ale (Leffe Blonde, Duvel), a rare and bitter sour red (Rodenbach), an amber (Palm, De Koninck), or a brown (Leffe Bruin). *Saison* beers are "seasonal" (summer-brewed), lightly alcoholic pale ales.

**Lagers** *(Pils):* Light, sparkling, Budweiser-type beers. Popular brands include Jupiler, Stella Artois, and Maes.

*Lambics:* Wild-yeast beers. *Lambics*—popular in Brussels—get their start in open vats, where they're exposed to naturally occurring wild yeasts in the air. Some brand names include Cantillon, Lindemans, and Mort-Subite ("Sudden Death").

*Lambics* are often blended with fruits to counter their sour flavor. Fruit *lambics* include cherry *(kriek)*, raspberry *(frambozen)*, peach *(pêche)*, or blackcurrant *(cassis)*. People who don't usually enjoy beer tend to like these tart but sweet varieties, similar to a dry pink champagne. *Gueuze*—a dry, sour, double-fermented *lambic* nicknamed "Brussels champagne"—is more of an acquired taste.

**White** (*Witte* or *Witbier*): Milky-yellow summertime beers made from wheat. White beer, similar to a Hefeweizen, is often flavored with spices such as orange peel or coriander.

**Trappist and Abbey Beers:** Heavily fermented, malty, monk-brewed beers. For centuries, between their vespers and matins, Trappist monks have been brewing beer. Three typical ones are *Tripel,* with a blonde color, served cold with a frothy head; *Dubbel,* dark, sweet, and served cool; and *Enkel,* made especially by the monks for the monks, and considered a fair trade for a life of celibacy. These styles originated at the Westmalle monastery; other official Belgian Trappist monasteries are Rochefort, Chimay, Orval, Achel, and Westvleteren (the last one's brews are often voted the "best in the world" and are hard to find). "Abbey beers" *(abdijbier)* emulate the Trappist style, but are produced at other monasteries or by commercial brewers; St. Bernardus is one popular abbey beer. Try the Trappist Chimay Blauw/Bleu—extremely smooth, milkshake-like, and complex.

**Strong Beers:** The potent brands include Duvel ("devil," because of its high octane, camouflaged by a pale color), Verboten Vrucht ("forbidden fruit," with Adam and Eve on the label), and the not-for-the-fainthearted brands of Judas, Satan, and Lucifer. Gouden Carolus is good, and Delerium Tremens speaks for itself.

**Mass-Produced Beers:** Connoisseurs say you should avoid the mass-produced labels (Leffe, Stella, and Hoegaarden—all owned by AB InBev, which owns Budweiser in America) when you can enjoy a Belgian craft beer (such as Westmalle or Chimay) instead.

## Other Alcoholic Drinks

Belgians drink a lot of fine **wine**, but it's almost all imported. In general, Flanders prefers Bordeaux wines (which used to be delivered to the busy Flemish ports of Bruges and Antwerp), while inland Wallonia prefers Burgundy wines (which were delivered overland).

The distilled grain alcohol *jenever* (yah-NAY-ver) is spiced with juniper berries and often called "continental gin" or "Dutch gin" in English. (English traders eventually created a similar drink and called it simply gin.) *Jonge jenever* (young) is sharp and served chilled; *oude jenever* (old) is mellow and more commonly poured at room temperature (the terms refer to whether they use the older or newer distilling technique). I prefer *oude jenever*, which is smooth and soft, with a more mature flavor—like a good whisky. *Jenever* can be sipped, or it can be chugged with a *pils* chaser (this combination is called a *kopstoot*—headbutt; or you can sink the shot of *jenever* into the beer to create a *duikboot*—submarine).

## Nonalcoholic Drinks

Belgian restaurants typically charge for tap **water** or refuse to serve it. Since you're paying anyway, you might as well spring a bit more for mineral water, still or sparkling (Spa brand is popular). Many cafés/bars have a juicer for making fresh-squeezed **orange juice.**

Belgians love their **coffee,** enjoying many of the same drinks (espresso, cappuccino) served in American or Italian coffee shops. Coffee usually comes with a small *speculoos* spice cookie. A *koffie verkeerd* (fer-KEERT, "coffee wrong") is an espresso with a lot of steamed milk—the closest thing to a latte.

# Staying Connected

One of the most common questions I hear from travelers is, "How can I stay connected in Europe?" The short answer is: more easily and cheaply than you might think.

The simplest solution is to bring your own device—mobile phone, tablet, or laptop—and use it just as you would at home (following the tips below, such as getting an international plan or connecting to free Wi-Fi whenever possible). Another option is to buy a European SIM card for your US mobile phone. Or you can use European landlines and computers to connect. Each of these options is described next; more details are at www.ricksteves.com/phoning. For a very practical one-hour talk covering tech issues for travelers, see www.ricksteves.com/mobile-travel-skills.

# How to Dial

### International Calls

Whether phoning from a US landline or mobile phone, or from a number in another European country, here's how to make an international call. I've used one of my recommended Bruges hotels as an example (tel. 50-444-444).

**Initial Zero:** Drop the initial zero from international phone numbers—except when calling Italy.

**Mobile Tip:** If using a mobile phone, the "+" sign can replace the international access code (for a "+" sign, press and hold "0").

### US/Canada to Europe

Dial 011 (US/Canada international access code), country code (32 for Belgium), and phone number.

▶ To call the Bruges hotel from home, dial 011-32-50-444-444.

### Country to Country Within Europe

Dial 00 (Europe international access code), country code, and phone number.

▶ To call the Bruges hotel from Germany, dial 00-32-50-444-444.

### Europe to the US/Canada

Dial 00, country code (1 for US/Canada), and phone number.

▶ To call from Europe to my office in Edmonds, Washington, dial 00-1-425-771-8303.

## Domestic Calls

To call within Belgium (from one Belgian landline or mobile phone to another), simply dial the phone number, including the initial 0 if there is one.

▶ To call the Bruges hotel from Brussels, dial 50-444-444.

## USING A MOBILE PHONE IN EUROPE

Here are some budget tips and options.

**Sign up for an international plan.** To stay connected at a lower cost, sign up for an international service plan through your carrier. Most providers offer a simple bundle that includes calling, messaging, and data. Your normal plan may already include international coverage (T-Mobile's does).

Before your trip, call your provider or check online to confirm that your phone will work in Europe, and research your provider's international rates. Activate the plan a day or two before you leave, then remember to cancel it when your trip's over.

**Use free Wi-Fi whenever possible.** Unless you have an un-limited-data plan, you're best off saving most of your online tasks

## More Dialing Tips

**Toll and Toll-Free Calls:** Note that calls to a European mobile phone are substantially more expensive than calls to a fixed line. International rates apply to US toll-free numbers dialed from Belgium—they're not free.

**More Phoning Help:** See www.howtocallabroad.com.

| European Country Codes | | | |
|---|---|---|---|
| Austria | 43 | Ireland & N. Ireland | 353 / 44 |
| Belgium | 32 | Italy | 39 |
| Bosnia-Herzegovina | 387 | Latvia | 371 |
| Croatia | 385 | Montenegro | 382 |
| Czech Republic | 420 | Morocco | 212 |
| Denmark | 45 | Netherlands | 31 |
| Estonia | 372 | Norway | 47 |
| Finland | 358 | Poland | 48 |
| France | 33 | Portugal | 351 |
| Germany | 49 | Russia | 7 |
| Gibraltar | 350 | Slovakia | 421 |
| Great Britain | 44 | Slovenia | 386 |
| Greece | 30 | Spain | 34 |
| Hungary | 36 | Sweden | 46 |
| Iceland | 354 | Switzerland | 41 |
| | | Turkey | 90 |

PRACTICALITIES

for Wi-Fi. You can access the internet, send texts, and even make voice calls over Wi-Fi.

Most accommodations in Europe offer free Wi-Fi, but some—especially expensive hotels—charge a fee. Many cafés (including Starbucks and McDonald's) have free hotspots for customers; look for signs offering it and ask for the Wi-Fi password when you buy something. You'll also often find Wi-Fi at TIs, city squares, major museums, public-transit hubs, airports, and aboard trains and buses.

**Minimize the use of your cellular network.** Even with an international data plan, wait until you're on Wi-Fi to Skype, download apps, stream videos, or do other megabyte-greedy tasks. Using a navigation app such as Google Maps over a cellular network can take lots of data, so do this sparingly or use it offline.

Limit automatic updates. By default, your device constantly

---

## What Language Barrier?

People speak Dutch in Bruges, Ghent, and Antwerp—but with a Flemish accent. You will meet some French-only speakers in Brussels, but it's generally a minor issue: You'll find almost no language barrier in Belgium, as all well-educated folks, nearly all young people, and almost everyone in the tourist trade also speak English. Regardless, it's polite to use some Dutch or French pleasantries (see the survival phrases in the appendix).

---

checks for a data connection and updates apps. It's smart to disable these features so your apps will only update when you're on Wi-Fi. Also change your device's email settings from "auto-retrieve" to "manual" (or from "push" to "fetch").

When you need to get online but can't find Wi-Fi, simply turn on your cellular network just long enough for the task at hand. When you're done, avoid further charges by manually turning off data roaming or cellular data (either works) in your device's Settings menu. Another way to make sure you're not accidentally using data roaming is to put your device in "airplane" mode (which also disables phone calls and texts), and then turn your Wi-Fi back on as needed.

**Use Wi-Fi calling and messaging apps.** Skype, WhatsApp, FaceTime, and Google+ Hangouts are great for making free or low-cost calls or sending texts over Wi-Fi. With an app installed on your phone, tablet, or laptop, you can log on to a Wi-Fi network and contact friends or family members who use the same service. If you buy credit in advance, with some of these services you can call or send a text anywhere for just pennies per minute.

Some apps, such as Apple's iMessage, will use the cellular network if Wi-Fi isn't available: To avoid this possibility, turn off the "Send as SMS" feature.

### USING A EUROPEAN SIM CARD

With a European SIM card, you get a European mobile number and access to cheaper rates than you'll get through your US carrier. This option works best for those who want to make a lot of local calls, need a local phone number, or want faster connection speeds than their US carrier provides. It's simple: You buy a SIM card in Europe to replace the SIM card in your "unlocked" US phone or tablet (check with your carrier about unlocking it) or buy a basic cell phone in Europe.

SIM cards are sold at department-store electronics counters, some newsstands, and vending machines. If you need help setting it up, buy one at a mobile-phone shop (you may need to show your passport). Costing about $5-10, SIM cards usually include prepaid

## Tips on Internet Security

Make sure that your device is running the latest versions of its operating system, security software, and apps. Next, ensure that your device and key programs (like email) are password- or passcode-protected. On the road, use only secure, password-protected Wi-Fi hotspots. Ask the hotel or café staff for the specific name of their Wi-Fi network, and make sure you log on to that exact one.

If you must access your financial info online, use a banking app rather than accessing your account via a browser. A cellular connection is more secure than Wi-Fi. Avoid logging onto personal finance sites on a public computer.

Never share your credit-card number (or any other sensitive information) online unless you know that the site is secure. A secure site displays a little padlock icon, and the URL begins with *https* (instead of the usual *http*).

calling credit, with no contract and no commitment. Expect to pay $20-40 more for a SIM card with a gigabyte of data.

There are no roaming charges for EU citizens using a domestic SIM card in other EU countries. Theoretically, providers don't have to offer Americans this "roam-like-at-home" pricing, but most do. To be sure, buy your SIM card at a mobile-phone shop and ask if non-EU citizens also have roam-like-at-home pricing.

When you run out of credit, you can top up your SIM card at newsstands, tobacco shops, mobile-phone stores, or many other businesses (look for your SIM card's logo in the window), or possibly online.

### WITHOUT A MOBILE PHONE

It's possible to travel in Europe without a mobile device. You can make calls from your hotel and check email or browse websites using public computers.

Most **hotels** charge a fee for placing calls—ask for rates before you dial. You can use a prepaid international phone card (usually available at newsstands, tobacco shops, and train stations) to call out from your hotel. Dial the toll-free access number, enter the card's PIN code, then dial the number.

You'll only see **public pay phones** in a few post offices and train stations. Most don't take coins but instead require insertable phone cards, which you can buy at a newsstand, convenience store, or post office. Except for emergencies, they're not worth the hassle.

Most hotels have **public computers** in their lobbies for guests to use; otherwise you may find them at public libraries (ask your hotelier or the TI for the nearest location). On a European keyboard, use the "Alt Gr" key to the right of the space bar to insert the extra symbol that appears on some keys. If you can't locate a special character (such as @), simply copy and paste it from a web page.

## MAIL

You can mail one package per day to yourself worth up to $200 duty-free from Europe to the US (mark it "personal purchases"). If you're sending a gift to someone, mark it "unsolicited gift." For details, visit www.cbp.gov, select "Travel," and search for "Know Before You Go." The Belgian postal service works fine, but for quick transatlantic delivery (in either direction), consider services such as DHL (www.dhl.com).

# Transportation

Figuring out how to get around in Europe is one of your biggest trip decisions. Cars work well for two or more traveling together (especially families with small kids), those packing heavy, and those delving into the countryside. Trains and buses are best for solo travelers, blitz tourists, city-to-city travelers and those who want to leave the driving to others. Smart travelers can use short-hop flights within Europe to creatively connect the dots on their itineraries. Just be aware of the potential downside of each option: A car is an expensive headache in any major city; with trains and buses you're at the mercy of a timetable; and flying entails a trek to and from a usually distant airport.

Because of the short distances and excellent public transportation systems in Belgium, I recommend connecting Antwerp, Ghent, Bruges, and Brussels by train. Frequent trains connect each of these cities faster and easier than you could by driving. But for other destinations, a car could be a good alternative. Arrange to pick up your car in the last big city you'll visit, then use it to lace together small towns and explore the countryside. For more detailed information on transportation throughout Europe, see www.ricksteves.com/transportation.

## TRAINS

The easiest way to reach nearly any Belgian destination is by train. Connections are fast and frequent. Because Belgium is bilingual, the rail system has a complicated identity; it's NMBS in Dutch but SNCB in French (luckily, it has a good English website—www.belgianrail.be). InterCity (IC) trains are speedy for connecting big cities, and the high-speed Thalys is the fastest (the speed comes at a price; see "Reservations for Rail-Pass Holders," later). InterRegio (IR) trains connect smaller towns and make more stops along the way. Throughout Belgium, smoking is prohibited in trains and train stations.

# Rail Passes and Train Travel in Belgium

A Eurail **Benelux Pass** lets you travel by train in Belgium, the Netherlands, and Luxembourg for three to eight days within a one-month period. Discounted rates are offered for two or more people traveling together and for youths (ages 12-27). Up to two kids (ages 4-11) can travel free with each adult.

Rail passes are best purchased outside Europe (through travel agents or Rick Steves' Europe). For more on the ins and outs of rail passes, including prices, download my **free guide to Eurail Passes** (www.ricksteves.com/rail-guide) or go to www.ricksteves.com/rail.

For short trips within the region, individual **point-to-point train tickets** may save you money over a pass. Use this map to add up approximate pay-as-you-go fares for your itinerary, and compare that to the price of a rail pass. For international trains, significant discounts on point-to-point tickets may be available with advance purchase.

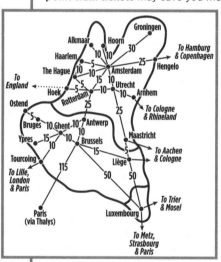

Map shows approximate costs, in US$, for one-way, second-class tickets on faster trains.

PRACTICALITIES

## Schedules

To get train schedules in advance, consult the Belgian rail site: www.belgianrail.be (tel. 025-282-828). The German Rail (Deutsche Bahn) website is also useful and has comprehensive schedules for almost anywhere in Europe (www.bahn.com).

At train stations, check the TV screens listing upcoming departures. The direction of the train is identified by its final station. If you can't find your train, or are unclear on departure details,

visit an information booth or enlist the help of any official-looking employee.

## Tickets

**Buying Tickets:** Belgian train ticket machines take US credit cards as long as they have a chip and PIN. It's also possible to purchase tickets at www.belgianrail.be with a US credit card (print them out at home or download the Belgian rail app and have everything on your mobile phone).

**Ticket Deals:** If you're not traveling with a rail pass, consider the region's money-saving deals. In Belgium, youths under age 26 can get a Go Pass (€51 for 10 rides anywhere in Belgium). A similar deal is available for anyone 26 or over for €76. Both youths and seniors (age 65+) can get a same-day round-trip ticket to anywhere in Belgium for €6 (but the senior version is not valid before 9:00 on weekdays and all day Sat-Sun in July-Aug). There are also weekend discounts for round-trips (50 percent off, valid Fri after 19:00). For more information, visit www.belgianrail.be.

**Bike Fees:** If you're traveling with a bike, you'll pay extra to bring it on the train. In Belgium, bikes cost €5 extra for a one-way trip, and €8 round-trip.

## High-Speed International Trains

Fast **Thalys** trains connect Brussels with Amsterdam, Cologne, and Paris (www.thalys.com). The **Eurostar** train zips between London and Brussels in 3 hours—faster and easier than flying (www.eurostar.com). French **TGV** trains link Brussels with Charles de Gaulle Airport, outside Paris, in under two hours (www.tgv-europe.com).

These fast-train services are expensive, but they do offer significant price discounts, with restrictions, on tickets reserved in advance (most available three months ahead, Eurostar available nine months ahead). Each company sells tickets online or through US agents such as www.ricksteves.com/rail. In Europe, you can buy tickets at any major train station in any country or at any travel agency that handles train tickets (expect a booking fee). Note that Thalys tickets between Brussels and Paris and Eurostar tickets between Brussels and London can qualify you for a discounted regional train connection in Belgium. For more on these trains, see page 207.

### Rail Passes

All rail passes that cover Belgium also cover the Netherlands and Luxembourg. Collectively, they're called "Benelux," and count as one country as far as rail passes are concerned. Most visits to Belgium don't cover enough miles to justify a rail pass, but if your itinerary extends beyond this relatively small region, adding Benelux to a multicountry rail pass could make sense.

For more detailed advice on figuring out the smartest rail pass options for your train trip, visit www.ricksteves.com/rail.

**Reservations for Rail-Pass Holders:** For the most part, you can hop on nearly any Belgian train with just your rail pass in hand. But the fast Thalys trains that run between Brussels and Amsterdam, Cologne/Dortmund, and Paris do require paid reservations and a rail pass that covers both ends of the trip. (Point-to-point tickets also cost more on Thalys trains than other trains on these routes.) On Brussels–Amsterdam and Brussels–Cologne/Dortmund trains, you can avoid this extra cost simply by choosing a regular non-Thalys train, which doesn't require seat reservations. The Brussels–Paris direct route, however, is served only by Thalys trains and is not covered by the Benelux rail pass—reserve as far ahead as possible for that stretch.

### BUSES

While you'll mostly use trains to travel in this region, you can also consider buses. There's no unified national bus company for Belgium—various destinations are served by different companies. Flanders is served largely by De Lijn (www.delijn.be), while French-speaking areas have TEC (www.infotec.be). Flanders has one set price for city bus tickets—€3 for one hour. If you plan to use city buses in Bruges, Ghent, and Antwerp, consider getting a

**PRACTICALITIES**

10-ride ticket for €16—it's good all over Flanders. Eurolines and Flixbus buses connect Belgium to other European cities (www. eurolines.be, www.flixbus.com).

## TAXIS AND RIDE-BOOKING SERVICES

Most European taxis are reliable and cheap. In many cities, two people can travel short distances by cab for little more than the cost of bus or subway tickets. If you like ride-booking services such as Uber, their apps usually work in Europe just like they do in the US: Request a car on your mobile phone (connected to Wi-Fi or data), and the fare is automatically charged to your credit card. For more about taxis in Brussels, see page 120.

## RENTING A CAR

It's cheaper to arrange most car rentals from the US, so research and compare rates before you go. Most of the major US rental agencies (including Avis, Budget, Enterprise, Hertz, and Thrifty) have offices throughout Europe. Also consider the two major Europe-based agencies, Europcar and Sixt. Consolidators such as Auto Europe/Kemwel (www.autoeurope.com—or the sometimes cheaper www.autoeurope.eu) compare rates at several companies to get you the best deal.

Wherever you book, always read the fine print. Ask about add-on charges—such as one-way drop-off fees, airport surcharges, or mandatory insurance policies—that aren't included in the "total price."

### Rental Costs and Considerations

Figure on paying roughly $250 for a one-week rental for a basic compact car. Allow extra for supplemental insurance, fuel, tolls, and parking.

**Manual vs. Automatic:** Almost all rental cars in Europe are manual by default—and cars with a stick shift are generally cheaper. If you need an automatic, request one in advance. When selecting a car, don't be tempted by a larger model, as it won't be as maneuverable on narrow, winding roads or when squeezing into tight parking lots.

**Age Restrictions:** Some rental companies impose minimum and maximum age limits. Young drivers (25 and under) and seniors (69 and up) should check the rental policies and rules section of car rental websites. If you're considered too young or too old, look into leasing (covered later), which has less stringent age restrictions.

**Choosing Pickup/Drop-off Locations:** Always check the hours of the locations you choose: Many rental offices close from midday Saturday until Monday morning and, in smaller towns, at lunchtime. When selecting an office, plug the address into a mapping website to confirm the location. A downtown site is generally cheaper—and might seem more convenient than the airport. But pedestrianized and one-way streets can make navigation tricky when returning a car at a big-city office or urban train station. Wherever you select, get precise details on the location and allow ample time to find it.

**Picking Up Your Car:** Before driving off in your rental car, check it thoroughly and make sure any damage is noted on your rental agreement. Rental agencies in Europe tend to charge for even minor damage, so be sure to mark everything. Find out how your car's gearshift, lights, turn signals, wipers, radio, and fuel cap function, and know what kind of fuel the car takes (diesel vs. unleaded). When you return the car, make sure the agent verifies its condition with you. Some drivers take pictures of the returned vehicle as proof of its condition.

## Car Insurance Options

When you rent a car in Europe, the price typically includes liability insurance, which covers harm to other cars or motorists—but not the rental car itself. To limit your financial risk in case of damage to the rental, choose one of these options: Buy a Collision Damage Waiver (CDW) with a low or zero deductible from the car-rental company (roughly 30-40 percent extra), get coverage through your credit card (free, but more complicated), or get collision insurance as part of a larger travel-insurance policy.

Basic **CDW** costs $15–30 a day and typically comes with a $1,000-2,000 deductible, reducing but not eliminating your financial responsibility. When you reserve or pick up the car, you'll be offered the chance to "buy down" the deductible to zero (for an additional $10–30/day; this is sometimes called "super CDW" or "zero-deductible coverage").

If you opt for **credit-card coverage,** you must decline all coverage offered by the car-rental company—which means they can place a hold on your card for up to the full value of the car. In case of damage, it can be time-consuming to resolve the charges. Before relying on this option, quiz your card company about how it works.

If you're already purchasing a **travel-insurance policy** for your trip, adding collision coverage can be an economical option. For example, Travel Guard (www.travelguard.com) sells affordable renter's collision insurance as an add-on to its other policies; it's valid everywhere in Europe except the Republic of Ireland, and some Italian car-rental companies refuse to honor it, as it doesn't cover you in case of theft.

For more on car-rental insurance, see www.ricksteves.com/cdw.

**PRACTICALITIES**

## Leasing

For trips of three weeks or more, consider leasing (which automatically includes zero-deductible collision and theft insurance). By technically buying and then selling back the car, you save money on taxes and insurance. Leasing provides you a brand-new car with unlimited mileage and a 24-hour emergency assistance program. You can lease for as little as 21 days to as long as five and a half months. Car leases must be arranged from the US. One of several companies offering affordable lease packages is Auto Europe.

## Navigation Options

If you'll be navigating using your phone or a GPS unit from home, remember to bring a car charger and device mount.

**Your Mobile Phone:** The mapping app on your phone works fine for navigation in Europe, but for real-time turn-by-turn directions and traffic updates, you'll need mobile data access. And driving all day can burn through a lot of very expensive data.

The economical work-around is to use map apps that work offline. By downloading in advance from Google Maps, Apple Maps, Here WeGo, or Navmii, you can still have turn-by-turn voice directions and maps that recalibrate even though they're offline.

You must download your maps before you go offline—and it's smart to select large regions. Then turn off your data connection so you're not charged for roaming. Call up the map, enter your destination, and you're on your way. Even if you don't have to pay extra for data roaming, this option is great for navigating in areas with poor connectivity.

**GPS Devices:** If you want the convenience of a dedicated GPS unit, consider renting one with your car ($10-30/day). These units offer real-time turn-by-turn directions and traffic without the data requirements of an app. The unit may come loaded only with maps for its home country; if you need additional maps, ask. Also make sure your device's language is set to English before you drive off.

A less expensive option is to bring a GPS device from home. Be sure to buy and install the European maps you'll need before your trip.

**Maps and Atlases:** Even when navigating primarily with a mobile app or GPS, I always make it a point to have a paper map. It's invaluable for getting the big picture, understanding alternate routes, and filling in when my phone runs out of juice. The free maps you get from your car-rental company usually don't have enough detail. It's smart to buy a better map before you go, or pick one up at a European gas station, bookshop, newsstand, or tourist shop.

## DRIVING

**Road Rules:** Traffic cameras are everywhere in Belgium; speeding tickets for even a few kilometers over the limit are common. Kids under age 12 (or less than about 5 feet tall) must ride in an appropriate child-safety seat. Seat belts are mandatory for all, and two beers under those belts are enough to land you in jail. Be aware of typical European road rules; for example, many countries require headlights to be turned on at all times, and nearly all forbid hand-held mobile-phone use. In Europe, you're not allowed to turn right on a red light unless a sign or signal specifically authorizes it, and on expressways it's illegal to pass drivers on the right. Ask your car-rental company about these rules, or check the "International Travel" section of the US State Department website (www.travel. state.gov, search for your country in the "Country Information" box, then click on "Travel and Transportation").

**Fuel:** Gas (*benzine* in Dutch, *essence* in French) is expensive—about $6 per gallon. Diesel (*diesel* or *dieselolie* in Dutch, *gazole* in French) is about the same—$6 per gallon—but diesel cars get better mileage, so try to rent a diesel to save money. Be sure you know what type of fuel your car takes before you fill up. Gas is most expensive on freeways and cheapest at big supermarkets. Some of the filling stations in Belgium are unmanned, and your US credit cards should work at self-service gas pumps if you have a chip and a PIN code. If not, look for stations with an attendant or be sure to carry sufficient cash in euros.

**Parking:** Finding a parking place can be a headache in larger cities. Ask your hotelier for ideas, and pay to park at well-patrolled lots (blue *P* signs direct you to parking lots). Parking structures usually require that you take a ticket with you and pay at a machine on your way back to the car. These machines accept euro coins (and sometimes bills); US credit cards with a chip and PIN should work.

## FLIGHTS

To compare flight costs and times, begin with a travel search engine: Kayak.com is the top site for flights to and within Europe, easy-to-use Google Flights has price alerts, and Skyscanner.com includes many inexpensive flights within Europe.

**Flights to Europe:** Start looking for international flights at least four to six months before your trip, especially for peak-season travel. Depending on your itinerary, it can be efficient and no more expensive to fly into one city and out of another. If your flight requires a connection in Europe, see my hints on navigating Europe's top hub airports at www.ricksteves.com/hub-airports.

**Flying Within Europe:** Flying between European cities has become surprisingly affordable. Before buying a long-distance train or bus ticket, first check the cost of a flight on one of Europe's airlines, whether a major carrier or a no-frills outfit like EasyJet and Ryanair, along with Brussels Airlines (www.brusselsairlines.com). Be aware of the potential drawbacks of flying with a discount airline: nonrefundable and nonchangeable tickets, minimal customer service, time-consuming treks to secondary airports, and stingy baggage allowances. To avoid unpleasant surprises, read the small print about the costs for "extras" such as reserving a seat, checking a bag, or checking in and printing a boarding pass.

**Flying to the US and Canada:** Because security is extra tight for flights to the US, be sure to give yourself plenty of time at the airport. It's also important to charge your electronic devices before you board because security checks may require you to turn them on (see www.tsa.gov for the latest rules).

# Resources from Rick Steves

## Begin Your Trip at RickSteves.com

My mobile-friendly **website** is *the* place to explore Europe in preparation for your trip. You'll find thousands of fun articles, videos, and radio interviews; a wealth of money-saving tips for planning your dream trip; travel news dispatches; a video library of my travel talks; my travel blog; my latest guidebook updates (www.ricksteves.com/update); and my free Rick Steves Audio Europe app. You can also follow me on Facebook and Twitter.

Our **Travel Forum** is a well-groomed collection of message boards where our travel-savvy community answers questions and shares their personal travel experiences—and our well-traveled staff chimes in when they can be helpful (www.ricksteves.com/forums).

Our **online Travel Store** offers bags and accessories that I've designed to help you travel smarter and lighter. These include my popular carry-on bags (which I live out of four months a year), money belts, totes, toiletries kits, adapters, guidebooks, and planning maps.

Our website can also help you find the perfect **rail pass** for your itinerary and your budget, with easy, one-stop shopping for rail passes, seat reservations, and point-to-point tickets (www.ricksteves.com/rail).

## Rick Steves' Tours, Guidebooks, TV Shows, and More

**Small Group Tours:** Want to travel with greater efficiency and less stress? We offer more than 40 itineraries reaching the best destinations in this book...and beyond. Each year about 25,000 travelers join us on about 1,000 Rick Steves bus tours. You'll enjoy great guides and a fun bunch of travel partners (with small groups of 24 to 28 travelers). You'll find European adventures to fit every vacation length. For all the details, and to get our tour catalog, visit www.ricksteves.com or call us at 425/608-4217.

**Books:** *Rick Steves Belgium* is just one of many books in my series on European travel, which includes country and city guide-

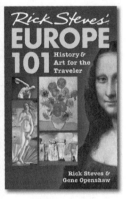

books, Snapshots (excerpted chapters from my bigger guides), Pocket Guides (full-color little books on big cities), "Best Of" guidebooks (condensed, full-color country guides), and my budget-travel skills handbook, *Rick Steves Europe Through the Back Door*. A more complete list of my titles—including phrase books, cruising guides, and more—appears near the end of this book.

**TV Shows and Travel Talks:** My public television series, *Rick Steves' Europe*, covers Europe from top to bottom with over 100 half-hour episodes—and we're working on new shows every year (watch full episodes at my website for free). Or, to raise your travel I.Q., check out the video versions of our popular classes (covering most European countries as well as travel skills, packing smart, cruising, tech for travelers, European art, and travel as a political act—www.ricksteves.com/travel-talks).

**Radio:** My weekly public radio show, *Travel with Rick Steves*, features interviews with travel experts from around the world. It airs on 400 public radio stations across the US, or you can hear it as a podcast. A complete archive of programs is available at www.ricksteves.com/radio.

**Audio Tours on My Free App:** I've produced dozens of free, self-guided audio tours of the top sights in Europe. For those tours and other audio content, get my free **Rick Steves Audio Europe app,** an extensive online library organized by destination. For more on my app, see page 5.

# APPENDIX

## Holidays and Festivals

This list includes selected festivals in major cities, plus national holidays observed throughout Belgium. Many sights and banks close on national holidays—keep this in mind when planning your itinerary. Before planning a trip around a festival, verify the dates with the festival website, the Belgian national tourist office (www.visitbelgium.com), or my "Upcoming Holidays and Festivals in Belgium" web page (www.ricksteves.com/europe/belgium/festivals).

| | |
|---|---|
| **Jan 1** | New Year's Day |
| **Feb/early March** | Carnival (Mardi Gras) |
| **April** | Easter Weekend (Good Friday-Easter Monday): April 19-22, 2019; April 10-13, 2020 |
| **May 1** | Labor Day |
| **May** | Ascension and Procession of the Holy Blood, Bruges: May 30, 2019; May 21, 2020 |
| **Mid-May** | Zinneke Parade, Brussels (even years only, procession with music, dance, and floats, www.zinneke.org) |

| May/June | Pentecost and Whit Monday: June 9-10, 2019; May 31-June 1, 2020 |
|---|---|
| June | Brussels Film Festival (www.brff.be) |
| Late June/ early July | Ommegang Pageant, Brussels (historic costumed parade to Grand Place, www.ommegang.be) |
| Mid-late July | Ghent Festivities (free concerts, fireworks, street performers, market, www.gentsefeesten.be) |
| July 21 | Belgian Independence Day (parades, fireworks) |
| Aug | Brussels Summer Festival (concerts, street performers, www.bsf.be) |
| Aug | Musica Antiqua Festival, Bruges (medieval music, www.mafestival.be) |
| Aug 15 | Assumption Day (procession in Bruges) |
| Mid-Aug | Carpet of Flowers, Brussels (celebrated even years only, www.flowercarpet.be) |
| Mid-Oct | Ghent Film Festival (www.filmfestival.be) |
| Nov 1 | All Saints' Day |
| Nov 11 | Armistice Day |
| Dec | "Winter Wonders" Christmas Market, Brussels (www.plaisirsdhiver.be) |
| Dec 6 | St. Nicholas Day (Sinterklaas; processions and presents for children) |
| Dec 25 | Christmas |

APPENDIX

# Books and Films

To learn more about Belgium past and present, check out a few of these recommended books or films.

## NONFICTION

*The Guns of August* (Barbara Tuchman, 2004). This Pulitzer Prize-winning chronicle follows the outbreak of World War I and events along the Western Front, including Belgium.

*In Flanders Fields: The 1917 Campaign* (Leon Wolff, 1958). In a classic account of the Flanders battle at Passchendaele, Wolff details how Allied forces captured a few thousand yards at the cost of tens of thousands of lives.

*King Leopold's Ghost* (Adam Hochschild, 1999). This best-seller provides a clear-eyed examination of Belgium's exploitation of its Congo colony.

*A Tall Man in a Low Land: Some Time Among the Belgians* (Harry

Pearson, 1999). Pearson offers a wry look at contemporary Belgium through the eyes of an outsider.

*The Wisdom of the Beguines: The Forgotten Story of a Medieval Women's Movement* (Laura Swan, 2016). Swan explores *beguinages*, communities of like-minded women who aided their towns' poor and vulnerable.

## FICTION

*The Abyss* (Marguerite Yourcenar, 1968). One of Belgium's greatest novelists tells the story of an atheist in Renaissance Bruges.

*The Adventures of Tintin* series (Hergé, 1929-1976). These classic comics feature the irrepressible boy reporter and his dog.

*The House of Niccolò* series (Dorothy Dunnett, 1999). This three-volume series traces an audacious apprentice who rises to lead a mercantile empire in 15th-century Flanders.

*The Lady and the Unicorn* (Tracy Chevalier, 2003). Uncover the creation story of the famous *Lady and the Unicorn* tapestries, which were woven by a master craftsman in Brussels.

*Pallieter* (Felix Timmermans, 1916). A Flemish classic, this "ode to life" details a young man's journey recovering from a life-threatening disease.

*Resistance* (Anita Shreve, 1995). In Nazi-occupied Belgium, the wife of a resistance fighter shelters an American bomber pilot.

*The Square of Revenge* (Pieter Aspe, 2013). Bruges' medieval architecture conceals a bizarre mystery for Inspector Van In to solve.

## FILMS

*The Adventures of Tintin* (2011). Steven Spielberg's adaptation of the beloved Belgian comic book hero follows Tintin on a treasure hunt for a sunken ship.

*The Battle of the Bulge* (1965). This historical drama starring Henry Fonda recounts the surprise Nazi attack on the Western Front in 1944.

*Get Out Your Handkerchiefs* (1978). Shot in the Ardennes, this wacky romantic comedy starring Gérard Depardieu won the Academy Award for Best Foreign Language Film.

*If It's Tuesday, This Must Be Belgium* (1969). A comedic group of travelers from the US races through seven countries in 18 days on a bus tour.

*In Bruges* (2008). This dark comedy was filmed...in Bruges.

*The Monuments Men* (2014). In this action-drama, a WWII platoon goes on a mission to rescue Nazi-stolen art treasures—including Bruges' Michelangelo piece *Madonna and Child* and the Ghent Altarpiece.

# Conversions and Climate

## Numbers and Stumblers

- Europeans write a few of their numbers differently than we do. 1 = $\mathcal{1}$, 4 = $\mathcal{4}$, 7 = $\mathcal{7}$.
- In Europe, dates appear as day/month/year, so Christmas 2020 is 25/12/20.
- Commas are decimal points and decimals are commas. A dollar and a half is $1,50, one thousand is 1.000, and there are 5.280 feet in a mile.
- When counting with fingers, start with your thumb. If you hold up your first finger to request one item, you'll probably get two.
- What Americans call the second floor of a building is the first floor in Europe.
- On escalators and moving sidewalks, Europeans keep the left "lane" open for passing. Keep to the right.

## Metric Conversions

A kilogram is 2.2 pounds, and 1 liter is about a quart, or almost four to a gallon. A kilometer is six-tenths of a mile. I figure kilometers to miles by cutting them in half and adding back 10 percent of the original (120 km: 60 + 12 = 72 miles, 300 km: 150 + 30 = 180 miles).

| | |
|---|---|
| 1 foot = 0.3 meter | 1 square yard = 0.8 square meter |
| 1 yard = 0.9 meter | 1 square mile = 2.6 square kilometers |
| 1 mile = 1.6 kilometers | 1 ounce = 28 grams |
| 1 centimeter = 0.4 inch | 1 quart = 0.95 liter |
| 1 meter = 39.4 inches | 1 kilogram = 2.2 pounds |
| 1 kilometer = 0.62 mile | 32°F = 0°C |

## Clothing Sizes

When shopping for clothing, use these US-to-European comparisons as general guidelines (but note that no conversion is perfect).

**Women:** For pants and dresses, add 32 in Belgium (US 10 = Belgian 42). For blouses and sweaters, add 8 for most of Europe (US 32 = European 40). For shoes, add 30-31 (US 7 = European 37/38).

**Men:** For shirts, multiply by 2 and add about 8 (US 15 = European 38). For jackets and suits, add 10. For shoes, add 32-34.

**Children:** Clothing is sized by height—in centimeters (2.5 inches = 1 cm), so a US size 8 roughly equates to 132-140. For shoes up to size 13, add 16-18, and for sizes 1 and up, add 30-32.

## Fahrenheit and Celsius Conversion

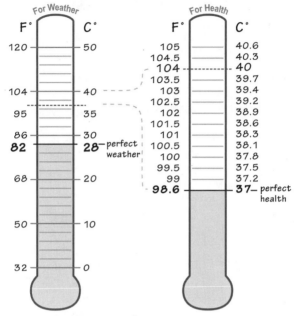

Europe takes its temperature using the Celsius scale, while we opt for Fahrenheit. For a rough conversion from Celsius to Fahrenheit, double the number and add 30. For weather, remember that 28°C is 82°F—perfect. For health, 37°C is just right. At a launderette, 30°C is cold, 40°C is warm (usually the default setting), 60°C is hot, and 95°C is boiling. Your air-conditioner should be set at about 20°C.

### Belgium's Climate

First line, average daily high; second line, average daily low; third line, average days without rain. For more detailed weather statistics for destinations in this book (as well as the rest of the world), check www.wunderground.com.

| J | F | M | A | M | J | J | A | S | O | N | D |
|-----|-----|-----|-----|-----|-----|-----|-----|-----|-----|-----|-----|
| 41° | 44° | 51° | 58° | 65° | 71° | 73° | 72° | 69° | 60° | 48° | 42° |
| 30° | 32° | 34° | 40° | 45° | 53° | 55° | 55° | 52° | 45° | 38° | 32° |
| 9 | 11 | 14 | 12 | 15 | 15 | 13 | 12 | 15 | 13 | 10 | 11 |

APPENDIX

# Packing Checklist

Whether you're traveling for five days or five weeks, you won't need more than this. Pack light to enjoy the sweet freedom of true mobility.

## Clothing

- ☐ 5 shirts: long- & short-sleeve
- ☐ 2 pairs pants (or skirts/capris)
- ☐ 1 pair shorts
- ☐ 5 pairs underwear & socks
- ☐ 1 pair walking shoes
- ☐ Sweater or warm layer
- ☐ Rainproof jacket with hood
- ☐ Tie, scarf, belt, and/or hat
- ☐ Swimsuit
- ☐ Sleepwear/loungewear

## Money

- ☐ Debit card(s)
- ☐ Credit card(s)
- ☐ Hard cash (US $100-200)
- ☐ Money belt

## Documents

- ☐ Passport
- ☐ Tickets & confirmations: flights, hotels, trains, rail pass, car rental, sight entries
- ☐ Driver's license
- ☐ Student ID, hostel card, etc.
- ☐ Photocopies of important documents
- ☐ Insurance details
- ☐ Guidebooks & maps

## Toiletries Kit

- ☐ Basics: soap, shampoo, toothbrush, toothpaste, floss, deodorant, sunscreen, brush/comb, etc.
- ☐ Medicines & vitamins
- ☐ First-aid kit
- ☐ Glasses/contacts/sunglasses
- ☐ Sewing kit
- ☐ Packet of tissues (for WC)
- ☐ Earplugs

## Electronics

- ☐ Mobile phone
- ☐ Camera & related gear
- ☐ Tablet/ebook reader/laptop
- ☐ Headphones/earbuds
- ☐ Chargers & batteries
- ☐ Phone car charger & mount (or GPS device)
- ☐ Plug adapters

## Miscellaneous

- ☐ Daypack
- ☐ Sealable plastic baggies
- ☐ Laundry supplies: soap, laundry bag, clothesline, spot remover
- ☐ Small umbrella
- ☐ Travel alarm/watch
- ☐ Notepad & pen
- ☐ Journal

## Optional Extras

- ☐ Second pair of shoes (flip-flops, sandals, tennis shoes, boots)
- ☐ Travel hairdryer
- ☐ Picnic supplies
- ☐ Water bottle
- ☐ Fold-up tote bag
- ☐ Small flashlight
- ☐ Mini binoculars
- ☐ Small towel or washcloth
- ☐ Inflatable pillow/neck rest
- ☐ Tiny lock
- ☐ Address list (to mail postcards)
- ☐ Extra passport photos

## Dutch Survival Phrases

Northern Belgium speaks Dutch, but for cultural and historical reasons, the language is often called Flemish. Most people speak English, but if you learn the pleasantries and key phrases, you'll connect better with the locals. To pronounce the guttural Dutch "g" (indicated in phonetics by h), make a clear-your-throat sound, similar to the "ch" in the Scottish word "loch."

| English | Dutch | Pronunciation |
|---|---|---|
| Hello. | Hallo. | **hah**-loh |
| Good day. | Dag. | dah |
| Good morning. | Goedemorgen. | **hoo**-deh-mor-hehn |
| Good afternoon. | Goedemiddag. | **hoo**-deh-mid-dah |
| Good evening. | Goedenavond. | **hoo**-dehn-ah-fohnd |
| Do you speak English? | Spreekt u Engels? | shpraykt oo **eng**-ehls |
| Yes. / No. | Ja. / Nee. | yah / nay |
| I (don't) understand. | Ik begrijp (het niet). | ik beh-**hripe** (heht neet) |
| Please. (can also mean "You're welcome") | Alstublieft. | **ahl**-stoo-bleeft |
| Thank you. | Dank u wel. | dahnk oo vehl |
| I'm sorry. | Het spijt me. | heht spite meh |
| Excuse me. | Pardon. | **par**-dohn |
| (No) problem. | (Geen) probleem. | (hayn) **proh**-blaym |
| Good. | Goede. | **hoo**-deh |
| Goodbye. | Tot ziens. | toht zeens |
| one / two | een / twee | ayn / t'vay |
| three / four | drie / vier | dree / feer |
| five / six | vijf / zes | fife / zehs |
| seven / eight | zeven / acht | **zay**-fehn / aht |
| nine / ten | negen / tien | **nay**-hehn / teen |
| What does it cost? | Wat kost het? | vaht kohst heht |
| Is it free? | Is het vrij? | is heht fry |
| Is it included? | Is het inclusief? | is heht in-**kloo**-seev |
| Can you please help me? | Kunt u alstublieft helpen? | koont oo **ahl**-stoo-bleeft **hehl**-pehn |
| Where can I buy / find...? | Waar kan ik kopen / vinden...? | var kahn ik **koh**-pehn / **fin**-dehn |
| I'd like / We'd like... | Ik wil graag / Wij willen graag... | ik vil hrah / vy **vil**-lehn hrah |
| ...a room. | ...een kamer. | ayn **kah**-mer |
| ...a train / bus ticket to ____. | ...een trein / bus kaartje naar ____. | ayn trayn / boos **kart**-yeh nar ____ |
| ...to rent a bike. | ...een fiets huren. | ayn feets **hoo**-rehn |
| Where is...? | Waar is...? | var is |
| ...the train / bus station | ...het trein / bus station | heht trayn / boos **staht**-see-ohn |
| ...the tourist info office | ...de VVV | deh fay fay fay |
| ...the toilet | ...het toilet | heht **twah**-leht |
| men / women | mannen / vrouwen | **mah**-nehn / **frow**-ehn |
| left / right | links / rechts | links / re**h**ts |
| straight ahead | rechtdoor | **reht**-dor |
| What time does it open / close? | Hoe laat gaat het open / dicht? | hoo laht haht heht **oh**-pehn / di**h**t |
| now / soon / later | nu / straks / later | noo / strahks / **lah**-ter |
| today / tomorrow | vandaag / morgen | **fahn**-dah / **mor**-hehn |

## In a Dutch Restaurant

The all-purpose Dutch word *alstublieft* (**ahl**-stoo-bleeft) means "please," but it can also mean "here you are" (when the server hands you something), "thanks" (when taking payment from you), or "you're welcome" (when handing you change). Here are other words that might come in handy at restaurants:

| English | Dutch | Pronunciation |
|---|---|---|
| I'd like / We'd like... | Ik wil graag / Wij willen graag... | ik vil *hrah* / vy **vil**-lehn *hrah* |
| ...a table for one / two. | ...een tafel voor een / twee. | ayn **tah**-fehl for ayn / t'vay |
| ...to reserve a table. | ...een tafel reserveren. | ayn **tah**-fehl ray-zehr-feh-rehn |
| ...the menu (in English). | ...het menu (in het Engels). | heht meh-**noo** (in heht **eng**-ehls) |
| Is this table free? | Is deze tafel vrij? | is **day**-zeh **tah**-fehl fry |
| to go | om mee te nemen | ohm may teh **nay**-mehn |
| with / without | met / zonder | meht / **zohn**-der |
| and / or | en / of | ehn / of |
| special of the day | dagschotel | **dah**s-hoh-tehl |
| specialty of the house | huisspecialiteit | **hows**-shpeh-shah-lee-tite |
| breakfast | ontbijt | **ohnt**-bite |
| lunch | middagmaal | **mid**-dah-mahl |
| dinner | avondmaal | **ah**-fohnd-mahl |
| appetizers | hapjes | **hahp**-yehs |
| main courses | hoofdgerechten | **hohfd**-heh-reh-tehn |
| side dishes | bijgerechten | **bye**-heh-reh-tehn |
| bread / cheese | brood / kaas | brohd / kahs |
| sandwich | sandwich | **sand**-vich |
| soup / salad | soep / sla | soop / slah |
| meat / chicken / fish | vlees / kip / vis | flays / kip / fis |
| fruit / vegetables | vrucht / groenten | fruht / **hroon**-tehn |
| dessert / pastries | gebak | heh-**bahk** |
| I am vegetarian. | Ik ben vegetarisch. | ik behn vay-heh-**tah**-rish |
| mineral water / tap water | mineraalwater / kraanwater | min-eh-rahl-**vah**-ter / **krahn**-vah-ter |
| milk / (orange) juice | melk / (sinaasappel) sap | mehlk / **see**-nahs-ah-pehl (sahp) |
| coffee / tea | koffie / thee | **koh**-fee / tay |
| wine / beer | wijn / bier | vine / beer |
| red / white | rode / witte | **roh**-deh / **vit**-teh |
| glass / bottle | glas / fles | *h*lahs / flehs |
| Cheers! | Proost! | prohst |
| More. / Another. | Meer. / Nog een. | mayr / noh ayn |
| The same. | Het zelfde. | heht **zehlf**-deh |
| The bill, please. | De rekening, alstublieft. | deh **ray**-keh-neeng **ahl**-stoo-bleeft |
| Do you accept credit cards? | Accepteert u kredietkaarten? | **ahk**-shehp-tayrt oo kray-deet-**kar**-tehn |
| Is service included? | Is bediening inbegrepen? | is beh-**dee**-neeng in-beh-*h*ray-pehn |
| tip | fooi | foy |
| Tasty. | Lekker. | **leh**-ker |
| Enjoy! | Smakelijk! | **smah**-keh-like |

## French Survival Phrases

When using the phonetics, try to nasalize the <u>n</u> sound.

| English | French | Pronunciation |
|---------|--------|---------------|
| Good day. | *Bonjour.* | bohn-zhoor |
| Mrs. / Mr. | *Madame / Monsieur* | mah-dahm / muhs-yuh |
| Do you speak English? | *Parlez-vous anglais?* | par-lay-voo ahn-glay |
| Yes. / No. | *Oui. / Non.* | wee / nohn |
| I understand. | *Je comprends.* | zhuh kohn-prahn |
| I don't understand. | *Je ne comprends pas.* | zhuh nuh kohn-prahn pah |
| Please. | *S'il vous plaît.* | see voo play |
| Thank you. | *Merci.* | mehr-see |
| I'm sorry. | *Désolé.* | day-zoh-lay |
| Excuse me. | *Pardon.* | par-dohn |
| (No) problem. | *(Pas de) problème.* | (pah duh) proh-blehm |
| It's good. | *C'est bon.* | say bohn |
| Goodbye. | *Au revoir.* | oh ruh-vwahr |
| one / two / three | *un / deux / trois* | uhn / duh / trwah |
| four / five / six | *quatre / cinq / six* | kah-truh / sank / sees |
| seven / eight | *sept / huit* | seht / weet |
| nine / ten | *neuf / dix* | nuhf / dees |
| How much is it? | *Combien?* | kohn-bee-an |
| Write it? | *Ecrivez?* | ay-kree-vay |
| Is it free? | *C'est gratuit?* | say grah-twee |
| Included? | *Inclus?* | an-klew |
| Where can I buy / find...? | *Où puis-je acheter / trouver...?* | oo pwee-zhuh ah-shuh-tay / troo-vay |
| I'd like / We'd like... | *Je voudrais / Nous voudrions...* | zhuh voo-dray / noo voo-dree-ohn |
| ...a room. | *...une chambre.* | ewn shahn-bruh |
| ...a ticket to ___. | *...un billet pour ___.* | uhn bee-yay poor ___ |
| Is it possible? | *C'est possible?* | say poh-see-bluh |
| Where is...? | *Où est...?* | oo ay |
| ...the train station | *...la gare* | lah gar |
| ...the bus station | *...la gare routière* | lah gar root-yehr |
| ...tourist information | *...l'office du tourisme* | loh-fees dew too-reez-muh |
| Where are the toilets? | *Où sont les toilettes?* | oo sohn lay twah-leht |
| men | *hommes* | ohm |
| women | *dames* | dahm |
| left / right | *à gauche / à droite* | ah gohsh / ah drwaht |
| straight | *tout droit* | too drwah |
| pull / push | *tirez / poussez* | tee-ray / poo-say |
| When does this open / close? | *Ça ouvre / ferme à quelle heure?* | sah oo-vruh / fehrm ah kehl ur |
| At what time? | *À quelle heure?* | ah kehl ur |
| Just a moment. | *Un moment.* | uhn moh-mahn |
| now / soon / later | *maintenant / bientôt / plus tard* | man-tuh-nahn / bee-an-toh / plew tar |
| today / tomorrow | *aujourd'hui / demain* | oh-zhoor-dwee / duh-man |

## In a French Restaurant

| English | French | Pronunciation |
|---------|--------|---------------|
| I'd like / We'd like... | Je voudrais / Nous voudrions... | zhuh voo-dray / noo voo-dree-ohn |
| ...to reserve... | ...réserver... | ray-zehr-vay |
| ...a table for one / two. | ...une table pour un / deux. | ewn tah-bluh poor uhn / duh |
| Is this seat free? | C'est libre? | say lee-bruh |
| The menu (in English), please. | La carte (en anglais), s'il vous plaît. | lah kart (ahn ahn-glay) see voo play |
| service (not) included | service (non) compris | sehr-vees (nohn) kohn-pree |
| to go | à emporter | ah ahn-por-tay |
| with / without | avec / sans | ah-vehk / sahn |
| and / or | et / ou | ay / oo |
| special of the day | plat du jour | plah dew zhoor |
| specialty of the house | spécialité de la maison | spay-see-ah-lee-tay duh lah may-zohn |
| appetizers | hors d'oeuvre | or duh-vruh |
| first course (soup, salad) | entrée | ahn-tray |
| main course (meat, fish) | plat principal | plah pran-see-pahl |
| bread | pain | pan |
| cheese | fromage | froh-mahzh |
| sandwich | sandwich | sahnd-weech |
| soup | soupe | soop |
| salad | salade | sah-lahd |
| meat | viande | vee-ahnd |
| chicken | poulet | poo-lay |
| fish | poisson | pwah-sohn |
| seafood | fruits de mer | frwee duh mehr |
| fruit | fruit | frwee |
| vegetables | légumes | lay-gewm |
| dessert | dessert | day-sehr |
| mineral water | eau minérale | oh mee-nay-rahl |
| tap water | l'eau du robinet | loh dew roh-bee-nay |
| milk | lait | lay |
| (orange) juice | jus (d'orange) | zhew (doh-rahnzh) |
| coffee / tea | café / thé | kah-fay / tay |
| wine | vin | van |
| red / white | rouge / blanc | roozh / blahn |
| glass / bottle | verre / bouteille | vehr / boo-tay |
| beer | bière | bee-ehr |
| Cheers! | Santé! | sahn-tay |
| More. / Another. | Plus. / Un autre. | plew / uhn oh-truh |
| The same. | La même chose. | lah mehm shohz |
| The bill, please. | L'addition, s'il vous plaît. | lah-dee-see-ohn see voo play |
| Do you accept credit cards? | Vous prenez les cartes? | voo pruh-nay lay kart |
| tip | pourboire | poor-bwahr |
| Delicious! | Délicieux! | day-lees-yuh |

For more user-friendly French phrases, check out *Rick Steves' French Phrase Book and Dictionary* or *Rick Steves' French, Italian & German Phrase Book.*

APPENDIX

# INDEX

INDEX

# MAP INDEX

# Start your trip at

## Explore Europe

At ricksteves.com you can browse through thousands of articles, videos, photos and radio interviews, plus find a wealth of money-saving travel tips for planning your dream trip. And with our mobile-friendly website, you can easily access all this great travel information anywhere you go.

## TV Shows

Preview the places you'll visit by watching entire half-hour episodes of Rick Steves' Europe (choose from all 100 shows) on-demand, for free.

*your travel dreams into affordable reality*

## Radio Interviews

Enjoy ready access to Rick's vast library of radio interviews covering travel

tips and cultural insights that relate specifically to your Europe travel plans.

## Travel Forums

Learn, ask, share! Our online community of savvy travelers is a great resource

for first-time travelers to Europe, as well as seasoned pros. You'll find forums on each country, plus travel tips and restaurant/hotel reviews. You can even ask one of our well-traveled staff to chime in with an opinion.

## Travel News

Subscribe to our free Travel News e-newsletter, and get monthly updates from Rick on what's happening in Europe.

# Audio Europe™

# Pack Light and Right

*Gear up for your next adventure at ricksteves.com*

### Light Luggage

Pack light and right with Rick Steves' affordable, custom-designed rolling carry-on bags, backpacks, day packs and shoulder bags.

### Accessories

From packing cubes to moneybelts and beyond, Rick has personally selected the travel goodies that will help your trip go smoother.

**Shop at ricksteves.com**

## *Experience maximum Europe*

## Save time and energy

This guidebook is your independent-travel toolkit. But for all it delivers, it's still up to you to devote the time and energy it takes to manage the preparation and logistics that are essential for a happy trip. If that's a hassle, there's a solution.

## Rick Steves Tours

A Rick Steves tour takes you to Europe's most interesting places with great

# great tours, too!

## with minimum stress

guides and small groups of 28 or less. We follow Rick's favorite itineraries, ride in comfy buses, stay in family-run hotels, and bring you intimately close to the Europe you've traveled so far to see. Most importantly, we take away the logistical headaches so you can focus on the fun.

travelers—nearly half of them repeat customers—along with us on four dozen different itineraries, from Ireland to Italy to Athens. Is a Rick Steves tour the right fit for your travel dreams? Find out at ricksteves.com, where you can also request Rick's latest tour catalog. Europe is best experienced with happy travel partners. We hope you can join us.

### Join the fun

This year we'll take thousands of free-spirited

# A Guide for Every Trip

## BEST OF GUIDES

*Full color easy-to-scan format, focusing on Europe's most popular destinations and sights.*

Best of England
Best of Europe
Best of France
Best of Germany
Best of Ireland
Best of Italy
Best of Spain

## COMPREHENSIVE GUIDES

*City, country, and regional guides with detailed coverage for a multi-week trip exploring the most iconic sights and venturing off the beaten track.*

Amsterdam & the Netherlands
Barcelona
Belgium: Bruges, Brussels, Antwerp & Ghent
Berlin
Budapest
Croatia & Slovenia
Eastern Europe
England
Florence & Tuscany
France
Germany
Great Britain
Greece: Athens & the Peloponnese
Iceland
Ireland
Istanbul
Italy
London
Paris
Portugal
Prague & the Czech Republic
Provence & the French Riviera
Rome
Scandinavia
Scotland
Spain
Switzerland
Venice
Vienna, Salzburg & Tirol

HE BEST OF ROME

ie, Italy's capital, is studded with
an remnants and floodlit-fountain
es. From the Vatican to the Colos-
, with crazy traffic in between, Rome
derful, huge, and exhausting. The
s, the heat, and the weighty history

of the Eternal City where Caesars walked
can make tourists wilt. Recharge by taking siestas, gelato breaks, and after-dark
walks, strolling from one atmospheric
square to another in the refreshing evening air.

Pantheon—which
t dome until the
y 2,000 years old
y over 1,500).

Athens in the Vat-
es the humanistic

ladiators fought
other, entertaining

Rome ristorante,
at St. Peter's
riously.

trat in a cat

Rick Steves guidebooks are published by Avalon Travel, an imprint of Perseus Books, a Hachette Book Group company.